TWENTIETH CENTURY
ECONOMIC HISTORY
OF EUROPE

PAUL ALPERT

SCHUMAN · NEW YORK

FOR MY WIFE

ACKNOWLEDGMENTS

I SHOULD LIKE to express my gratitude to Professor William Orton, to Dr. Samuel Smith, and to Dr. John Shubin for their kindly appreciation, advice, and suggestions.

I wish also to thank Mr. Alfred S. Myers for his excellent editorial work.   PAUL ALPERT

CONTENTS

II. FROM DEPRESSION TO WORLD WAR II

III. EUROPE'S ECONOMY DURING WORLD WAR II

IV. EASTERN EUROPE SINCE THE END OF WORLD WAR II: POPULAR DEMOCRACY, TRANSITION TO COMMUNISM

V. WESTERN EUROPE SINCE THE END OF WORLD WAR II: RECONSTRUCTION AND ATTEMPTS AT UNIFICATION

INTRODUCTION

THE MAIN REASON that induced me to write this book, designed for the American public, is the value of the contemporary economic history of Europe as a particularly instructive example. The material is based on a course given at the Graduate School of New York University.

It is widely acknowledged today that the world has been in a state of transition ever since the close of the period of the classical liberal capitalism of the nineteenth century, which came to an end in Europe in 1914 and in the United States probably in 1929. From that time on, factors such as private business monopolies, as well as monopolies of organized labor and farmers, began to grow so powerful as to obstruct the normal functioning of the capitalist economy based on free competition and fluidity of prices. All countries are faced with the problem of adapting their economies to these changes, which imply the necessity of conciliating economic security with political freedom.

There is, in my opinion, no possible uniform pattern of adjustment which could be adopted by all countries, for each economy has to be adapted according to the national characteristics of the respective country, its geographical position, its social and economic structure, the balance of power between the different forces of its economy, and similar factors. Nevertheless, comparisons of divergent experiences of various countries is most interesting.

In these circumstances, there is special significance in the experience, during this period, of Europe, containing, as it does, the most anciently civilized countries of the Western World, which, with the exception of the United States, are also the most highly industralized, and which constitute a region where this phase of transition started earlier than in the United States and under more difficult conditions.

Thus, the American public may well be interested in a description and analysis of the different ways in which the main countries of this region—Great Britain, France, Germany and Russia—have been, and still are, trying to handle and solve this problem, their attempts, failures and successes.

The first and foremost importance of the subject consists in its relation to their own similar problems, and in its providing examples to be followed or to be rejected, but always giving matter for useful thought. The discussion may also give some inside knowledge of the present problems of the important region above referred to. Because of the growing economic and political interdependence between all parts of the world, such knowledge is a necessary condition for understanding not only the situation in Europe, but the international situation as a whole. Such knowledge, too, is especially essential for this country if it is to succeed in its function of leadership of the Western World.

I FROM WAR TO DEPRESSION

1 THE ECONOMIC STRUCTURE OF GREAT BRITAIN, FRANCE, GERMANY, AND RUSSIA IN 1914

GREAT BRITAIN

The nineteenth century, from the political as well as from the economic point of view, should be correctly defined as the period extending from 1815 to 1914. It was a time of British hegemony. While the British Navy ruled the seas and prevented any major war on a scale comparable to the Napoleonic wars which had preceded the nineteenth century and the world wars which had followed it, in the realm of economic life Great Britain's industrial, commercial and financial supremacy was even more complete and unchallenged than her naval might during the greater part of this period. As a matter of fact, the structure of the whole world economy during the nineteenth century had been based on the exchange of goods and services between Great Britain and the rest of the world.

This economic supremacy was partly due to an earlier industrialization. Great Britain had been the pioneer of industrial revolution and, as a consequence, during the first part of the century, enjoyed nearly a monopoly in large-scale modern industry, and especially in exports of industrial goods. This monopoly gradually disappeared as other industrial countries, such as Germany and the United States, particularly, developed their production. Nevertheless, British industrial exports continued to hold an

3

especially strong position. Other important factors were the position of Great Britain as the world's greatest importing and exporting country; the predominance of its merchant marine; the financial supremacy of the city of London; and the monetary supremacy of sterling, a consequence of the fact that the gold standard, which had gradually spread during this period from Great Britain to the rest of the world, was for all practical purposes a sterling standard managed by the Bank of England.

The basis of British industrial supremacy was coal. British coal deposits not only were rich but also were most conveniently located near the sea, which facilitated exports as well as industrial manufacturing out of raw materials imported from overseas. During this whole period Great Britain had been the greatest coal-producing country in Europe, while since 1906 its production had become second in the world to that of the United States. However, it remained the world's greatest coal exporter. In 1913 British coal production amounted to 287 million tons and exports to 90 million tons.

During that period, coal was the main if not the only source of power for industry and transport, so that this commodity found large markets in all countries lacking adequate domestic resources. Coal thus became a considerable stimulant for the development of the British merchant marine, providing it with a convenient and profitable export cargo. The possibility of loading coal on all cargo ships leaving the country, instead of sending them in ballast, indirectly cheapened the freight rates for British imports and thus the cost of imported raw materials and foodstuffs. Other industrial countries did not have bulk exports as easily marketable.

The development of the British merchant marine had also been favored by the vast opportunities for maritime transport resulting from the economic progress achieved during this period by the principal parts of the British Empire. This progress was true also of other overseas countries where the British flag enjoyed special advantages, owing either to political influence or to other factors such as the existence of favorably located British ports like Singapore and Hongkong. Thus, at the end of the nineteenth century, the British merchant marine still had a dominant position, in spite of increasing competition, mainly from Germany in the Atlantic and from Japan in the Pacific. In 1913 it amounted to about 18 million tons, that is, nearly half of the total world tonnage.

The iron and steel industry—where most of the production methods had been first developed in Great Britain (e.g. the Bessemer method)—was also one of the main factors of British industrial strength. Even though the British iron and steel production had already been overtaken by that of the United States in the 1890's, and by Germany shortly after 1900, Great Britain still remained the greatest exporting country of iron and steel products and had maintained its supremacy in production and, above all, in machinery exports of all kinds. Especially in shipbuilding its position was one of absolute supremacy; the British shipyards possessed 80 percent of the world capacity.

In textiles, particularly in cotton, the industrial production of which had also originated in Great Britain, that country had also maintained a predominant place throughout the century. It had nearly half of the world capacity of cotton spinning and weaving. The volume of its exports, especially to the Far East, was enormous, in spite of a gradually increasing competition—particularly by Japanese exports in mass-production, low-cost lines—and revival of domestic production in India.

As a basis of British economic supremacy, trade was as important as industry. In the first half of the nineteenth century Great Britain had already been the leading trading country of the world, but it achieved an enormous expansion of its foreign trade after the abolition of the Corn Laws in 1845. It then put an end to tariff protection of home-grown food and thus sacrificed its agriculture to the development of its world trade.

The introduction of free trade reduced the cost of food, and thus the wage bill of British industry, improving its competitive position on foreign markets and stimulating British exports. On the other hand, as population and industrial activity in Great

5

Britain increased, this policy offered a big and steadily expanding market to its trading partners and provided them with the sterling exchange required to pay for their imports of British manufactures. Consequently Great Britain, which imported 60 percent of its food and enormous quantities of raw materials of all kinds, became the world's greatest importing country and the largest market for raw materials and produce from all parts of the world.

Owing to the existence of this centralized market, London became a center of international distribution. A great many countries found it more convenient, and even cheaper, to purchase there the raw materials and exotic foodstuffs, like tea, which they required, than to order them directly in the producing countries. Deliveries therefrom would have been more costly, either owing to the lack of direct maritime connection or because of the comparatively small quantities concerned. This reexport trade became very important and made a significant contribution to the prosperity of British overseas commerce, as well as to the volume of freight carried by the British merchant marine.

During the greatest part of this period, imports had exceeded exports and the deficit of the balance of trade steadily increased. This deficit, however, was more than compensated for by invisible receipts: income from shipping, reexports, finance and insurance services and, most important of all, the income from foreign investments. Thus Great Britain's balance of payments always had an important surplus.

In the average of the years 1910-1914 the British balance of trade was, in millions of pounds (£):

Imports	Exports	Imports surplus	Reexports
714	570	144	107

Finance was an equally important element of British economic prosperity. London was the world's greatest money market, and so by far the largest part of all international trade, even between "third" countries, was financed by means of bills of exchange in sterling drawn upon, and discounted by, London banks. The con-

6

centration of short-term capital for such operations in London enabled the Bank of England to influence the general trends of the world economy through variations of its discount rate. In this way it played an important part in maintaining, during most of this period, a considerable degree of monetary and price stability.

London was also the world's greatest capital market, owing to the fact that the surplus of the British balance of payments was being invested abroad. British foreign investment policy was generally guided by trade considerations. Investments were made mainly in private companies established for the purpose of developing the natural resources of overseas countries, which would open new sources of supply for Great Britain's imports and provide new markets to its exports of manufactures. Therefore, in the first part of the nineteenth century, investments of British capital had already made an important contribution to the building of the railroads in the United States and later in Argentina, as well as in Canada and all other parts of the British Empire. They were also the basis of the development of gold mines in South Africa, of rubber plantations in Malaya, and of all sorts of productive ventures in all parts of the world. Most of these investments had achieved their purpose of the development of productive resources and, as a consequence, were highly remunerative. The total income from foreign investments, the value of which amounted by 1913 to 4 billion pounds ($20 billion gold), was thus steadily increasing.

The economic history of great Britain during the nineteenth century offers a perfect and complete example of the application of the theories of classic liberal economics, in so far as economic development was the result of the free action of economic forces only, without any interference from political or other factors. As a matter of fact, state intervention in the economy had been nearly nil; not until 1910 had the first important social security laws been introduced by Lloyd George. Industrial combinations were scarcely in existence and the trade unions, even though steadily increasing in power, were still very far from having a monopolistic influence. The success which was achieved by the British economy during this period, and which was considered due to its particular resemblance to the ideal of liberal economists, was striking: Great Britain's standard of living was the highest in Europe, and scarcely inferior to that of the United States, in spite of the latter's considerable superiority of resources per capita, as well as the fact that the British population had doubled since 1860.

FRANCE

In France, material conditions, as well as psychological (perhaps even more important), were extremely different from those in Great Britain.

The main difference between the two countries, however, was psychological. As a rule, the French people were more interested in, and attracted to, political ideas and theories, even if abstract, than to economic activity and its concrete results. This general statement does not imply that the great mass of average Frenchmen, in their respective fields of economic activity, did not work as hard as members of the same classes and professions in other countries. As a matter of fact, they worked at least as hard, possibly harder, and at any rate longer hours. The industriousness of the French peasant is proverbial; the Anglo-Saxon institution of the week-end for relaxation was unknown in France until about 1929. Whereas in Great Britain the great majority of the young men of the middle class—and even the younger sons of the aristocracy not endowed with titles and estates—went into business and established or developed undertakings in the country itself or overseas, most young men of similar condition in France, the educated bourgeoisie, the so-called "elite," preferred to go into politics, law, normally the first step leading to a political career, or the civil service. This was especially true of the most brilliant of them.

There were obviously many significant exceptions. The most

important were the disciples of Saint Simon, a philosopher of the early nineteenth century, whose doctrine stressed the importance of economic progress as a foundation for the improvement of political conditions. Some of the members of Saint Simon's group were leading pioneers of economic development achieved during the nineteenth century. The best known were de Lesseps, who built the Suez Canal and started the building of the Panama Canal, and the Pereyre brothers, who established the basis of the French railway system.

As a general rule, however, only a small minority of the French bourgeoisie devoted their energy and their financial means to constructive economic activity. Consequently there was a much slower rate of economic progress than in Great Britain, as well as a much more considerable impact of political factors and motives in the field of economics. Purely economic considerations carried far less weight with the general public than political factors, since they were less well known and understood.

Another important psychological factor was the French national characteristic of extreme individualism, which became an impediment to mergers and concentration of business undertakings, an essential prerequisite of modern large-scale production.

In France, material conditions also were much less favorable for economic development than in Great Britain. Most important in this respect was, and still is, the insufficiency of coal resources to cover domestic requirements. In 1913, coal production amounted to only 41 million tons, while consumption was 63 million tons. This shortage was a handicap particularly to the development of heavy industries. Another very important factor was the very small rate of population growth since the enormous losses incurred during the period of the war of the Revolution and the Napoleonic era; in the latter part of this period, population became completely stationary. Thus French economy did not benefit from the stimulating effect of a rapidly growing domestic market.

These reasons provide the main explanation of the fact that industrial progress in France was much slower than in Great Britain and did not go as far. Still it should be stressed that industrial revolution in France had been contemporary to that in Great Britain, and that the French intellectual participation in industrial development, i.e., its share in creative technical inventions, had been very considerable. Some significant French inventions were: sodium, by Leblanc; photography, by Daguerre; rayon, by Chardonnet; the steam turbine, by Laval; motion pictures by Lumière, to name a few. But in France the spirit of economic enterprise was less developed than technical ingenuity, and in many cases originally French inventions were applied on a large scale in other industrial countries, such as especially Germany or the United States.

The main difference in economic policy between Great Britain and France was the refusal of the latter to sacrifice its agriculture to prospects of increased foreign trade and industrial exports. France maintained tariff protection for agriculture, as well as for industry. The main theoretical reason for such a policy was the desire to maintain social stability by preserving the existence of a strong independent peasant class, a class which long ago had disappeared in Great Britain; the main practical reason was, of course, the considerable political influence of this peasantry.

In so far as the general efficiency of the whole economy, and even of agriculture by itself, was concerned, the results of the policy of tariff protection were rather indifferent. Agriculture in Great Britain, in order to survive even on a reduced scale against foreign competition, had to rationalize its production, to concentrate it on the best soils and on the products most suited to them, as well as on those for which world competition was least dangerous and comparative cost of domestic production most favorable. Such products were meat, dairy produce, fruit, vegetables, and so on. British agriculture had been able to accomplish this adjustment, which obviously had been very difficult and costly, because of its structure; it consisted mainly of large farms which operated as capitalistic undertakings, and which had therefore been able to

10

make the heavy investments required. On the other hand, the French peasants, sheltered by the tariff, did not have to make a similar effort of adjustment and modernization. In any event, they would have been unable to achieve it, lacking the capital it required. Thus technical progress in French agriculture was relatively slow. For this reason—as well as owing to the lack of specialization and to the utilization for crops of all categories of soil, even those relatively little suited for them—yields were generally lower in France than in either Great Britain or Germany.

The high level of food prices, resulting from tariff protection, and a relatively inefficient production of staple products were a handicap for industrial exports.

In spite of all these difficulties, French industrial production underwent a considerable development, and during the greater part of the nineteenth century had been second only to that of Great Britain; it had, however, been overtaken during the latter part of that century by the United States and Germany. French industry was especially successful, not in large-scale production, but in the manufacture of high-quality and luxury products, in which artistic taste and craftsmanship could produce the best results. The structure of French industry, consisting mainly of small, sometimes very small, undertakings, was also especially well adapted to such production. Thus the most successful French industries, which enjoyed a world-wide reputation and exported on a considerable scale, were silk, perfumes, lace, china, dresses, articles of fashion, and so on. Similarly, French agriculture, while inefficient in the production of staple products like cereals, excelled in the production of specialties, as, for example, many different sorts of wine and cheese.

Most large-scale industries had been developed in order to supply only the protected domestic and colonial markets. The one exception in this respect was the iron and steel industry, which, after discovery at the end of the nineteenth century of the rich phosphoric iron-ore deposits in Lorraine, considerably expanded

11

its production and began to export, even though on a smaller scale than either Great Britain or Germany. The latter, however, at this time included the richest part of the Lorraine deposits, which had been annexed in 1871.

Iron and steel production of these three countries in 1913 amounted in millions of tons to:

	Iron ore	Pig iron	Raw steel
Great Britain	16.2	10.4	7.7
France	21.7	5.3	4.6
Germany	28.6	16.7	17.6

In spite of the relatively slow rate of economic progress in France, the accumulation of savings was considerable, owing mainly to the thrifty character of the French people. Since opportunities for profitable investment in the French economy were comparatively limited, the amount of capital available for foreign investment was very important. Paris, therefore, became the biggest international financial center except London, and the total amount of French capital invested abroad was by 1913 about 9 billion gold dollars.

The fields and the distribution of French foreign investment, however, were extremely different from those of the British type. While, in Great Britain, foreign investments were made mainly by big capitalists, well-informed as to economic trends in general and the prospects of their investments in particular, the savings which were the source of the French foreign investments were accumulated by a multitude of small investors (*petits épargnants*) who were generally economically illiterate. Consequently, the average French investors disliked the uncertain yields and the risks of private enterprise; they preferred the security, even with limited yield and without any possibility of profit, which government appeared to offer. As a result, the greatest part of French foreign investments took the form of loans to foreign governments. The tendency toward such a type of investment was encouraged by the

French government, which thus obtained an important instrument for its international policy. Encouragement was given by the Paris banks, also, which were the intermediaries for such transactions, and to which foreign governments, even if in bad financial shape, could offer much greater commissions than any legitimate private company, which had to consider its costs-and-profits possibilities. It was rather natural, therefore, that the country which was by far the greatest single beneficiary of French foreign investments, and which absorbed over 25 percent of their total, was Russia, the great ally of pre-war France. Most of the balance was loaned to all sorts of governments: Turkey, Austria-Hungary, the Balkan States, Latin-America, and others. Events did not justify the somehow candid confidence of the French investors in the honesty and solvability of governments, and by far the majority of these foreign investments was to be lost after World War I.

The French balance of payments during this period had always a substantial surplus, as the deficit of the balance of trade was more than offset by tourist traffic and income from foreign investments.

In considering the development of French economy and comparing it to that of Great Britain, it should be stressed that not only conditions but even the aims of economic policy were not entirely identical in the two countries. Great Britain obviously achieved a much greater development and a higher standard of living; however, it is evident today that this progress had been based on exceptionally favorable conditions which could not be considered as necessarily permanent, and which thus increased the fragility of the British economy. France, on the other hand, maintained a much higher degree of social as well as economic stability, owing to the existence of a strong middle class of peasants and townsmen, artisans and shopkeepers. This independent middle class, generally satisfied even with its limited way of life, formed the majority of the population, while the urban proletariat was only a minority, a condition just the reverse of that in Great Britain and in Germany.

13

GERMANY

The rise of Germany as a great economic and industrial power occurred much later than that of Great Britain or of France. It coincided with the economic and political unification of Germany. The economic unification, achieved through the Zollverein, the German customs union established by 1830, became the basis of the political unification in the Reich, established by Bismarck in 1870. This coincidence was a major reason for the tendency toward using state intervention as a means of furthering and stimulating economic development, a trend which was much stronger in Germany than in any other country of Western civilization, and which also became much earlier apparent there. It explains, moreover, the conviction which dominated German economic life, namely, that the existence of a powerful state was an essential condition of economic prosperity, and that it should therefore be also a major objective of economic activity. This conviction was a constant *leitmotiv* of German economic policy, from Friedrich List, who established the Zollverein, to Dr. Schacht during the Hitler period.

The economic development of Germany gained many advantages from the experience of its older competitors. Its economy could thus be organized on more efficient and rational lines. The natural conditions were extremely favorable: abundant deposits of coal and iron ore, as well as of raw materials for the chemical industry, such as lignite and potassium; a central location in Europe, facilitating trade and traffic; a substantial rate of population growth, providing a steady increase of the domestic market, and so on. The economic expansion of the Reich had therefore been very considerable.

A main characteristic feature of German economic development, which was one of the principal reasons for its brilliant suc-

14

cess, was the systematic application of science to agriculture and industry. This was not present in a comparable degree, during the same period, in either the French or the British economy. Another characteristic factor in Germany was the importance of state interference. The state had constructed, and owned, most of the railway system, as well as a great number of mines and other undertakings. Even more important was the tariff policy, which inaugurated in Europe the educational tariff protection aiming at fostering the growth of new industries. The trend toward industrial combinations in monopolistic cartels was also a specifically German characteristic. Such cartels were established mainly in order to maintain high prices on the home market, and to conquer foreign markets by the use of dumping. Thus, the steel industry used to grant to engineering firms rebates on the steel used for the manufacture of exported machinery. Such cartels could be established only under tariff protection, and the German laws not only allowed but even favored them, while in Great Britain and France they were unlawful. These cartels, the development of which was a consequence of the German characteristic of discipline and the faculty of organization, had been an important favorable factor in German economic expansion.

A most remarkable feature of Germany's economic development was the fact that, while rising in the short space of forty years to become the first industrial power of the European Continent, Germany did not sacrifice its agriculture to its industry. Owing mainly to the application of technical progress to agriculture—especially through an enormous increase in the consumption of potash and phosphate fertilizer, which Germany produced in considerable quantities—that nation succeeded in achieving an important increase of crop yields. German agriculture was consequently able to maintain a reasonable degree of prosperity, even though obviously only under the protection of a relatively high tariff. The prosperity was shared, during this period, by the big estates of the East, which enjoyed conditions best suited to the application of modern farm techniques, as well as by the small farms

15

of Western Germany, the technical level of which was relatively high, owing to an excellent system of rural education.

The expansion of agricultural production in Germany had been such that, in spite of the increase of the population from 39 million in 1870 to 68 million in 1914, 75 percent of the food consumption was covered by domestic production. The percentage of domestic production was 85 for cereals and 93 for meat.

During this period, the industrial development of Germany was tremendous, proceeding at a rate comparable only to that which marked the development of the United States. Coal production, which in 1870 had amounted to 4.5 million tons, by 1913 had reached 190 million tons of hard coal, to which should be added 87 million tons of lignite. In Europe, German coal production became second only to that of Great Britain. Iron and steel production had been stimulated by the annexation, in 1871, of the rich phosphatic iron-ore deposits of Lorraine, which, combined with the coke resources of the Ruhr, placed Germany first among the steel-producing countries of Europe, and second only to the United States among all the steel-producing countries of the world. Even more considerable was the development of industries, such as chemicals, based to a great extent on German inventions. For most products of the chemical industry, such as, in particular, dyes and pharmaceuticals, German producers had achieved a complete domination of the world market. The German dye cartel, out of which later developed the I. G. Farbenindustrie, enjoyed a *de facto* world monopoly. Germany held nearly as strong a position in the manufacture of heavy electrical machinery—owing to the inventions and to the industrial establishments for which Siemens was responsible—as well as in optical goods, precision instruments, toys, and some other products.

This German industrial production found very easy outlets in foreign markets, and German foreign trade achieved an expansion similar to the industrial development. Within a short time, industrial exports won domination of markets in eastern and southeastern European countries, where Germany had the advantage of

16

geographical proximity. German goods also began, with steadily increasing success, to compete with British products in overseas markets, where certain factors favored their penetration. Among these were their high quality, due to modern equipment and organization methods; relatively lower prices, made possible by a somewhat lower wage level; and, above all, the cartel policy of dumping. Already, about 1900, there had been complete failure of a British attempt to exclude German goods from the British Dominions by making mandatory the mention of their origin "made in Germany."

As German requirements of overseas raw materials steadily increased, the expansion of the German merchant marine went parallel to the development of industrial production and foreign trade. German shipping had ready freight available for export (coal, which the Reich could export as well as Great Britain, and several other bulk commodities), as well as for import. German ships also enjoyed an advantage that was due to the central location of their country, which enabled them to leave their home ports without a full cargo and complete it by calling at English or French harbors. There, as they required only a complement of freight or passengers, they could quote very low rates. Thus the German merchant fleet became, in liners as well as in cargo ships, second only to Great Britain.

A natural consequence of this tremendous economic growth was the rise of Germany as a financial power. While in her balance of trade there was a small deficit, there was, nevertheless, owing to invisible receipts, a large surplus of the balance of payments available for foreign investment. German investments abroad amounted to about $6 billion in 1914, and they were located mainly in southeastern Europe and in Turkey. They were about equally divided between government loans and business ventures; the most important of the latter was the "Bagdadbahn," a railroad from Constantinople to the Persian Gulf.

In the years preceding World War I, Germany had the greatest population increase, as well as the highest ratio of economic

17

progress, of all the great industrialized countries of Europe. Already it was the strongest power of the European Continent, economically, politically and militarily, and it is obvious that, if World War I had not occurred, Germany would have gradually increased her power, in both absolute and relative terms, and would have achieved by peaceful means a position of hegemony in Europe.

But in these circumstances, strikingly similar to those which arose twenty-five years later, the German leaders, statesmen, generals and big businessmen lacked patience and foresight. Possibly they were blinded by their success, or perhaps by the pathological lust for power which had been a constant tradition of Prussian militarism. They wanted to obtain everything at once: domination of the seas by a big navy policy—which was obviously a deadly menace to Great Britain; domination of the Balkans, which was due to be resisted by Russia; and penetration in the Middle East, which was another challenge to Britain; as well as interference in Morocco, which was in the French sphere of interest. Thus they themselves fostered the very coalition which opposed them, and which for one generation destroyed the German dream of world domination.

RUSSIA

Russia entered the stage of modern capitalist economy only in the second half of the nineteenth century, after the abolition in 1861 of peasant serfdom. That step put an end to an age of slave labor with its low cost, and even lower productivity, and resulted in the adoption of capitalistic methods and techniques.

Since then, Russian economy could be characterized mainly by a striking contrast: While capitalistic industry, taking advantage of most favorable natural conditions, achieved a very decided expansion of production, especially in the twentieth century, since the establishment in 1905 of a constitutional regime, it is never-

18

theless true that the great mass of the peasantry (including even in 1914 over 80 percent of the total population) was still living psychologically, as well as economically, in a pre-capitalistic era.

The emancipation of the serfs had not solved, either from the economic or from the social point of view, the question of ownership and cultivation of the land. The peasants generally received practically all the land which they had cultivated for themselves while under serfdom. The arrangement, however, included a consideration to be paid over a period of nearly fifty years. The ownership of this land, moreover, was not granted individually to each peasant, but collectively to the village community, the *mir*, which was in principle to distribute it according to existing needs —that is, the number of family-member mouths to be fed. Also, in principle, though not always in practice, all cultivated land belonging to one community was periodically redivided, in order to give to each member of the community a share of land corresponding to the size of his family. Such a system was most unfavorable for improvement in farming technique, as no peasant was sure of keeping the plot of land he was cultivating, and therefore none was willing to make improvements the benefits of which he might not be able to reap. In addition, the principle of sharing the land according to the size of the family stimulated even more the already very high birth rate, and thus aggravated the problem of rural overpopulation.

Under the prevailing very low level of agricultural technique, the quantity of land per head of agricultural population was insufficient, with the result that most peasants were confined to subsistence farming on an extremely low plane of consumption. It is natural that under such conditions land hunger was the most passionate urge of Russian peasantry, and that they unanimously demanded a new and global redivision of all land. This insistent demand included the land which, during the period of serfdom, they had cultivated for the landlords, and which the latter had retained. However, such a redistribution could not have provided a real solution, as the estates of the gentry had been constantly de-

19

clining since the loss of their serf manpower, and by 1917 their share of total arable land amounted only to 16 percent, while the peasant holdings included over 75 percent, state and church ownership accounting for the rest. But it should be noted that the big estates provided the greatest part of the food surplus used for feeding the city population and for export of agricultural products, mainly cereals, of which pre-war Russia was one of the greatest world exporters.

The real solution of the agricultural problem could have been provided only by the following definite and constructive moves: a change in the status of ownership, providing incentives for improvement of techniques and increase of productivity; a policy of settlement of the considerable area of virgin land available in eastern areas, especially in Siberia; and absorption of rural surplus labor through industrialization. In the system of the *mir,* in which the community and each of its members were collectively responsible for payment of taxes and debts, the *mir* was reluctant to let its members leave—indeed, had the right to prevent them from leaving.

The necessity of such a land reform had been recognized by the Tzarist government, only very late, after the rural disorders of 1905. In 1907, the prime minister, Stolypine, began introduction of a plan which, on the one hand, facilitated emigration and resettlement of peasants on new land and, on the other hand, enabled all members of the rural community to leave the *mir* and to claim their share of land as individual property. It then had to be allotted to them, not in widely scattered strips, as before, but in one compact holding, thus facilitating cultivation. This reform, which was obviously favorable to the rich and efficient peasants, who had the best opportunity to avail themselves of the possibility to become independent farmers, had been applied gradually and met with considerable success. In the short space of seven years, until 1914, 24 percent of all peasant households had taken advantage of its provisions. It is probable that, if it could have been continued

for another ten years, the structure of Russian agriculture would have been completely transformed and greatly strengthened.

However, it should be stressed that, even though the reform in the short period of its implementation achieved considerable results, and in particular increased productivity of the new independent farms (*xhutors*), it did not change the psychology of the peasant population. Nor did it still their craving for the land of the estates, a craving which was particularly strong among the small and less efficient farmers remaining in the *mir,* but which was shared even by the independent farmers who continued to claim that land as their just due. Thus deep seeds of social unrest remained in the great mass of the rural population.

Industrialization in Russia had made rapid progress since the emancipation of the peasants and the beginning of the period of railroad building in the 1860's, which created the basis for the establishment of a modern economy in the whole vast territory of the Empire. Indeed, industrial development in Russia, especially after 1900, had proceeded at a pace which exceeded by far that of all Western European countries, and which can be compared only to that of the United States. It was favored by: abundant mineral resources; availability of agricultural raw materials, such as cotton in Turkestan—production of which covered, by 1914, more than half of the requirements of the national industry—as well as wool, flax, and so on; cheap labor; and a domestic market which, in spite of the low purchasing power of the masses, was still gigantic, and which was protected by a high tariff.

Starting practically from nothing, Russia in some fifty years of industrial development had reached fourth place in the world as a producer of cotton manufacture, ranking only after Great Britain, the United States and Germany. This industry of hers was concentrated mainly in the region of Moscow. Russia had fifth place in the production of iron and steel, mainly in the Donets basin, where coal and iron were found together. The iron and steel industry had been developed mainly with foreign capital, particularly French and Belgian. Pig-iron production amounted in 1913 to 4.5 million tons, approximately equal to that of France; Russian coal production in that same year was also fifth in the world, with 29 million tons, and by 1916, stimulated by war requirements, had even increased to 36 million tons.

Notwithstanding this rapid progress, however, and the very high level of technical efficiency of some industrial undertakings, particularly in textile and other consumer-goods industries, production was insufficient to meet the main requirements of the nation. Especially, equipment of all kinds was imported, and this dependence on outside sources was to prove an important cause of weakness during the 1914-1918 war.

Development of industry and trade resulted in the creation of a small class of extremely prosperous merchants and manufacturers. The middle class of engineers and technicians, however, which exercises the main creative functions in modern technical civilization, was developing only slowly and was still limited in numbers and in influence.

On the other hand, industrialization resulted in the development of a proletariat, which was not very numerous compared to the total population, but which was concentrated in a few big cities and industrial regions. This class, composed of peasants whom lack of land had brought into the cities, was not accustomed to participating in the Westernized civilization of the upper classes. The proletariat of the Western nations had long ago assimilated that civilization. Besides, the low living standard of this peasant class prevented it from partaking of all the material and intellectual benefits of the existing civilization. That low living standard was natural in a period of early capitalist development, similar to the first half of the nineteenth century in Western Europe, when Marx was composing his main theories.

Without any traditions of attachment to the state or to the nation, by whom it felt itself to be exploited without being conscious of receiving any compensation, the proletariat of Russia was to become naturally attracted to Marxism, the most revolutionary of proletarian doctrines. This doctrine stimulated the self-respect of the Russian workers, promised them liberation and revenge and thus attracted them, while already by that time it had lost a great part of its appeal to the more developed and less exploited masses of workers in the countries of the Western world.

2 THE IMPACT OF WORLD WAR I
ON THE EUROPEAN ECONOMY

BEFORE 1914, most economists were convinced that a general war
of long duration would be impossible because its excessive cost
would create the danger of bankruptcy for belligerent countries
and thus force them to put an end to the fighting. An especially
convincing demonstration of the economic absurdity of war, which
appeared to prove its impossibility, was contained in a well-known
book by Norman Angell, *Grand Illusion,* published shortly before 1914. The course of events after 1914, however, proved how
gravely mistaken was this theory, which had been based on the assumption, typical of capitalist mentality, that economic motives
were the most decisive in guiding the action of nations, as well as
of individuals.

As a matter of fact, the experience of World War I proved that,
although the actual cost of the conflict was much greater than
could ever have been imagined, financial considerations and fear
of bankruptcy were unable not only to stop the war but even to
shorten its duration. This, in spite of the fact that the direct financial war expenditures alone amounted to $156 billion for the
Allies and $63 billion for the Central Powers. As long as the war
lasted, the belligerent nations willingly sacrificed the greatest part
of their national income, that is, the fruit of their toil, as well as
their national wealth accumulated through generations, to satisfy
their political and nationalist feelings and passions.

24

Those emotions were stimulated by the danger threatening the preservation of the independence and security of their respective countries, as well as by the will to reach the essential objectives of traditional national policy-ideals, shared by the great majority of their respective populations, as, for example, domination of Central Europe by Germany; reconquest of Alsace-Lorraine by France; and acquisition of the *terra irridente* by Italy. The nations' economic resources proved to be only means, freely spent for achievement of these political objectives. During the whole nineteenth century, people became accustomed to believing that economic factors were of paramount importance, a belief resulting from the obvious fact that, during this period, economic progress had been everywhere in the world the greatest single influence on the course of events. But the 1914-1918 war forced people to remember the old truth that economic factors and motives are normally far from being the strongest in the life of nations. That truth became especially obvious in a period when all the forces of the nations were strained, and all their resources spent for destructive, not for constructive, purposes.

All economic activity in the belligerent countries became subordinated to the national interest—namely, military victory—through the establishment of the so-called war economy. It may be interesting to note that this name is of German origin, *Kriegswirtschaft*, as is also the concept which it describes. This subordination of all activity to one objective introduced basic, and, in their essence, quite revolutionary changes in the structure of the pre-war capitalist economy of the countries concerned.

First of all, the intricate mechanism of international and especially European economy, based on a continuous exchange of goods, services and capital, had from the start become completely disrupted. Thus all belligerent countries, instead of continuing to rely on the world market for the supply of the goods they required, made strenuous efforts to become, as far as possible, self-sufficient. They wanted to substitute domestic production for goods previously imported, as importing became impossible or difficult, owing to blockade or submarine warfare, or simply too expensive in terms of foreign currencies in short supply. On the other hand, export prohibitions were applied to commodities required for military purposes, as well as those which could be useful to the enemy countries. Direct trade with the enemy was, of course, prohibited.

The intervention of the state in economic matters was an even more drastic violation of the basic rule of capitalist economy: the rule of free enterprise, conducted with a view to a profit determined by the action of the price mechanism, in a free market, without any consideration of noneconomic factors. Under war conditions, this intervention steadily increased in scope until it became a complete direction of all economic activity by the state, with the one object of achieving its political aims. Thus, the state stimulated development of products essential to the war effort, and discouraged, restricted, or even completely suppressed those which it considered useless for this objective, and which, from this point of view, caused a wasteful consumption of raw materials and labor.

The state controlled foreign trade and supervised the organization of the import of essential commodities. It took over from private enterprise the merchant marine, as under wartime conditions shipping had become a venture too dangerous for private business. The state was also obliged to control distribution, by introducing priorities and rationing, in order to insure to all the population, at nominal prices, the most efficient utilization of available resources, as well as minimum supplies of food and essential consumer goods. In so far as these basic commodities were concerned, rationing abolished to a considerable extent the inequality which results from differences in monetary incomes, and which is an essential feature of capitalist economy. Distribution thus became a sort of public service.

The state-controlled and state-directed war economy of this period, which was adopted by all belligerent countries for reasons of political and military expediency, offered the first example in

26

modern history of an economy entirely planned in the light of political objectives. Results proved that such an economy not only was workable but could succeed.

The organization of war economy proceeded along similar lines in all major belligerent countries. However, it had been first developed in Germany, which had been cut off at the beginning of the war from its major sources of supply, owing to its inferior sea power and also to its geographic position, surrounded as it was by enemy countries.

As early as August 1914, Walter Rathenau, a big industrialist, Chairman of the German General Electric Co. (A.E.G.), submitted to the German General Staff a plan of economic mobilization. He suggested the establishment of war-raw-materials sections (*Kriegsrohstoff Abteilungen*) which would be in charge of strategic materials, such as food and raw materials in short supply. These sections would be empowered to requisition domestic production and stocks, to purchase abroad, and to control utilization of the respective materials, priority being given to use for war purposes. They could also organize production of substitute materials. Part of these functions were fulfilled by semipublic war-economy companies (*Kriegswirtschaftsgesellschaften*) which were established out of peacetime cartels, and which were also in charge of the distribution of the commodities produced by their respective industries.

State control was also extended to transportation, to utilization of manpower, and to practically all other aspects of economic activity. Owing to the habits of discipline inherent in the German character, the organization of the war economy there encountered fewer difficulties and thus proved more successful than in most other countries.

War production in Germany underwent a considerable expansion, in spite of the obstacles with which the German economy as a whole was faced; and it continued to increase until 1917. On the other hand, all other categories of industrial production steadily declined, owing to lack of manpower, deterioration of equipment

27

due to lack of maintenance and replacement, and a decline in productivity resulting from the deterioration of the food situation, especially after the winter of 1917 (*Rübenwinter*).

Agricultural resources also decreased, notwithstanding the most careful husbandry, which took the following forms: bread rationing, introduced soon after the beginning of the war; the mixture of bread grains with potatoes, which resulted in a great deterioration of the quality of bread; the so-called K.K. bread; restriction of alcohol and even of beer production; and concentration of production on cereals. Domestic production declined considerably, owing to the following factors: lack of manpower, in spite of the utilization of 800,000 war prisoners; lack of draught power, due to the requisition of 2 million horses for the army; and lack of fertilizer, mainly phosphates and nitrate. The shortage of nitrates, however, had been alleviated as a result of the invention by Haber of synthetic nitrate, which enabled Germany to replace the products formerly imported from Chile. As to food imports, they had declined by 1917 to less than 10 percent of prewar. Still, granted all the obvious economic difficulties and hardships which the German people had to face, food shortage was not a major factor in deciding the issue of the war. While, after the end of hostilities, the German Nationalists pretended and claimed that Germany lost the war only because of starvation (*Aushungerung*), the fact remains that she was defeated on the battlefield. This claim was made in order to stimulate in the people a fierce pride and desire for revenge.

In Great Britain, introduction of the war economy had been especially difficult, as the measures which it implied were absolutely alien to the character and the secular traditions of the people. The British took time to realize the requirements of the situation, and to make the necessary adjustments. At first, indeed, the slogan they used was "Business as usual." The level of exports was maintained, and an attempt was even made to expand exports in order to replace, on overseas markets, German goods cut off by the blockade.

The gravity of conditions began to come home to them only

28

during the munitions crisis of the spring of 1915. Then the Defense of the Realm Act gave to the government wide powers of control. Lloyd George, who became Minister of Munitions, introduced priorities as to the utilization of raw materials and labor; interfered with trade-union rules, and obtained from the unions a "no strike" pledge; and prohibited export of vital materials required for war purposes. In order to improve labor-management relations and to stimulate productivity, tripartite manpower and production committees were established in the war industries. Coal production declined at the beginning of the war because of the decrease in exports; and as soon as war production expanded, coal resources became insufficient. Considerable effort had to be made to stimulate production in the mines. Miners were exempted from conscription; domestic consumption of coal was rationed; and exports were restricted. Coal could be exported only to Allied countries for their legitimate requirements, or to neutrals in exchange for vitally needed import commodities, such as Swedish iron ore. While production in war industries expanded, production of consumer goods drastically declined because of manpower and raw-materials deficiencies. The latter were due to reduction of imports resulting mainly from the necessity of conserving shipping space.

Agricultural production, on the contrary, considerably increased, as the result of a determined effort to stimulate its development by subsidies and other means. The output of vegetal foodstuffs, in particular, expanded, owing to a great extent to increased mechanization in the industry. Production of wheat, for example, in 1918 had reached a level 60 percent above the pre-war average; the increase for oats was 50 percent, and for potatoes 40 percent. In spite of all this, however, rationing had to be applied, as it was essential to reduce the level of imports considerably.

The most difficult situation arose in shipping. Out of the approximately 18 million tons of British merchant ships, about 500,000 tons had been seized by the enemy and 4 million tons requisitioned by the Admiralty for military transport. The remaining tonnage, which would have been scarcely sufficient, even under normal conditions, for all requirements, began to suffer increasing losses as enemy submarine activity became more disastrous. At the beginning of hostilities, the government had to undertake the insurance of hulls against risks of war. In spite of the enormous rise in freight rates, which caused an increase in the cost of imports, the new shipbuilding undertaken was completely inadequate to cover losses. In 1916, the government extended its control of shipping by requisitioning, at fixed rates, part of the cargo space available on all ships. All voyages had also to be approved by the government, which could decide to send any ship to the destination which it considered to be the most important. Finally, in 1917, the government decided to build and run a state-owned merchant fleet consisting of standardized ships. These were built in Great Britain, as well as in the United States, and they were the first application of an idea used later, during World War II, on an even larger scale, for construction of the now famous Liberty ships. In spite of all these efforts, however, new building remained inferior to losses until April 1917, when the maximum of submarine-warfare losses was reached, with 545,000 tons sunk. Later on the crisis was overcome, largely owing to the production of American shipyards.

Of the three great Western European belligerent powers, France had been the country most affected by the war, because a great part of her most productive agricultural and industrial areas had been occupied by the enemy almost from the very beginning.

Under these particularly difficult conditions, the achievements of French industry had been extremely impressive. Notwithstanding the loss of more than 50 percent of the coal and steel resources, production of war materials underwent an enormous expansion. In the Allied group, France was the leading country in production of aircraft and artillery; the United States Expeditionary Force at first was equipped with French planes and guns. New industries were established to meet war requirements or to replace goods formerly imported from Germany, such as chemicals, electric ferro-alloys, and so on. In order to replace coal, hydroelectric-power production was considerably expanded. In the new muni-tion plants, application of mass-production methods, until then scarcely used at all in France, was generalized; and some of these methods became the basis of new modern industries after the war. The Citroen automobile factories, for example, were initially es-tablished during the war as munition plants.

On the other hand, agricultural production in France decreased markedly, owing in part to the loss of some of the most fertile ter-ritories, but above all to the conscription into the army of 75 per-cent of the peasants and of a great part of the available horses. Al-though there was a considerable increase in imports, a very strict rationing had to be introduced.

Foreign trade, especially imports, were entrusted to state-con-trolled *consortiums,* i.e., trade associations that included all the producers of the respective industries; these *consortiums* were also in charge of the distribution of imported supplies.

The war which was being waged by one coalition of powers against another made apparent the necessity of state direction and intervention in regard to economy, not only on the national level but even on an international scale. Interallied economic coopera-tion was the first example of international economic planning.

The initial attempt at such cooperation was made by effecting, in common, purchases in neutral countries, in order to avoid overbid-ding, or by pooling resources which were in short supply. On August 15, 1914, the first Allied organ for this purpose was estab-lished, the Interallied Commission of Supply (*Commission Interal-liée de Ravitaillement*). In November 1916, the Interallied Wheat Executive was established and entrusted with the responsibility of making purchases for civilian and military requirements, allocat-ing supplies between the different Allied countries, and providing the shipping required. In August 1917, a similar Executive was es-tablished for meats and fats. In November 1917, the War Purchase and Finance Council was created and entrusted with the pooling of Allied financial resources and the obtaining of credits from the United States. In the same month, the most important of all interallied war boards was also established, the Allied Maritime Transport Council. Its importance was due to the crucially essential character of shipping and its particularly dangerous bottleneck situation, as well as to the nature of the executive powers vested in this board. It had complete authority to allocate shipping space belonging to all Allied countries, with a view to the most efficient utilization for the common interest.*

The financial consequences of the war had also been a shattering blow to the structure of capitalist economy. The tremendous losses of accumulated national wealth and productive resources, including the many millions of men killed and crippled—a natural result of this most wasteful form of consumption—produced financial effects as disastrous as the economic results of the war, the destruction of monetary and financial stability.

As soon as World War I began, the enormous budgetary deficits, which were the unavoidable consequence of war expenditure, direct and indirect, were the main basis of a steadily increasing inflation. While budgetary deficits increased the amount of distributed income, whereas the quantity of goods available for consumption had decreased because of concentration of production on war requirements and reduction of imports, prices naturally rose. The cost of military supplies purchased by the state therefore increased also, and the result was another rise in the budgetary deficit. Thus the vicious spiral of inflation continued its course. Only at a later stage had the progress of inflation, at first unhampered, been restrained through the introduction of rationing and price controls. The latter, however, were far from being effective, owing to the inability of governments to reduce the amount of monetary supply.

Of the Western European belligerent countries, Great Britain —which had not suffered any actual physical devastation, and which had a strong tradition of conservative budgetary policy—was

* In Russia, organization of war economy was along similar lines, though in general much less efficient than in Western European countries.

the only one to cover a significant part of its military expenditure by an increase in taxation, mainly in the rate of income tax (see Table I, page 34). In all other countries the strain of the war was very considerable. As a result, taxable resources declined, owing to the decrease in consumable and taxable production, while, on the other hand, new civilian expenditures caused directly or indirectly by the war (such as relief for refugees, subsidies, and so on) steadily increased. For these countries, any attempt to increase taxation in order to cover even part of their military expenditure would have been a political, if not a physical, impossibility.

It was therefore natural that in the countries faced by such conditions the solution of the problem of compensating war expenditures with new revenue and balancing the budget was postponed to the post-war period. It was also natural that in France, as well as in Germany, politicians responsible for the management of the national budget were tempted to declare that eventually, after the victorious issue of the war, the cost of this expenditure would be covered by the enemy. Such a proposal was obviously due to be most appealing to the population of these countries, not only because it would offer the prospect of easing the burden of their taxation, but also because they were convinced that the enemy of their respective countries was the culprit responsible for the war, and that therefore it was perfectly just and proper that he should pay its cost.

The most laconic expression of this policy was made by the French Minister of Finance, Klotz, who, upon being questioned in Parliament about military expenditures, said: *"Le boche paiera"* (The Hun will pay).

Thus, belligerent countries covered their war expenditures by means of loans, and a steadily increasing proportion of these loans consisted of short-term issues which caused credit inflation and even direct borrowing from central banks. That, in turn, resulted in a similar expansion of currency issue and direct monetary inflation. The amount both of the public debt and of the currency circulation thus increased considerably (see Table I).

33

TABLE I*

WAR EXPENDITURES AND BUDGETARY DEFICITS

	Total Expenditures	War Expenditures	Revenue	Deficit
	UNITED KINGDOM			
	(in millions of pounds)			
1914-15	535	328	211	324
1915-16	1590	1435	305	1285
1916-17	1825	1600	499	1326
1917-18	2290	1975	638	1652
1918-19	2972	2550	842	2130
	FRANCE			
	(in millions of francs)			
1914	10,371	6,526	4,196	6,175
1915	22,120	14,712	4,130	17,990
1916	36,848	23,853	4,932	31,916
1917	44,661	28,662	6,186	38,475
1918	56,649	36,120	6,791	49,858
	GERMANY			
	(in millions of marks)			
1914 †	9,651	6,936	3,344	6,307
1915	26,689	23,908	2,712	23,978
1916	28,780	24,771	3,063	25,716
1917	53,261	42,188	9,076	44,185
1918	45,514	33,928	8,479	37,035

CURRENCY CIRCULATION

(in millions of units of national currencies at the end of the year)

	France	Germany	Great Britain
1913	5,714	2,902	34.6
1914	10,043	5,862	79.6
1915	13,216	8,360	144.9
1916	16,580	11,438	196.8
1917	22,336	18,246	266
1918	30,250	33,069	399.2

PUBLIC DEBT AND PRICES

Public debt in millions of national currency			Wholesale prices, annual average	Cost of living, annual average
France			(1914 = 100)	(1914 = 100)
1914	at end of year	39,023	100	100
1915	"	n.a.	137	120
1916	"	n.a.	185	135
1917	"	103,896	257	163
1918	"	123,795	333	213
Germany			(1913 = 100)	
1914	31 March of year	5,158	96	
1915	"	16,955	139	
1916	"	39,856	148	
1917	"	69,211	159	
1918	"	105,304	198	
1919	"	156,452	274	
United Kingdom			(1914 = 100)	
1914	31 March of year	706	99	n.a.
1915	"	1,162	100	100
1916	"	2,129	123	123
1917	"	3,696	159	146
1918	"	4,925	207	176
1919	"	6,188	228	203

* Source: *Public Debt 1914-46*, United Nations, 1948.

† Budget year from 1 April to 31 March.

Apropos of this state of affairs, Great Britain issued, in addition to Bank of England notes, currency notes of the Treasury and the amount of these notes was by far larger than that of the banknotes issued. In Germany, currency circulation amounted in 1918 to 33 billion marks, in contrast to 5.8 billion marks in 1914. In France, currency circulation had also increased from 5.7 billion francs in 1913 to 30 billion in 1918.

This enormous monetary expansion obviously implied the suspension of the gold standard, which was attributable to the statutory rule of a minimum gold reserve for currency issued, as well as to the desire of belligerent countries to preserve their gold resources and not to risk depletion through the operation of the gold standard. Germany was the only belligerent country in which monetary legislation had been adapted beforehand to wartime conditions and thus did not require modification, since reserves required for currency issued could include not only gold but also treasury notes.

The value of the currencies of belligerent countries depreciated, as compared to that of neutral countries which had remained on the gold standard, such as the United States,* or even other neutrals, where, because there was only limited military expenditure, budgetary and price inflation was much smaller.

For France and Great Britain, however, the consequence of the effective depreciation of their currencies, as expressed in their exchange rates, was somewhat veiled, owing to the pegging of these rates after 1916, in relation to the United States dollar, at a level only slightly lower than the pre-war parities. This pegging was made possible at first through private loans obtained in the United States. Later on, when America had entered the war, it was continued as a result of an interallied financial agreement. However, this apparent stability could persist only as long as the interallied agreement was maintained in force, and the rates of these currencies were due to depreciate to their natural level as soon as the agreement would be terminated at the end of the war.

The main elements of the nineteenth century capitalist economy—free enterprise, unhampered by state interference or state control; international exchange of goods, services and capital; and monetary stability—were thus abolished, restricted or at least shattered as a consequence of World War I.

* Neutral up to April 1917.

The main problem which remained to be solved during the post-war period was whether economy could be rebuilt on exactly the same principles as before. This question did not arise immediately after the war, when a positive answer to it appeared to be taken for granted. However, it was to dominate the course of events during the next twenty years.

3 THE RUSSIAN REVOLUTION AND ITS INFLUENCE ON THE SOCIAL STABILITY OF THE REST OF EUROPE

THE COMMUNIST REVOLUTION of October 1917 occurred in Russia in a way which not only did not justify the predictions of Karl Marx, but which was completely contrary to them. Communism had gained victory, not as expected, in the most highly developed industrialized country with the most mature capitalist structure, but in a country where capitalism had just begun and where the peasantry, which was the vast majority of the population, was still living in a precapitalist era.

The victory of Communism was due to the political genius of Lenin, who grasped the extraordinary chance which circumstances offered him to seize control. These circumstances included the deep discontent and weariness of the soldiers, that is, of the masses of mobilized peasants. Most of these soldiers had no feeling of solidarity toward the state, as they shared practically no participation in the civilization of which the state was the basis. They wanted only to end the war as soon as possible, and at any price, and to implement land reform—in other words, to share among the peasants all the land which did not yet belong to them.

The provisional government of Kerensky did not satisfy this craving of the great majority of the Russian people. His motives were honorable but, as events proved, rather unrealistic. He wanted to remain faithful to the Western Allies, and refused to implement land reform, even though it was part of his program, before the election of the Constituent Assembly, which could not meet before the end of the war. Lenin, on the other hand, did not hesitate to take up these demands of the people, even though sharing of the land among individual peasants was contrary to the original Marxist program, which advocated collective ownership. Thus he gained the support of the masses.

The somewhat unexpected success of the Communist Revolution, which had been acknowledged at its beginnings by some of the Soviet leaders, certainly does not impair its historical importance or the magnitude of the transformation which resulted from it. It has, however, some importance in a consideration of the Marxist doctrine and its appeal to different nations and classes.

The consequences of the Communist Revolution in Russia will be discussed later (Chapter 10), while the present chapter will be devoted to the influence of the Russian Revolution on the rest of Europe, which had remained capitalist.

As a matter of fact, outside of the direct, destructive consequences of the war on capitalist economy, the latter had also been endangered by the establishment in Russia—as an indirect result of the war—of a regime based on the Marxist doctrine and absolutely opposed and hostile to capitalism.

Until the October 1917 Revolution, Marxism had been considered on the whole only as a theoretical doctrine, which had a great appeal to and influence upon the proletariat. That appeal consisted not in the scientific character of this doctrine—which according to Marx differentiated it from those of his predecessors, such as Owen or Proudhon—but, on the contrary, in its mythical, quasi-religious conclusions. These constituted a sort of redemption of the proletariat, rehabilitating in their own consciousness the value and importance of their contributions to society and civilization.

In the hierarchy of the capitalist economy and society, the proletariat was on the lowest possible level, which in the early period of capitalism was very low indeed. Workers were considered purely as manpower, little more than human robots, more or less on the same level with motive forces, such as horsepower and waterpower. Their work was considered as an ordinary commodity and its price, the wage rates, fluctuated with the market trends. According to the views of prominent classical authors of capitalist economy, such as Ricardo, and also, above all, according to the practice of capitalist economy during the first half of the nineteenth century, wages could not rise above pure subsistence level. The wage rates, however, could fall very much below subsistence level and even to nothing when supply of labor exceeded demand. Unemployed were supposed by capitalist economists to die off until supply and demand were again balanced. This was not purely abstract theory, as the unemployed had no rights whatsoever to assistance, and no legal claim on capitalist society, which used them when their labor was needed and rejected them when it was not wanted.

The workers naturally felt a deep resentment against the capitalist order, in which they were thus exploited and mistreated and, in fact if not in theory, completely excluded from enjoying any of its cultural or political rights or achievements. This oppression had also produced in them a deeply rooted inferiority complex. Since they were considered in capitalist society as the lowest class and since their work was classified in the lowest category, the workers themselves believed in this inferiority of their class and, though suffering from it, accepted it as more or less justified. Even though they resented the oppression which was to some extent a consequence of this classification of their work, and revolted against it, the workers tried whenever possible to effect escape, for themselves and their children, from manual labor and to rise to other classes and occupations.

The Marxist doctrine, which was based on the definition of all value as being created by labor, and proclaimed that the surplus value obtained by the capitalist employers was stolen from the workers, reversed the former depressing *inferiority* complex into a *superiority* complex filling them with pride and exaltation. Marx proclaimed that the workers were the only productive class of society, and that the upper classes of the capitalist order, which

40

exploited the proletariat, were mere parasites fattening upon the proceeds of the workers' toil. The proletariat, not its oppressors, was thus the most important, or even the only important, class of society. Far from deserving the low position which they held under the capitalist order, the workers had the right to be the ruling class of society, whose existence was due to their toil.

The replacement of the proletariat's former inferiority complex with a superiority complex of its own immensely strengthened its moral position in the class struggle, since now the oppression from which it suffered appeared not only cruel from a moral point of view, but also absurd from a supposedly scientific point of view.

This dialectical achievement of Marxism explains its appeal to the working class in the middle of the nineteenth century, when even in the Western European countries most progressive from a political, economic and social point of view the proletariat was really oppressed, and the term, "wage slavery," was not far from reality. The appeal of Marxism was much greater than that of socialist theories, which pleaded only for moral reasons for the granting to the workers of a greater share of the national income.

The same reasons also explain the attraction which Marxism— in spite of its outdated character and the disproving by actual experience of many of its basic theories—still has in countries which are economically in a phase of early capitalism similar to conditions which existed in Western Europe a hundred years ago. In those countries, exploitation of the workers is obvious, and their standard of living extremely low, while a small and apparently parasitic class of capitalists, or feudal landowners, enjoys an incomparably higher standard; and the active, strong middle class, which elsewhere in modern highly industrialized countries is the backbone of the social and of the economic structure, is not even in existence. Such a country was Russia in 1917, and Spain in the 1930's. Even today most of the countries of the Far and the Middle East, as well as of Latin America, are in that category. In the industrialized countries, on the contrary, conditions which, since

41

the days of Marx, have changed entirely and in a direction very different from what he foresaw, have reduced the appeal of the Marxist creed. First and foremost, instead of the gradual proletariatization of the whole population except for a small and steadily dwindling big capitalist group, and a generalization of poverty, there has been an unprecedented rise in wealth, national income and standards of living. The improvement in the standard of living benefited the workers, as well as the other classes of the population.

This improvement was due to a series of accompanying factors, the importance of which varied according to the different countries concerned. The main factors were: a change in the general moral attitude which no longer permitted considering labor as a simple commodity, and which recognized the necessity of satisfying minimum requirements, even of the unemployed; state legislation, which was adopted under the influence of this change of attitude, and which introduced regulations about minimum wages and maximum hours, as well as various social security benefits; the power of organized labor, which won from employers better working conditions and higher wages; and finally, the growing importance of a high purchasing power for the workers themselves, in providing a large domestic market for products of industry and agriculture. Nobody could pretend that the workers could be still considered outcasts in a capitalistic society, even though the improvement in the proletariat standards of living, while steadily increasing, was still insufficient and a continued struggle for further progress was fully justified.

In even greater contradiction to the forecasts of Marx was the steady growth in the importance, power and prosperity of the middle class. This middle class consisted to a great extent of the following old elements: some partly rural groups; small and medium farmers, as well as urban dwellers; small and medium industrialists and tradesmen; and professional people. A new and even more important element, however, had been added to the middle class in the salaried professions, namely, the managers and

42

technicians of modern industry and trade undertakings. Owing to its inventive and organizing ingenuity, this class had the greatest share in the establishment of the new industrial economy. Even if it did not receive the greatest share in the profits of this economy, it certainly did not consider itself as oppressed by capitalism and, because of this attitude, it offered a great material and psychological obstacle to the penetration of Marxist doctrine.

It is necessary to point out that capitalism and Communism, in spite of complete opposition to each other in their practical conclusions, are based upon the same philosophical premises: the paramount importance of economic and material factors and motives in the life and activity of individuals and nations. This concept, originating in Bentham's definition of utilitarianism, dominated the practical operation of the capitalist economy. The existence of this mentality in that economy facilitated the adoption, by the victims of this order, of a philosophy based on the reality from which they had suffered—a philosophy that reversed reality in their favor. Thus, in Marxism that concept became the basis of a new philosophic system: historic materialism, a doctrine that explains history by material factors only, all other factors—such as political doctrines, religions, and so on—being considered merely as "ideological superstructures" of secondary importance.

Accordingly, Marxism completely rejected the traditional system of national states, considering it only as a political superstructure of capitalism, a sham façade for capitalist domination. It denied the feeling of national solidarity as purely artificial and fostered by capitalists, and advocated its replacement by the only natural international class solidarity, namely, the solidarity existing between the workers of the different countries of the world.

World War I inflicted another denial of Marxist hopes and forecasts by demonstrating that national solidarity, based on an ancient tradition of common language, culture, origins, history, and the like proved in a decisive crisis to be much stronger than any international solidarity of the working class. In all belligerent countries with a highly industrialized capitalist economy, even

43

the socialist workers' parties were nearly unanimous in accepting the necessity of fighting for the defense of their homelands. As a counterpart to the acceptance by the proletariat of its patriotic duties, it was promised improvement of its conditions, for the post-war period, such as introduction of the eight-hour day in France, and establishment of at least some measure of economic security through unemployment relief (dole) in Great Britain.

While the experience of the war had strengthened national unity and class collaboration in the belligerent countries of Western Europe, the impact of the Bolshevik Revolution on the social relations in these countries produced quite the opposite effect. It stimulated the class struggle. The demonstration by this Revolution of the possibility of obtaining an alternative to capitalism, through the establishment of a Communist dictatorship of the proletariat, enormously increased the appeal and the driving power of the most revolutionary parties of the working class. Before the war, the practical policy of the Socialist parties was directed much more toward increasing the share, and improving the condition, of the workers inside the capitalist economy than toward the destruction of that economy. As a consequence of the Russian Revolution, however, powerful groups arose amidst the proletariat striving with fanatical zeal for destruction by violence of the capitalist order and of the whole structure of society based upon it.

A natural counterpart of this stimulating influence of the Soviet Revolution on the radical wing of the proletariat was the deep repulsion and hatred which the tendencies and the acts of the Bolshevik leaders created in all other classes of society, in all the countries of Western civilization. Save in the case of a small minority of big capitalists, this aversion did not result only, or even mainly, from the fear of losing their private property. Especially the middle class, where this feeling of repulsion was particularly significant, had been the main creative force in the establishment of modern society based on political democracy and capitalist economy in the frame of national states. This class was proud of its creation and of the immense progress achieved toward improved economic standards of living and political freedom, and was deeply attached to the principles upon which these achievements had been based. It was thus especially outraged by the destruction, in Russia, of the whole structure of the national state and of civilization, which it generally respected and cherished. It was appalled, too, by the complete subordination, and even partial extermination, of the Russian middle-class intellectuals (*intelligentsia*), as well as by the establishment of the dictatorship of the proletariat, a class which it considered to be its inferior and certainly the least likely to be qualified to rule the destinies of the economy and of the state.

The middle class in all these countries became therefore strongly opposed to the international proletarian revolutionary movement. This opposition was especially violent in countries where the issue of the war had stimulated nationalist feelings and resentment, as well as weakened the structure of the state and of the capitalist economy. Among such countries, for example, were Germany, Austria and Italy. There, this attitude of the middle class was to be the psychological basis of Fascism.

4 THE POST-WAR RECONVERSION PERIOD 1918–1920, "BACK TO NORMALCY"

As WE LOOK back today, with our present experience, on the period which followed World War I, it seems obvious that a return to the pre-war peacetime economy should have been accomplished slowly and gradually, with the greatest possible cooperation both between the different factors in each national economy: business, labor and government, and between nations. This would seem especially true in view of the complete disruption of the pre-war pattern of the capitalist economy, in its international aspect, particularly in Europe, as well as in the national economy of the individual belligerent countries.

International cooperation was necessary for success in the major and immediate short-term task, namely, alleviation of the shortages of key commodities and prevention of inflation, and also for the long-term task of coordination of reconstruction of the world economy, taking into account the permanent change in its structure that resulted from the war. The most important of these changes, especially as affecting Western European economy, were: alterations in frontiers, mainly in Germany and France, resulting in changes in productive capacity, export and import requirements, and so on; the loss of Russia as an important market for industrial exports after the 1917 Revolution, as well as the complete loss of all foreign capital invested there, mainly by France; and the loss by all Western European countries of a considerable part of their overseas investments, in the case of Great Britain and France spent to purchase supplies in the United States. As for Germany, all her foreign assets had been confiscated as reparations, in accordance with the Treaty of Versailles.

While all these changes had weakened the economy of Western European countries, their main rivals—the United States and Japan—had benefited from the war, expanding their industrial production and conquering overseas markets. During the war, those markets had been starved of their normal European imports of manufactured goods, as the factories of Europe were working for war production and not for export. Moreover, because of lack of industrial goods previously imported from Europe, industrialization in many overseas countries made considerable progress, and thus reduced future markets for European exports when they could be resumed.

Yet, in spite of all these obvious reasons in favor of a gradual process of adjustment, the change-over from war economy had been extremely abrupt. The great mass of the public, impatient to do away with the discomforts of restrictions and to come back to pre-war prosperity, supported the efforts of business to abolish as soon as possible all controls that restricted prices and profits. Most of the wartime measures, therefore, were very rapidly dispensed with. There only remained in force measures which were supported by powerful interests whom they benefited, such as rent control in France, as well as agricultural subsidies for several years. In Great Britain, in spite of the support given to the principle of free trade, the MacKennah duties * were maintained.

The boards of interallied cooperation were also rapidly terminated, with the one exception of the Maritime Transport Council. This was maintained till the end of the year 1919, because of the universal lack of shipping and the enormous requirements for

---

* Introduced in 1915 to create revenue and reduce nonessential imports, and thus to husband shipping; amounted to 33 percent on automobiles, watches, optical instruments, and certain other goods.

47

sea transport, which were increased by the repatriation of the United States and Dominion armies from Europe.

The interallied financial and monetary agreement with the United States was suspended in March 1919. As a consequence, the exchange rates of pound sterling and of the franc, which had been pegged near the pre-war parities (£1 = $4.83, and $1 = frs. 5.18), immediately declined to less than $4 for £1 and 17 frs. for $1 by the end of 1919. This decline in the rates of European currencies was still more violent in Germany; by the end of 1919, the mark descended to a value of 79 marks to the dollar.

These conditions may be attributed to two principal causes: First, the domestic inflation which had developed during the war, and which, owing to the tremendous budgetary expenditure on reconversion and reconstruction (the latter especially in France), was still increasing. Second, the disequilibrium in the balance of payments between Western Europe and overseas countries, especially the United States. For the two-year period 1919-1920, the balance of payments of Europe (of which Western Europe contributed more than 90 percent) was the following: imports, $19.7 billion; exports, $7.7 billion; deficit of the balance of trade, $12 billion. However, this deficit was reduced to $8 billion, owing to invisible items: services $2.2 billion, and income from foreign investments, $1.8 billion.

This disequilibrium resulted from the enormous demand of former belligerent countries, where consumption levels during the war had been extremely reduced, and where home production recovered only slowly for goods of all kinds, but especially for food and raw materials which could be imported only from overseas. Thus, the situation in Western Europe, as to the dollar shortage, was very similar to conditions after World War II, and nearly as grave. However, at that time the resources available to Western Europe for bridging this gap in its balance of payments, though diminished to pre-war, were still far from being exhausted. Indeed, by liquidation of some foreign assets and the use of a few private loans, the gap had been closed.

48

Another similarity between the situation after 1918 and the present one is the fact that then, also, Eastern and Central Europe —that part of the Continent producing and exporting food and raw materials—had suffered even greater destruction and dislocation than Western Europe. Agricultural production thus recovered very slowly, and exports to Western Europe remained practically nil for several years after the end of the war. The very slow recovery in this region was due partly to continued military operations (civil war in Russia and in Hungary, war between Poland and Russia) but it was also due to a certain extent to the land reforms initiated in most of the countries of this section. Here the big estates that formerly produced most of the exports had been divided, and there had been a temporary decrease in production and, especially, in the sales of agricultural produce on the market. This was also an important factor of increase in overseas imports of Western Europe.

From the point of view of production, recovery in Western Europe after World War I was very slow, much slower than after World War II. This slow rate of progress was due, in considerable degree, to a series of factors such as lack of raw materials of industry and of fertilizer for agriculture, as well as dislocation of national economies resulting from change of frontiers. But there were also difficulties of reconversion, which were due to the absence of planning and direction for reconstruction, as well as to an unsettled labor situation. Labor having claimed and failed to receive the improvement in conditions promised during the war—such as shorter hours and higher wages—a series of important strikes were fought out, especially in Great Britain.

In 1919, then, the level of industrial and agricultural production in Western Europe was still much below pre-war, and even lower compared with the progress achieved by the United States.

Owing to the tremendous excess of effective demand over supply, world economy experienced a very strong inflationary boom in 1919-20. In Western Europe, inflationary pressures resulting from commodity shortages were aggravated by labor troubles, which

49

decreased production and increased cost but above all were stimulated by an excessive supply of money resulting mainly from budgetary deficits. Consequently, rise of prices was extremely abrupt. (In France, the wholesale price index rose, from the end of 1919 to the end of 1920, from 356 to 509).

PHYSICAL VOLUME OF PRODUCTION IN 1919, PER CAPITA OF POPULATION (1913 = 100) *

	Agriculture	Industry
Germany	62	61
France	83	66
Great Britain	89	88
Belgium	78	91
Italy	73	74
United States	112	114

* Clough & Cole, *Economic History of Europe*. Heath, 1946.

This post-war boom, however, was due to collapse as soon as the most urgent requirements had been satisfied. Consumer excess purchasing power (savings accumulated during the war) was rapidly exhausted because of the rise in prices, and the same process occurring in each national economy was also expressed in the reduction in purchases in overseas products, owing to the growing shortage of hard currencies.

The 1920-21 depression originated not in Europe but in overseas countries producing food and raw materials. These countries were the first to be hit by the curtailment of European purchases overseas, especially as their productive capacity had been expanded to meet war requirements. The new industrial countries were severely hit, the most important being Japan, which had enormously increased production and exports to replace lacking European goods, and which was strongly affected by the return of European competition. The slump, which first started in Japan, spread rapidly, to Europe.

The country most affected by the slump was Great Britain. Because of the paramount importance of its overseas trade, it suffered from the curtailed purchasing power of its main customers, due to the fall in food and raw material prices. The basic British industries most affected by the slump were cotton—with its enormous export volume—shipbuilding, and coal. As the result of decline in production, mass unemployment spread for the first time through Great Britain and, for the whole period between the two world wars, became the most serious calamity of British life. The impact of the world slump was much less felt in France, where reconstruction of the war-devastated areas began to stimulate all industrial activities. It was scarcely felt at all in Germany, however, where increasing inflation stimulated exports and industrial production.

After the 1920-21 depression, the period of reconstruction began in Europe, during which each country attempted to restore its pre-war position in relation to production and currency stability, as well as foreign trade. The latter factor resulted to a certain extent in a revival of pre-war international economic relations.

The main feature common to this economic reconstruction in all countries was the fact that the development was pursued with a purely national outlook, without any consideration of what was happening elsewhere. The unavoidable result of such a policy was duplication of productive capacity. Especially when changes of frontiers had divided formerly integrated industrial entities, on both sides of the new frontiers the former entities were restored through erection of a new plant. Thus, when the textile industry of the former Austro-Hungarian Empire—the spinning mills of which were located in Austria proper and the weaveries in Bohemia—was divided between Austria and Czechoslovakia, the Austrians built new weaveries and the Czechs new spinneries. This was done instead of agreeing to continue the former industrial division of labor, by preferential custom agreements. The same thing happened with Lorraine, which, when returned to France, contained mainly pig-iron furnaces; finished steel was manufac-

51

tured in the Ruhr. Steel mills, then, were erected in Lorraine and pig-iron furnaces in the Ruhr. This enormous duplication of industrial capacity was generally undertaken without sufficient consideration of markets or costs, as geographical location of the new mills generally was less favorable than of the old ones built on the basis of the most economic division of labor. Such circumstances implied the necessity of high custom duties and prepared the way for future overproduction difficulties.

5 REPARATIONS AND WAR DEBTS

THE EFFORTS of all former belligerent countries to return to pre-war conditions of national and international economy were hampered by a sinister inheritance from the war: the problem of war debts and reparations.

The history of war debts and reparations and of their absurd and catastrophic results cannot be understood on the basis only of financial and economic factors, such as difficulties of transfer and balance of payments. The intricacy of this problem and the final impossibility of arriving at a really satisfactory solution seem to be due even more to differences of opinion on the political, legal and moral aspect of the problem than to the opposition of material interests. This fact is one of the most convincing examples in history of the deep psychological meaning behind the maxim of Luigi Pirandello, the famous Italian playwright: "Everybody has his own truth."

The point of view of the Western European Allies—that is, of France, Belgium, Italy and, to a slightly lesser extent, Great Britain—was the following: As Germany was responsible for the war, she was due to repair the damage she had caused. That viewpoint was supported by a considerable amount of willful destruction committed by the Germans in Belgium and in France. There, in order to ruin their enemies and to prevent any easy recovery, they practiced the "scorched earth" policy by flooding mines, felling fruit trees, and inflicting other serious damage on property and land. The Western European thesis was incorporated in the text of the Versailles Treaty, which in its Article 232 contained the so-called "war-guilt clause" stating, in effect, that because Germany was guilty of having started the world war, she was therefore obliged to compensate the victims of her aggression. The amount of the damage to be compensated for was tremendous in spite of the fact that, under the influence of the United States, reparations had been limited to the cost of the actual devastations and of war pensions, instead of payment by Germany of the total cost of the war for the Allies as had been originally requested by the Western European powers.

As to Germany, her nationalist feeling had been deeply stultified by the war-guilt clause. Believing that she had fought a just and defensive war, she was revolted by the fact that her victorious enemies not only wanted to extract from her a war indemnity, but pretended to justify this indemnity by imposing on the Reich an admission of exclusive guilt, absolutely unjustified from the German point of view. She would probably have grudgingly accepted such a penalty—if limited in amount and time—as a natural consequence of her defeat, as Germany herself had extracted substantial war indemnities from Russia and Rumania. The revolt of German nationalist opinion against the attitude of the Allies was to a certain extent justified from the German point of view. In other words, the Versailles Treaty, though undoubtedly more just than the treaties at times imposed by victorious Germany, as well as the status quo of 1914, still conformed mainly with the interests of the Allied victors and therefore, for the Germans, was far from absolute justice.

The Germans consequently considered the war-guilt clause a hypocritical statement imposed by the Allies in order to justify the reparations, which were intended to become the principal means of exploiting Germany and making her a slave of the victors for nearly sixty years. The revolt against the moral condemnation of the war-guilt clause was thus reinforced by the revolt against payment of the reparations, which the Germans naturally considered as the main, or even the only, cause of their miseries and sufferings. Thus the war-guilt clause and the reparations were of considerable influence in assisting the revival of nationalism, development of xenophobia, and the birth of Nazism.

As to the Allied war debts, the American government and public opinion considered the credits granted, during the war, by the United States Treasury to other Allied governments as normal financial obligations, which naturally were supposed to be repaid according to the original terms of credit agreements. On the contrary, the Western European Allies considered that these sums had been spent for the common war effort, and that, especially before the massive participation of American troops on the battlefields— which took place only in the summer of 1918—these loans had been used for arming and feeding their soldiers who had fought, and also died, in large numbers for the common cause. Having been devastated and impoverished by the war, they felt it to be an acute injustice to be obliged to reimburse these sums to a country whose sacrifices in the war had been relatively slight, but whose wealth and productive capacity had, on the contrary, considerably expanded. This European point of view found justification in historical precedent since, in the past, financially strong nations had always subsidized the armies of their poorer allies. England, especially, had a long tradition of granting to her allies important sums (à fonds perdus) without ever demanding reimbursement.

The insistence of the United States upon receiving payment of its war debts increased the necessity that reparations be paid in excess of the payments due to America, since there was no possibility, economical, and still less political, that countries such as France, Belgium or Italy could pay war debts out of their own war-devastated economy.

These were the psychological attitudes of the different groups of countries interested in the problem of war debts and reparations.

The difficulties resulting from these various points of view were

55

enormously increased by the attitude of the United States. While insisting on repayment of war debts, America refused to accept payment in the only normally possible form in which payment could be effected, namely, a surplus of goods and services. Instead of accepting an import surplus, the United States desired to protect her industry from foreign competition and therefore maintained her traditional export surplus without realizing that her change of position from a debtor to a creditor country implied a change in foreign trade policy, as well as in the balance of trade. Thus during this period the United States twice increased her protective tariff, by the Fordney-McCumber Act in 1922 and by the Hawley-Smoot Act in 1930.

As a result of this policy, the United States, having an important surplus in her trade balance and an even more considerable surplus in her balance of payments, had substantial resources available for foreign investment. She invested most of it in Germany, a country which now required capital for industrial reconstruction and for reparation payments and was ready to pay especially high interest rates. Most of the money thus lent to Germany was used for payment of reparations and, to a great extent, came back to the United States in payment of war debts. However, this extraordinary and absurd circuit of capital could last only as long as the United States continued to make new loans on a large scale. As soon as new foreign investments stopped, after the beginning of the American depression, this absurd international credit pyramid gradually collapsed and not only did payment of reparations and war debts come to an end, but also all the new capital invested in Germany was frozen, and finally wiped out.

It seems a piece of cruel irony of history that, because the United States had insisted on payment of war debts and at the same time refused payment in goods, American capital was induced to invest and to lose in Germany far greater sums than those which the United States was due to receive. The American investor thus not only financed reparation payments to his former Allies and war-debts payments to the United States Treasury, but also to a great extent he financed the development of German industrial capacity which a few years later was to become the basis of Hitler's war machine.

A summarized history of war debts and reparations will help to illustrate the preceding developments. The total amount of reparations had not been determined by the Versailles Treaty, partly because of the difficulty of arriving at an agreement, and partly because the amount of the damage to be paid could not yet be established. The Reparations Commission was entrusted with establishing the total amount due. Germany was also to pay occupation costs. However, as an interim payment a sum of $5 billion was to be paid immediately in gold, foreign securities, and deliveries of commodities, mainly coal to compensate for decrease of Allied coal production due to war devastation.

The first tentative estimate of the amount of reparations made by the Reparations Commission was 269 billion gold marks, payable by annuities of a minimum of 3 billion marks. The Germans protested against the immensity of this sum and it was reduced several times, till in May 1921 the final amount of reparations was put at 132 billion gold marks, payable in annuities of a fixed amount of 2 billion marks, increased by the proceeds of 26 percent of German exports. This figure, announced to Germany as an ultimatum, was accepted by her government. But difficulties rapidly became insurmountable: the necessity of making some reparations in cash precipitated the fall of the mark; the industrialists of the Ruhr were opposed to the deliveries in kind to France and Belgium, wanting to keep all the coke to develop German steel production (a quite similar situation developed after World War II); and the repeated failure of Germany to make the promised coke deliveries led to the French occupation of the Ruhr, which, together with German passive resistance, paralyzed Germany's economy and completely destroyed the mark.

The time, then, was ripe for compromise. Indeed, compromise was desired: (1) by the Anglo-Saxon powers, which wanted the recovery of Germany as a prerequisite of recovery as a whole; (2)

by the Germans, who now became convinced that, in order to obtain evacuation of the Ruhr by the French troops, they would have to agree to pay the reparations; and (3) by the French, who by the costly occupation of the Ruhr did not succeed in getting more reparations, and who were very eager to reach an agreement enabling them to obtain this result.

A commission of financial experts, presided over by a Chicago banker, Charles Dawes, studied the reparations problem and the general situation of Germany and drew up a plan which was finally accepted by all the powers concerned. The main principles of the Dawes Plan were the adaptation of reparations to Germany's capacity to pay, and the obligation of the Allies to accept payment in goods—that is, by means of a German export surplus—which, as well as a balanced budget and a stable currency, were the basic conditions required for the success of the scheme. At the start of the Plan, in 1924, Germany received an international loan of $200 million, mainly subscribed in the United States, for reestablishment of her new currency, the Reichsmark, on a gold standard. The Dawes Plan established a normal reparations annuity of 2.5 billion gold marks, an amount, however, which would be reached only gradually in the fifth year; it started at 1 billion for 1924. But this normal annuity could be increased or decreased according to the German economic situation as measured by a prosperity index. Germany had to offer its internal revenue, as well as its railways, as a lien against payment of reparations. A reparations agent appointed by the Allies resided in Berlin and controlled the fulfilment of the Plan. An American banker, Gilbert Parker, acted in this capacity.

During the implementation of the Dawes Plan, between 1924 and 1927, the Western European Allies made agreements with the United States for settlement of their war debts. The United States Treasury granted conditions which, from its point of view, were rather generous, abandoning the greatest part of the accumulated interest, and even part of the principal, and making the rest payable in sixty-two annuities. For all countries concerned, with the

58

exception of Great Britain, the amount payable as war debts was less than what they received as reparations; however, it absorbed a considerable part of what was due them for reparation of their war devastation. By far the worst feature of the war-debt agreements with the United States was the refusal of the latter to connect reparations and war debts and to make payments of the latter conditional on receipt of the former.

The Dawes Plan did not establish the total amount of the reparations; it was supposed to be only a temporary solution. But a final solution of the problem was desired by all parties concerned, and thus in 1929 another international expert committee, presided over by the American banker Owen Young, drew up a new plan. Based on the very favorable experience of the Dawes Plan during five years, it represented an effort really to provide a final solution. This Young Plan omitted the "escape clauses" which existed in the Dawes Plan—such as the prosperity index—and which permitted variation in the amount to be received or paid.

The Young Plan put the total amount of reparations at 121 billion gold marks to be paid in 59 annuities of 2.1 billion marks each. Part of this amount was supposed to be converted into interest-bearing bonds and to be issued on the international capital markets, an arrangement which would enable the creditor countries to get in cash part of the amount due them. A small loan, called the Young Loan, had actually been issued. As a counterpart to the definite obligation assumed by Germany to pay the sum stipulated in this Plan, she got a reduction in the amount of the annuities, the termination of international financial control by the reparations agent and, above all, the complete evacuation of her territory by Allied troops.

The last French troops left the Rhineland in September 1930. Unfortunately their departure coincided with a great victory of the Nazis in the national elections, as well as with the stoppage of foreign loans and credits which in a few months caused a complete breakdown in Germany's economy, making default unavoidable. At this moment, President Hoover proposed to the European

59

Allied Powers a one-year moratorium on reparations, in order to avoid a German financial crash which would have aggravated world depression as well as endangered American private capital invested in the Reich. To make the proposal at all acceptable, he had to recognize the relationship, heretofore denied by the American authorities, between reparations and war debts and to extend the moratorium also to the latter. However, as a result of financial panic and flight of capital, the situation in Germany, far from improving, only deteriorated and, when the moratorium expired, there could be no possibility of resuming reparations payments. In line with their general attitude on this problem, all the Western European Allies—with only the temporary exception of Great Britain—also defaulted on their war-debt payments to the United States.

A last conference on the reparations problem, held in Lausanne in 1932, practically wiped out reparations by reducing them to the sum of 3 billion gold marks, which were supposed to be issued as an international loan. The acceptance of these terms by the Western European Allied powers, however, was conditional upon the abandonment by the United States of her war-debt claims. As the United States did not agree to this point, the Lausanne agreement was not implemented and this was the end of reparations.

A balance sheet of reparations payments will give the following results: from Versailles until the Dawes Plan, Germany had paid about 25 billion marks in gold, foreign securities, commodities and foreign exchange obtained from the sale of marks. From 1924 to 1931, she paid 11.15 billion marks—about 6 billion to France and 2.4 billion to the British Empire. During the same period, 1924-31, she had borrowed about 25 billion marks from abroad, most of it from the United States and the rest from Great Britain, Switzerland, the Netherlands, Sweden, France, and other nations. In 1931, Germany defaulted on this private foreign debt, first by freezing it, then by prohibiting transfers even of interest payments, etc. Practically this whole foreign debt was wiped out.

These 25 billion marks enabled Germany not only to pay reparations and to extend her productive capacity, but also to make important investments abroad estimated at about 10 billion marks. These German foreign investments were not wiped out by default, but were to be most useful in strengthening German economic and also political influence in the countries concerned. The investments were made in neighboring countries of southeastern Europe, in South America, and even in the United States, where I. G. Farbenindustrie acquired considerable interests.

As to the United States, her Treasury finally recovered as war debts a total sum of $2,735 million. The losses of the private American investors, however, had been of a much higher amount. Of greater importance by far than the financial loss involved were the consequences of the reparations and war-debts problem in the disintegration of the financial and economic international relations, a disintegration which prepared the way for political tension and conflict.

6 GREAT BRITAIN DURING THE PERIOD
1921–1931: DEFLATION AND STAGNATION

THOUGH GREAT BRITAIN had not suffered physical devastation in World War I, her economy was greatly weakened as a consequence of the war. The loss of her economic supremacy was Britain's war devastation.

After the Armistice of November 1918, Great Britain had a large share in the boom of prosperity, owing to the pressure of pent-up demand. Her industries worked full time for domestic and export markets starved of manufactured goods; prices, wages and profits rose; and unemployment was at a low point of 2 percent of employable workers, as compared to a pre-war average of 4 percent.

But this prosperity was very short-lived and, as soon as the fall in prices of primary products had shattered the purchasing power of overseas markets, there began for Britain a period of chronic depression, the most disastrous feature of which was mass unemployment. It lasted, with only slight improvement, even during the climax of world prosperity, until World War II.

The decline of the British economic position in the world was due to three series of factors:

The loss of financial supremacy by the City of London to New York, due to liquidation of a considerable part of the most remunerative foreign investments (about £1 billion) in the first years of World War I, which had been made in order to pay for American supplies; a lesser flow of new capital formation and surplus of balance of payments; and a loss of monetary prestige, caused by the depreciation of sterling while the United States dollar remained convertible in gold.

The decline in exports was due to development (during the war, while British exports were halted) of industrial exports of Japan (mainly in the Far East) and of the United States, mainly in Latin America, and was due also to increasing industrialization in former overseas markets, such as India, the Dominions and even Latin America. British industrial exports were affected by this industrialization abroad more than those of the other great industrial countries, because they consisted to a great extent of basic staple products, such as cotton goods, the production of which could be developed in the earliest stages of industrialization. Thus British exports declined, if not in terms of value in sterling then in terms of volume, and did not recover their pre-war level even at the height of the prosperity of the 1920's, when world trade had reached again its pre-war maximum.

British exports, compared to pre-war, had been:

	in £ millions	quantum % of 1913
1913	570	100
1921	703	50
1927	709	79
1929	730	82

The decline of British industrial production was also considerable as compared to pre-war. This decline was due partly to decrease of exports, but to a great extent to the fact that British industry was organized mainly to provide satisfaction of basic needs. Demand for her products had enormously expanded, it is true, while satisfaction of such needs became gradually possible for the formerly underprivileged classes and nations. However, once satisfaction of such needs was reasonably complete, demand did not increase any more with rise in purchasing power, which was devoted to the satisfaction of other needs of a less urgent character. On the contrary, increase of purchasing power could sometimes even decrease demand for staple necessities * when a new and more attractive way of satisfying this demand became available. Thus, consumption of cotton was considerably affected by the enormous expansion of rayon during the period under consideration.

Hence, the level of British industrial activity underwent a considerable decline as compared to pre-war. Even in 1925, the best year for British industry in the 1920's, the index of general industrial production and mining reached only 86 percent of 1913.

Decline in production and exports was particularly important in coal, which had been the cornerstone of British industrial power. Coal consumption had been reduced through the practice of fuel economy—thus, the quantity of coal consumed for production of a kilowatt hour of electricity decreased from 3.5 kg. to less than 1 kg.; and by increased competition of gas and fuel oil for industry, domestic heating, and especially for shipping, where coal was completely displaced, with the resultant loss of the very substantial bunker trade. Competition of other coal-producing countries was also much more severe. The Ruhr coal, sent as reparations to France and Italy, took the place of former British exports, while Polish coal exports, benefiting from much lower wage rates, conquered important British markets in Scandinavia. The competitive position of the British coal industry was particularly difficult both because of its inefficient organization (over 3000 mines, most of them small and with outdated equipment) and because of the highest wage rates and the shortest hours in Europe.

The British coal industry was thus in a state of constant depression. Already in 1919, a commission of inquiry appointed by the government recommended nationalization of the mines, in order to concentrate and rationalize production. This solution was not adopted, however; instead, the state paid a temporary subsidy. When the subsidy was terminated, in May 1926, the

* Decline in consumption of such basic necessities does not mean that all demand measured by human needs was fully satisfied, but only effective demand, that is, purchasing power.

miners rejected the wage reduction requested by the owners, refusing to be victimized for the inefficient organization of the industry. The resulting coal strike, which also caused a short-lived general strike, lasted for six months and cost Britain 100 million tons of coal and the permanent loss of a great part of her export markets. The continuous depression of the coal industry had very dire results for its future. The bad financial position of the mines, which operated more often at a loss than at a profit, impeded new investment, as well as modernization and rationalization of production equipment and methods.

In addition, the considerable proportion of unemployed miners, which since 1921 had never been below 10 percent, discouraged influx of new young forces into mining. Even the sons of the miners deserted into other professions providing easier work more secure employment, and sometimes even better pay. Thus was prepared for the near future a serious manpower crisis, which did not become apparent so long as production was at a low level, but which was suddenly revealed during World War II. Coal production stagnated during most of this period and was considerably below pre-war level: The 1913 figure of 287 million tons was never reached again; production fluctuated from a minimum of 207 million tons to a maximum of 232 tons reached in 1938; the average volume of exports was 40 million tons, instead of 90 million before the war.

Decline of coal exports was one of the main reasons for the depression in shipping, British ships having lost the privilege of a coal cargo readily accepted everywhere for outgoing voyages. However, the main reason for the shipping crisis was the enormous increase in world tonnage resulting from the mass production of standardized cargo ships, especially in American shipyards during the last years of the war and in the post-war boom. Thus, world tonnage in 1921 was 65 million tons against 45 million tons in 1913, while the volume of international trade carried was much smaller. It reached the 1913 peak only in 1929, and immediately declined again as soon as world depression began.

Shipbuilding suffered naturally most heavily from the crisis which included superabundance of shipping. For the 10 years after 1920, scarcely any new ships had been ordered by British shipowners in British yards, where the proportion of unemployed was over 50 percent of total workers of the industry.

Cotton, which was the greatest export consumers'-goods industry was affected in a steadily increasing degree by competition from industrial countries with much lower wage rates—Japan and India for example—as well as from newer textiles, such as rayon. Consequently, production and exports of cotton goods steadily declined.

	Cotton yarn (in millions of pounds)		Cotton cloth (in millions of yards)	
	Production	Exports	Production	Exports
1913	1922	1432	8044	6673
1924	1352	942	5426	4625
1927	1047	197	3320	2407
1937	1350	159	3386	1922

Iron and steel production and exports also declined, handicapped by the lack of domestic iron ore and suffering from heavy competition mainly from France, Belgium and Luxembourg, which had greater ore resources, more modern equipment, and lower wage rates. Production and exports of machinery and other equipment, though well maintained, progressed less rapidly than those of the main competing countries, i.e., the United States and Germany.

While these old basic industries, born and developed in the nineteenth century, suffered thus more or less severely from continuous depression or stagnation, new industries created and developed in the twentieth century enjoyed considerable prosperity. Such industries as electrical apparatus and appliances, chemicals, automobiles, etc. catered on the whole to less essential needs than the old industries, and produced not necessities but goods providing greater comforts or luxuries. They were thus capable of greater expansion in the event of rising purchasing power of the market.

These industries could hold their own against most foreign competition on the domestic and export markets. They were established in Great Britain at the same time as in the main competing countries, and were organized with a more or less similar degree of efficiency and productivity, with the possible exception of those in the United States, where the larger home market especially favored mass production. However, they were primarily organized to cater to the home market, and could not claim to obtain a special privileged position on foreign markets comparable to that possessed previously by the traditional British export industries.

The British monetary policy also added to the difficulties of British industry. After World War II, Great Britain decided to restore the pound sterling to its pre-war parity, in order to re-establish the financial supremacy of "The City" (London), and also —though this was a minor consideration—to restore the value of British foreign investments made in sterling currency. This policy implied a lengthy and painful deflationary adjustment, including: balancing of the budget by maintaining a very high level of taxation; increasing the burden of the public debt; and, a natural consequence of the gradual revaluation of the currency, a continuous and even steadily increasing deflation. The final restoration of the gold standard had been accomplished in 1925, when Winston Churchill was Chancellor of the Exchequer. While he was later criticized for this measure, it had been unanimously approved beforehand by a committee containing members of all parties, including Labor.

After World War I, as well as today, Great Britain with admirable courage accepted a policy of painful austerity, in order to restore her previous greatness. During that former period, however, the sacrifices implied by this policy were far from equitably distributed. While deflation favored financial interests, it created a great handicap for British industrial exports, increasing their cost in foreign currency. At the same time, cost reduction through wage decreases was possible only in a very limited degree, owing to powerful resistance by trade unions. On the other hand, revaluation of the pound favored foreign imports, making them cheaper in terms of sterling; and, since only a very small part of British industrial production enjoyed tariff protection, through the key products or the McKennah duties, imports of foreign manufactured goods increased to a very considerable extent.

Revaluation of sterling did not succeed in reestablishing the world supremacy of "The City." The financial center of the world had finally shifted to New York. London, however, after Great Britain's return to the gold standard, attracted a considerable amount of foreign funds in search of short-term investment. These funds were owned mainly by foreign central banks which, according to the gold exchange standard widely accepted at that period, could cover their currency issue with foreign exchange convertible in gold, as well as with gold itself. Having complete confidence in the stability of sterling, and in the possibility, whenever necessary, of converting their holdings into gold, these central banks benefited from the interest accrued on their deposits. The greatest holding, amounting to about £200 million, belonged to the Banque de France.

The London banks, however, in the management of these foreign funds, did not show themselves worthy either of this confidence or of the great tradition of conservative progress in British banking. Since the possibility of using these funds profitably in financing foreign trade had declined as compared to pre-war, British bankers permitted themselves to become attracted by the high interest rates existing abroad, especially in the debtor countries of Central Europe—Germany, Austria, and the rest. Without giving sufficient consideration to the shaky financial structure of these countries, which could generally remain solvent only as long as foreign capital continued to flow in, they invested there considerable sums which, as the situation in these regions deteriorated, were to become frozen and lost. The irresponsible investment policy of the London bankers thus paved the way for Great Britain's monetary disaster in 1931.

In spite of all these difficulties, Great Britain still had during this period a favorable balance of payment. In 1927, while the balance of trade had a deficit of £392 million, income from shipping was £140 million; from other services, £78 million; and from foreign investments, £270 million. Thus there remained a net surplus of £96 million. But Great Britain was in the position of a capitalist living partly on income from capital, while a great part of his productive resources remain idle. The part of the population drawing its livelihood from the new industries was reasonably prosperous; the regions where these industries were located (such as Coventry and Greater London) grew and prospered; and the classes living from foreign investments and finance were very prosperous indeed—yet, a great part of the working class formerly employed in the old industries was permanently on the dole. After 1921, the total number of unemployed was always above 1 million. In 1922, it amounted to 2,015,000 or 17.7 percent of all the workers insured; in 1925, 1,322,000 or 11.2 percent; and in 1929, 1,466,000 or 2.2 percent.

Unemployment insurance, first introduced in Great Britain shortly before 1914, extended at first only to the main industries. After World War I its scope was enlarged, and finally it was supplemented by relief payments (dole) payable when the insurance benefits were exhausted, after six months of unemployment. After 1921, the dole became a permanent feature in the life of the British working class. Granted during most of this period only after checking the absence of other resources (the so-called means test), which the unemployed considered humiliating and which they deeply resented, the dole was just enough to keep the unemployed and their dependents alive, not enough to give them a minimum decent standard of living.

Permanent mass unemployment and subsistence on the dole led to a disastrous physical and moral deterioration of the victims of this calamity. In many formerly thriving industrial communities of the old industrial areas—as, for example, in South Wales, Northumberland and Scotland—often the majority of the population lived on the dole. These were the so-called depressed areas, as much devastated as if they were in material ruins. There, grown-up workers literally rotted in depressing idleness, with the demoralizing feeling of utter uselessness, while the young grew up without any prospect of finding employment, being placed on the dole immediately upon leaving school.

Some liberal economists, especially the French theoretician Jacques Rueff, have asserted that the dole had been the main cause of British unemployment, in so far as it established a minimum floor below which wages could not decline. In the absence of a dole, wages and costs would have declined and sooner or later reached the level on which production would have become profitable. Its increase would then have absorbed unemployment. It seems very doubtful, however, if application of this theory, which is based on the complete assimilation of labor to a commodity, could have solved the British crisis. Wage-cutting could not have improved the competitive position of British export industries, unless possibly wages had been reduced to Japanese standards, a procedure which was morally and politically impossible. The British people believed in giving to their workers minimum decent living standards, and this belief had been strengthened during World War I when the soldiers had been promised a Britain "fit for heroes to live in." It is true, however, though this was not a part of Rueff's argument, that the cost of British wages had been artificially increased by revaluation of sterling, which was an additional handicap to British exports.

Chronic mass unemployment, which was a main feature of British life during this period, and the failure of capitalist economy until 1939 to absorb it, to put back to productive work the unemployed—practically outcasts thrown out as useless by capitalist society—was largely responsible for the growth of anti-capitalism in Great Britain. Those same factors were responsible for the development of the Labor Party, until after the end of

World War II it was swept into power with the main object of preventing return of unemployment. This also explains the attitude of British opinion and of government in considering unemployment as a sort of Public Enemy No. 1 and aiming at full employment, regardless of cost.

7 FRANCE DURING THE PERIOD 1921–1929: INFLATION AND RECONSTRUCTION

In WORLD WAR I, France had suffered devastation which, even if not comparable to that of World War II—being concentrated in the northeastern areas occupied by the Germans, where most of the war had been fought—was nevertheless very substantial. The war damage included destruction of 900,000 buildings of all kinds; 9000 factories; 200 coal mines; and 34 iron-ore mines flooded; 6000 bridges; and 1500 kilometers of railway track. To this direct physical destruction should also be added the loss of the greatest part of foreign investments, in part as a result of liquidation to pay for war purchases in America, but to a greater extent as a consequence of the Russian Revolution, which wiped out over 25 percent of all French foreign investments. Losses nearly as severe were suffered by French investors in Turkey and the Balkans, as a result of currency depreciation.

Even much more disastrous, especially in the long run, for a country with a low birth rate, was the loss of 1,400,000 young men. This terrible loss of the flower of her manhood, from which France was far from having recovered when World War II began, was the main reason for the country's increasing weakness after 1919.

On the other hand, France had recovered Alsace-Lorraine, with its highly developed textile industry in Mulhouse and the rich iron-ore deposits in Lorraine. These, added to the rest of Lorraine, Normandy and the Pyrenees, made France the first iron-ore producer of Europe. There was also a fine iron and steel industry, which increased total capacity of steel production by about 30 percent.

In France, reconstruction of devastated areas was considered, and very rightly so, to be of absolutely paramount importance. In order to enable private owners of destroyed property to rebuild it, the state undertook to compensate them for the full amount of the damage—that is, the full cost of reconstruction—only on the condition, however, that such reconstruction be effectively carried out. This very generous compensation offered the possibility for the owners concerned to rebuild their destroyed plants at the expense of the state, frequently with a much greater capacity and, naturally, always with much more modern equipment and organization. As a result, productive capacity in the reconstructed areas considerably increased and improved. The state was to be reimbursed by the German reparations for its advances to the owners. However, fortunately for France, the government did not limit reconstruction expenditure to the amount of reparations received. In fact, reparations covered only about 40 percent of the total cost or reconstruction, which amounted to over 130 billion francs. The rest was practically paid for through budgetary deficits, i.e., credit and currency inflation.

In principle, reconstruction was financed by long-term loans floated by a special state credit institution, Crédit National. The total amount of these loans was 44 billion francs; but the short-term debt created during the war, the Bons de la Défense Nationale, also increased and the state continued borrowing from the Bank of France, thus increasing monetary circulation. Thus, from the end of 1921 to the end of 1925, total public debt had increased from 177,879 million francs to 292,915 million francs; and currency issued had increased from 36,417 million to 49,993 million. Budgetary deficit, caused not only by reconstruction expenditure but also by the cost of military occupation of the Ruhr, swelled the inflationary pressure and the exchange rate of the franc deteriorated, at first slowly and then more and more rapidly, from 11.11 francs to the dollar in 1919, to a maximum of 42 francs to the dollar in July 1926.

Although the financial and monetary crisis steadily grew, the economic situation of the country was basically sound. The balance of payments had been passive only in 1919 and 1920, during the period of extraordinary post-war imports for the reconstitution of stocks. But very soon production of agriculture was restored and imports of food could be curtailed. Industrial production also rapidly recovered and soon exceeded pre-war levels. Exports were stimulated by depreciation of the currency and expanded considerably, while cost of living and wages rose more slowly. By 1925, exports were equal to imports, leaving all income from tourist trade, from other services, and from the still considerable foreign investments as a very substantial surplus.

It would seem surprising that, under these conditions, the financial situation of the country was so unsatisfactory. But the picture becomes clearer when one realizes that the main reasons were psychological and political. The French middle class of tradesmen, craftsmen and peasants is, in politics, principally Leftist, even radical, but in financial matters extremely conservative, believing absolutely in balanced budget and stable currency. As André Siegfried has excellently expressed this contradiction in the French character, "The average Frenchman has his heart at his left, but his pocketbook at his right." This psychological feature of the French had often been used by reactionary forces supported by the banks, the so-called money wall (*mur d'argent*), to overthrow Leftist governments whose financial policy was generally far from orthodox, by engineering a monetary panic which created a claim by the public for return to conservative finance, that is, also, conservative government.

The last example of such obstruction by big business was the period 1924-26. Then, after the victory at the polls of the Leftist bloc (*cartel des gauches*) with a relatively modest program of social reform, such as introduction of social security, the government had been strongly opposed by industry and finance leaders who proceeded to institute massive capital exports. Thus French exporters left the proceeds of their exports in foreign banks, a situation which led to strong pressure against the franc. Several changes of cabinet, resulting mainly from the monetary crisis, led in July 1926 to a big panic that caused a catastrophic fall of the franc, about 40 percent in a week. This panic led to the formation of a large coalition government under a conservative statesman Poincaré, who was highly orthodox in financial matters, and who enjoyed the confidence of the general public, as well as of the big money interests. The main aim of the new government was to save the franc.

As soon as the Poincaré government was established, and even before any effect of the substantial tax increases—made in order to balance the budget—could be felt, French capital began to come back. The exchange rate of the franc recovered so rapidly that business interests became alarmed, fearing that revaluation would involve the country in a heavy deflation and impede exports.

Thus already, in December 1926, Poincaré was able to stabilize the franc de facto by giving to the Banque de France the authorization to buy all foreign currency offered at the rate of somewhat more than 1/5 of the pre-war parity (about 25 francs to the dollar). Scarcely a year earlier, a foreign loan of $100 million was used in an attempt to stabilize the franc by selling foreign exchange at a fixed rate. The attempt failed, because the flight of capital rapidly exhausted the proceeds of this loan. The situation now, however, was completely reversed. The amplitude of this capital repatriation, and also of the then existing surplus of the French balance of payments, is shown by the fact that in the 18 months from December 1926 to June 1928, when the franc had been legally stabilized at the same rate, the amount of foreign exchange (mainly dollars and sterling) bought by the Bank of France exceeded 40 billion francs. At the same moment, the total gold and foreign-exchange holdings exceeded 80 billion francs

75

($3.2 billion) and were above pre-war. The budget was balanced; above all, the economy was extremely prosperous, the basis of this prosperity being perfectly sound.

Recovery of French production had been highly successful, owing to a great extent to modernization and expansion through reconstruction. Agricultural production, stimulated by subsidies, had reached pre-war level by 1925. Not only did it nearly cover the needs of domestic consumption for staple foods like wheat, but it developed exports of specialties (cheese, butter, early vegetables, fruit and traditional exports of wine) directed mainly to Great Britain. Development of industry was considerably greater; in 1925, the index of industrial production was already at the level of 125 (1913=100) and increased to 160 in 1929. The coal mines of the north having been completely reconstructed, their productive capacity was expanded and in 1929 production reached a maximum of 50.5 million tons as against 41 million in 1913. Iron and steel production, too, was considerably developed, stimulated by the return of Lorraine. Compared to prewar production, in 1929 it was:

(in million metric tons)

	Iron Ore	Pig Iron	Steel
1913	22	5.3	4.6
1929	51	10.36	9.7

The automobile industry, partly because of reconversion of munition plants back to automobile production by Citroen, became very large and during the 1920's France had the greatest production and exports of automobiles in Europe, second in the world only to the United States. A similar though less spectacular development occurred in rayon, aluminum and other fields. Manufacture of chemicals, especially dyes, formerly nearly a monopoly of Germany, developed considerably. Production of woolen textiles expanded, competing successfully with that of Yorkshire. Last, but not least, production and exports of luxury articles took a considerable upswing.

76

All this expansion of production resulted in a material increase in exports, stimulated at first by the gradual depreciation, and later by stabilization, of the franc at a relatively low level. Thus, in 1927 exports reached the level of 166 (compared to 1913=100) while imports for the same year were only 117. Later on, however, imports increased considerably more than exports; but, if the balance of trade, after having a surplus for 2 or 3 years, again became passive—which was normal for a highly industrialized creditor country—surplus of balance of payments remained substantial. Foreign trade and general prosperity benefited also from development of the colonial empire, which, owing to preferential tariffs, became an important market for French industrial products. It supplied considerable amounts of raw materials, such as peanuts from Senegal, for the fat and oil industry of Marseilles, phosphates for fertilizer from North Africa, and so on.

To the proceeds of exports should be added the income from the substantially expanded tourist traffic, which in 1929 reached about 10 billion francs ($400 million), and also the income from foreign investments, which were still appreciable in spite of war losses, and which were again increasing as France began to make new investments, though unfortunately again mainly in government loans to such countries as Rumania, Poland, etc.

Such was the extraordinarily bright picture of French economy during the 1920's. But that was not all. Unlike many other countries, especially Great Britain, France had no unemployment whatever. In order to achieve the task of reconstruction and meet the increasing requirements of industry and agriculture, about 2 million foreign workers had been introduced into France between 1921 and 1929. Although these workers arrived under temporary contracts, most of them remained in the country.

In spite of this apparently excellent economic situation, however, France was suffering from a most dangerous weakness, the economic as well as the political consequences of which were to become gradually more and more serious. This weakness was its demographical situation, enormously aggravated by the losses of the war. Its total population was stationary, its active population was even slightly declining, as the number of old men arriving at retirement age was greater than the number of youngsters reaching working age. Consequently, the home market did not offer normal opportunities for expansion, a fact which discouraged economic progress.

The young generation, being limited in numbers, more and more preferred the less arduous and socially more respected white-collar professions to primary industries. Naturally, therefore, agriculture and mining began to suffer from manpower shortage. Insufficiency in the number of technicians available for emigration to French overseas territories impeded the economic development of those areas. Immigration of foreign labor did not offer a completely satisfactory substitute for absence of population growth, as immigrants were unstable and some left the country, partly because France had no tradition of immigration and naturalization of foreigners similar to that existing in the United States. Naturalization was obtained only with considerable difficulty, and foreign immigrants were not sufficiently encouraged to settle in France.

Other causes of economic weakness were: shortage of most important industrial minerals (with the one exception of iron ore), which impeded especially the development of concentrated heavy industry; continued specialization of most French industries in individualized, not mass-production, items, a policy that reduced the scope of their markets and increased difficulties of competition on the world market; and finally the tradition of overall tariff protection, which induced French industrialists to be satisfied with their limited but sheltered domestic markets, instead of expanding to meet the arduous competition on the world market.

Still, by the end of this period, even in relation to the factors just discussed, the protectionist tradition, a significant change in favor of progress toward a greater participation in world trade, appeared to be developing. In 1927 there was signed a Franco-

German trade agreement which was an effort by the two leading protectionist industrial countries of the European Continent to return to the pre-war pattern of increased international trade. This attempt was to be made through reducing and consolidating tariff duties on a great number of items and returning to the "most favored nation" clause. Only the future could reveal that this important step toward a return to a freer international trade was a swallow which did not cause spring to arrive.

8 THE GERMAN INFLATION

AT THE END of the war, the German financial and monetary situation was not only not worse, but even slightly better than in France, if not than in Great Britain. Thus the amount of currency issued was of the same order of magnitude, about 30 billions in 1919 and price level even lower, only 200 (1913=100), as against 300 in France. As to the economic situation of the country, also compared to France, it was even better, since Germany had not suffered any significant war devastation. Thus, her productive apparatus remained unimpaired, otherwise than by the loss of Alsace-Lorraine and Upper Silesia, important for industry, and other territories which were lost to Poland, and which were valuable for their agricultural production.

At the end of 1918, therefore, there was no reason to suppose that in a few years Germany would be the victim of hyperinflation, the greatest and the worst the world had ever seen. It was to be equaled later, after World War II, in countries like Hungary and Greece. What was the cause of this unprecedented monetary catastrophe? Opinion on the subject was, and still is, divided more or less in the same way as it was concerning reparations and war debts. The German point of view is very straightforward, namely, that reparations destroyed the mark. The French opinion is obviously quite the opposite, i.e., that the Germans themselves engineered inflation in order to make reparations pay-

80

ments impossible and thus rob the Allied creditor nations of the sums due them. Both theories contain considerable elements of truth; an impartial, objective explanation is naturally much more complex.

It is undoubtedly correct that the necessity of making heavy reparations payments in cash, once the foreign assets had been liquidated, depressed the value of the mark abroad, marks being offered on the international market in order to obtain foreign exchange. This currency depreciation stimulated rise of prices, increased the budgetary deficit, and led to increase of monetary circulation. It should be stressed, however, that for a very considerable time these massive sales of marks abroad, which were due to depreciate their rate of exchange, were compensated for by massive purchases by foreign speculators. The respect of these speculators for the efficiency and capacity of the German people and their economy led them to a blind confidence in the ability of the Germans and also in their willingness to restore the original value of German currency. These foreign purchases contributed, if not toward maintaining the stability, at least toward slowing down the decline, of the mark. In so far as by this speculation, the result of which was disastrous for the foreign purchasers, the foreigners supplied Germany—practically without any counterpart whatsoever—with considerable sums in foreign currencies, the loss of the foreigners corresponded to a gain to the Reich. The latter thus obtained, without any consideration, a substantial part of the foreign exchange required for reparations payments.

It is also evident that the German government did not make a serious effort to compensate inflationary pressure by increasing taxation, which would have reduced domestic money supply to such an extent as to enable the nation to make reparations payments. That such a policy was possible was proved by the experience of the Dawes Plan, a few years later, especially as reparations payments corresponded to reduction in military expenditures under the disarmament clauses of the Versailles Treaty. Military

81

expenditures in the last years before World War I were on a level comparable to reparations payments after that war. Increase in taxation would have been facilitated also by the considerable industrial prosperity of Germany, which was stimulated by inflation.

The general index of production rose from 61 in 1920 to 72 in 1921 and 86 in 1922, which, taking into account the loss in territory, corresponded to a level of activity at least equal to pre-war. Exports had also doubled from 1921 to 1923. Instead of reducing inflationary pressure by taxation, however, the German government of the Weimar Republic even materially increased the available money supply by paying enormous indemnities to owners of industrial properties located in the seized territories, in order to enable them to replace their lost plants.

In the fight against inflation, the German government was guilty of gross negligence and/or incompetence. However, in examining the origins of inflation in Germany and applying the old Roman legal saying used in penal law, *cui prodest* (Whom does it benefit?), interesting conclusions can be arrived at. The inflation had benefited, to an extraordinary extent, the classes which still remained by far the most powerful economically, even though they had apparently lost their political power as a result of the breakdown of the imperial regime. Obviously those classes continued to exert a strong if not decisive influence on the policy of the new republican government.

These classes—the big industrialists, mainly the heavy-industry magnates of Western Germany, and the big landowners, the "Junkers" of Eastern Germany—benefited to a fabulous extent from the inflation which had wiped out some 40 billion marks of pre-war bonds and mortgage debts, and which provided really unbelievable opportunities for speculative profits. It was estimated that in the years 1921-23 the big industrialists alone took from other classes of the German population over 25 billion marks. The method used for this enrichment was exceedingly simple: The industrialists borrowed from the banks sums in marks which they repaid when the currency had been depreciated; this procedure made loans most profitable, even at high rates of interest. The borrowed sums were used either for financing exports, the proceeds of which were naturally not repatriated, or for bargain purchases of all sorts of property, the price of which did not follow the depreciation of the mark.

The most important of such bargain properties were real estate and, even more, business undertakings: either small-scale firms which had no means of getting bank credits and thus, with currency depreciation, found themselves out of cash; or even large joint stock companies which remained prosperous, but whose dividends had not been adjusted to the rate of currency depreciation. The latter situation caused the depression of stock-exchange quotations of their shares well below their real value, and made them an easy and most valuable prey for bargain-hunters with sufficient ready cash. Thus, during this period, gigantic concentrations of undertakings of all kinds, the so-called *konzerns,* were built up by enterprising industrialists. These *konzerns* were established without any logical reason, such as vertical or horizontal concentration, but only according to opportunities of bargain-hunting.

The greatest of these *konzerns* was built by Hugo Stinnes, who before World War I had a medium-sized business in coal trade and transport on the Rhine. By the end of 1923, he controlled a great part of the coal and steel industry of the Ruhr, the *Rhein-isch Westfalishe Electricitaets Gesellschaft,* the greatest public-utilities concern of continental Europe, as well as a great number of businesses of all kinds, such as ocean shipping lines, automobile factories, banks, insurance companies, newspapers, and so on. The total number of workers of the *konzern* embracing this vast scope of activities was well above one million.

The considerable share of responsibility of the big industrialist class in the inflation policy can be assumed in view of their strong and even decisive influence even on the most Leftist of the governments of the Weimar Republic, their self-interest, and their prejudices. It is certain that to them the appeal of a policy

83

of steady currency depreciation was very great indeed. It presented them with unlimited profit possibilities and offered the prospect of evading reparations payments and thus taking revenge on the Allied enemy powers. As to the risks to the general welfare of the country entailed by the policy of destruction of the currency, they were easily accepted by this class as long as they did not apply to its own interests. Attempts to win advantage out of a general catastrophe engineered for the purpose (*Katastrophenpolitik*) not only is a line of policy for which a special term exists only in the German language, but above all it is an attitude typical of Germany, of which Hitler was later to offer an even more striking example.

Even if this analysis were limited to the realm of concrete indisputable facts, it is at once evident that big business victoriously resisted all attempts of government to improve the currency and budget situation by increasing taxation. Such increase would obviously have applied mainly to business excess profits. Big business also encouraged the government of the Republic to pursue, as to reparations, an uncompromising policy which could only be considered by the Allies as provocation and sabotage, and which naturally stimulated them to take reprisals that were to be fatal to the German currency. Thus the refusal to make the promised deliveries of coke to Belgium and France—which in January 1923 had caused occupation of the Ruhr—had been made by Chancellor Kuno, a former director of the Hamburg-American Line, who more than any other contemporary German politician was an obedient tool of big business.

The big industrialists also took the initiative in the passive resistance in the Ruhr, without however bearing its cost! The general strike proclaimed there was financed by subsidies of the government which enabled management to continue payment to the striking workers of their normal wages. The cost of these subsidies exhausted the last resources of the Reich treasury, while industrial production, owing to the strikes, considerably declined. For the year 1923 it averaged only 51 (1913=100). As to the

84

mark, its fall, at first gradual, steadily increased in pace and by the spring of 1923 became abrupt, declining 10 to 20 percent a day. While in 1921 (June 30) the United States dollar was worth 62.50 marks, by the middle of 1922 it was worth 277.78 marks, and by the middle of 1923 over 100,000 marks. In November 1923, stabilization had finally been effected at the rate of 4.2 billion marks per United States dollar.

Long before this end, the mark was no more fulfilling the function of a currency. At the beginning of the inflationary movement, prices lagged behind currency depreciation and thus attracted bargain-hunters, Germans and foreigners. Conditions provided them with the opportunity to make enormous profits, not only from purchase of business undertakings, but also from real estate—considerably depreciated because of rent control—and from the purchase of all sorts of manufactured goods. Germany, as a satirical journal with some bitterness proclaimed, was the object of a universal liquidation sale at bargain prices.

At a later stage, however, prices fluctuated parallel to the currency depreciation, changing as fast as twice a day, together with the quotation of the dollar. Wages were paid on a sliding scale established weekly, but still lagged behind prices. The printing presses could not follow the terrific speed of currency depreciation in its final stages, which was a symbolic symptom of the disappearance of the liquid resources of the economy. The value of banknotes was sometimes changed by means of a rubber stamp, transforming millions into billions. During the same period, municipalities and even big business undertakings started issuing their own emergency currency (*Notgeld*), in order to have enough notes available for payment of their wage bills. But in spite of all these measures, the effective value of the currency issued steadily shrank until at the moment of stabilization it amounted to only 16 million gold marks, that is, less than ½ percent of the currency in circulation before World War I.

The social and economic consequences of the German inflation were tremendous. It destroyed to a great extent the backbone

85

and moral foundation of capitalist economy: Confidence in the stability of money and savings. This breakdown offered to capitalists opportunity for speculative profits which not only were immoral in themselves, but which also were contrary to the normal "rules of the game" of capitalist economy. The main victims of inflation were not the workers, whose wages were adjusted to currency depreciation, though with a time lag, but the middle class. These were the white-collar workers—whose salaries were much less adjusted, owing to less unionization—in particular, state officials; small tradesmen who, not enjoying easy bank credits lost part of their liquid resources; and above all, the renters, whose savings (being invested in bonds, mortgages, insurance policies, etc., measured in marks) depreciated and finally became entirely worthless.

This middle class, though proletariatized by the inflation which had deprived it of its former economic basis, did not feel at all a solidarity with the proletariat, the mass of the manual workers. From them it was distinguished, first, by its political attitude, strongly nationalistic; and secondly, by a feeling of superiority resulting from a better education and higher functions (from its point of view, more important) which it fulfilled in economic activity or in the service of the state. The middle class considered proletariatization a degradation, and felt deep resentment and hatred toward those whom it considered responsible for the catastrophe of which it was the victim. These objects of their hatred were naturally those whom they had already hated before, such as the Allied powers who wanted to enslave Germany by exacting reparations payments, as well as those whom the middle class thought to be the German accomplices in this scheme. The accomplices were the international socialists, the politicians, who, by accepting the demands of the Allies and starting the policy of implementation of the Versailles Treaty (*Erfüllungspolitik*), had become traitors to the Fatherland. Last but not least of those hated by the victims of inflation were the Jews, the traditional scapegoats, accused of betraying Germany to the Allies, as well as of profiteering. The truth is that the greatest profiteers during this period, big industrialists like Stinnes, were pure Arians, while the big banks where Jewish participation was relatively important, were victims of inflation in which they lost a substantial part of their capital.

Out of this ruin of the middle class caused by inflation came thus the first successes of the Nazi movement. The initial attempt of a putsch by Hitler took place in Munich in November 1923; even though it failed, the seeds of the Nazi creed remained to grow and flourish in the near future.

The stabilization of the mark by Dr. Schacht had been achieved in November 1923, when already for some time any real domestic currency had been lacking, trade transactions being made more and more often on the basis of the United States dollar or of the gold mark as a purely accounting currency. Dr. Schacht, having neither gold nor foreign-exchange resources, imagined a purely fictitious coverage for his new currency, the *Rentenmark,* the parity of which was the same as that of the pre-war mark. The issue of *Rentenmarks,* limited to 1 billion, was supposed to be covered by a general mortgage on all the land and industrial properties of the Reich. This coverage obviously had not the slightest degree of liquidity, which had been supposed to be the main quality required of a sound currency coverage. In spite of this most unorthodox procedure, the *Rentenmark* was a great success, owing partly to the confidence gladly given by the public, who had been desperately longing for a stable currency, and partly to the strict limitation of the currency issue which in one stroke replaced inflation with deflation.

About the same time that Dr. Schacht stabilized the mark, passive resistance collapsed in the Ruhr, where also the general strike terminated, since the subsidies paid by the state to the strikers had ended. The heavy industry of the Ruhr entered into an agreement with the Franco-Belgian industrial Authority, the *Micum,* and had to promise to deliver considerable quantities of coal. Thus, it became obvious even to the most national-

87

istic Germans, that a general agreement on reparations, too, was unavoidable if Allied occupation and intervention in the economic activity of the Ruhr were to end. To a considerable extent, the occupation of the Ruhr had fulfilled its purpose. However, it had been very costly for France, and the French themselves very much preferred an agreement by which they would obtain reparations without intervention in the actual management of the Ruhr industries. From both sides, then, the necessity of a compromise was recognized. The Dawes Plan was such a compromise, more or less mutually acceptable. Still nationalistic feelings were hurt by the international controls over the German economy which that Plan introduced. The nationalists also opposed the Dawes Plan as implying the confirmation of agreement to pay reparations, which, however, was to be repudiated before long.

9 GERMAN PROSPERITY ON LOAN, 1924–1930

In 1924, after the stabilization of the currency and the acceptance of the settlement of the reparations problem through the Dawes Plan, the German economy found itself without debt, but also without any working capital. The liquid resources, as well as the debt, had been wiped out by inflation. Germany suffered from a severe deflationary crisis, both because of the lack of liquid funds, and because after stabilization prices were no longer below world level and no longer provided a stimulant for industrial production and exports. In particular, all the monstrous industrial empires created without any consideration of productive coordination—purely as a result of bargain-hunting and of the flight from the mark into the so-called real values (*Realwerte*)—suffered immediately from the lack of productivity of their components and very rapidly broke down. The Stinnes Konzern, biggest of all, crashed in the spring of 1924.

German economy was in desperate need of fresh capital which, domestic reserves having been wiped out, could be provided only by foreign lending. Capital was needed not only for the restoration of liquid resources, but also, and to a much greater extent, for investment purposes. Productive apparatus, especially in industry, even though not affected by war devastation, had not been adapted to the technical progress achieved abroad (particularly in the United States). Industrial equipment and organization were considerably out of date, which was a serious handicap to competition of German manufactured goods on world markets. If Germany was to be able to develop her exports to an extent sufficient to pay for her imports of food and raw materials, as well as to achieve the export surplus required for payment of reparations, then substantial capital investment for development, modernization and rationalization of her productive capacity was obviously essential. This required massive import of foreign capital.

These foreign capital imports, i.e., loans, had been started by the Dawes loan of $200 million, granted in 1924 for currency stabilization. The proceeds of this loan were used to replace the *Rentenmark* with a more orthodox currency, the *Reichsmark,* of the same parity but with a normal coverage in gold and in foreign exchange convertible into gold. This loan, recommended by the international experts who drafted the Dawes Plan, had been issued and subscribed mainly on the Wall Street market, but to a lesser extent on all other international capital markets. The success of the Dawes loan opened to German borrowers the doors of capital markets, and in the next five or six years Germany succeeded in borrowing abroad some 25 billion Reichsmarks.

It is interesting to note that, although the main attraction for foreign investors was the high interest rates, and for the banking houses floating the loans it was the heavy commissions paid by German borrowers, such a flow of foreign capital would have been impossible without a general confidence in German soundness and honesty. Even at that period, this confidence might have appeared somewhat misplaced in view not only of later general events, but also of the recent experience of total inflation, whereby foreign as well as domestic debts were wiped out. Such a confidence did not find justification in the use made of all borrowed moneys by the Germans; a great part of the loans floated by German cities or lesser governments was spent for unproductive purposes, as in the construction of ostentatious public buildings. Nor did that confidence find justification in the deterioration of the German balance-of-payments position resulting from these loans.

In 1929, annual interest payments on the net debt of some 15 billion Reichsmarks—about 10 billion of the total amount borrowed had been used for rebuilding of German assets abroad—amounted to over 900 million Reichsmarks, to be covered by export surplus, while in 1913 Germany had from its foreign investments an income of one billion marks.

However, the modernization, rationalization and expansion of German industrial productive capacity, achieved mainly with the aid of foreign borrowed capital, was a considerable technical success. Owing to modernization of equipment, together with the introduction of new production methods, on the American pattern, particularly the assembly line, productivity per worker increased appreciably. During the period from 1907 to 1925 this increase had amounted to only 11 percent. From 1925 to 1929 it reached 25 percent; this rapid improvement in productivity was mainly due, however, to a 38 percent increase in the total horsepower installed during the same period. In spite, then, of the loss of important industrial areas as compared to pre-war (Alsace-Lorraine, Upper Silesia and the Saar, which until 1935 was separated from the German economy), industrial production exceeded pre-war, amounting in 1928 to 102 (1913 = 100).

Increase of production had been particularly substantial in the heavy capital goods industry, where improvement of lignite production had more than compensated for the loss of important hard-coal resources in Silesia and the Saar. Lignite was used as a source of cheap fuel especially for electric power. A great part of the electric power consumed in Berlin came from the thermal plant built on the lignite deposit of Golpa-Czornewitz, in Saxony. Lignite was also the basic raw material for important industries, such as production of synthetic oil and rubber, which, however, were to develop at a somewhat later period. Compared to pre-war (1913 = 100) the index of production of lignite in 1928 was 190, of electricity 412, of aluminum 657, and of rayon 633.

Rationalization in coal mining made gigantic strides, so that the industry substantially overtook major European competitors.

91

In 1928, in the Ruhr, 78 percent of all coal was mined by machines, while in Great Britain in the same year only 20 percent was mechanically mined. Annual output per worker had increased, as a result of this rationalization in the Ruhr, from 175 tons in 1925 to 315 tons in 1929. An even greater progress had been achieved in utilization of coal. Thus, in spite of the loss of important coal-mining areas, production of coke from hard coal reached 40 million tons in 1929, against 32 million in 1913. This increase resulted in a corresponding expansion in the output of by-products such as tar, benzol, ammonia, etc., used mainly as raw materials for the production of various chemicals. The surplus gas which was produced in the coke ovens, and which could not be absorbed by the local heavy industry, was sent by means of pipe lines to the big cities, like Cologne or even Hannover, even at a considerable distance from the mining areas. As a result of this progress in the utilization of coal, more than 60 percent of the coal produced was chemically treated—not simply burned as fuel. Such procedure resulted not only in a much more rational and remunerative use of coal as a source of fuel, but above all preserved important materials otherwise wasted.

The progress of the German coal industry, accomplished mainly through this rationalization in production and utilization of coal, had also been stimulated by its organization in a tightly knit cartel (*Rheinisch Westfälischer Kohlensyndicat*), membership in which had since 1919 been made mandatory by the government of the Weimar Republic. This cartel did not interfere in the organization of production by the different mining companies. It did, however, have absolute control of the distribution of German coal on domestic and foreign markets, dividing those markets between the different coal fields. It established common sales agencies, especially in foreign countries; and above all it managed the price-fixing policy in a manner most suitable to achieve expansion of German exports, namely, by the use of dumping whenever necessary and possible.

Production in 1929, when it reached its maximum for the period under consideration, had developed as follows, as compared to pre-war:

(in millions of tons)

| Hard coal | 1929 | 163 | 1913 (old frontiers) | 190 | new frontiers | 141 |
| Lignite | " | 175 | " " " | 87 | " " | 87 |

Production of iron and steel items had also made considerable progress. Owing to the indemnity received by the former plant owners from the government, in compensation for the plants lost in Lorraine, the ironmasters of the Ruhr built new iron furnaces and thus reestablished the complex productive capacity which the frontiers drawn up in the Versailles Treaty had split. The proceeds of foreign loans enabled the industrialists of the Ruhr to achieve this aim completely and, above all, to make their new plants the most modern and the most efficient in Europe.

But from now on, the domestic raw-material basis for German iron and steel production was insufficient, and about two-thirds of the iron ore required had to be imported from Sweden, Lorraine and Spain. In order to reduce this dependence on imports, the German steel industry expanded utilization of the Siemens Martin method, which uses scrap iron instead of pig iron in the production of steel. One-half of the total German steel production during that period was manufactured by the Siemens Martin method.

Production in 1929, as compared to pre-war, amounted to:

(in thousands of tons)

| Pig iron | 1929 | 15.344 | 1913 (old frontiers) | 16.800 | new frontiers | 10.760 |
| Raw steel | " | 18.273 | " " " | 17.147 | " " | 11.768 |

A similar but even greater development took place in other categories of heavy industry that were less, or not at all, affected by territorial losses. Some of these categories were, for example, chemicals, electric engineering and machinery. In contrast, in most light consumer-goods industries, production was either below or only slightly above pre-war level. The only industry in this instance that expanded was rayon.

93

The expansion of the production and the foreign sales of German industry was assisted by the development of the system of cartels, which, already very powerful before World War I, still increased in numbers and in influence. The government of the Weimar Republic made an attempt to regulate the activity of the cartels, in order to protect the public against possible abuses of monopolistic power. A special cartel law was voted by the Reichstag, establishing a tribunal which was intrusted with the investigation of cartels, and particularly of complaints against them. If any cartel's policy was considered contrary to the public interest, the tribunal was empowered to dissolve the organization by declaring its charter void. However, this law did not achieve any effective limitation of the power of the cartels nor any protection of the interests of consumers. On the contrary, the provision of the cartel law authorizing the government to make membership in a cartel mandatory, if it considered such action to be in the public interest, had been used for some of the most important of these bodies and had considerably enhanced their power. In 1923, the total number of industrial cartels in Germany was about 1500.

Outside of this organization into cartels, common to all industries, in some of the most important industries expansion benefited by concentration through mergers and combinations. Thus, the *Vereinigte Stahlwerke,* established on the pattern of the United States Steel Corporation, represented a concentration of more than half of the total German steel productive capacity, a production equal to that of Great Britain.

In the chemical industry it was a combination of nearly all the existing big undertakings that established the I. G. Farbenindustrie, a gigantic horizontal and vertical merger, possessing a quasi monopoly in such different products as heavy chemicals, dyes, pharmaceuticals and the like. This trust, the biggest in the world, at least as measured by value of production and number of workers employed (over 300,000), rapidly reestablished its connections and participation in foreign countries destroyed or lost during the war. The favorite method of penetration of this organization, used

94

also, though on a smaller scale, by other German corporations, was through patent agreements.

The I. G. Farbenindustrie enjoyed a position of technical leadership, possessing first-class specialized laboratories, so that it could offer to its foreign competitors, on advantageous terms, the bait of license rights to its patents. These license agreements, however, implied for the foreign concerns which purchased them abandonment of their own research in the particular field of such patents, as such research offered no more prospects of commercial advantage.

The agreements implied, also, limitation of production and productive capacity to the requirements of their domestic markets, while the I. G. Farbenindustrie kept the exclusive right to export to all markets not covered by patent agreements. This was true even regarding licensing agreements with concerns of comparable size and importance, such as the Imperial Chemical Industries of Great Britain and the DuPont de Nemours of the United States. To the former, Farben abandoned the markets of the British Empire and to the latter the whole American Continent. This German combine still kept commercial control over the continent of Europe as well as most of Africa and Asia. But above all, those two concerns, the greatest competitors of the I. G. Farbenindustrie in the whole world, agreed to leave further progress in the respective fields to research by the German concern.

This policy of the I. G. Farbenindustrie was for the time being a source of enormous monopolistic profits, as well as a means of strength for the German economy in time of peace and, especially, in time of war. It was a correlative source of weakness, however, for the countries with which these agreements were concluded, especially in time of war. A typical example of such an agreement was the one made between I. G. Farbenindustrie and the Standard Oil Company of New Jersey for establishment of a common subsidiary, the Standard I. G. Farbenindustrie, in which both participating companies pooled their patents on liquid fuel. As a result, Standard Oil, having obtained a license for I. G. Farben's

95

cracking processes, abandoned all attempts of its own to develop synthetic fuel production.

In the United States, the I. G. Farbenindustrie controlled a number of sizeable industrial undertakings, for example, General Aniline Corporation and Agfa-Ansko. It had also important share-holdings in many others, including some of the most important concerns of the American chemical industry.

In Europe, its foreign holdings had been concentrated in a Swiss holding the I. G. Chemie, established mainly in order to make less apparent German domination of foreign concerns.

The important participations in, and control of, foreign concerns by the I. G. Farbenindustrie and other German trusts had been made possible only by the influx of foreign capital. It was therefore comparatively easy for such corporations to water their capital with excessive issues of shares and bonds, as well as to obtain from German banks long-term credits, which were often made with the proceeds of foreign short-term loans.

Besides the I. G. Farbenindustrie, some of the outstanding examples of German industrial expansion abroad were the following: The Vereinigte Glanzstoffwerke, the rayon trust which controlled rayon factories in the Netherlands, Belgium and France, as well as in the United States; the electricity trust of the A.E.G. (Allgemeine Elektrizitaets Gesellschaft), with controlling influence in Switzerland, Spain and South America; and Krupp, which had used the proceeds of a loan issued in the United States to win control of the Swedish armament concern, Bofors.

Owing to the influx of foreign capital, Germany had the possibility, in the financing of its foreign trade, of engaging in aggressive competition with other industrialized exporting countries, by granting credits—mainly for the purchase of equipment—on more favorable terms and for longer periods than her competitors. Such credits, financed either through bank loans or directly by the big manufacturing firms concerned, had been granted in particular to the Soviet Union, which obtained a three-year credit of 500 million Reichsmarks for the purchase of equipment required for the fulfilment of its first Five Year Plan. From the German point of view, such a generous credit policy for exports to Russia was justified (1) by the importance of the Russian market as the greatest outlet for German capital-goods exports; and (2) by the very close relationship existing during this period between the German heavy industries (particularly the concerns specializing in armament production) and the Soviet authorities.

Since the time of the German-Russian Treaty of 1922, German industry had established in Russia a large number of subsidiaries, mainly concerned with the manufacture of such armaments as it was absolutely impossible to produce in the Reich, for the time being, because of the activities of the Allied Control Commission. The production of these plants, created as a result of this German-Soviet cooperation, was shared in equal parts by both partners. This cooperation, which had been established by the German firms concerned under the direction of the military authorities of the Reich, and which was a secret equally well guarded by both sides, had lasted until the arrival of Hitler in power, in 1933. One of the best known results of this cooperation had been the establishment by Junkers of the first modern airplane factory in Russia, located near Moscow.

The German armaments industry also established subsidiaries in other neutral countries, where research and production of new models could be pursued without the interference of Allied control. Such subsidiaries were the Fokker airplane plants in the Netherlands, and the Bofors artillery factory in Sweden which, as above mentioned, had been brought under the control of Krupp.

German agriculture did not share the expansion and prosperity achieved by industry. Though having considerably benefited from inflation, which had wiped out its mortgage debt, agriculture very rapidly became heavily indebted again, principally because of capital expenditures required for modernization of its equipment. In spite of the maintenance of very high rates of protective duties for agricultural products, the big cereal-producing estates of the region east of the Elbe (Ostelbien) especially suffered from unremunerative prices and from lack of manpower. German farm workers emigrated from these areas—most of which are at present under Polish administration—where wages paid to farm labor were low, and where they were kept in a state of semifeudal dependence upon the big landowners (Junkers). The worker emigrants drifted to the big cities, and were replaced only by seasonal Polish workers. The Junkers, in spite of all their antipathy to the democratic government, did not hesitate to claim assistance, which they declared the only possibility of saving the eastern territories for the German nation.

The Weimar government could have refused this request, let the big estates go bankrupt, bought them up and divided them between the farm workers. The small farms which could thus have been created, if worked intensively and with more emphasis on stockbreeding than on cereal growing, would have become economically sound propositions. Such a course would have been a great success politically as well as economically, and in particular would have consolidated democracy and economic stability, as well as solidifying the German character of the eastern territories. The Weimar government, however, did not adopt that course. Instead, it agreed to satisfy the claims of the Junkers, and granted them assistance in the form of low interest loans and even outright grants by the treasury. The result of this policy was to be politically as well as economically most disastrous.

During this period, 1924-30, Germany succeeded in reestablishing and expanding its productive capacity, the economic basis of its future war potential. However, from a purely economic point of view, the great accompanying prosperity enjoyed by Germany was artificial and most uncertain. This prosperity resulted mainly from the substantial import surplus, in which was reflected the heavy influx of foreign capital. German prosperity could have been maintained only if Germany, as a result of modernization of its economy, could have developed an export surplus sufficient to meet the interest payments on its political and commercial foreign debts. But even if she could have achieved such a surplus, and

98

it had actually reached this aim in 1929-31 (see table following), would foreign countries have had the purchasing power and the willingness to absorb such an increase in German exports? Such willingness and capacity would have depended on the degree of prosperity existing in principal German foreign markets and on their readiness to accept German goods, either spontaneously, or because of a political or economic dependence on Germany, which would have made the Reich the only source of supplies open to them. But none of these conditions existed when the world depression disrupted Europe's economy; purchasing power then declined everywhere, and foreign loans abruptly stopped. A few years later, Dr. Schacht made a successful attempt to create a basis of a more permanent economic prosperity for Germany, by insuring to the Reich stable foreign markets in countries brought into a state of economic dependence. In 1930, however, the breakdown of German economy was unavoidable.

The development of German foreign trade during the years 1923-32 was as follows:

(in millions of Reichsmarks)

	Imports	Exports	Surplus + Deficit −
1923	6.150	6.102	−48
1924	9.625	6.585	−3.040
1925	12.362	8.799	−3.563
1926	10.001	10.414	+413
1927	14.143	10.219	−3.924
1928	14.001	12.276	−1.725
1929	13.447	13.483	+36
1930	10.393	12.036	+1.643
1931	6.727	9.599	+2.872
1932	4.067	5.739	+1.672

10 SOVIET RUSSIA UNTIL
THE FIVE-YEAR PLANS

THE ECONOMIC SLOGANS, the use of which secured to the Bolshevik Revolution the support of the workers and of the majority of the mobilized peasants, were, besides immediate peace, control of factories by the workers and control of land by the peasants. It must be acknowledged that, after the victory of the October Revolution, these demands had been met nearly at once. This resulted, however, not so much from faithfulness of Soviet authorities to the principles they had proclaimed, as from a spontaneous movement of the masses, to which the authorities had to give in.

Thus the movement of distribution among the peasants of land belonging to big landowners, to the state, or to the church had already started before the Bolshevik Revolution. It was rapidly achieved during the winter of 1917-18, and was legalized by a decree of February 1918. While in principle this decree proclaimed nationalization of the land and abolition of private land rights, it did grant permanent right of cultivation to all persons willing to till the land with the assistance of their families. The use of hired labor was prohibited.

In industry, also, even before the decree of June 1918 had nationalized all large-scale undertakings, the latter had been taken over by the workers and their representatives, generally trade-union committees, which either completely replaced former management or, at least, supervised its administration in a most interfering way. A natural result of such a state of affairs was a rapid decline in labor discipline and productivity, and a complete disorganization of all industrial production. This breakdown of industry was also due to the fact that for some time, although the state had proclaimed nationalization of industry, it had not created any central organization which could coordinate the different plants managed by workers' committees and fit all undertakings and industries into a general pattern of economy.

Still other causes of the catastrophic decline in industrial production were (1) the civil war, which started immediately after the Bolshevik Revolution and for three years devastated the country, separating the industry of the big cities of North and Central Russia from their fuel (Donets coal and Baku oil) and raw materials (cotton from Turkestan); and (2) mobilization of a large proportion of the workers into the Red Army. In addition, a great number of others abandoned the cities, where the food situation steadily deteriorated until it became disastrous, and many returned to their former village communities and even participated in the distribution of land. Total migration from the big cities to the countryside was estimated at 8 million persons. This migration, hunger, epidemics, and the flight abroad of part of the upper middle class caused the population of St. Petersburg to decline from 2.4 million in 1916 to 600,000 in 1920, and the population of Moscow to drop from 2.2 million to 1 million.

While industrial production was nearly paralyzed, because of the reasons above, production of agriculture also declined. This was due in part to the normal consequences of the continuation and aggravation of the war as a civil war (such as lack of manpower, of draught power, and of fertilizer and equipment); but it was due also to destruction of the most progressive and efficient units of production, the estates of the landlords and the big individual farms that used hired labor. These farms were the *khutors* of the rich peasants, called *kulaks*.

Even greater was the impact on agricultural production of the Soviet policy of food collection. Until the Bolshevik Revolution,

101

food collection for feeding the big cities was no problem, as the slight decline by 8 percent in 1917 of agricultural production, compared to 1913, was more than compensated for by the stoppage of exports. Conditions deteriorated with the disruption of the big estates, but especially with the implementation of the law on grain monopoly (May 1918), which made it mandatory to deliver to the state-delivery organization all grain exceeding minimum requirements, for food and seeds, of agricultural producers. It was obvious from the start that these deliveries could not be voluntary, but would have to be imposed by force of arms. This was because significant surpluses could be available practically only on the relatively big and efficient farms of the *kulaks*. Owing to steady depreciation of the currency, official prices paid for grain deliveries had become purely nominal, and this, added to the decline in industrial production, made it impossible for the peasants to purchase even a minimum quantity of the industrial products that they required.

Control on implementation, by the rich peasants, of these deliveries, which were in fact tantamount to confiscation, was at first intrusted to the rural proletariat, the landless peasants and farm workers, whose committees had dictatorial powers. They abused those powers in exercising a cruel and economically most ill-conceived tyranny, looting and devastating prosperous and efficient farms, and often robbing them of grain required for seeds. At the same time, they kept for themselves the small quantities of industrial products received from the cities, and often even the greatest part of the confiscated grain itself. From the standpoint of the feeding of the urban proletariat, such actions by its rural counterpart were thus most unsatisfactory. For this purpose, the Soviet authorities therefore had to organize special "collection troops" consisting mainly of industrial workers, who were armed with machine guns and even artillery. They requisitioned food in the countryside by methods that would have done credit to the most ruthless enemy army of occupation.

These collection troops succeeded in breaking the resistance of
102

the peasants and increasing the total of deliveries from 1.8 million tons in 1918-19 to 3 million in 1919-20, thus insuring to the cities a minimum supply, even though very small. In 1916-17, deliveries had reached 8.7 million tons. However, this radical action also resulted in completely liquidating all stocks of grain in rural areas, thus making famine a certainty, in the event that the next harvest should fail.

On the other hand, even if resistance of the peasants—manifested in hundreds of revolts in all parts of Russia throughout 1919 and 1920—could be crushed by superior force, such force could not prevent the peasants' natural reaction to the wholesale robbery of their produce. That reaction took the form of their refusal to grow any surplus grain. Thus they cut the planted area to the minimum required to provide for themselves and their families. This restriction of area, even barring a failure of the harvest, was bound to cause famine in urban, as well as in rural, areas. In the summer of 1921, as a result of the conditions described above, and of a drought in the rich Volga region, grain production declined to 51 percent of pre-war. This could easily be foreseen as early as the beginning of 1921, when Lenin decided to put an end, for the moment, to the policy of introducing Communism at once and at any price, and called for a pause in the so-called New Economic Policy, or *Nep*.

In his speech of March 15, 1921, at the Congress of the Communist Party, Lenin very frankly confessed the reasons for the proposed change of policy: the failure of grain deliveries, which drove the peasants to the suicidal attempt to starve out the cities and the government. The peasants could obviously be appeased and put back to production only by offering them industrial goods for their surplus food. But industrial production under workers' management, conducted without any consideration of productivity and cost, was nearly nil. In 1920, as compared with 1913, total volume of production was only 12.8 percent; production of pig iron had declined to 115,000 tons as against 4.5 million; and production of cotton cloth to 126 million meters as against 1625 million. The general discontent resulting from such a situation was expressed not only in peasant revolts, but even more in the insurrection of the sailors of the Baltic Fleet, who in October 1917 had been a major factor in Bolshevik victory. This insurrection had not yet been suppressed when Lenin proclaimed the Nep.

In agriculture, the most important change brought about by the Nep was termination of the mandatory grain deliveries which had been made by the peasants, and which were replaced by a tax in kind. This took only a fixed amount of the grain, while the peasants got the right to dispose at will of the rest of their harvest— that is, to sell it on the market. Other important measures reestablished stability of peasant holdings, prohibiting new redistribution of land, which had often been attempted by poor peasants during the preceding years. Finally, the peasants received the right to farm their land as they liked, a concession which put an end, for the time being, to the pressure that had been put on them to drop individual, and adopt collective, farming methods.

As soon as the worst consequences of drought and famine had been overcome, that change of policy very rapidly brought a considerable recovery in agricultural production, thus eliminating difficulties in food supply to the cities. Consequently, area sown in grain increased from a minimum of 66.2 million hectars in 1922-23 (in 1913, 94.4 million hectars) to 93.7 million hectars, or nearly pre-war level, in 1926-27; net grain production, after deduction of seeds, increased from a minimum of 42.3 million tons in 1921-22 (in 1913, 80.1 million tons) to 78.3 million tons in 1926-27.

However, in spite of this recovery in overall production to about pre-war level, not only was there no improvement in the structural deficiencies of Russian agriculture—namely, rural overpopulation, bad division of the land, and low technical levels—but they had actually been aggravated by the new distribution of land. As a result of the division of the big estates, the total *area* of peasant farms had increased by less than 25 percent; but owing to this new distribution, as well as to increase in population, the total *number*

104

of such farms had increased by 1927 to 24-25 million as against only 16 million in 1913. The average size of the farms had thus declined, increasing even more the subsistence-farming nature of Russian agriculture and decreasing drastically the quantities of produce which it was able to market. Thus, in 1926-27, out of an overall production nearly equal to pre-war, the share of commercialized produce was only 13.3 percent instead of 26 percent in 1913. Such a situation not only prevented renewal of grain exports on any significant scale, but even created difficulties in providing adequate supplies for the rapidly growing urban population.

In the field of industry and trade, the main changes due to the Nep were the following: Private activity, especially in small-scale industry and retail trade, was authorized; small industrial firms which had been nationalized either were returned to former owners or were leased to other private persons. All large-scale industrial and commercial undertakings, however, remained in state ownership and management, with the exception of a few (mainly mining) concerns for which concessions had been granted to foreign capitalists. The structure of state industry was completely changed: workers' control, and equality of wages irrespective of productivity and cost, were abolished. Each plant was put under a responsible manager. Working discipline and a differentiated wage scale were restored. All the undertakings of each industry were combined in one trust, the central office of which controlled the whole industry. The General Council of National Economy coordinated the different economic activities. Finally, the greatest stress was put on overall increase in production, on a reduction in cost, and the profitable operation of state industries.

As a result of this policy, industrial production also recovered, and by 1926-27 the pre-war level of production was again reached as a whole, and even considerably exceeded in some industries, such as coal mining and cotton-cloth manufacture.

The main objective of the Nep—recovery of production from its catastrophic level of 1920—was thus achieved. But once this immediate result was attained, the main question to be answered

105

was: Since the stage reached was one of transition and uncertainty, what would be the policy pursued from now on?

By most Western observers the Nep had been considered as a confession of the failure not only of the Communist policy pursued during 1917-20, but of Communism as a whole. The partial restoration of private ownership and initiative in trade and agriculture was expected to be only the first step toward a complete return to a capitalist economy. Such a development was what many Communists feared. The intentions of Lenin, however, when he initiated the Nep, were quite different. The dropping of the policy of ruthless socialization, and partial return to private initiative and ownership, were under existing circumstances the only practical means to restore production and thus save Russia and its Communist rulers, the former from a complete breakdown and the latter from annihilation. But the Nep was never intended to mean a return to capitalism, or even a permanent compromise between socialist and capitalist factors of economy. It was meant purely as a sort of tactical retreat, in order to enable the economy to recover, and thus to provide the possibility, once this recovery was achieved, of a renewal of socialization. Lenin was, of course, aware of the danger inherent in the fact that the Nep was strengthening capitalist forces, but he was convinced that the Communist state, preserving the key sectors of large-scale industry and foreign trade, would not be seriously endangered. Events proved him to be right.

The new turning point came by 1927. At that time began the drafting of the first Five-Year Plan of economic reconstruction and industrialization, which was implemented from October 1, 1928, on.

The new change of policy was due to a series of political and economic factors. Progress in the stabilization of Western Europe had destroyed Russia's earlier hopes of an imminent world revolution, so that coexistence of Communist Russia within a mainly capitalist world had to be faced. Stalin had conquered his opponents, including Trotzky, with his theory of permanent revolution, and he now proclaimed the necessity of organizing socialism in one country. This policy appeared particularly feasible in Russia because, with its vast territory and resources, it could easily be made self-sufficient, that is, independent of the capitalist world. In order to achieve self-sufficiency, however, a gigantic effort of industrialization was required to enable Russia to produce the major industrial goods it required both in time of peace and in time of war. Such industrialization—essentially, expansion of large-scale industry, the main socialist sector of Soviet economy—was due to change the balance of power inside the economy by increasing the number and, even more, the economic strength of industrial workers, as compared to the still individualist peasants.

Finally, the effort of industrialization offered to Communist-educated youth a substitute outlet for their enthusiasm over the idea of world revolution, which for the time being had to be postponed. Socialist construction, reaching and exceeding the technical and industrial achievements of capitalist countries, especially the United States, became a most stimulating target for the young Communist.

This industrialization was naturally to be achieved at the expense of the foes of Communist policy, i.e., the capitalist elements, who, owing to the Nep, had achieved a considerable degree of prosperity and, as regards the kulaks in rural areas, even a substantial economic power. By the end of the Nep, the kulaks were already starting, even though illegally, to transform the structure of farming by a return to the Stolypin big-farm system. Their procedure was to lease land illegally from small peasants whom, also illegally, they employed as farm workers. Even though containing the possibility of increase in production and badly needed commercialized surpluses, this development was of course most dangerous from the point of view of the Soviet authorities. In order to prevent such a spontaneously capitalist solution of the structural deficiency of Russian agriculture, a socialist solution had to be imposed. The kulaks had to be destroyed, as well as their counterpart in the cities, the new bourgeoisie created by the Nep.

The struggle against the kulaks was due to an economic, as well as to a political, necessity. Industrialization was to inflict heavy sacrifices upon agriculture, since imports of foreign manufactured equipment had to be paid for by exports, mainly of agricultural produce. As food surpluses, under the existing structure of agriculture, were insufficient, a return to a ruthless policy of requisitioning was applied, carrying a threat of renewed famine in the countryside. In addition, a structural reform of forced collectivization was instituted, intended to provide in future the food surpluses for feeding the cities, and to make available surplus labor for expanding industry. This new struggle of industrialization and forced collectivization lasted for the greater part of the period 1928-39, and resulted in a complete transformation of the Russian economy.

11 AGRICULTURAL EUROPE FROM WAR TO DEPRESSION

THE BREAKDOWN of the empires of Russia and Austria-Hungary, at the end of World War I, resulted in a great shake-up and reapportionment of territory. In the whole vast area of eastern and southeastern Europe—between the frontiers of Russia on the one hand and Germany and Italy on the other—a series of new small and medium-sized states was established. There was also an extension of already existing states, such as Serbia and Rumania. In all these states created or extended by the peace treaties of 1919, the formerly oppressed nationalities organized their own independent existence.

This new territorial structure implemented for the nations concerned the ideal of national self-determination, even though to a great extent denying it to substantial minorities. From the economic point of view, however, it was far from being preferable to the previous one. Thus, it resulted in the disruption of the fairly balanced economic unit of Austria-Hungary, and in the detachment from Russia of regions where there had been developed activities mainly for the Russian market, such as the Polish textile industry.

Most of these states, with the main significant exception of Czechoslovakia, had the following principal characteristics:

They were economically unbalanced, with a more or less strong predominance of agriculture. The percentage of population dependent on agriculture was 55.5 for the whole area, with 60.8 in Poland and 68.4 in Rumania, but only 36.6 in Czechoslovakia.

This agriculture consisted, in varying degrees, of big estates belonging to landlords and of small peasant farms, but it was in both cases on a very low level of technical development and productivity.

As a consequence of the change in sovereignty, and under the influence of the Russian Revolution, land reform—that is, division of part of the big estates between the peasants—had been more or less implemented. This implementation had been most complete in countries where most of the landlords were of a nationality alien to the nation ruling the new states, as, for example, in the Baltic countries. Such land reform was implemented in most of these countries without any considerable assistance in capital or technical advice being given to the peasants for adjustment and modernization of their production methods. That was partly due to the fact that peasants, even though they constituted the majority of the population, still did not exert influence in proportion to their numbers in most of these new states, which, again with the exception of Czechoslovakia, were democracies in name only.

Thus land reform, which at first had disrupted agricultural production, had as a lasting effect an increase in subsistence farming and decrease in commercialized food quantities available, especially for export. Yields were very low per unit of arable land, and even lower per head of agricultural population. The reasons were: generally excessive land distribution, which was steadily aggravated by the rapid growth of population; lack of technical knowledge for applying improved methods of cultivation, like crop rotation; and lack of capital essential for machinery and fertilizer. Therefore, while output per hectar of wheat, compared to that of France—which may be considered as an average for Western Europe—was only slightly lower in 1930, the fact remains that, measured in output per head of agricultural population, the difference was tremendous and provides the true picture of low pro-

110

ductivity and resulting low standard of living, as well as of rural overpopulation. Here are actual comparative figures:

	Yield per hectare	Output per head of agricultural population
	(in metric quintals)	
France	14.8	19.6
Rumania	10.6	11.3
Poland	11.5	9.1

A natural result of such a situation was the fact that even though agriculture was by far the most important activity of all these countries, the export surplus of agricultural produce, mainly grain, was relatively low. Moreover, the surplus existed only because of the extremely low consumption levels. Besides, the cost of agricultural products exported was relatively high, and these products could compete only with the greatest difficulty with those of overseas countries, whose agriculture was highly mechanized. They could be exported to Western Europe, their only possible outlet, only as long as prices remained relatively high, which was the case during most of the period of the 1920's, as agricultural production in Western Europe was slow to recover from the decline due to the war.

Industrial development should have provided the main remedy for most of the agricultural difficulties of this area. It would have: (1) absorbed the surplus of manpower, thus allowing a more rational system of farming; and (2) provided domestic sources of supply for equipment, as well as an enlarged domestic market for agricultural produce. Contradictory as it may sound, the results of industrialization, however, during the whole inter-war period, had been highly unsatisfactory. This, too, in spite of the fact that natural resources for industrial development are substantial in most of the countries concerned. It was excessive nationalism, employed in building up the economy of the newly established countries, that was mainly responsible for this failure. Each country,

111

as soon as it had achieved independence, at once decided to strive for economic self-sufficiency in all fields, and erected high tariff walls to protect its existing industries and above all to foster establishment of new ones.

Thus, it was impossible to achieve a regional cooperation toward industrialization which, by specializing the different countries of the area in the products for the manufacture of which they enjoyed the greatest natural advantages, would have made possible the establishment of new industries with low cost and prospects of large markets. Even the economic cooperation existing heretofore in the relatively large economic unit of the Austrian Empire was abruptly discontinued, since the new states stubbornly refused to adopt the preferential customs agreement that had been considered by the Western powers. On the contrary, each one of them tried to exclude, by high tariff duties, the products which it formerly received from its neighbor countries, developing, instead, its own production in order to replace these imports.

To a great extent, such industrial expansion amounted to a wasteful duplication of already existing facilities, with little consideration either of cost or of markets. Most of the new industries, because of their artificial character, were limited to the small domestic market of the countries concerned, and proved to be of little advantage to these countries themselves. As a matter of fact, these high-cost industries, artificially fostered and maintained, could neither absorb a significant part of the rural surplus population nor provide the manufactured goods or the domestic market required for the development of agriculture.

The economic development, as well as the social stability of a major part of this area—especially countries like Poland, Rumania and Hungary—was greatly handicapped by the weakneses of the middle class, which, in the countries of Western civilization, was the main element of progress toward economic development and political democracy. This situation was a result of a semifeudal structure of society, to some extent still persisting.

112

The gap between the landowners and the peasants had been traditionally bridged by national minorities, Germans and Jews, who were by far the greatest part of he urban population monopolizing most trades and handicrafts. This situation still persisted in considerable degree, in spite of the efforts of the governments to build up a national middle class. As a result, a great part of the existing middle class did not fulfil its normal functions in the development of economic activity. Far from enjoying the politcal support and influence necessary to favor its efforts, in most countries of the area, that class was the victim of marked discrimination, if not persecution, which hardly encouraged it to invest its available capital in new ventures.

Exploitation of the area's major mineral resources was mainly pursued by foreign capital (examples: oil in Rumania and copper in Yogoslavia). The raw materials produced were generally exported without being processed in the country of origin, which was thus deprived of the possibility of establishing industries for the development of which natural conditions existed.

Foreign capital granted as loans at high interest rates, mainly by France, the political ally of most countries of the region, also enabled their governments for the time being to maintain an, even though shaky, equilibrium of their economy and of their finances. Such equilibrium, however, was not only achieved on the basis of extremely low production and consumption levels, but also, in its international aspect, was subject to: (1) maintenance of a high level of world prices for export grain, which alone enabled them to market in Western Europe their main export item, and (2) continuation of foreign loans. As soon as these conditions ceased to exist, the economy of these contries was due to crash.

In the area under discussion, however, there were two countries which offered two different patterns of what might have been achieved in the field of economic development in the whole area. These countries were Czechoslovakia and Lithuania.

Czechoslovakia started under particularly favorable circum-

113

stances, as it had inherited the most industrialized as well as the most highly developed agricultural areas of Austria-Hungary. In that country, the basis of a prosperous and stable agriculture was an intelligent agricultural policy, which, in turn supported the prosperity of industry. Land reform was implemented by granting technical and financial assistance to farmers to enable them to modernize their production and to concentrate on the most profitable crops, such as sugar beets.

Even more significant, however, was the example of Lithuania, a small and purely agricultural country without any mineral resources whatsoever. Its pre-war agriculture was based mainly on grain crops harvested by the big estates. A comprehensive land reform wiped out the big estates owned mainly by Polish, Russian and German landowners, while the leaders of the rural cooperative movement had organized the major part of the peasantry and thus enjoyed a great political influence. These leaders understood that maintenance of the previous system of cultivation on new small farms with a soil of relatively low fertility would condemn the peasants to a very low-standard subsistence farming. Therefore they decided to change completely the economic basis of agriculture, shifting it from food cereals to livestock raising and fodder crops, thus imitating Denmark, where natural conditions were somewhat similar.

In about ten years, as a result of a systematic effort, a complete structural change had been accomplished, and Lithuanian agriculture had become highly efficient. It specialized in the production of dairy and livestock products (butter, eggs, bacon, etc.) which, exported, fetched excellent prices, mainly in Great Britain. Thus the Lithuanian farmers and the whole country were provided with a standard of consumption considerably above that of most of the other countries of the area. Somewhat similar efforts had been made also in Lettland, Poland and other countries. The attempt, however, was less systematic and therefore met with less success.

114

II FROM DEPRESSION TO WORLD WAR II

12 EUROPEAN FACTORS OF THE WORLD ECONOMIC DEPRESSION, 1929–1932

DURING the first decennium after the end of World War I, the general trend in European and world economy had been in favor of reestablishment of the pattern of international economic relations that had existed before 1914. This tendency reached its climax and came to an end by 1927-28. At that time, volume of international trade had again attained its previous maximum of 1913; and the League of Nations called, in Geneva, an international economic conference for the purpose of general reduction of tariffs.

This by no means meant that pre-war world economy had been reestablished. It meant only that from then on the tendency toward such reestablishment receded until, as soon as the world depression started, it became completely reversed.

It should also be pointed out that, although the volume of international trade had recovered in 1928 to its pre-war level, the relative importance of international exchange of goods, as compared with world production, had declined. The reason was, that volume of world production had not only recovered to pre-war, but had increased in 1928 by 25 percent over 1913. This situation, namely, less recovery and development of international trade than of production, was the natural consequence of the fact that, in reconstruction of their economy after the war, each country stressed first and foremost developments of

117

domestic production, in order to replace excessive reconstruction imports and thus reestablish the equilibrium of its balance of payments.

Only when this first essential target had been practically reached was more attention given to restoration of international trade: to expansion of imports as well as of exports. This return to more liberal foreign trade policies, however, had been hampered by the changes which had resulted in each national economy from the drive for increased production. Thus, new domestic sources of supply, developed to replace former imports, could obviously not be sacrificed. Nor could new protective tariffs, established in order to stimulate domestic production, be abolished; in fact, they were reduced only with the utmost difficulty, and against the stubborn resistance of all the interests concerned. As a general rule, then, the considerable increase in the level of tariff protection which had occurred during the first post-war years could be only halted; it could not be substantially reduced.

By the end of this period, however, considerable hope for a stronger revival of international economic relations was expressed, and received a marked impetus from the international economic conference called by the League of Nations in May 1927. But this conference did not fulfill the hope which it had stimulated; in particular, it did not result in a reversal of the trend toward increase in tariffs. In fact, many of the countries participating in the conference increased their tariffs beforehand, in order to have a bargaining margin. In many cases, reductions effected as a consequence of recommendations of the conference were less than the increases which had preceded them. Conference recommendations, however, concerning consolidation of tariff rates and return to the "most-favored nation" clause had considerable influence on some commercial treaties concluded during this period, especially on the Franco-German treaty of September 1927.

This agreement, concluded between the two leading protectionists countries of Europe, achieved not a little improvement in trade conditions between those two countries. They consequently stabilized their tariff rates, sometimes reduced them, and extended the benefits thus obtained for each other to all other countries, by restoring the most-favored nation clause, which before 1914 had been the chief instrument of generalization of tariff reduction. Since the end of the war this clause had been generally abandoned. It was replaced, in most countries, by a policy of reciprocity that applied reduction of protective duties only to countries which were direct parties to agreements, and which offered as a counterpart similar advantages. The return to that clause, in the application of the Franco-German treaty, was thus considered very significant; but, in spite of the hope it had stimulated, this agreement remained only an isolated example, and a return to more liberal general policies did not materialize.

It should be noted that, in addition to the general obstacles and limiting factors hampering a revival of international trade, Europe's part in this trade had somewhat declined—from 60 percent in 1913 to about 50 percent in 1930 (56 percent of world imports and 46 percent of world exports).

This decline was both a direct and an indirect consequence of the war, which, while it had devastated the economy of Europe, had stimulated economic activity on all other continents. The most important factors of the decline were: industrialization overseas and increased competition from American and Japanese export industries, which had reduced export markets for European manufactured goods; the loss of industrial and, even more, of financial supremacy to the United States; and the steadily deteriorating balance-of-payment position of the Western European industrialized countries. Their imports of food and, still more so, of raw materials were constantly increasing, while they could pay for them only with a lesser volume of industrial exports and a very much smaller income from foreign investments. As a result, the security margin, i.e., the surplus of their balance of

119

payments, was considerably reduced; and since new capital available for investment abroad was consequently decidedly limited, this surplus could not be much increased. Western European industrialized countries thus occupied a relatively fragile economic position, which manifestly weakened their power of resistance in case of a large-scale world depression.

Taken as a whole, Europe, and especially the highly industrialized countries of Western Europe, still represented one of the greatest concentrations of wealth (second only to the United States) and of productive capacity. Equal, and in some respects superior, to that existing during the same period in North America, this capacity was, however, dispersed among a great number of different countries. The economies of European countries, far from being coordinated, became more and more contradictory, as a result of increasing tariff duties and of duplication of industrial development. The trend of industrial development favored large-scale production requiring large domesttic markets, such as the one which existed in the United States, or which the Soviet Union started to build up through its industrialization plans. But a similar development in Western Europe was hampered by insufficiency in the size of the domestic market of each country, a factor which was for all of them a steadily increasing handicap.

This handicap could be overcome by an economic union of the whole, or the greater part, of the continent of Europe. For the first time, there entered the realm of practical politics the idea of a European Federation, a "Pan-Europe," which for many centuries had been a favorite ideal of political philosophers such as Thomas More, Abbé St. Pierre and others. Its first and foremost propagandist was the Count of Coudenhove-Kalergi, who had started his campaign as early as 1922. The initial practical proposal in this field had been made in May 1930 by the French Foreign Minister, Aristide Briand. With a view to completing his lifetime aim of Franco-German reconciliation and European peace, begun at Locarno in 1925, he attempted to establish a

European customs union, which would have provided the economic basis for the political unification of Europe, in a way similar to that in which the Zollverein, a century before, had provided the basis for the political unification of Germany.

It is obvious today that if Briand's proposal had been accepted, most of the political and economic disasters of the next few years could have been avoided. Such a customs union would have been most important in providing Germany with an export market sufficiently large to enable the Reich to continue interest payments on its foreign debt. The large economic influence which Germany might have attained through such a development of her exports could have been offset by the economic power of other industrialized countries—such as Great Britain, France, Italy and Belgium—and thus could have been prevented from becoming the basis of a political and economic supremacy of the Reich. On the other hand, maintenance and development of prosperity in all European countries would have reduced instead of strengthened their nationalist resentment and the trend toward social and political disintegration, and thus would have acted as a powerful factor for the maintenance and consolidation of peace and democracy. This would have been especially true in countries which, like Germany, were eventually to be most strongly affected by the depression that resulted mainly from insufficient foreign markets.

Public opinion, however, was not ready for such a European customs-union proposal. The governments of these countries and the business interests concerned were even less prepared for it, and for the sacrifices it implied in sovereignty and economic favors—such as high prices due to tariff protection, guaranteed domestic markets, and so on. Besides, this plan was strongly opposed by Great Britain, which considered it impossible to become a member of such an organization that could endanger its economic relationship with the rest of the Commonwealth. She wanted, further, to prevent the establishment of a continental customs union of which she would not be a member, fearing that British economy would be adversely influenced by it. Thus Briand's proposal was not even discussed by the League of Nations. It was merely referred to a committee, which did not even present its report on the subject, and nothing whatever was done to prevent the catastrophe that was imminent.

The world depression did not originate in Europe but in the food-and-raw-materials-producing overseas countries. Restoration of European farm production, however, was one of the main reasons for the decrease in foreign sales by the overseas agricultural producers, who had considerably expanded their production during the war in order to care for European requirements. The agricultural and raw-materials exports crisis, which had started as early as 1928, became a world depression on an unprecedented scale after the breakdown, in October 1929, of the speculative stock-exchange boom of Wall Street. It was that which destroyed the unsteady balance of American prosperity. The first repercussions of the depression on European economy took the form of a fall in farm prices. This especially affected the economic stability of the agricultural producing and exporting countries of Central and Eastern Europe. They sold their produce to Western Europe and were also its customers for manufactured goods, as well as its debtors. In those debtor countries, agriculture was generally organized on the basis of peasant small-scale production, which had higher costs than those of the large-scale mechanized agriculture of the main overseas producers like the United States, Canada and Argentina. As a consequence of the fall in world prices, these countries were obliged to sell at a loss and were unable to cover, with the proceeds of their exports, their import requirements and the interest payments on their foreign debt.

They therefore had to default on their foreign debt as well as severely to curtail all their imports. As prices of farm products fell, and the exporting countries tried to press their sales in order to obtain foreign exchange, the markets of Western European food-importing countries were swamped by imports from overseas, from East Central Europe, and from the Soviet Union. This latter country was also at that period under the obligation to export cereals, at nearly any price, in order to pay for equipment ordered for implementation of the first Five-Year Plan.

Agriculture in Western Europe was severely affected by this heavy dumping and had to be protected by increase in tariffs, and especially by the introduction of import quotas establishing a quantitative limitation of imports. In spite of these protective measures, the purchasing power of domestic agriculture in these countries considerably declined. At the same time, there was an even more drastic decline in their exports to the agricultural exporting countries, especially East and Central Europe, formerly large customers of Western European industry.

The first direct effect of the American depression on Western European economy was the disastrous decline in exports to the United States of high-quality consumers' goods. For these America had sometimes been not only the greatest foreign market, but even the outlet for most of the output of the industries concerned. Among such goods were: Limoges and Bavarian china, Calais lace, Nuremberg toys, Swiss watches, Irish linen, British cloth, etc. The decline in United States imports, resulting from decrease in the purchasing power of their market, was still aggravated by the drastic increase in protective duties imposed by the Hawley-Smoot tariff, which was adopted by Congress in 1930. Because of decline in American imports, several important industrial areas of Europe that specialized in the production of the respective export goods, became depressed areas, and the majority of the population joined the ranks of the unemployed.

Decline in exports to the United States, and also of invisible exports (consisting in expenditures of American tourists), had extremely serious effects on the European balance of payments. Its equilibrium had been shaky already, as the import deficit and the additional burden of interest payments on commercial and political debts were temporarily bridged by American capital exports. The depression which reduced current dollar income also stopped the flow of that American capital to Europe. Thus, the international credit pyramid, built on the absurd basis of the circuit of war debts, reparations and American credits to Germany, was due to crash. The breakdown could not but shatter the financial and monetary structure of the whole world, but especially of European debtor countries. This happened not only in Germany and other countries of Central Europe, but even in Great Britain.

The crack-up occurred in 1931. Somehow, it had been delayed by short-term bank credits, which had continued to be granted for some time after the flow of long-term investment had stopped.

In May 1931, the Osterreichische Credit Anstalt, the biggest bank of Austria, went bankrupt. It had had considerable funds frozen in neighboring agricultural countries ruined by the fall in farm prices. This crash had immediate repercussions in Germany, mainly in destroying the confidence of foreign creditors in the solvency of their German debtors. Most of those debtors were the Berlin banks, which had reloaned to Austria and other countries of Central Europe part of the sums borrowed on short term from American and Western European banks. The flight of foreign capital which followed this bankruptcy began rapidly to endanger not only Germany but even Great Britain. She also had borrowed important sums, mainly from France, and reloaned them to Germany and other countries of Central Europe. The moratorium on war debts and reparations—declared on the initiative of President Hoover in June 1931—did not stop the capital rush, which finally brought Germany under exchange control and sent Great Britain off the gold standard.

The policies of the various European countries in their fight against depression differed considerably one from another, and should therefore be examined separately. Their only common feature, during this period extending from 1930 to World War II, was the complete reversal of the trend toward greater inter-

124

national economic cooperation. Now, each country tried to achieve and maintain prosperity by means of an exclusively, or at least mainly, national policy, paying little attention to considerations of international cooperation. The natural and inevitable end of this policy was World War II.

13 GREAT BRITAIN DURING THE PERIOD 1931–1939: DEVALUATION, PROTECTION, RECOVERY

GREAT BRITAIN, which since 1920 had been suffering from a chronic stagnation and mass unemployment, was the country first and foremost affected by the world depression 1929-31. This was the natural consequence of the fact that out of all great industrialized countries, Great Britain sent the largest proportion of its exports to overseas food-and-raw-materials-producing countries, and was also their greatest creditor. These debtor countries, located mainly in the British Commonwealth and Latin-America, were the first victims of the fall in primary prices that started the depression rolling. Great Britain was affected by the reduction of their purchasing power—which obliged them to cut their imports—and also by the suspension of their debt service, and the decrease of freight carried in the form of their exports and imports.

The British market became swamped with a flood of foreign imports of all kinds, the dumping ground for exports of all foreign countries in desperate need of convertible foreign exchange. In a world of steadily shrinking purchasing power and mounting trade restrictions, it was the only market still remaining open to foreign imports. Of all British imports, 83 percent could enter without payment of any customs duties; and there were no quantitative restrictions of imports, such as quotas. Moreover, the foreign exporters were certain to receive payment in currency

126

convertible into gold, which thus could be used to compensate balance-of-payments deficits with other countries.

This huge influx of imports—which depressed the domestic price level—endangered the stability and cut the sales of British agriculture, as well as of the formerly very prosperous industries catering to the domestic market.

The depression affected British industry and continued to get steadily worse, affecting the number of unemployed, which increased to a maximum of some 2,500,000 during the winter of 1931-32. Add to this number the dependents of those individuals, and from 6 to 7 million people—about one-fourth of the whole working-class population—were reduced to the dole. Following upon a ten-year period of stagnation and mass unemployment, the moral and material effects of such a crisis on the political and social structure of society were so vast as to be incalculable. In most other countries such conditions would probably have sowed the seeds of violent social disturbances.

During the summer of 1931, the financial and monetary crisis still further aggravated Great Britain's economic situation. This crisis was a consequence of the lack of prudence in the lending policy of the city banks, which had loaned considerable sums to countries where interest rates were high. In so doing, they neglected the fact that these rates were to a great extent justified by the risks of non-repayment, which had to be faced, taking into consideration the very unstable financial and economic equilibrium of the debtor countries. During the crisis, these risks actually did materialize when the debtor countries concerned declared a moratorium on their payments abroad and introduced exchange control. Then the funds loaned were immobilized— frozen, according to a very expressive neologism, which was later to be consecrated in international agreements.

This situation frightened the foreign depositors. These were banks and central banks, such as the Banque de France, which was the most important of them; and they maintained enormous sight or short-term balances in sterling, which, according to the

127

method of the gold exchange standard were part of the reserves backing their currency issue. The foreign depositors, therefore, began to withdraw their balances, converting them into gold. In addition to this flight of foreign capital, there was also at this moment a flight from sterling of British capital. It resulted from two factors: the opposition of capitalist interests to fiscal and social policies of the MacDonald Labor Government, and the lack of confidence of the British capitalists themselves in the future of the British economy.

Thus, in two months the Bank of England lost over £200 million of its gold reserves, in spite of a gold credit of £50 million by the Banque de France and the Federal Reserve Bank of New York. By September 20, 1931, its gold stock had declined to £130 million. A further depletion of the gold reserve being considered too dangerous, it was decided to suspend the gold standard. At this moment, one of the most tragic in British history, an economic Dunkerque, most foreign observers (even the most sympathetic to Britain's plight, such as André Siegfried) thought that the era of British greatness was gone forever.

Yet at this very same moment of deep gloom, British policy built the foundation of a recovery that enabled Great Britain to start a surprising come-back and to strengthen its economy, which otherwise might not have been able to meet the strenuous effort required during World War II. On this occasion, the British people once more proved that there was still success in their traditional policy of waiting to act till the last possible moment, and then "muddling through." This time, however, they adopted, not from motives of doctrine, but from sheer necessity, a completely new approach, throwing overboard their long-standing economic and monetary policies of gold standard and free trade.

The abandonment of the gold standard, however, far from being a deliberate measure, had been adopted under the absolute necessity of preserving the remainder of the gold reserve. This step resulted in a considerable depreciation of the pound, which at first the authorities neither encouraged nor resisted. But the

128

government at once established an Exchange Equalization Fund, which some time later was to become the chief medium of a policy of managed currency. It was maintained by a method of "flexible stability" at a level which was most proximate to the point of equilibrium between demand and supply of currency, and which could therefore be maintained with the least effort. At first, however, the intervention of the Exchange Equalization Fund was limited only to moderating fluctuations, without opposing the basic trend. Thus, in about a year after the abandonment of the gold standard, the pound declined by about 40 percent. Then the point of equilibrium was apparently reached. After that, and until the beginning of World War II, currency fluctuations were very limited.

The depreciation of the pound improved the situation of the British economy by cutting it off from the depressing influence of the continued fall in world prices of primary products measured in dollars. That price fall lasted as long as the United States remained on the gold standard—or until the spring of 1933. On the other hand, the expected rise in import prices did not materialize. In a country like Great Britain, where imports are of such paramount importance, a rise would have meant a similar increase in the cost of living. For most exporters of primary goods, the British market was of such importance that, in order to maintain the volume of their sales there, they tried to cut their prices (measured in gold currency) and thus keep them stable in terms of sterling. Such a policy was made possible for some of the most important trade partners of Great Britain by following Britain's own lead in depreciating their currency. A similar course had been followed by all countries of the British Commonwealth, as well as by Egypt, the countries of Scandinavia and some in Latin America. Thus, British costs and prices in sterling remained stable, justifying the proud confidence of the average Englishman in his currency. Many people in England did not understand that the pound had depreciated, and maintained that it was still worth twenty shillings.

129

This stability of prices in sterling corresponded to a cut in terms of gold currencies proportional to the fall of the pound. It therefore gave to British exporters considerable advantage in competition with countries which maintained the parity of their currencies, such as the United States and France. On the other hand, costs of exports of these countries to Great Britain were increased, and thus discouraged.

A few months after the abandonment of the gold standard, Great Britain also abandoned free trade by adopting, in the Import Duties Act of February 1932, a general protective tariff. Until then, protective duties had been relatively exceptional. Examples were the McKenna duties introduced in 1915, and the duties on key products introduced in 1921 to foster production in a few industries which before the war had been practically German monopolies: dyes, opticals, etc. From then on, however, only 25 percent of goods imported remained untaxed; these products were mainly raw materials and a few foodstuffs.

The basic rates of the new tariff were relatively moderate, compared with those of other major industrialized countries: Germany, France and especially the United States. The general rate was 10 percent, but much higher duties were levied on some important industrial goods. For example, the duty on iron and steel products was 33 percent. High duties were also applied on articles which were not yet manufactured in Great Britain, but which could eventually be produced there at a reasonable cost. This was an application of the theory of educational tariff policy, formulated a century earlier by Friedrich List, the founder of the German Zollverein. Imports of luxury goods were also heavily taxed.

Introduction of the general tariff enabled Great Britain to enlarge the system of imperial preference in its economic relations with the Commonwealth, but only after protracted negotiations at the Imperial Conference of Ottawa in the summer of 1932. Until then, the Dominions which granted preferential treatment to British industrial exports could not receive any effective reciprocal treatment from the mother country. Now, however, with imports of foreign foodstuffs liable to duty, preferential treatment could be granted to Empire exporters. The agreements with the Dominions sometimes included quantitative limits (quotas); Great Britain assumed the obligation to import minimum quantities at fixed tariff rates. Later on, during World War II, these quota agreements were extended to guarantee also the prices paid for the quantities imported, which were bulk purchases of commodities negotiated by the respective government authorities. As a result of the Ottawa agreement and the preferential treatment received and granted, British trade with the Empire expanded considerably. Thus, in 1938 half of the total British exports went to the Empire, instead of only one-third as in 1913; and the share of the Empire in British imports was 40 percent instead of 25 percent.

Further, introduction of tariff protection also provided Great Britain with greater bargaining possibilities in negotiating with foreign countries. Previously, the latter had had no reasons whatsoever to grant any favors to British exports, as no counterpart to such favors could be granted; and anyway, their own exports already enjoyed the best possible treatment: free entry on the British market. In a number of trade agreements concluded mainly with countries, such as Denmark, which depended to a considerable extent on the British market, Great Britain obtained more favorable conditions for her exports. In return, she granted reduction of duty on the import of a limited quantity of produce from the respective foreign countries. Under such circumstances, much more favorable than those existing previously, British foreign trade began an impressive recovery. Great Britain's share in the international trade of the world, which had been 15 percent in 1913 and had declined to 10 percent in 1930, increased to 14 percent in 1938.

Production in industry and in agriculture also developed markedly. It also underwent a process of modernization and rationalization, achieved, to a great extent, under the impulse and with the assistance of the state.

131

British agriculture had been very severely affected since the end of World War I, but in particular, since the beginning of the depression, by cutthroat foreign competition. This was most devastating, not only for cereals production, where British farmers suffered a natural disadvantage compared to overseas producers, but even for products such as meat, where their competitive position was normally reasonably good. Only with a few items, like dairy products and fruit, did the British producers benefit from the increase of consumption by the domestic market, as compared to pre-war.

The first measure of state intervention in agriculture was the subsidy for sugar-beet production, already introduced in 1924, and aimed at the creation of a rotation crop for wheat, in order to stimulate production of cereals, or at least prevent its decline.

The agricultural policy adopted by the British government on the initiative of Mr. Hudson, Secretary for Agriculture during the greater part of the period until 1939, had as its main features: the establishment of a guaranteed price for home production, sufficiently remunerative to stimulate production; a price guarantee, implemented by the payment of a subsidy to producers, and financed by a levy established either on total consumption of the respective products, or only on imports which were limited to fixed quotas for Dominion and foreign sources of supply. This system functioned through so-called marketing agreements, which were negotiated and concluded by the state and the producers' associations, and in which the state also pledged its assistance for improvement of efficiency in production and distribution. Funds for these purposes were made available under the Agricultural Credit Act. Thus, for British producers the price of wheat was guaranteed at 45 shillings a quarter ($1.37 per bushel). The deficiency payment required in order to cover the difference in relation to the market price, was collected by means of an excise milling tax. A similar system was applied with respect to other cereals, as well as to meat, butter, bacon, etc.

The introduction of protection facilitated rationalization of

132

industry. This process the state strongly stimulated and supported, although it did not intervene as directly as in the case of agriculture. Thus, in some instances, introduction or maintenance of tariff protection was conditioned by the pledge of the respective industries to adopt rationalization plans. Also, owing to the support of the state, funds for the financing of industrial rationalization schemes were made available by subsidiaries especially established for this purpose either by the Bank of England or by the big commercial banks: the subsidiary established by the Bank of England was the Securities Management Trust; the one by the commercial banks was the Bankers Industrial Development Corporation.

The best results of rationalization were achieved in the iron and steel industry. A new integrated iron and steel plant, the most modern in Europe, was built in Corby, in a location where it could use domestic iron ore mined in the neighborhood. This construction and the modernization of other plants reduced the production cost of British steel, and production of iron and steel expanded considerably. Pig-iron production thus increased from 6,600,000 tons in 1928 to 10,890,000 in 1939. In the same period, raw-steel production increased from 8,315,000 tons to 13,400,000.

The reorganization in the cotton, wool and shipbuilding industries was limited to the concentration of production in the most efficient plants; the others were bought up and dismantled. Recovery of production in the industries mentioned was not so considerable, owing to a permanent decline in the foreign demand. However, because of reorganization, these industries, which had been technically in a state of decay and financially nearly bankrupt, were restored to a condition of efficiency and solvency.

These reorganization schemes were sometimes implemented through combinations, such as the merger of Vickers-Armstrong in the steel industry. They were also frequently achieved through the conclusion of marketing agreements, or cartels (e.g., for steel and chemicals), which regulated competition on the domestic

133

market, while permitting participation in international cartels (such as the European raw-steel cartel), intended to enable British producers to maintain, without ruinous price competition with exporters of other countries, their share of world exports for their respective products. Participation in such international cartels brought about general improvement in the competitive position of British industries in world trade, and was therefore approved by the government. As to the domestic market, however, the government required that reorganization schemes accomplished through cartels must make up, by increased efficiency, for the cost of eliminating the plants closed down and dismantled. They were not permitted to pass on any price increase to consumers.

In spite of these efforts of the British government to utilize the cartel organization as a means of rationalizing industry and of preventing all abuses of monopoly, the dominating position on the home market achieved by the industries concerned still seems to have produced, at least to a certain extent, the natural effects to have been expected, namely: decrease of the stimulants for cost reduction; improvement in efficiency; and expansion of production.

In the coal industry, rationalization was especially difficult because of the dispersion of ownership and management. No effective progress in organization of coal mining could be achieved during the period under consideration. A first step toward future reorganization was accomplished, however, by an act in 1938 which nationalized the ownership of the soil and abolished the royalties to be paid by the mines.

A considerable expansion was achieved by new industries. Thus, automobile production more than doubled in 10 years. With a production of about 400,000 cars a year, it took a position second only to that of the United States. Comparable progress was made in the production of rayon, electrical machinery, airplane engines, chemicals, and other goods.

The government made a substantial effort to attract new industries to depressed areas, by opening credits, making grants,

134

and building industrial facilities (the so-called trading estates), as well as by re-educating labor. In spite of this effort, however, and the considerable recovery of industrial production achieved, unemployment decreased only very slowly. In 1938, which was a year of recession in world trade, the number of unemployed still amounted to as much as 1,700,000.

Great Britian thus survived and overcame the catastrophic crisis of 1931, and gradually achieved a considerable degree of recovery even if not of prosperity. This result, however, was accomplished by utilizing methods absolutely opposite to the traditional liberal and internationalist policies which had been the basis of her former supremacy during the nineteenth century. To sum up, those new methods were: managed currency and adoption of a general tariff protection, as well as a trend, fostered and directed by the state, toward rationalization of agricultural and industrial production by means of cartel-like marketing agreements.

It has been pointed out that such a development not only was opposed to the classical liberalism, but had considerable resemblance to the policy pursued, during the same period, in Nazi Germany. There was, however, something much more important than this superficial similarity in technical measures applied in the two countries—namely, the essential difference in the spirit in which they were implemented. In Great Britain, this policy was pursued through methods of democratic cooperation, without compulsion or violence. Thus the most important and vital part of the liberal tradition was maintained. In that fact lies the essential difference between this British experience, together with the somewhat similar American New Deal, and the totalitarian economy.

14 FRANCE DURING THE PERIOD 1930–1939: OVERVALUED CURRENCY, DEFLATION, SOCIAL DISTURBANCES

THE ATTITUDE of France toward foreign trade during the depression, if compared to that of Great Britain toward the same problem, provides an example extremely typical of both countries. More than that, it gives a symbolic picture of their difference in situation and in psychological approach to economic problems in general. Thus, whereas Great Britain sacrificed the stability of her currency to the prospects of maintaining and expanding her trade, France tried to protect her domestic market by increasing tariffs and introducing quota limitations of imports, as well as by maintaining, above all, the stability of the franc. This purely defensive attitude is entirely typical of French psychological reactions to economic problems. It is a natural result of the lack of stimulus for expansion, caused in turn by the lack of increase in population.

In all fairness, however, the comparison made above should be qualified, in so far as the decision of the French to maintain the stability of the franc at nearly any cost resulted, to a great extent, from the fact that their currency had already been devaluated by 80 percent a few years earlier. A new depreciation would thus have completely ruined the confidence of the people in their own currency. In Great Britain, on the other hand, in spite of the depreciation of the pound compared to foreign moneys, confidence in the currency was not endangered, especially as its purchasing power on the domestic market was well maintained. On the contrary, France being an importing country on a much smaller scale than Great Britain, her devaluation could not have affected world raw-materials prices to the same extent and kept them stable in the devalued currency. Import prices would inevitably have risen, causing a similar rise in the general price level and a considerable inflationary pressure.

At the beginning of the world depression, French economy had been relatively little affected, since the home market was well protected against foreign competition. It remained very prosperous for some time, as a result of the industrial reequipment boom that followed stabilization of the franc. Gradually, however, especially after 1930, the French economy began to suffer, in particular, from decrease in exports and tourist expenditures.

One of the first effects of the depression on French economy was trouble for several big business undertakings, as, for example: in transport, the *Compagnie Aéropostale* (airline to South America) and the French steamship line, *Compagnie Générale Transatlantique;* and in banking, the *Banque Nationale de Crédit,* a branch banking establishment which had deviated from the traditional ultraconservative policy of the big French banks. Faced with bankruptcy, these concerns appealed to the state for assistance. It was granted for motives of public interest, in order (1) to maintain essential transport services; and (2) to prevent a rush on *all* banks and a complete loss of public confidence in the banking system. The latter would have occurred if the depositors of the bankrupt bank had not been compensated. Such protection of big business in distress was necessary and already had been applied for a long time to railroads, where deficits if any were paid by the state. Nevertheless, action of this kind supplied an important argument in favor of socialization, an argument which was to be put forward a few years later by the Popular Front.

French agriculture, also—even though protected by high tariffs and import quotas against foreign competition—felt the impact of the world depression. This was due partly to the excessive protection itself, which had been concentrated in a most irrational way on staple products, such as wheat, the price of which was already more than 150 percent above world prices. Thus, wheat production was made highly remunerative, even for farmers with soil least adapted to production of this cereal. Domestic production of wheat was therefore considerably expanded, while consumption of bread in France, already the highest consumption of all the countries of Western civilization, could not increase and even declined slightly. This policy resulted in a completely absurd overproduction of domestic wheat and in an unsalable surplus, with a cost far above world prices. Thus, in spite of establishment of an official minimum price of wheat of 115 francs per metric quintal, effective prices went well below, though not low enough to make French wheat competitive on the world market.

The very unsatisfactory remedy for this absurd situation which was finally adopted included artificial increase in consumption through lowering of the milling rate; subsidies for export; and mandatory limitation of wheat growing. A similar situation arose with respect to wine, when overproduction had resulted principally from an enormous increase in production in Algeria. It began when French wines were temporarily devastated by a bug called the phylloxera. Owing to favorable climatic conditions, Algerian production developed to become a most formidable competition to French mass-production cheap wines. Because of the customs-union arrangement between Algeria and France, Algerian imports could be neither taxed nor limited by quotas, and export markets for such wines were not available. Finally, solution of this problem was attempted through limitation and even reduction of production, subsidies being paid for destruction of grape plants.

These examples demonstrate that, in spite of tariff protection, French agriculture was far from being prosperous. The state, which simply followed the line of least effort, was satisfied to provide agriculture with a wall of all-round protection, which the respective interests violently claimed, and which for political reasons the state could not refuse. But, contrary to the course followed by Great Britain, the state failed to stimulate agricultural production—particularly, specialization in the fields to which it was best adapted, and where it could have gained in prosperity and efficiency as well as in competitive capacity in relation to foreign production. Such a result could have been achieved through a policy of discrimination in protection, insuring remunerative prices to production which deserved to be encouraged, while discouraging with lower protection the least efficient, marginal production which should be reduced, possibly granting subsidies for switching to other products. However, this policy, though recommended by several experts, had never been applied, so French agriculture continued to consist as before of a mass of small-scale, diversified farms mostly with low yields, but nevertheless endowed with great stability during a period of depression.

In all fairness, however, it should be pointed out that French agricultural policy during this period had two major justifications. The first was the fact that maintenance of a stable agriculture was more a social than an economic problem. The second was that the problem to be solved in France arose from surpluses, and could not be met in the same manner as in Great Britain or Germany. The French policy as to surpluses was no worse, and no better, than the policy pursued during the same period in the United States.

Agriculture in the French overseas possessions suffered from similarly excessive production costs. They existed mainly as a result of the customs union with France where prices of equipment were considerably above world level. The most important of the products affected were: peanuts from West Africa; sugar and coffee from the West Indies and Madagascar; feed from Indo-China; and cereals and wine from North Africa. On the other hand, it was possible to sell at world prices mineral products such as phosphate and iron ore from North Africa; tin and rubber from Indo-China; nickel from New Caledonia; and hardwood

139

from Central Africa. Development of wine growing in North Africa was an example of the lack of a rational integration between the economy of France and that of her possessions; products developed overseas were actually competitive with, not complementary to, those of the mother country. France and her Empire provided each other with a relatively stable market at remunerative prices, because of protection. During the depression, economic relations became even closer. The Empire supplied at this time one-third of French imports and absorbed 40 percent of French exports.

Notwithstanding this increase in Empire trade, however, industrial depression in France steadily deepened, owing to continuous decline in exports. French foreign trade had been especially hard hit by the closing of the free British market owing to: (1) the introduction of protection, and (2) the stimulus provided to British competition on the world market by the depreciation of the pound. The purchasing power of the French home market for domestic industrial goods also declined, because of the agricultural depression and of increase in foreign competition, which, in spite of tariff protection, could still undersell the French producers. To these factors should be added the loss of income from foreign investments, due mainly to the insolvency of the countries of Central and Eastern Europe, where most of the new French foreign investments were made.

Thus mass unemployment, a condition absolutely irregular in a country which normally had to import annually several hundred thousand foreign workers, steadily increased. At the climax of the depression, the number of assisted totally unemployed was about 600,000. The number of non-assisted totally or partially unemployed was estimated at over 1,000,000. Considering the demographical condition of the country, these figures, even if not high compared to those of other countries, were absolutely catastrophic.

The reaction of government and public opinion, alike, to the unemployment problem in relation to foreign workers was most short-sighted. The first measure adopted was the suspension of all immigration of foreign workers. This, after all, was at least understandable, even though in certain activities, such as agriculture, a continuous flow of foreign labor was absolutely essential. However, as unemployment increased, even worse mistakes were made. The French workers were unconscious of, or unwilling to consider, the fact that immigration of adult workers was the cheapest and the only practicable way to provide France with labor, the productive factor most in short supply, required for the normal expansion of the French economy. Even more, they completely lacked confidence in the possibility of such an expansion, and they feared the competition of foreign workers for the limited amount of work available in a stagnant economy—an attitude unfortunately rather typical of France.

The French working class therefore demanded, and the government agreed to, repatriation of foreign workers. Over 100,000 residing in France, and their families, were repatriated. This policy caused the loss to French economy of the productive power of these workers. But, more than that, it shattered the confidence of the foreign workers remaining in France in the permanence of their residence and, indirectly, their desire to be assimilated and become French citizens. This attitude could only be explained, not excused, by the fact that, unlike the United States, France lacked a tradition of handling and assimilating a mass immigration. In France, immigration was a relatively new phenomenon that came about because of the low birth rate and the heavy losses, in the war, of men of working age. Up to 1914, France had been accustomed only to providing asylum for, and assimilating, political emigrants fleeing from persecution: Poles, Italians, etc. in comparatively small numbers. The policy of mandatory repatriation of foreign workers resulted in disastrous consequences for the French economy in a later period when the foreign workers still residing in France were called back by the governments of their respective countries.

Especially after 1933, the economic depression was aggravated

141

by the overvaluation of the franc as compared with other currencies. It was affected mainly because of the depreciation of most other major currencies, the last one being the United States dollar in the spring of 1933. Others, such as the Reichsmark, though in theory maintained at their previous parity, were depreciated for use in foreign trade by means of several ingenious devices.

After the spring of 1933, France was the only major country still remaining on the traditional gold standard, without any restriction or alteration whatsoever. With a few other countries, such as Switzerland, Netherlands and Belgium, France had created the so-called gold bloc. This situation brought some satisfaction in the way of prestige, especially when for a few years the French franc became the basic currency of the world. However, the real economic and financial strength of the country—the effective basis of the gold-franc prestige—was not such as to allow for any length of time the costly and useless luxury of maintaining an overvalued currency, from which France suffered during this period 1933-36, even more than Great Britain during the preceding period.

While the French economy was thus being seriously affected by a steadily increasing deflationary depression, the budgetary situation was also growing worse. The deficit was considerable; the tremendous surpluses accumulated as a result of Poincaré's tax increases during prosperity had been recklessly spent. To a great extent they had been squandered on purely demagogic propositions. One of these was the Veterans' pensions, which were actually expected to be granted, in due time, to an entire generation—some 5 to 6 million recipients in a nation of 40 million inhabitants! The amount of the individual pension could thus be only insignificant, of no importance to anybody; but to the nation these pensions were important—they created a considerable and steadily increasing burden on the budget. Any repudiation of this obligation, however, was politically impossible, for it would have been a sort of denial of the sacred right of the Veterans to the gratitude of the nation.

Even the monetary situation of France was also deteriorating. Since 1926, and until the depression, the gold and foreign exchange reserves had steadily increased, as a consequence of the repatriation of the formerly emigrated capital and important balance-of-payment surpluses. The maximum of the gold reserves was reached after the total conversion of the foreign exchange holdings of the Banque de France into gold in the spring of 1932; it amounted to some 130 billion francs, or about 5.2 billion gold dollars.

Very soon after the beginning of the depression, however, the trend of gold and capital movements became reversed. As soon as it became evident that France could not indefinitely maintain the overvalued parity of her currency (while in the United States and Great Britain improved economic conditions and reviving monetary stability had restored confidence of capitalists), France began to lose gold. These gold movements were due to some extent to the small deficit of the French balance of payments, which resulted during these years from the decline of income from foreign investments and tourist expenditures. But it was mainly due, and to a steadily increasing extent, to the flight of capital. These gold losses shattered the prestige of the franc and generalized still more the opinion that its devaluation was unavoidable.

Some of the best financial specialists among French statesmen, such as, in particular, Paul Reynaud, eventually understood the absolute necessity of proceeding to a new devaluation. Effected in time, it would have adjusted the franc to the new level of all other currencies, and thus would have prevented the painful and dangerous process of deflation. Such a policy, however, was most unpopular with nearly all shades of French public opinion, which still remembered only too well the losses incurred by the mass of the small investors (*rentiers*) during the previous devaluation. The ruin of the *rentiers* by the inflation was deeply resented in a nation in which, before World War I, not only the middle class, but even some of the workers, had cherished the hope of retiring as small investors. Inflation had thus shattered a national dream and so was deeply hated. For once the big capitalists, represented especially on the Board of Governors of the Banque de France, shared the prejudices of the small bourgeois, though for somewhat different reasons. They were afraid that a new currency depreciation would wreck the basis of the capitalist order.

Therefore, Parliament rejected not only Paul Reynaud's idea of devaluation, but even the much more modest plan for stimulation of economy through credit expansion, proposed by Flandin; and in June 1935 a conservative politician, Pierre Laval, became Prime Minister with a mandate to save the franc through a policy of deflation. As such a policy was rightly supposed to be most unpopular and Parliament was reluctant to take direct responsibility for it, Laval obtained the authority to implement this deflation by decrees (*décrets lois*). The deflationary measures taken by Laval included violations of the basic rules of the capitalist system (such as the inviolability of private contracts), possibly as severe as those resulting from inflation. For example, Laval reduced by 10 percent all prices and fixed incomes, such as rents, fixed-interests payments from bonds and shares, and wages and salaries, even those of state officials, whose rights were guaranteed by statute.

Laval's policy failed to achieve its primary objective: balancing of the budget. The decrease in revenue was greater even than the cut in expenditures, because of the aggravation of the depression. But politically and socially, even more than financially, his policy was a costly failure. True, it must be acknowledged that in France the 10 percent reduction in wages was more than compensated for by the fall in the cost of living since the beginning of the depression; and that the purchasing power of the wage-earners employed, as well as the productivity of labor, was as high as ever. But people were normally more concerned with the nominal amount of their income than with its purchasing power. Consequently, the wage cut and the semi-dictatorial way in which it had been achieved had created deep resentment. This resentment was felt not only by the working class and the very radical small officials, but as well by the majority of the middle class, peasants and shopkeepers, who were also suffering ·from deflation, and who were offended in their democratic traditions by the methods of Laval. Thus Laval's deflationary policy was the main reason for the Popular Front, just as Brüning's deflation in Germany had in somewhat similar circumstances paved the way for Hitler.

The Popular Front was a most heterogeneous coalition. Established for the main purpose of contesting, with a common list of candidates, the election of May 1936, it consisted of the following:

(1) The Socialists, who were the only party with a serious program of social and economic reforms and, who in particular, agreed to devaluation of the franc.

(2) The Radical-Socialists, who, in fact, in the American sense of these terms, were not radicals, and even less, socialists. They were a rather conservative middle-class party without any aim of social or economic reform whatsoever, but simply animated with the desire to come back into power.

(3) The Communists, who were following for the first time the new tactics of coalition, and who did not have any positive aim at all. They were naturally most reluctant to assist the success of social reform, which would have reduced the attractiveness of revolution. Thus, in the coalition they practically played the role of the Trojan horse, adopting purely demagogic attitudes. Therefore, though certainly not sharing the fetishistic adulation of the man in the street for "our little franc," they opposed devaluation for no other reason than that it was unpopular with the masses, and their opposition prevented it from being successful.

The common economic program of the Popular Front was most sketchy. It contained a few nationalizations, but these were limited and were planned more for political than for economic reasons. For example, nationalization of the Banque de France was planned in order to break the influence of financial capitalists; and nationalization of the war industries in order to put an end to the pro-militarist influence of armament manufacturers. The plans of the Popular Front for economic recovery were based on ideas borrowed mainly from the New Deal in the United States. This stressed the necessity of increasing purchasing power, especially of the working class, by means of rise of wages and reduction of working hours, and thus distributing the same amount of work among a greater number of workers. Such a theory, which might have been correct for an economy suffering from mass unemployment and having a surplus of manpower, was especially absurd in France. There, in spite of depression and of a relatively considerable unemployment, in some industries shortage of manpower (especially of skilled labor) remained a permanently characteristic feature of the economy. Owing to this situation, a flat reduction in the number of hours worked was bound to result in a similar decrease in production. Any hope to increase by this method the purchasing power of wages was thus completely absurd.

The absolute failure of this policy was made even more inevitable, and was aggravated, by the refusal to synchronize its start with the devaluation of the franc. Such a procedure would have stimulated economic activity and provided the economy with the margin required in order to absorb the planned direct wage increase, as well as the indirect (through reduction of hours). As a result of the policy, when the planned reforms had been implemented, the economy was unable to bear the cumulative increases in labor cost: 10 percent direct wage increase, to cancel the cut made by Laval's decrees; reduction of working hours from 48 to 40, with the same weekly pay, equivalent to an increase of 17 percent in the hourly wage rate; and granting to all wage-earners 2 weeks of annual leave, amounting to 4 percent of yearly earnings. Total increase in wage cost was thus over 30

146

percent. Increase in total distributed purchasing power—resulting mainly from the rise in wages, while industrial production declined—caused strong inflationary pressure. This still further aggravated the flight from the franc and finally, after a few months, made devaluation unavoidable.

This devaluation was effected in September 1936, under the worst possible conditions, not as a deliberate measure, but as an enforced result of both exterior and domestic inflationary pressures, and in the midst of a badly disorganized economy. It completely failed to achieve its main objective, namely, to relieve the economic situation of France. On the contrary, it contributed toward an undermining of confidence in the currency and toward stimulation of the flight from the franc, which already had been increased by political events. Because of the considerable rise in domestic prices, the first devaluation of the franc did not even succeed in restoring its international purchasing-power parity. Several successive devaluations, effected during the next three years, were required in order to restore the balance between the domestic and the world-market purchasing-power parity of the franc.

In relation to the United States dollar at its present parity, the franc declined from 15.15 in September 1936 to 37.15 at the eve of the war, in 1939. At that time, it was again devalued, together with sterling, to a parity of 43 to the dollar. These successive devaluations, however, did bring to the French Treasury important bookkeeping surpluses resulting from revaluation at a lower parity of the steadily declining, but still considerable, gold reserves of the Banque de France. But these extraordinary surpluses were far from sufficient to compensate for budgetary deficits, as the budgets were overtaxed by steadily increasing expenditures mainly for social purposes and, after 1938, also for rearmament. The rise in budget revenue was much slower, being stimulated by rising prices but hampered by economic stagnation. This unhappy budgetary situation increased the still considerable

147

inflationary pressure, and also aggravated the lack of confidence in the currency.

The economic and financial difficulties of France during this period were made substantially worse by the atmosphere of civil strife in which the economic and social program of the Popular Front had to be implemented. The starting point of this strife goes back to the Rightist Fascist riots of February 1934, which forced out of power the Leftist government, put into office by popular vote, and made necessary a return to a national coalition government, in which conservatives favorable to a "big capitalist" point of view held a dominant position. The formation of the Popular Front was a counterstroke against the reactionary governments born of the February riots. However, even after this victory at the polls, an important group of working-class leadership, partly influenced by Communist as well as by Anarchist tendencies, decided to gain acceptance of their demand by direct action, namely strikes. The tradition of *action directe* of Sorel was still alive in French labor unions. The repeated failures of Leftist governments in recent years to fulfill their promises was the cause of this attitude. It sprang mainly from loss of confidence in the capacity and willingness of Parliament and government to keep their election pledges to the workers.

The employers refused when the workers demanded that they implement at once all the pledges of tremendous improvements in the conditions of the workers which were contained in the program of the Popular Front, and which would have amounted to an enormous increase in the wage bill of business. Thereupon, an unprecedented strike wave swept through all France. Mines, factories and even big stores not only were closed but were occupied by their striking staffs, for the whole duration of the strike, which lasted several weeks. The principal aim of these first "sit-down" strikes was, to a great extent, a show of strength of organized labor to stimulate its recruitment, as well as intimidation of employers. Thus, the number of members of the C.G.T. (the General Federation of Labor) increased in a few months from

148

1.5 million to 5 million. It was also a manifestation of the conviction of the mass of the workers that their relationship to, and interest in, the respective plants to which they devoted all their active life was not inferior to the legal right of ownership.

These strikes, which started in June 1936, were a source of considerable embarrassment to the Léon Blum Popular Front government. It had just come into power and, though recognizing the illegal character of the strikes, could not very well use military force against millions of strikers who had just voted for it. The government thus tried to conciliate workers and employers. But, since the claims of the workers were included in the government's own program, they had to be accepted, and were ratified in the so-called Matignon Agreements. These reforms ordinarily would have been introduced gradually, and all necessary precautions would have been taken not to disturb revival of economic activity. But now they had to be imposed all at once, without any preparation, and with no chance of alleviating the force of their impact. As a result, costs of all industrial production drastically increased.

Much more serious, however, were the effects of the strikes and of their settlement (through a victory of the workers) on the working discipline; indirectly on productivity of labor, which considerably deteriorated; and, most important of all, on the relations between different classes of the French nation. Relations between workers and employers had never been really good in France, owing to the very general lack of social understanding on the part of the French employers, as well as to the fact that both sides were more interested in, and more conscious of, the irreconcilable differences in their political convictions, than in the considerable material advantage which would accrue to both of them from cooperation for development of production. This attitude has already been stressed as a typical French characteristic.

These strained relations provided the psychological background of the sitdown strikes. The strikes naturally created a

149

deep resentment in the employer class, which considered them as an illegal spoliation of their property rights and of their prerogative of management. Some owners and managers were at first even forcibly detained by sitdown strikers. Moreover, the strikes filled the employers with an overwhelming fright of another victory of the workers, which might wipe them out completely—possibly even literally, as in Russia. The employers thus harbored toward the workers a deep hatred and longing for revenge. From that moment on, while a substantial part of the leaders of the working class preferred allegiance to their class (as interpreted by a government of a foreign power) rather than allegiance to their own country, a considerable part of the capitalist class, also, at least passively, preferred the interests of its class to the well-being of the nation. *"Plutot Hitler que Stalin ou Blum"* ("Hitler rather than Stalin or Blum") was, alas, a slogan rather popular with some reactionary capitalist groups. Such a cleavage, corresponding practically to a state of cold civil war, naturally greatly weakened both the economy and the political action of the country. It provides, in particular, the explanation of such an absurd policy (from the French point of view) as the attitude of nonintervention in Spain, since, in case of an active intervention, the civil war would have immediately started in France, too.

The results of the social reforms of the Popular Front had thus been disastrous from all points of view, owing not so much to their inherent defects as to the circumstances under which they had to be implemented. The other category of reforms—the nationalizations—were scarcely more successful. The nationalization of the Banque de France made of the bank of issue practically a government agency, but did not substantially decrease the power of financial capitalism. The nationalization of the railroads, which had already been controlled and financed by the state, did not change much more than their name. The nationalization of the war industries, however, resulted in complete disorganization of production in the war plants at a moment when maximum production was more than ever required. It included such absurd features as nationalization of the tank workshop of the Renault automobile factory, while the rest of the plant was kept under private ownership and management, and was implemented against the obstinate resistance and even sabotage of the owners, being also handicapped by the bad labor discipline of the workers.

In the years 1937 and 1938, economic activity and industrial production stagnated, limited by the shortening of the working hours and the unwillingness of business, frightened by fresh social disturbances, to undertake new investments. These were the conditions under which France had to face the Munich crisis. After its most inglorious end, the need for an increased effort for defense was generally recognized. On the initiative of Paul Reynaud, one of the few intelligent and patriotic conservative leaders, who became Minister of Finance in November 1938, the return to the 48-hour week was effected. This was after the failure of a general strike started by the unions to defend the gains of the labor victories of 1936. However, the workers were paid overtime rates for the hours worked above 40. In spite of these measures, and because of the existing circumstances, revival of production was slow. Accordingly, France entered World War II with an economy weakened by nearly ten years of uninterrupted depression, with an outdated productive apparatus, and with a completely insufficient war production.

These material factors, as well as the moral reasons mentioned above, were the main cause of the events of June 1940. During the first months of the war, in spite of the passive obstruction of the Communists, production considerably expanded. Coal production, during the first quarter of 1940, reached the rate of 55 million tons, never equalled before or, as yet, after. As to the war industries, proper reconversion was achieved, and mass production was started in the spring of 1940. These results, however, came much too late to enable France to halt the German invasion.

151

15 GERMAN ECONOMIC BREAKDOWN PUTS THE NAZIS INTO POWER

THE PROSPERITY of the German economy during the latter part of the 1920's was still extremely unstable, though very considerable. Not only production but also consumption levels and the people's standard of living had risen substantially, and were about the highest on the continent of Europe. Stabilization of that prosperity depended either on a development of exports that would provide a surplus sufficient to cover payments for commercial and political debts, or on the continuation of the influx of foreign capital required to bridge the gap of the balance of payments. Before the beginning of the depression, the second of the possible solutions was being implemented; and, though exports had considerably expanded, the deficit was still considerable and mainly covered by new capital imports.

When the depression began, the terms of trade became more favorable to Germany, as prices of imports (food and raw materials) fell much more sharply than prices of the exported manufactured products. Owing partly to these favorable circumstances, Germany for the first time succeeded in achieving important export surpluses—1643 million Reichsmarks in 1930. In 1931 the figure was 2872 million. These amounts were nearly sufficient to cover the annual service of her foreign debt. But while Germany's balance-of-trade and balance-of-payments situation was improving, the improvement was more than offset by the reversal of the trend of international capital movements.

152

Foreign capital became frightened by the aggravation of the economic situation in the agricultural countries of Eastern and Central Europe. Their solvency had been endangered by the fall in their export prices, and capital began to withdraw from them. These withdrawals also affected Austria, whose economy possessed a solidarity in common with that of the agricultural countries, most of which had formerly been part of the Habsburg Empire. The latter, moreover, was a substantial creditor, supplier and customer of those countries. The panic spread to the foreign creditors of Germany, partly because considerable German funds had been loaned to Austria, mainly in the form of short-term credits granted by the big Berlin banks. The threat, too, of the withdrawal of the tremendous sum of short-term credits granted to German borrowers by the American and Western European banks became a terrific danger to the stability of the new German currency, the Reichsmark. The Reich had no substantial gold or foreign-exchange resources to counterbalance this foreign debt. The new foreign investments, made mainly by big business concerns, such as the I.G.Farbenindustrie, out of the proceeds of foreign loans, did not provide such a counterbalance.

These foreign investments were practically always long-term or, as more correctly named, permanent propositions. Besides, they were mostly made in such a way as to be practically out of reach in the event—which did not materialize—that the government of the Reich might want to requisition and to liquidate them in order to provide foreign exchange. A similar method was used, especially by the British government, during World War II. This dissimulation of foreign assets had been obtained by the use of devices such as establishment of more or less fictitious holding companies incorporated in small and neutral countries, in which control of foreign holdings was apparently vested.

During the first seven months of 1931, withdrawals of foreign capital from the Reich had reached the sum of 1.9 billion Reichsmarks, with a resultant loss to the Reichsbank of nine-tenths of its gold reserves! Thus, while some 10 billion Reichsmarks of foreign short-term credits still remained in Germany, all means for covering new withdrawals were now exhausted.

In this emergency, the German government applied at home a policy of strict deflation and appealed for assistance to the Western powers. In July 1931, Chancellor Bruning visited Paris. This was undoubtedly one of the most dramatic lost opportunities of modern history. It is quite possible, of course, that it would have been too late to save German economy and German democracy from catastrophe, even if France, which at the time was the only country in Europe able to render the financial assistance required, had been willing to do so. It is obvious that if, at that moment, Briand had still been in power, the largest possible assistance would have been rendered. This aid might have alleviated the German financial and economic crisis and thus also have prevented the victory of Nazism. But, beyond that, such an act of generosity might even have put an end to the traditional Franco-German enmity and thus have established a basis for European peace and cooperation.

However, as is frequently the case in history, it happened on this occasion that similar trends in different countries did not coincide, and that statesmen of one country did not find in other countries the partners whom they needed for success. Thus, when Briand, in Locarno in 1925, was trying to éstablish Franco-German cooperation and friendship, he had to deal with Stresemann, who, as his diaries later proved, wanted to rebuild German supremacy and tried to double-cross Briand by his *finanzieren* policy. Again, it was the irony of fate that when Bruning, the most sincere and honest of the statesmen of Weimar Germany, came to Paris to beg for assistance, Briand, though still Minister of Foreign Affairs, was already ill and dying, and Pierre Laval, the *maquignon auvergnat* horsedealer, was Prime Minister and master of French policy. It is also tragic to realize that the man who, ten years later, was to be the main artisan of Franco-German "collaboration"—in which he did not hesitate to trade his country's honor and freedom—did not grasp the opportunity of true and

154

honorable collaboration when it was offered to him under such infinitely more favorable conditions. But then, of course, he would have needed vision and generosity, which were not in the line of a horsedealer's policy.

Bruning's visit was therefore a failure, and the only assistance which resulted from it was a small credit of $100 million in gold, opened to the Reichsbank by the Banque de France, in association with the Bank of International Settlements, the Federal Bank of New York and the Bank of England. The alleviation of the German monetary situation due to this credit was, however, insignificant.

Some weeks earlier, Bruning had also appealed to the United States. On the initiative of President Hoover, a one-year moratorium for German reparations and war debts was arranged, starting on July 1, 1931. But this suspension of payments on Germany's political debt, instead of restoring the confidence of her commercial and financial creditors, merely encouraged them to rush the withdrawal of the balance of their credits during this period.

At last, then, nearly all reserves being exhausted, Germany suspended her payments abroad from July 1931 on, protecting her currency by a strict foreign-exchange control. The remaining foreign credits were thus frozen. The alternative to exchange control, i.e., depreciation of the Reichsmark, a solution similar to that adopted a few months later in Great Britain, was politically and psychologically impossible for Germany. Coming so soon after the tragic experience of total inflation, it would have ruined all confidence in the currency and started the flight from the Reichsmark, not only by the foreign creditors but also by the Germans.

In the meantime, Bruning had made a tremendous effort to save the financial stability of the Reich. He applied a policy of deflation even more drastic than that employed a few years later by Laval in France, and also much more complete. It extended to prices, wages, rents, bond interests and share dividends. It also involved the breaking up of cartels in order to reduce the prices fixed by them; the abolishment of subsidies to big eastern land-

155

owners, etc. This deflation, however, failed to reach its main target, as the budget, with unemployment relief expenditure steadily increasing, remained unbalanced. Moreover, its influence on the German economy was most disastrous. It drastically reduced the purchasing power of all classes of the population, and stopped investment by reducing profit prospects, thus nearly paralyzing all economic activity. The catastrophic fall of exports also considerably aggravated the depression. From 1929 to 1932, the value of exports declined by 8 billion Reichsmarks, a sum equal to 10 percent of the total value of German production (gross national product) in 1929, and nearly 20 percent of its value in 1932. This decline affected practically all industrial exports.

The fall of exports was due to a combination of many factors. Among the foremost were: the decline in purchasing power of the agricultural producers of Central and Eastern Europe, which had been important customers of German industry; the increase in protection by the big industrialized countries: France, by the introduction of import quotas; Great Britain, by the adoption of its new tariff; and the United States, by the considerable increase in duties resulting from the Hawley-Smoot tariff of 1930.

The greatest decline in production and in exports took place in the capital-goods industries, where progress had been particularly considerable during the period immediately preceding. Thus, during the 3 years from 1929 to 1932, the climax of depression, production decreased by one-half or even two-thirds, as follows:

Production	1929	1932
Pig iron (*in thousands of tons*)	15,344	5,281
Raw steel " " " "	18,278	7,115
Hard coal (*in millions of tons*)	163	105
Lignite " " " "	175	123

The decline in consumer-goods production was nearly as severe, owing to the decrease in domestic purchasing power and in exports.

This depression naturally resulted in a disastrous increase in mass unemployment which, at its maximum in 1932, reached the figure of 6,014,000 of registered and assisted unemployed. There were about 1,000,000 more who were not registered, and who were therefore without any assistance from public authorities. The unemployed, with their families, at this moment constituted nearly one-third of the total German population. This increase in unemployment was partly due to the rationalization of industry, which resulted in an additional technological unemployment of some 2,000,000 workers, who had been displaced as a result of improvements in equipment and organization. The rest of the unemployment was due directly to the depression.

The immense effort of rationalization and modernization undertaken by German industry during the 1920's had been a costly economic and financial failure, due to a considerable extent to the high cost of capital borrowed for this purpose: 6 to 7 percent on the average. Interest payments at such a high rate could not be paid out of earnings, as the expansion of production, made possible by the rationalization, did not materialize to the extent expected and planned. The reason was twofold: the insufficient purchasing power of the domestic market, and the failure to develop and maintain sufficient export markets. However, the financial consequences of rationalization were mostly the loss of Germany's foreign creditors. Their investments were first frozen, and later on wiped out, while the German economy still remained in possession of a productive capacity considerably increased, and substantially improved in efficiency.

German industry had tried to win, by means of increased exports, the large markets required to enable it to utilize fully its newly created productive capacity in large-scale production, on a pattern similar to that of the United States. Thus it would have been possible to achieve the increase in earnings that it had expected from the rationalization drive. In these objectives, German industry failed. This failure contributed to a change in political outlook of most big industrialists. It stimulated them to turn away from their already very lukewarm acceptance of interna-

157

tional cooperation through foreign trade and to come back to their traditional nationalist craving for domination. Having been unable to obtain by peacetime competition the markets necessary for their increased production, they became more and more inclined to conquer them by gaining domination of a sufficiently vast area of Europe.

This instinctive tendency of German big business was supported by writers, such as Ferdinand Fried. They formulated the theory of large spaces (*Grossraum*), required in order to obtain a market big enough to absorb the large-scale production, which became more and more the condition for the success of modern industry. Fried claimed for Germany, as the greatest industrial power on the continent of Europe, the natural right to create such a large space by achieving domination of the neighboring vital space (*Lebensraum*) that she needed for this purpose.

The tragic misery from which the great mass of the German population suffered, after the beginning of the depression, supplied the chief basis for the extraordinary development of anticapitalist movements, like Communism and National Socialism. The propaganda of such movements had been facilitated by the fact that the recent disastrous inflation had weakened, if not destroyed, the confidence in the values of the capitalist order in a great part of the middle class, which had been its chief victim.

However, contrary to what had happened in Russia, the strength and appeal of the nationalist movement were much stronger than those of the proletarian Communists. The Communists attracted only part of the working class, principally the unemployed, as the majority of the occupied workers remained faithful to the Social-Democrats, who had improved their standard of living. But, by the emphasis put on the proletarian class motive, and the rejection of the traditional national feelings, the Communists repelled the rest of the German nation, especially the peasants and the urban middle class.

As to the nationalist anticapitalist movement, it had a powerful appeal for all classes of the German population, and it did not

158

repel any class as such. Its attraction was strongest for the youth of the proletariatized middle class. Even more than the working class, these young people had been suffering from the depression, as they were less protected, by either the power of their trade unions, or by social-security legislation. Even though they did receive such social-security benefits as unemployment relief, the necessity of accepting it caused them resentment and deep humiliation. Therefore they bitterly hated the social and political order which they held responsible for this state of affairs. As a matter of fact, their eventual misery, with the utter hopelessness of outlook and lack of opportunity for employment, or of prospects of success of new individual ventures, was due to some extent to a national disaster: the loss of the war. Among the consequences were the loss of overseas colonies and the set-back caused to German economic expansion abroad, which formerly provided ample opportunities to young German businessmen and technicians. Yet, the revolt against the capitalist order, even though it had brought these youth such misery and hopelessness, could not be accepted by them if it were presented only as an internationalist class revolt against the nation. It had to be represented as a nationalist revolt against foreign (supposedly) international capitalism, which to a certain extent was really responsible—and was believed by the youth to be entirely responsible—for their sufferings. Against this international capitalism and its supposed domestic accomplices, the Jews—who were now more than ever used as scapegoats—the hatred and resentment of this class were increasing as depression deepened.

The National-Socialist movement had a few direct ideological predecessors, such as H. Stewart Chamberlain, an Englishman who became a naturalized German and in his philosophical and historical writings tried to prove the superiority of the German race. More immediate predecessors were a group of young businessmen and officials, such as Walter Rathenau (a Jew himself) and Koeth von Moellendorf, author of a memorandum on corporative economy. They had tried to interest public opinion, during

159

World War I, in ideas of national German supremacy and state-directed economy. Moreover, ever since Fichte's famous "Speeches to the German nation" (*Reden an die deutsche Nation*), more than a hundred years ago, this idea of the superiority of Germany as a nation had been steadily propagated by many generations of professors and teachers in universities, high schools and public schools. It had thus deeply influenced the psychology of the whole nation.

In such circumstances, and with this psychological and material background, it was natural that there should have developed a movement exactly fitting the tendencies of this most dynamic part of the nation—the suffering, and therefore the revolutionary, middle-class youth. The Nazi ideology fitted in with the nationalist prejudices of this class—its resentment over having lost the war and over being supposedly unjustly exploited by the victorious nations as a consequence of the imposed war-guilt clause. That ideology fitted in, also, with the class fear of proletarian dictatorship and the resulting aversion toward the proletarian movement, condemned as internationalist, with its antipathy toward the Jews, which was partly due to envy.

The extraordinary success of National-Socialism was due to a great extent to its "mythic," quasi-religious appeal to the Germans, very similar to the attraction of Marxism for the proletariat. For example, in the Nazi myth, the German nation was described as the "Christ of the Nations," victim of unjust oppression, while, according to the myth, it was in fact the only one fit for domination, the chosen nation, just as the proletariat, according to Marxism, was the chosen class. Thus was transformed into a superiority complex the inferiority complex strongly, even though unconsciously, felt and resented by the mass of the German nation, in relation to victorious former enemy countries, as well as by the proletariat in relation to the capitalists. This transformation offered a tremendous psychological satisfaction to the individuals concerned and attracted them to the movement, which had thus not only reestablished but even exalted their self-respect

160

and self-confidence. These movements also, by attributing their sufferings to the wickedness of their enemies, offered them an explanation fitting their traditional prejudices as well as their intellectual level. The remedy which these movements held out to the suffering masses of their followers was as simple as it was obvious: In order to conquer their enemies, they must unite, pledging their full support to the movement which alone could be their savior.

In Germany capitalism had been much more firmly intrenched than in Russia and, above all, its breakdown was due not to an exterior factor, such as an unpopular and practically lost war, but mainly—if not entirely—to an interior crisis resulting from the normal cyclical fluctuations of the capitalist economy. Also it was much easier to note in Germany a psychological phenomenon which is one of the main factors responsible for the development, and too often for the victory, of totalitarian movements. This phenomenon was the breakdown of the traditional optimistic self-confident outlook shared heretofore by most individuals of all classes in industrialized countries with a relatively high general standard of living, but shared especially by individuals of the middle class. That breakdown was a result of the disintegration of the capitalist economy and of the sufferings it brought.

This former optimism was born of a habit of mind developed ever since the beginning of capitalist economy, of monetary stability and of economic progress—conditions which offered, to individuals willing to make the necessary effort, if not a complete guarantee, at least a very good chance to reap through material success the reward of that effort. The opportunity to achieve material success and prosperity, most people were naturally inclined to believe, was due to their own ability, and not to favorable economic conditions. In countries where economic progress had been particularly great, this idea of opportunity filled most individuals with a somewhat candid self-confidence, even if, in the great mass of common men, it was not consciously felt. They were proud of their ability which, it appeared to them, gave the power to conquer all obstacles, to build their lives as they pleased, to be masters

161

of their destiny and of the whole material universe. All this the gigantic new technical inventions seemed to place at their feet.

As already indicated, optimistic self-confidence had already been badly shattered in Germany by the weakening of the capitalist economy resulting from the loss of the war and from inflation. It was completely destroyed during the great depression. Then, millions of people were faced with economic catastrophe that had wiped out their livelihood, sometimes the painfully established result of many years of strenuous effort. All their expectations and hopes for the future crushed, they staggered under this annihilating blow, which stunned them all the more because most of them did not understand exactly what had happened or why. Thus, they realized their utter helplessness as individuals, the complete impossibility of saving themselves from the disaster by any means of their own.

These psychological reasons provide the main explanation why masses of formerly independent, self-assertive individuals now began to crowd into collective movements, such as Nazism, which not only provided them with an apparently adequate explanation of their disaster, but above all promised them relief from it. By way of natural recompense for this promise of relief, the suffering masses gladly surrendered to the movement their formerly cherished prerogatives of freedom of action and freedom of thought, which had anyhow proved useless, and even embarrassing in their present plight.

The instinct of power, which, for individuals in a capitalist economy, was expressed through a craving for material success—in other words, "lust for wealth"—was also collectivized, in logical consequence of this surrender by the individuals to the collective movement. It was transposed into the deification of the power of collectivity: movement, party, or state. In this new concept, the collectivity had to be omnipotent, in order to be able to conquer every obstacle and enemy and to save from disaster the masses who expected salvation from its action. It followed that concentration of all power in the collectivity had to be achieved at any cost.

162

Thus the craving for wealth, which in capitalist economy is the main stimulant of individual effort, had been replaced in a totalitarian order of state and economy by a collective craving for power, with an immensely increased moral and material impact on the life of the people and the structure of society. In totalitarian states, this collective will for power becomes the basis of a sort of "categorical imperative" of a new moral conception. It sweeps away the distinction between good and evil—which not only since the Gospel, but since the beginning of civilization, has been the basic rule for the social relationships of mankind—and replaces it with the ant-like distinction between what is useful and what is harmful, respectively, to collectivity and the ruling class.

Roughly summarized, that is the psychological basis of the development of all totalitarian movements, especially of the Nazi movement, and of its attraction for the youth of the middle class, which since the beginning was its main support. All these feelings and emotions, already described, were shared deeply by the chief components of this youth: the unemployed professionals, underpaid officials, and shopkeepers and artisans, in, or on the verge of, bankruptcy.

Nazism, however, appealed also to all other classes of the German population. It had a strong attraction for the peasants, who were nationalists by tradition, and who were pleased by its ideas of economic self-sufficiency through expansion of domestic food production. It appealed to the workers, to whom the Nazi doctrine promised liberation from capitalist domination and oppression, though naturally by means different from those of the Communists. And it should be stressed that capitalist domination, especially the supremacy of the least creative speculative capitalism bred by inflation, had been deeply felt and resented by the workers, as well as by the middle class, during the Weimar period. Fifteen years of republican government, with Socialist participation, had not brought any improvement in this respect. The Nazis offered to the workers the prospect of ending economic insecurity

163

and the catastrophe of mass unemployment, through mobilization of all the resources of the economy including, in particular, manpower for work in the service of the state.

As to the inequality resulting, in capitalist society, from the difference in incomes between wage-earners and employers, that was to be overcome in the Nationalist-Socialist economy by the incorporation of both categories, with different but equally important functions, into the universal army of the servants of the state. In this army there was to be no real independence for any privileged group, but the same rule of discipline and strict obedience for all. Thus, between all members of the Nazi movement there was to be established a psychologically very important moral equality in which all the subjects of the Third Reich were to share. And though this equality was an equality in servitude, it still had a great value for those suffering from the inequality of the capitalist order.

Finally, the Nazi movement, even if it did not completely appeal to the two strongest elements of pre-war Germany, nevertheless benefited from their support. Those two elements, which had kept a great part of their former influence, were the heavy industry and the big landowners of Eastern Germany. A great number of the big industrialists resented the power of organized labor, which, by enforcing wage increases, had deprived them of a great part of the profits expected from the rationalization. The Ruhr industry therefore began to lend financial support to the Nazi movement after the successful big steel strike in December 1928. It also sympathized with the Nazi aims of rearmament and political expansion, which promised them profitable armament orders and prospects of an expanded market.

The last steps which brought Hitler to power had been taken, however, on the initiative of the eastern landowners, the Junkers. Fearing the withdrawal of the subsidies supporting their bankrupt estates, they used their influence on President Hindenburg in order to bring down the governments of Bruning and General von Schleicher, when the latter attempted to stop the subsidies

164

and to divide the Junkers' estates in order to establish a peasant class in Eastern Germany.

Even if the two last-named groups were far from adhering to the Nazi doctrine, they were instrumental in establishing that regime. They had expected that when Hitler came into power, they could control his policy and keep him only as a figurehead, in which intention they obviously had been completely mistaken.

16 THE NAZI ECONOMY: BUILDING OF
THE GERMAN WAR MACHINE

THE ECONOMIC DOCTRINE of National Socialism was extremely vague, the only fixed idea being its nationalist tendency. Its direct anticapitalism was limited to the liberation of national economy from the so-called "interest slavery" (*Zinsknechtschaft*). In fact, Nazi anticapitalism applied mainly to foreign or Jewish capital. Thus, before coming into power, the Nazis had shown a strong opposition to the mainly Jewish department stores. This opposition, however, rapidly ceased as soon as the department store became Arianized.

The main aim of the Nazi economy was the achievement of economic self-sufficiency: the autarchy through development of agricultural and deficient industrial production. The real purpose of this policy was obviously the strengthening of German economic power in time of peace; and even more in case, and for the pursuit, of war. The Nazi government had the good fortune to be able to use, for the building of its economy, the inventive genius and resourceful mind of one of the world's foremost economic and financial experts, Dr. Hjalmar Schacht. To his direction during the period 1933-38 was due, to a great extent, the impressive degree of achievement reached.

When Hitler came into power, in January 1933, the situation of the German economy was extremely difficult, especially considering the aims to be pursued through National-Socialist policy.

166

Germany was still in the throes of a stringent deflation, though some timid efforts for a credit expansion had been attempted by the von Papen government, through the issue of short-term works bills for the financing of public works. But a much more considerable credit expansion was required in order to achieve a complete recovery of production and the realization of full employment.

The German currency, however, was overvalued in comparison with those of most other great economic powers, and a new devaluation was out of the question, because of political and psychological reasons, as well as reasons of prestige. On the other hand, Germany had to maintain an export surplus sufficient to provide for payment of interest on its foreign debt, the capital of which had been frozen according to the Standstill (*Stillhalte*) Agreements concluded in September 1931 with the foreign creditors. Those agreements, though applying explicitly only to short-term debts, had been applied also, whenever necessary, to long-term debts. At the same time, however, Germany had to pay for increased imports required for a recovery of domestic production, and particularly for considerably expanded imports of strategic raw materials necessary for military purposes. On the contrary, resources available for export gradually declined as industrial production was more and more changed over to direct or indirect rearmament.

The monetary policy of Dr. Schacht was proclaimed by the Nazis to be an example of the successful application of their monetary theory. This was the theory of the liberation of the currency from the slavery of the gold standard, and the replacement of gold, as the basis and guarantee of currency stability, by work and production, the Nazi currency being the "production standard." As a matter of fact, the gold resources of the Reichsbank continued to decline, owing to the partial repayment of short-term credits and the maintenance, until June 1933, of the interest service, to a minimum of 156 million Reichsmarks reached by the end of 1934. However, the Nazis were to manifest later on, during

167

the war, a considerable inconsistency with respect to their doctrine. For example, denying all value and importance to gold, at the same time they looted occupied territories in an attempt, above all, to get gold.

As a matter of fact, Dr. Schacht's policy was based mainly upon an application of a monetary technique somewhat similar to the one he had used ten years earlier, while creating the Rentenmark. He estimated that, in the existing circumstances, a moderate expansion for productive purposes would stimulate general economic recovery and increase employment, and thus also increase tax revenue and savings so that a great part of the credits released would be absorbed. The functions of this money "circuit"—recapturing, by means of taxes and loans, the surplus of purchasing power injected into the economy—was facilitated by the stabilization of the wage rates. Total wage income increased considerably, however, in accordance with the rise in production and employment. The money circuit was also assisted through: (1) the limitation of dividend rates (to 6 percent as a general rule); (2) a policy of general price stability; as well as gradually (3) the increasing scarcity of high-class consumer goods, as production was more and more directed to war purposes.

It has to be acknowledged that the success of this policy had been very considerable indeed. Compared with its repercussions on the economy as a whole, and on production and employment in particular, expansion of credit had been relatively moderate. Thus, while the national debt had increased, during the period 1932-37, from 12 to 40 billion Reichsmarks, the national income had increased during the same period from 45 to 77 billion Reichsmarks, reaching again the level of the 1929 prosperity climax. Owing to the cheap money policy, however, which was an essential condition of credit expansion, interest rates had been reduced to such an extent that the proportion of interest service on the national debt to the national income had actually declined. In 1937 it amounted to only 1 billion Reichsmarks.

The effect of this credit inflation on the price level had also

168

been very moderate. The wholesale price index (1929 = 100) had increased only from 67.3 in December 1932 to 77.1, the average for the year 1938. In the meantime, however, the price level—in terms of gold in the other main industrial countries, competitors of Germany in their exports—had declined, owing mainly to devaluation, in the United States from 72 to 48.8, and in France from 70.5 to 45.1. Great Britain was an exception; there, depreciation of currency had occurred earlier. With its official parity still maintained in principle, the Reichsmark was thus considerably overvalued.

But this parity, in actual fact, was purely a fiction maintained for reasons of prestige. It was scarcely used any more, not even in foreign trade, which was transacted mainly through special devices. The rise in the price level from 1932 to 1937 was due, however, only partly to credit inflation. It was to an even greater extent the result of the subsidy policy used in order to stimulate domestic production of food and raw materials. As a general rule, the policy of credit expansion had been well balanced and very successful in the beginning, while it was used to stimulate remunerative productive activity, but it became gradually more dangerous and inflationary as it was more and more utilized to foster noneconomic war production.

The first aim of the Nazi economic policy was to absorb as speedily as possible the more than seven million unemployed. This aim provides the explanation for a series of measures introduced in the first year of the Third Reich, which did not aim at increasing production, such as: displacement of women in industry, which was also in accordance with the Nazi population policy; the introduction of a mandatory work year for youths, which was a temporary substitute for and preparation for military conscription, etc. Very soon, however, the emphasis was switched to increased output in all vital products of industry and agriculture, in order to achieve self-sufficiency along those lines.

In agriculture, the proportion of domestic production to consumption was 75 percent in 1933; it had been 85 percent in 1913,

169

with a larger territory and the same number of population. By 1936, this proportion had been raised to 81 percent. In 1934, under the stimulus of the leader of the peasantry, Walter Darré, German agriculture started the "battle of production" or, in nonmilitary terms, the effort to develop production of all important deficient foodstuffs. For this purpose, the Nazi authorities used as means of stimulation an increase in tariff duties, as well as subsidies for new plantings of oil seeds, textile fibers, fruit trees, and so on. The state also obliged the peasants to use for productive purposes all the available soil and, to that end, ordered the tearing down of walls separating fields belonging to different owners. Considerable progress was also achieved in increasing the use of fertilizer and improving the quality of seeds and breeding stock.

A serious impediment to increase of agricultural production was the shortage of farm labor, as Polish immigration was prohibited. In order to alleviate this shortage, the Nazi authorities introduced a mandatory year of agricultural labor for all youth (*Landjahr*), and tried to increase the recruitment of farm workers by raising wages and improving living conditions, as well as by favoring increase in mechanization.

The state also intervened in the consumption of agricultural produce in such ways as the following: by reducing consumption of imported foodstuffs and orienting them to the foodstuffs easiest available at any given moment ("consumption steering"), in order to achieve the best possible utilization of resources; by raising the extraction rate for cereals; and by prohibiting the use of bread grain for feed and distilling.

Marketing boards (*Reichsstellen*) were established to regulate the marketing of each category of German-produced foodstuffs. They had also the power to authorize imports of the respective products. The first of such boards had already been created in 1930 for small grains. Gradually this form of organization was extended to control all main products.

A strict regimentation of deliveries of agricultural produce by farmers was instituted, fixing quotas for each producer. Organiza-

170

tion of rationing had already been prepared at that period by requiring that each consumer must make his purchases at a certain shop. There alone he could buy what he needed. Especially severe restrictions were placed on foodstuffs, which were in short supply because of insufficient domestic production and reduction of imports. The consumption of butter, for example, could thus be easily reduced.

New legislation, based on Nazi ideology, and dealing with the organization of agriculture, established a class of hereditary peasants whose farms could be neither sold nor mortgaged. The main significance of this measure was political and demographical. These peasants, of pure Aryan blood, were supposed to become the basis of the demographic expansion of the German race. The economic results of this legislation for the farmers concerned were rather indifferent, as, owing to the impossibility for them to give any security for loans, they suffered from lack of capital.

All these different measures, combined, resulted in an increase of agricultural production, though not as much as might have been expected from the intensity of the effort spent. Agricultural yields in Germany, however, were already very high, and the law of diminishing returns did fully apply. Thus, from 1928-32 to 1935-39, average production of bread grains (rye and wheat) increased from 11,940,000 tons to 12,740,000 tons. This increase had been achieved as the result of: an improvement in yields, in spite of a slight reduction in area owing to the considerable surface of agricultural land taken over for military purposes (airfields and camps); and the substantial expansion of industrial crops: oil seeds such as soya, textile fibers, etc. The number of livestock increased by about 10 percent from 1926 to 1937. For example, increase in cattle was from 18,414,000 to 20,504,000; milk cows, from 9,474,000 to 10,224,000; and hogs, from 20,166,000 to 23,847,000.

On the other hand, this policy had resulted in a considerable rise in the prices which were paid by consumers, and which were sometimes 100 or even 200 percent higher than world prices. This was true even of foodstuffs such as sugar, for which Germany had normally a considerable export surplus that was sold abroad by means of "dumping," that is, at a much lower price. Taking into account the considerable reduction in imports of food, consumption of the more expensive high-quality foodstuffs in Germany had declined during the period of Nazi domination.

In industry, the economic policy of the Nazi government resulted in an enormous expansion of capital-goods production, while production of consumer goods increased at a much slower pace and remained below the maximum reached in 1929. Industrial exports also being considerably lower than before the depression, the market for the expanded output of capital goods was provided through the development of domestic industrial investment under the impulse and the direction of the state. Thus, from 1936-37 on (later figures are not comparable owing to territorial changes), production figures for all basic materials—hard coal, lignite, pig iron and raw steel—considerably exceeded the 1929 maxima. In 1938, the general index of industrial production reached 126 (1929 = 100).

At first, investments were mainly concentrated on public works financed by the state (motor highways), as well as on airplane- and motor-vehicles industries. The character and dimensions of industrial investment, however, gradually changed and after 1937, when Hitler had proclaimed his second Four-Year Plan, with the openly declared mainly military objective of making Germany independent of imports of raw materials, investment was more and more concentrated on development of production of substitute materials. The aim of the first Four-Year Plan—absorption of unemployment—had already been achieved.

Thus, a considerable effort was made to increase the use of domestic iron ore for steel production, in spite of its extremely low content, which made necessary a special concentration treatment, similar to that applied in South Africa to gold ore. A large and extremely modern iron-and-steel plant was established on this iron-ore basis in Salzgitter. Production of synthetic oil from hard coal, but especially from lignite (*Leuna*), was developed from the

172

experimental stage to large-scale industrial production. In addition, owing to systematic and extensive prospecting and boring, domestic natural-oil production had also considerably increased, though it still remained much less important than the new synthetic-fuel production. The production of synthetic rubber (*buna*) was developed, too, based on lignite; production of new synthetic textiles, such as fibrane (*Zellwolle*), out of wood became a large-scale industry; and production of rayon also expanded considerably.

Most, if not all, of these many substitute products were non-profitable, besides requiring heavy investments. Their expansion therefore had to be supported by the state. For this assistance different methods were used, either credits or direct grants for the capital cost; or price guarantees which were also guarantees of rentability. The latter were provided through state contracts of purchase, at fixed prices, of the production of the new industries (*Wirtshaftlichkeits-garantievertraege*), offering, by the fixity of the sales prices, a special incentive for reduction of cost by the most efficient producers. Sometimes these price guarantees were implemented by means of subsidies financed by a levy on the imports of the natural product, as, for example, oil or rubber. In several of the new industries, the state obliged the industrial groups concerned—such as textiles for synthetic wool, and coal and lignite for synthetic oil—to establish, jointly, companies for the new products. In some other cases, such as steel, the state itself had to participate directly in the establishment of the new production. This was done by combining, with the industrial group concerned, in a mixed-ownership company functioning under state control, such as the Hermann Goering Werke, created in order to develop production of steel based on low-content iron ore.

Goering had been intrusted since 1937 with the direction of the Four-Year Plan, whose main object was to prepare the war mobilization of all the resources of the economy. His influence on German economic policy gradually superseded that of Dr. Schacht, who finally resigned in 1938, a few weeks before the Munich crisis.

173

Schacht's successor as Minister of national economy and Governor of the Reichsbank, Dr. Funk, was a subordinate of Goering. Thus the whole ministry of national economy became purely the economic section of the War Resources Mobilization Board, headed by the *Reichsmarschall*.

The mobilization of the economy for war had been facilitated by the corporate organization of all branches of production. Agriculture was organized in the Food Corporation (*Nährstand*). Industry was organized both by specialties and by geographical regions. Each undertaking was under the authority of its specialty group (*Fachschaft*), as well as of the local Chamber of Commerce and Industry and the regional Chamber of Economy (*Gaukammer*). Both of these hierarchies were centralized in the Chamber of the Economy of the Reich (*Reichswirtschaftskammer*). Business was under strict state regulation. For example, control of membership was vested in mandatory cartels. The state also controlled investment, in so far as the establishment of new concerns or the enlargement of old ones could be undertaken only with the authorization of the state, according to a law already adopted in 1933. The Nazi authorities sometimes used the provisions of this law in an even broader way for reduction of industrial capacity. Thus, they applied it whenever they deemed increase of production undesirable, a wasteful use of resources and manpower, in view of the need for increasing German economic power. In 1934, for example, they enforced a reduction of German textile production.

In 1939, on the eve of the war, the government also made use of this law, in order to obtain rationalization of production, thus liberating manpower for the armed forces or for direct war production. This was accomplished through concentration in the so-called joint undertakings (*Gemeinschaftsbetriebe*) established, according to the orders of the government, by the combination of several concerns the production of which was considered by the state to be necessary for the state.

Another form of economic control was the regulation of build-

174

ing. In order to husband the maximum of resources and manpower for state projects, permits were given only for building considered as being in the interest of the state.

The application of the Nazi leader principle increased the independence of business management from control of capital; the prerogatives of the shareholders' meeting were reduced. Further, management was liberated from the intervention of elected labor representatives, the shop stewards. They were replaced by "men of confidence" (*Vertrauensmänner*) designated by the manager himself.

However, management was far from being free. According to the Nazi theory, management was considered not as a right that was the consequence of private ownership, but as a social function to be fulfilled in the interests of the nation. Thus, if a manager, because of incapacity or unwillingness, failed to implement the directives of the state—e.g., by failing to increase production—he could be removed and replaced with a manager appointed by the state, with no consideration for the wishes of the owners. While such cases did occur, they were very few. This was mainly because the managers were very careful not to disobey the orders of the state, knowing what would happen if they did. Thus, in fact, under the Nazi regime management was nearly as much under state control as in Soviet Russia; private enterprise for profit had no field of action whatsoever. The state direction of the activity of every business concern was implemented, in part, directly through distribution of state orders, mainly for armament industries. But the direction was also partly through the intermediary of the professional industrial groups, which allocated raw materials, fuel, and other materials, especially if imported.

The only difference between the Nazi and the Soviet system concerning organization of industry, both essentially instruments of state policy, was a difference in methods, not in principle. The Nazi state retained, in general, the system of ownership management. Thus, it could at once have at its disposal, for the purposes of its policy, the expert knowledge of the old managers. In Russia, on the other hand, most of such managers were physically exterminated, so that they had to be replaced with a newly trained class, obviously a slow and very costly process. Another advantage of the Nazi method was that it had yielded an important political benefit: It not only had avoided fierce resistance from the owner and manager class, but had easily won their obedient acceptance of the new regime.

As to the comparative cost to the community of these two different systems of management, the Nazi method was certainly no more costly, especially if efficiency of management is taken into account. Dividends were strictly limited and manager salaries, even if high, were proportional to production and scarcely higher than those of the managers of the state trusts in the Soviet Union.

For the workers, the main achievement of the Nazi economy was the complete elimination of unemployment. The stage of full employment had already been reached in 1937. From then on, there was even a shortage of manpower, which caused a considerable number of foreign workers, mainly Italian, to be sent to Germany. The economic security of the workers and the stability of their income were thus again guaranteed, which, for the great majority, was more than sufficient compensation for the loss of their democratic freedom. Total consumption by the working class, especially of foodstuffs, had not increased and probably was even slightly lower than during the climax of depression; however, consumption was now evenly and more justly distributed. There were no more masses of unemployed living on relief at a semi-starvation level, and with the demoralizing feeling of being outcasts, excluded from the creative work and life of the nation.

Looking back upon this dreadful misery, which had gripped them all with fear, the working class now gladly accepted the reduction in consumption requested by the Nazi state. To them, it was a worth-while sacrifice for the well-being and greatness of the community, which guaranteed and protected their existence and their right to work. Indeed, the workers were proud to make such a sacrifice. This state of mind explains the considerable success of

176

Goebbels' propaganda slogan, "The German people prefer guns to butter," which he used when he wanted to convince the Germans of the necessity of going without some hitherto usual luxury consumption, in order to be able to import raw materials required for the strengthening of the Reich.

The replacement of the free-trade unions by the *Arbeitsfront,* an organization of which both workers and employers were members, had reduced the effective protection of workers' rights; but it gave them a considerable satisfaction of prestige, and exalted their consciousness of belonging to the national community and of being a most important factor therein. A spectacular and most effective organization of vacation travel for workers during their annual leave, with pay—the "strength through joy" (*Kraft durch Freude*)—also stimulated the pride and feeling of national solidarity of the workers.

It is necessary to point out here a special fact. While, immediately after the end of the war and after the holocaustic termination of Nazism, it appeared as if there had never been a single Nazi in Germany (as no German would confess to having been one), it seems obvious that, prior to the war, the great mass of the nation, including the working class, was on the whole well satisfied with the Nazi regime. It had, after all, they argued, overcome the two greatest defects of the capitalist system: the lack of economic security, and the isolation of the proletariat from the rest of the nation. This experience should be well remembered by other peoples, for such a development may very well happen in other countries, if democracy fails as tragically to solve its economic problems as it did in the case of the Weimar Republic in Germany.

In foreign trade, exchange control and moratorium on foreign debts became a medium of economic expansion abroad, owing to the ingenuity of Dr. Schacht. The moratorium on short-term foreign debts had been first negotiated in July 1931 and had been periodically renewed until the beginning of the war. It included provisions for partial repayment and prorogation of the balance. Because of these gradual repayments, and also because of the de-

177

preciation by 40 percent of the main creditor currencies (dollar and sterling), the amount finally outstanding of these short-term debts had been reduced from 12 billion Reichsmarks in 1931 to 800 million by 1939.

However, practically, repayment could not be made in free Reichsmarks, convertible at the theoretical parity in foreign currencies, but only in the so-called "blocked" marks (*Sperrmark*). These, credited to blocked accounts, could be used only for payments of exports, which could be considered as additional to the normal German sales to the countries concerned. The rate of these blocked marks was obviously considerably below the official parity and declined steadily. By 1939 the discount on these marks amounted to 60 percent. Thus, these additional German exports were being subsidized, and the cost of the subsidies was being paid by the foreign creditors desirous of getting their money back from Germany, even at a considerable loss.

A similar system was used somewhat later, in July 1933. At that time, there was continuing deterioration of Germany's foreign-exchange position, resulting from the decrease of the national export surplus, and from the flight of capital due, in particular, to the persecution of the Jews. The system used this time was to suspend the transfer even of interest payments. The interest continued to be paid by the German debtors, but it was paid into a Conversion Office (*Konversionskasse für deutsche Auslansschulden*) established for the handling of German foreign debts. The accounts of the foreign creditors opened by these payments (*Konversionsmark*) at the Conversion Office, could also be used as part payment for additional exports at a considerable discount.

Another method for subsidizing German exports at the expense of the creditor nations of Germany, was to allow German concerns to purchase on foreign stock markets German bonds which were issued there, and which, because of the stoppage of transfers, had naturally depreciated considerably—then to resell them at par in Germany. German authorities also encouraged barter, or so-called private-compensation transactions, especially when in this way it

178

was possible to obtain essential raw materials. Besides this method of private compensation, exchange agreements intended to realize a general compensation of imports and exports had also been concluded with several countries.

At first, after introduction of exchange control, the German foreign-trade policy did not discriminate between the different countries of origin of imports. Thus, German importers obtained foreign exchange for payment of their imports at a fixed ratio of their former purchases in the same countries. As foreign-exchange resources dwindled, however, and also as the aims of the Nazi economic policy became more clarified, discrimination was applied to the categories of goods imported and exported, as well as to the countries from which these goods were imported or to which they were being sent.

In July 1934 a complete reorganization of German foreign-trade policy took place. The so-called "New Plan" subordinated all foreign-trade transactions to a system of regulation, which was to enable the authorities to use those transactions for the purpose of the general policy. All imports had to be authorized by the respective commodity boards (*Reichsstellen*), which delivered the certificates required for purchase of foreign exchange. As to exports, for all the most important goods export licenses were required; and even for all other goods authorization by the state authorities was practically indispensable. This was because German exports, becoming more and more expensive in relation to world prices, could practically not be effected without a direct or an indirect subsidy of the payment, of which the state had to approve the principle as well as the method.

By the system of export licenses and authorizations, the government was able to determine (1) the countries to which German goods could be sold with the greatest return to the German economy, and (2) the method of payment for these exports and what type of subsidy, if any, should be used (e.g., partial payment in blocked marks).

The main principle of the New Plan was the replacement of the

179

general uniform exchange-quotas system with a range of priorities. The available foreign exchange was allocated, in the first place, to finance imports of the goods most needed. This priority system, however, applied rigidly only to imports payable in foreign currency; imports which could be paid through exchange clearing or through payment in blocked marks were much less severely restricted. The chief aim of this system was to obtain at the best possible terms—and as far as possible from sources most likely to remain available even in case of war—the imports necessary for the development of the German economy, and especially for the expansion of Germany's war potential. This aim was rendered more difficult of achievement by the increasing concentration of German industrial production on rearmament. As a result, the quantity of goods available for export steadily decreased and their quality gradually deteriorated.

In order to achieve this aim, the German foreign-trade policy had exercised an extraordinary ingenuity. Its attitude, exceedingly flexible, varied according to such vital factors as the bargaining power of the respective trade partners; their degree of dependence on the German market; and the strength of their exchange position. In accordance with the variations of these different factors, the rate of depreciation of the Reichsmark categories used for payment of imports also varied.

The main methods used by the Nazi authorities in their dealings with the different categories of countries may be classified as follows:

In dealings with Western European countries, the Nazis were not interested in introducing an exchange clearing which might have reduced their receipts in free currency. This was logical, since those countries did not maintain any exchange restrictions, and with them Germany normally had export surpluses, for which she received payment in freely convertible foreign currency. However, partial clearing agreements with such countries had generally been concluded on the initiative of their governments, who wanted to protect their exporters from the effects of the steadily

180

more stringent German import restrictions. Thus, for the additional imports that Germany agreed to accept, they, in turn, agreed to receive payment—after the normal exchange quotas of her importers had been exhausted—in so-called special marks (Sondermark).

These were paid, at the Reichsbank, into the accounts of the central banks of the different countries concerned, and they could be used only for payment of certain specified German exports and for foreign-tourist expenditures in Germany. The Sondermark were naturally considerably depreciated, in relation to the official parity. On the other hand, the foreign central banks rapidly accumulated substantial balances of these Sondermark, as German importers took advantage of this possibility of comparatively unrestricted imports and purchased, in the respective countries, enormous quantities of goods of all kinds. Among such purchases were even commodities which did not originate in those countries —mainly overseas raw materials—but which, owing to exchange difficulties, they could not so easily buy in the country of origin. On the other hand, German exports of goods and services for payment in Sondermark were very limited. Since the Sondermark agreements had thus functioned in a very unsatisfactory manner for Germany's foreign-trade partners, and had made them once more, very much contrary to their intentions, creditors of the Reich, most of these countries insisted on replacing the Sondermark agreements with complete clearing agreements.

Such clearing agreements, concluded, in particular, with countries like France and Belgium, provided for the centralization of payments for all exports and imports in clearing accounts, opened with respective central banks. Out of the proceeds of the German exports, thus centralized, were supposed to be paid the imports into Germany and the interest on the bonds of the Dawes and Young loans issued in the country concerned. Provision was also made for the gradual reimbursement of the commercial debts previously incurred, such as debts on the Sondermark account. The assumption under which these agreements had been concluded

181

was that a German export surplus sufficient to provide funds required for all these purposes would be maintained.

However, for the same reasons as those applying to the Sondermark agreements, German purchases in clearing accounts, not limited by foreign-exchange quotas, suddenly increased. The German exports surplus dwindled, sometimes even disappeared, and the foreign countries concerned began to accumulate important credit balances on their clearing accounts. Once again, these countries had to request a change in the technique of the agreements, in order to protect themselves against German ingenuity, which always succeeded in obtaining from foreign-trade partners goods on credit, the repayment of which was most uncertain.

The final form of trade agreements between these countries and Nazi Germany consisted of payment agreements which were concluded, in particular, with Great Britain and France. By their terms, a fixed ratio was established between German exports and imports to and from the country concerned, leaving an export surplus sufficient to provide for payment of interest on the Dawes and Young loans, and for gradual liquidation of former commercial debts. The German government was pledged to allow payment in free exchange of German imports and of the financial payments agreed upon, provided they did not exceed a certain percentage of German exports which had been determined in the agreements. Such arrangements did function without any special difficulty until World War II, and proved satisfactory to Germany's partners. But they were even more favorable to Germany, since they guaranteed to the Reich an export surplus payable in free foreign exchange.

In the trade relations of Germany with this category of countries, the official parity of the Reichsmark was effectively applied. In order to enable German exporters to compensate for the over-evaluation of their currency, and to quote competitive prices in the foreign markets, the Nazi government paid them considerable subsidies. This procedure had been kept secret; the details became known only after the war. These subsidies were being financed by a levy on all German industrial production, including even service industries; the amount varied from 1 to 3 percent of the value of their output.

For the trade with overseas countries—mainly purchases of raw materials so far as imports were concerned—Germany had at first used the barter (private compensation) method to a considerable extent. Later on, especially after the introduction of the New Plan, the general-compensation system was employed. This consisted in paying for foreign imports in the so-called Aski marks—foreign accounts for domestic payments (*Aski-Ausländer Sonderkonten für Inlandzahlungen*). These Aski marks could be used only for payment for certain specified German goods, to be exported to the same country. Thus, for example, a Chilean exporter of copper was paid in Aski marks, which could be used for the purchase of German chemicals or optical goods to be exported to Chile. Because of the strict limitations put on its use, the Aski mark was always at a great discount, compared to the official parity. Its depreciation varied, however, according to the countries to which it applied.

The categories of German goods which could be purchased by payment in Askis were also different according to the countries where they had to be exported and, above all, according to the character of the foreign goods imported and paid for in these Askis. Thus the Askis, created for payment for imports of goods especially needed by the Reich, and originating in countries not particularly dependent on the German market, had a higher value (and could be used in payment for more valuable German exports) than those created to pay for imports of goods less required or/and exported by countries economically or politically dependent on Germany.

As a general rule, the depreciation of the Aski mark amounted to a subsidy paid by the German importer to the German exporter. The German authorities, however, tried wherever possible to use their bargaining power, in order to transfer the cost of at least part of this depreciation to the foreign-trade partners. In this they succeeded to a considerable extent, with a great number of countries.

Thus, the following are examples of results obtained in different categories of countries to which this procedure was applied:

American exports to Germany of raw materials, such as copper, oil and cotton, were not affected by the Aski procedure, either in their volume or in their value in dollars. Germany needed these commodities, and the American exporters, being independent of the German market, could not be induced to make special sacrifices in order to maintain their sales there. Consequently, depreciation of the Aski became a purely domestic matter of compensation between German importers and exporters.

In relation to Central or South American countries, the German authorities could drive a much harder bargain. There the necessity to sell the countries' products was more imperative, and the German market could be of greater importance, as in the case of coffee from Colombia. The Aski marks created for these imports became much less depreciated, or they were made usable only for purchase of less desirable German goods—eventually, also, at prices higher than the level of the world market, as the country concerned would be inclined, anyhow, to facilitate German exports in order to recuperate its Aski marks credits.

The Aski system was at first very widely used. Later on, however, the Nazi authorities restricted it to imports of essential raw materials. As to the German exports which could be paid for in Askis, the value of imported raw materials contained in such goods had to be paid for in free currency. The system undoubtedly constituted a type of dumping; and in March 1939 the United States applied to German exports paid for in Aski mark certain countervailing antidumping duties.

The most important and significant application of the Nazi foreign-trade policy, politically as well as economically, was made in the relations with the agricultural countries of Central and Southeastern Europe. These countries had been deeply affected by the depression, especially because their agriculture was handicapped by much higher costs and could not compete at prices existing after the depression. This, in turn, was due to a lack of the vast spaces of virgin land and the mechanized equipment of the main overseas producers.

Several attempts to solve the economic problems were made, but did not succeed. They were furthered mainly by France, which was a political ally of most countries of this area, and which also had considerable financial interests there, but which did not offer those countries an important market for their exports.

The first of these attempts, the proposal of a Danubian economic federation, was sponsored by Tardieu in 1930, and it would have reestablished the economic unity of the former Austro-Hungarian Empire. It failed, owing mainly (1) to the short-sighted resistance of Czechoslovakia, which was afraid of a revival of Austrian hegemony; and (2) to the opposition of Germany, which very accurately saw in this possible federation an obstacle to her future domination.

The second attempt was made at the Stresa Conference in 1933, and was sponsored jointly by France and Italy. The latter hoped at that moment to establish its influence in Central Europe, especially in Austria and Hungary. At Stresa, the proposal was made that Western European industrialized countries grant preferential treatment to Danubian products, mainly cereals. This proposition broke down, mainly from Great Britain's resistance, which was based on the fact that such treatment would have been contrary to the imperial preference system that had been consolidated, a few months earlier, at the Ottawa Conference.

The economic and financial situation of these countries thus became absolutely tragic. They had (1) suspended all payments on their foreign debts; (2) curtailed drastically even the most vital imports; and (3) introduced a strict exchange control. Germany was the country whose economy most complemented theirs and was also their greatest and nearest market, as well as their natural source of supply for manufactured goods. On the other side of the picture, this region offered Germany a source of supply of food

185

and certain raw materials. Moreover, this area was most conveniently situated for being kept open in time of war, and also offered a great opportunity for Germany to extend its influence and domination.

With these agricultural countries of Central and Southeastern Europe, then, Germany concluded general exchange clearing agreements which did not put any quantitative limits on either exports or imports. These agreements rapidly resulted in an enormous surplus of German imports, and substantial credit balances on clearing accounts were consequently accumulated by the central banks of the countries concerned. In connection with the payment of those balances, Germany was sometimes able to impose on the creditor countries the purchase of the least desirable of her manufactured products. For example, enormous quantities of aspirin were sold to Yugoslavia, and to Greece an extraordinary number of harmonicas, far in excess of any possible demand, and at inflated prices. These credit balances made the governments of these countries entirely dependent on Germany, as they became interested in maintaining the strongly inflated rates of the clearing mark, in order to preserve the value of their credits.

The governments concerned finally understood the danger of their being too closely entangled in Germany's foreign-trade devices, and very strongly desired to reduce exports to Germany, in order to have goods available to export for payment in free exchange. They did not dare, however, to effect this export reduction, fearing that Germany would then suspend her exports to the respective countries, and would thus render worthless their credit balances. These balances had also become the basis of a considerable inflation of the currencies of the countries concerned, as their central banks, in order to pay in domestic currency the exporters of goods sent to Germany, had to issue additional currency that was covered only by the balances on Germany's exchange clearing account. The high nominal prices in national currencies, which the Germans could easily pay, inflated the domestic price level;

186

thus made exports to other countries even more difficult; and therefore increased still more the dependence of those countries on Germany.

Under the pretense of guaranteeing stable markets to the agriculture of the Danubian countries, the Germans also concluded long-term contracts for products which they especially required, and which had to be especially planted for export to Germany alone. Soya beans in Rumania and Hungary are one example. Thus, they made certain that they could obtain the needed supplies at fixed prices, while giving no similar guarantee for the future prices of German exports to these countries. As a matter of fact, owing to the high-handed manner in which the Nazi authorities used the method of exchange clearing in their trade relations with this group of countries, the latter became, economically, semicolonial dependencies of the Third Reich, having lost all freedom of action in foreign-trade policy.

The development of German exports and imports, in relation to these countries was as follows:

Share of German exports going to Southeastern Europe: 6.5 percent in 1929; 4.6 percent in 1930; 11.4 percent in 1937.

Share of German imports originating in Southeastern Europe: 6.3 percent in 1929; 6.1 percent in 1930; 12.3 percent in 1937.

Later figures are not comparable, owing to changes in territory, but in 1938 Germany (including Austria for 9 months, and Sudeten for 3 months) took from this area 14.3 percent of its imports, and sent there 14.2 percent of German exports.

As to Germany's share in the foreign trade of this group of countries, it was as follows: Hungary, about 25 percent of imports and exports; Greece, about 30 percent of exports, over 25 percent of imports; Rumania, about 20 percent of exports and imports alike.

As regards the results of the economic policy of the Nazi regime, it should be emphasized that they were tremendously successful, particularly with respect to the main objective, the

187

strengthening of German power. That general statement is fully justified by an enumeration of the following concrete results of the Nazi policy:

Germany modernized and increased the productive capacity and efficiency of her economy; put her unemployed back to work and utilized to the utmost all her productive resources; obtained domination of important markets in Central and Southeastern Europe; * and penetrated into important markets in South America and other overseas countries.

This tremendous economic success—especially since it was added to a rapid rate of growth in population and in economic potential, as well as to the overwhelming military strength built up during these few years—made Germany by far the strongest power in Europe. It seems evident that, if peace had been maintained and Germany had devoted to peacetime production the greater part of her productive capacity, she would rapidly have gained economic and political supremacy in Europe, as well as the complete domination of all the smaller countries of Eastern Central, and even of Western, Europe. Such hegemony in Europe would have been achieved without any serious political or military risks, as Germany was already much too strong to be attacked by any power or group of powers in Europe. Besides, the dominant psychology of appeasement was so strong in the capitalist democracies that, through sheer fright, they would certainly have consented first to be outflanked, economically and politically, and then probably to be gradually subjugated.

As already once before, in 1914, however, the lack of patience and the pathological craving for military success and revenge drove Germany into war and defeat. Military victory, as a sort of final consecration of success, was required by the Nazi regime, which was based on exaltation of war as the highest test of a nation's strength and valor. From the start, the Nazis used their

* Mitteleuropa, that is, a Central Europe, dominated by Germany, was practically a reality. It was the dream of Naumann, a German nationalist writer of the period of World War I.

military power as a means of blackmail and in this manner made considerable political and strategic gains; so they did not stop when danger of resistance to this method was increased. Instead, they risked—and lost—everything. Once more in history, the course of events proved the Scriptural prophecy: "He that killeth with the sword must be killed with the sword."

17 SOVIET RUSSIA DURING THE FIVE-YEAR PLANS: VICTORY OF INDUSTRIALIZATON AND COLLECTIVIZATION

WITH THE PERIOD of the Five-Year Plans, inaugurated on October 1, 1928, there began for Soviet Russia a transformation of the entire economic and social structure of the country. At the beginning of this period, the principal characteristic features of Russian economy were still the same as before the Bolshevik Revolution, the only difference being in the state ownership of industry. By the end of it all, the main components of economic activity had undergone a complete change as to volume of production, geographical distribution, and relative importance of the various factors, as well as in their organization. This structural revolution was as important as the political revolution of 1917, which it complemented.

The Five-Year Plans—whose main objectives have been stated above—were the first attempt at a complete socialist planning of the development of Russian economy. During the period of war-Communism, organization of planning was a copy of the German war economy of World War I. This copy was not at all adjusted to Russia's conditions, and this fact, together with all the other difficulties of that period, was one of the main reasons for the complete failure of the policy. Now, however, there was a special organ for planning, the State Planning Commission (Gosplan), created in 1921, and its plans were definitely the result of careful study and investigation.

These Five-Year Plans were mainly a program of economic and, above all, industrial development of gigantic dimensions. The main stress was laid on expansion of heavy capital-goods industries, the importance of which was due to the following fact: Those industries alone could provide the tools required to make the Soviet Union independent of the West—in time of war, by producing armaments; in time of peace, by producing the new equipment essential to the continuation of industrial development. At the start of the Five-Year Plans, industrial development owed its beginnings to large imports of heavy machinery from the Western countries, especially Germany and the United States. The expansion of the heavy industries was providing the basis of the future economic and military power of the Soviet Union.

Expansion of light (consumer-goods) industries, which cater to needs of the population and its current well-being, was, on the contrary, absolutely neglected. As a matter of fact, production in these industries was curtailed at the very beginning. This was due partly to the concentration of all resources and manpower on heavy industry; but it was due also to the drive (also a major objective of the Plans) to make industry entirely state-owned and to eliminate all private and semiprivate enterprises. The latter had achieved, during the period of the Nep, a considerable degree of development and prosperity, and had supplied a substantial part of the total production of many important items of consumer goods.

Another major objective of the Five-Year Plans was the creation of new industries in the formerly purely agricultural and very sparsely populated regions of Eastern European Russia, Siberia and Central Asia. The effort toward this end was well justified by the immense natural resources of these areas, and also by strategical considerations for the establishment of a new industrial basis out of reach of any enemy aggression. The former main industrial areas were too close to the western borders to be considered safe. In fact, they had actually been invaded by the end of World War I.

191

Since these were the major aims of the Five-Year Plans, it must be acknowledged that they had been reached to a considerable extent, in spite of the tremendous difficulties encountered. Among the greatest obstacles was the lack of any industrial tradition and of trained manpower, including technicians.

The last reliable statistics applying to the pre-war territory of the Soviet Union were published for 1937. During 1928-1937—which constituted the period of the first Five-Year Plan (reduced to 4¼ years, October 1, 1928 to December 31, 1932) and of the first four years of the second Five-Year Plan—development in main lines of industrial production was as follows:

| | | | | 1937 in % of | |
Item	1913	1927-28	1937	1913	1927-28
Cotton cloth					
(*billions of meters*)	1.65	2.7	3.4	205	125
Oil (*millions of tons*)	9.2	11.6	30.5	335	263
Coal (*millions of tons*)	29.1	36.1	127.3	437	350
Pig iron (*millions of tons*)	4.2	3.3	14.5	345	440
Machinery and metal products					
(*billions of rubles of 1926-27*					
purchasing power)	1.1	2.0	27.5	2500	1375

The increase in production of industrial raw materials was thus very considerable, and production of finished capital goods literally soared, through the establishment of hundreds of new industrial plants for production of industrial and agricultural machinery formerly imported. The emphasis on capital-goods production was even stronger during the implementation of the Plans than had been originally intended. Thus, estimates for capital-goods production were overfulfilled to the extent of 126.7 percent of planned figures during the period of the first Five-Year Plan, and 121.2 percent during the period of the second. Consumer-goods production, on the other hand, remained below expectations by respectively 80.5 percent and 85.4 percent of planned figures.

Thus, during 1927-28, production of industrial consumer goods was more than double, in value, of total production of capital goods: 12.3 billion rubles as against 6 billion. In 1937, however, the respective importance of the two industrial categories was reversed: value of production of capital goods, 55.2 billion rubles; consumer goods, 40.3 billion. Besides, the increase of consumer-goods production reflected in these figures was considerably overestimated, as, by the end of the Plan period, they included all production, while previously a very substantial production of small private handicraft was not included in the statistics.

The development of new industrial areas became an important part of general industrial expansion, especially after the second Five-Year Plan. The most important objective had a twofold purpose: (1) to develop the coal basins of Kusnetzk in Western Siberia and Karaganda in Central Asia; and (2) to establish—on the basis of the Kusnetzk coal and the Ural iron-ore deposits—in the region of Magnitogorsk and Kusnetzk, one of the most modern and powerful centers of iron and steel production in the world.

This tremendous industrial development involved, of course, a heavy cost mainly in terms of reduced present consumption for the population. The proportion of investment expenditure in relation to total national income, during the period of the first two Five-Year Plans, had been estimated at about 28-30 percent as against only 8 percent in pre-1914 Russia, and as compared with a normal rate of about 15 percent in Western countries with a high rate of industrial development and high level of national income. The investment rate of 20 percent in post-war Britain implies maintenance of austerity, and is considered very painful. Besides, this very high rate of investment expenditure applied to the very low per capita income existing in Russia. It thus implied a very considerable reduction in consumption for the population, not only in consumer goods but even in food. This reduction was reflected in the re-establishment of a very

193

strict rationing system for food and other essential consumer goods.

The extremely high level of the sales tax on such consumer goods is another factor which enables us to measure the importance of the sacrifices in consumption which the population of Soviet Russia had to bear in order to make possible the implementation of the Five-Year Plans. This tax provided about two-thirds of the budget revenue. The total amount of sales tax collected was reached in 1935, when its level attained the peak of 175 percent of the total amount of sales without tax. That is, the purchasing power of Soviet wage-earners was only 36 percent of their nominal wages, since 64 percent was absorbed by the sales tax. The crushing effect of such a tax on consumption levels of even the barest necessities was even more evident from the fact that more than half of the proceeds of this tax was collected from grain, which was the source of bread and porridge, the principal staple foods of the Russian peasants and other workers.

Owing to this tax on bread, the relation in 1935 between the prices of grain (bought by the state from the peasant) and the price of bread (sold by the state to urban consumers) was as 1 to 6; in France, during the same year, the same price relation was 1 to 1.8. After 1935, changes in sales tax levels and their impact on price levels were only slight.

An important aspect of Soviet industrial development was the situation of industrial labor. The requirements of manpower were naturally enormously increased by the expansion of industry; and most of the new workers came from rural areas, especially after the beginning of the drive for mandatory collectivization. The working discipline of these new industrial workers was generally rather unsatisfactory. This was hardly surprising in view of the following facts: The level of real wages was extremely low, and living conditions, especially housing, were frequently appalling, even for Soviet standards. Particularly was this true in the new industrial centers, where mines and plants were built before any decent accommodations were provided for the workers, who at first, at least, had to live in tents or earthen huts. The turnover of workers seeking to change jobs, in order to find better living conditions, reached extraordinary proportions. As a result, all the efforts being made to increase productivity were seriously impeded. The situation reached its height during 1930-32, when the turnover during one year amounted to 150 percent of the total labor force. Even in later years it remained at about 100 percent of the aggregate labor figures.

In order to increase the stability of labor, the Soviet authorities applied strict repressive measures which culminated in the introduction, in 1938, of a special "workers' labor book." It is maintained, today, by the concern where the worker is employed. A change of employment can be made only with the agreement of the previous employing firm, which, if it does agree, returns to the worker his labor book with a stamp, "Liberated from employment in this undertaking." Any attempt to change employment without authorization is a penal offense punishable by a prison sentence. Thus, the status of the Russian working class is practically back to the status of serfs before their liberation, in 1861, with the minor difference that, instead of being attached to the land, the worker is now attached to a particular plant or mine.

It is necessary to stress, besides the general semiserf labor status, the following well-known fact—even though its dimensions cannot be accurately estimated: that a great part of the most difficult undertakings of the Five-Year Plans, such as the building of the great inland canals, had been accomplished with forced labor, supplied partly by political foes of the regime, but mainly by peasants who had resisted collectivization. This forced labor, under the Ministry of the Interior, that is, the M.V.D., or Secret Police, was also responsible for the bulk of lumber production in Northeast Russia (one of the main exports of the Soviet Union), as well as for all the production of gold, mainly in Eastern Siberia.

However, the main cost, in human suffering, of the production

195

achievements of the Five-Year Plans was borne by the rural population. The mandatory collectivization of agriculture, which was complementary to industrial development, resulted in a bitter struggle which ended with a complete victory for Communist domination. It was a victory achieved at a very heavy price for agriculture, as well as for the whole economy.

Already, during the period of war-Communism, 1917-20, the Soviet authorities made a great effort to foster collectivization of agriculture. The main elements to undertake collective farming were the poorest peasants and even certain groups of industrial workers. The latter, driven from the cities by famine, returned to the countryside and undertook to farm estates of former landlords as complete collective establishments, the so-called communes. There production, as well as consumption, was on a collective basis. Besides the collective farms, the Soviet authorities also had established, on some of the biggest and most efficient of the former estates, state farms (*sovkhose*). All the labor was composed of wage laborers, and the farms themselves were run in the same way as the industrial undertakings conducted by state-appointed managers. In spite of considerable effort to build up the collective farms (through subsidies, privileges in delivery of equipment and of manufactured goods, and lower rates for grain deliveries), their development was very limited. In 1920, of the total sown area in European Russia, only 4.6 percent belonged to state farms; 1.7 percent belonged to collective farms.

During the period of the Nep, when the government was more interested in furthering general increase of agricultural production than in changing its structure, the trend toward collectivization was actually reversed. The total number of collective farms declined from 15,819 in 1921 to 10,732 in 1925.

Collectivization of agriculture, and transformation of farming from a capitalist into a socialist sector of the economy, constituted one of the chief aims of the first Five-Year Plan. It was expected that the effort would be implemented gradually, as increasing production of mechanized farm equipment and tractors

196

would increase incentives for joining collective farms, which alone were able to use them. From the beginning of the Five-Year Plan, however, a severe strain resulted from difficulties in securing a supply of grain. This was due to the fact that, while requirements had considerably increased, a very limited share of harvested grain was being brought into the market for feeding the steadily rising urban population, as well as for exports. The latter had to be expanded, in order to provide the foreign exchange required for payment of equipment supplied by the countries of Western Europe. In order to cope with this situation, the Soviet authorities took severe repressive measures to enforce increased deliveries. The result was a strong pressure for collectivization, which was more and more accelerated as it was practically forced on the peasants.

This drive for collectivization started in 1929, when penalties for failure to implement required deliveries were increased. Refusal could be considered by the authorities to be an act of revolt against the state, and could lead to confiscation of all property and deportation of the peasant and of his family outside of his district. Under the pretense of placating the poor and medium peasants, and in order to overcome kulak resistance to deliveries, another even more drastic regulation permitted authorization of the village community to undertake deliveries on a village basis. The share of each peasant in such deliveries was also determined by the village community, in an open vote. Any refusal of an individual peasant to deliver his quota could lead to complete confiscation. Twenty-five percent of the proceeds of such confiscation were to be used toward establishing the poorest members of the village community on a collective farm.

Such measures stimulated a violent class struggle in the countryside. They did, however, succeed in increasing grain deliveries to the state, though at the cost of again creating hardship, and even famine conditions in many rural areas. They also resulted in wiping out entirely the class of the most efficient and prosperous peasants, the kulaks, and thus eliminated an important

197

potential political danger to Communist domination. This destruction of the kulak class was mainly a result of deportation, which affected hundreds of thousands of peasants, perhaps even several millions.

These repressive measures intimidated the great majority of peasants of the small and medium economic classes. In order to avoid being persecuted as kulaks, they chose the only available solution of their problem—joining the collective farms. Incidentally, the authorities did not define the term *kulak;* therefore they could apply it, at will, to any individual peasant of whose behavior they disapproved.

The number of collective farms thus increased at a tremendous pace. On July 1, 1928, the proportion of collective farms in the sown area had been 1.7 percent; it had increased a year later to 3.9 percent; on October 1, 1929, to 4.1 percent; on January 20, 1930, to 21 percent; and on March 1, 1930, to 58 percent.

Even though, according to the Plans, collectivization was supposed to extend only to main means of production—cropland, equipment and draught power (horses)—very often the peasants were also obliged to contribute all their livestock, and even poultry. They were most unwilling to contribute their livestock to the collective farms; and there was shortage of feed grain, lack of organization and of facilities to keep livestock on these newly planned farms, the general efficiency of which was at first quite indifferent. Because of those facts, the number of livestock declined in the following catastrophic proportions:

NUMBER OF LIVESTOCK
(in million heads)

	Horses	Cattle	Sheep and Goats	Hogs
1929	34	68.1	147.2	20.9
1930	30.2	52.5	108.8	13.6
1931	26.2	47.9	77.9	14.4
1932	19.6	40.7	52.1	11.6
1933	16.6	38.6	50.6	12.2

This mass loss of livestock amounted to the nearly complete destruction of animal husbandry, and was a terrible blow to Russian agriculture. The loss of half of the country's horses at a time when production of tractors was in only an early stage of development created an acute shortage of draught power on the collective farms. Delivery regulations prescribed that all surpluses above mandatory deliveries had to be sold to the state at official prices, which were most unsatisfactory, so that the peasants had little or no incentive whatsoever to increase their effort and to overcome the very serious difficulties which were impeding increase of production. The reward of such increased effort would have been insignificant. Thus, not only livestock but also agricultural crop production considerably declined. In spite of all this, the authorities, through the use of force, did succeed in obtaining the supplies required to distribute minimum rations in the cities. But there was a real famine in several of the richest agricultural regions of Russia, such as the North Caucasus, where the resistance to deliveries, as well as the repressive measures, had been most severe. It is probable that the very general discontent of the peasant population spread into the Soviet Army where most of the recruits were of peasant extraction. It may even have been responsible, to a considerable extent, for the conspiracy of several prominent generals, such as Marshall Toukachevsky.

The situation, however, gradually improved. In 1932, delivery regulations had already been modified, and the collective farms had been authorized to sell the surplus on the open market, after payment of a tax in grain. Increase in production of tractors and farm machinery led to the establishment of state machine and tractor stations, which rented their equipment to collective farms and were paid by a share of the harvest (generally 20 percent). Finally, in 1935, a new government decree explicitly limited collective production inside the collective farms and enabled, even encouraged, the peasants to develop animal husbandry on an individual basis. They were authorized, as a general rule, to keep one cow per family as well as small livestock, though no horses,

199

as well as to cultivate fruit and vegetable gardens on small plots adjacent to their houses. This reform stimulated recovery in the number of livestock. Another even more important factor in the improvement of the position of the peasantry was the decrease in numbers, through mass immigration into the cities of the old and the new industrial areas. From 1929 to 1938, the number of peasant families declined from 25.5 million to 20.3 million. In 1939, the total rural population of the Soviet Union amounted to 114.6 million, the same figure as in 1913, as against 126.5 million in 1929, while—owing to increase in sown area—the area sown, per capita of rural population, had increased from 0.98 hectar in 1913, and 0.79 hectar in 1929, to 1.23 hectar in 1939.

Thus, finally, the problem of rural overpopulation, which had been at first aggravated after the 1917 Revolution, had been more or less solved through collectivization, which thus achieved the following results: (1) improved to some extent the situation of the peasantry; (2) at the same time provided the manpower for the development of the new industries established during the Five-Year Plans, and the grain surpluses to feed it; and, above all, (3) brought the rural population, nearly as much as the industrial workers, under the control of the central government.

III EUROPE'S ECONOMY DURING WORLD WAR II

18 THE NAZI NEW ORDER IN EUROPE
DURING WORLD WAR II

IN GERMANY

The economy of Nazi Germany, prior to 1939, had been established, to a great extent, with a view to preparation for war. Therefore, when World War II actually started, very little reconversion was necessary. This was quite the opposite to what had happened in 1914. The economic war organization was already in existence and required only some small-scale overhauling or readjustment.

Thus, at the outbreak of the war, the general organization of the German economy remained practically unchanged; it was merely slightly tightened. The policy-making organ in the economic field was, and since 1937 had been, the Office of the Four-Year Plan. Its decisions were implemented by the Ministry of the National Economy, and the various organs of the corporative organization in industry and agriculture, including Commodity Boards (*Reichsstellen*), for foreign-trade control. Organization of the wartime economy was somewhat complicated by the intervention of the military authorities, in particular the Economic Division of the Supreme Military Command (*Ober Kommando der Wehrmacht*). In spite of the existence of a special coordination organ created at the beginning of the war, the Ministerial Council presided over by Goering, there was still considerable duplication of authority. The Army, through its inspection of armament industries (*Rüstungsinspectionen*), tried to control the war industries, which during the war included the greatest part of all industry. Toward the end of the war, when military operations came close to German territory, the influence of regional military authorities (*Reichsverteidigungskommissaren*) on the organization of the economy in the areas under their control, became important. Local leaders of the economy (*Wirtschaftsführer*) had also been appointed during that period, in order to help in effecting complete subordination of the economy to military needs.

As a general rule, however, the German war economy had been built up through utilization of the organizational structure that already existed. In industry, the mandatory cartels (*Reichsvereinigungen*), established since 1933 in the different industries, had their powers considerably increased. They became the main mediums of the application of direct state control of industrial production. Such agencies issued, in particular, the basic written orders that were required for all phases of economic activity: manufacturing and process orders with control of quantity and quality for industrial goods; purchase permits for raw materials; sales and delivery orders for agricultural produce; storage orders for inventories, etc.

Agriculture was even more strictly regulated. Its general organization, the Food Guild (*Nährstand*), was divided into three sections dealing respectively with the peasant (*Bauer*), the farm (*Gut*), and the marketing of farm produce (*Markt*). Associations of producers of each main agricultural product received full authority, from the beginning of the war, to plan production, use of the soil, consumption on the farms, and distribution. In each region were established **Food Offices** (*Landesernährungsämter*) divided into two sections. One dealt with procurement, and also decided to what extent agricultural production was really efficient and developed according to plan; the other section was empowered to control deliveries and food distribution.

Government control extended also to the capital market. Dividend and interest payments on bonds and shares were limited to

6 percent or, in some exceptional cases, to 8 percent. The main purposes of this limitation were: to restrict purchasing power available for consumption out of shareholders' income; to divert the greatest part of the profits of corporations to investment through autofinancing; and to reduce flotation on the capital market of issues of private companies in competition with government financing.

Control of labor was also very strict. Labor wages had been frozen, in principle, since 1933, and their rates could be changed only by a motivated decision of the labor trustee, a government supervisor. In 1935, the government introduced the labor book * as mandatory for all employable persons, making thus available to the authorities the record of their workers' employment and skills. This was obviously done in order to facilitate the mandatory allocation of labor, when it became necessary.

At first, the emphasis of Nazi legislation had been on liquidating unemployment. To that end, rules had been established: restricting industrial employment of women; making it mandatory for all concerns to employ a certain percentage of aged workers; and prohibiting migration to areas where unemployment was considerable. Later on, as unemployment gradually declined and then disappeared, the emphasis was shifted to increased stability of employment. In March 1939, in the most important industries, a new regulation made validity of dismissal or resignation notices dependent on approval of employment offices. Employment of skilled labor was authorized only when its skill could be fully utilized. Gradually, as labor shortages developed, the length of the working day was considerably extended (to 60 hours a week and sometimes more). At the beginning of the war, allocation of manpower was already in existence; the only new factor now introduced was the reversal of the former trend against the employment of women, and their number in industry again considerably

---

* Similar to that introduced in the Soviet Union at roughly the same time. This was described earlier.

increased. However, rules for their employment always took demographic motives into consideration.

Price control existed in Germany since 1931, when the Bruning government had established it with the intention of reducing the general price level. It had been maintained by the Nazi regime, which had utilized it chiefly for sustaining price stability in spite of the trend of costs increase, which resulted especially from the self-sufficiency policy. Thus, even if an industry requested a price increase, in order to compensate for rising costs, the authorities tried to see that this cost increase was absorbed by the producers, especially if production had increased. If price increases had to be granted after all, attempts were made to offset them by reduction of prices of other products bought by the same category of purchasers. Consequently, increase of prices of farm machinery was to be counterbalanced by a reduction of prices of fertilizer.

In 1936, the organization of price control, as well as the policy applied in this respect, was transformed by the establishment of an Office for Price Formation (*Preisbildungsamt*), headed by a *Reichskommissar* of great authority, Dr. Goerdeler, the Mayor of Leipzig. The principle of an absolute price freeze remained, and all requests for changes were investigated by local boards, authorized by the central office. They were granted only if found economically justified by cost of production, all the elements of which —such as interest of capital, depreciation, etc.—were determined by fixed rules.

The price policy applied, relative to war orders at the beginning of the war, at first was to agree to prices sufficient to cover costs plus a moderate profit considered legitimate for average producers. Obviously, this was not sufficient to give any profit to the least efficient producers. Sometimes it was not even enough to cover their costs. In 1942, when an effort was made to achieve the greatest possible increase in war production, the pricing system was modified. All producers were classified in five categories, according to their cost of production; and the prices paid to each category were sufficient to cover cost and a minimum profit. Those in the lowest cost category were favored only in so far as they received priority for allocation of raw materials and manpower.

The general tendency of German price policy, during the war, had been to reduce profits as much as possible. This procedure was motivated by the desire to prevent an inflationary expansion of income from profits, as well as for the following moral reasons: the desire to avoid excessive war profits, demoralizing to the population; and to maintain a minimum of equality in sacrifice. War risks and losses therefore were not taken into account in the establishment of prices of war orders, and an excess profit tax was introduced. Attempts were made to compensate for price increases on war production by reducing the prices of consumer goods.

The financial policy of the Nazi government had already achieved, even in peacetime, a much greater rate of increase in public revenue than in purchasing power of the population. The greatest part of the benefit resulting from the increase in production and employment was absorbed by the state, owing to Dr. Schacht's policy of the "money circuit." Thus, national income and its distribution between the state and the public had been as follows:

(1937 frontiers) *in billions of Reichsmarks*

	Total National Income	Available for Consumption	Absorbed by the State
1932	45	40.5	4.5
1939	77	50.0	27.0

Since the beginning of the war, the rate of absorption of national income by the state had again considerably increased. This increase resulted from new taxation (excess-profits tax, higher luxury taxes), and from mandatory savings (*Eherne Spargroschen*), which were imposed on business as well as on wage-earners. A certain proportion of their respective profits and wages was retained by the state for the duration of the war, and was to be repaid, tax-free, at the end of the war. Besides these mandatory

207

savings, the state could also collect all the surplus purchasing power available, as consumption at fixed prices was strictly rationed, and there was no outlet for savings other than deposits in banks or savings banks, which had to invest all their funds in government securities. The Nazi government thus financed the German war effort mainly by borrowing from institutions, without any direct appeal to the public by flotation of loans on the capital market.

In so far as data are available, development during the war of German national income, revenues and expenditures was as follows: *

(in billions of Reichsmarks)

	1938-39	1939-40	1940-41	1941-42	1942-43	1943-44	1944-45
Total national income	79.7	95.5	100	...	...	...	...
Total tax receipts	15.8	23.6	27.6	30.7	40.4	31.9	28.5
Borrowing	3.0	11.8	21.4	41.7	56.1	60.1	79.7
Total revenue	18.8	35.4	49.0	72.4	96.5	92.0	108.2
War expenditures	...	20.0	54.0	76.0	101.0	123.0	140.0
Total expenditures	18.8	52.0	77.0	101.0	128.0	153.0	176.0
Occupied-territories levies & secret borrowing *	...	16.6	28.0	28.6	31.5	61.0	67.8

* The amount of secret borrowing from institutions resorted to, during the last months of the war, had been estimated at from 20 to 40 billion Reichsmarks.

The total military expenditures during the war period had amounted to about 514 billion Reichsmarks, while the total of all expenditures during the war had been 687 billion Reichsmarks. This grand total included contributions from occupied territories of Western Europe, but did not include contributions and requisitions levied in Eastern Europe. According to German official figures, the German public debt on April 30, 1945 amounted to 380 billion Reichsmarks, but had been estimated by Lindholm at

* Source: Lindholm, "German finance during the Second World War," *American Economic Review,* March 1947.

473 billion; in September 1939, it amounted to 40.7 billion Reichsmarks.

Though exact data for the latter part of the war period are not available, it seems probable that during the greatest part of the war over 60 percent of the gross national product was absorbed by the war effort. Production considerably expanded during the war, while consumption was reduced to the utmost and the excess purchasing power was pumped back into the treasury of the Reich through the circuit of taxes and voluntary as well as mandatory savings. Consequently, in spite of the enormous potential inflation reflected in the budgetary deficit, and the increase of public debt and currency circulation, the price level remained stable.

It should be pointed out, however, that in spite of the considerable reduction in overall consumption, the German population, especially the workers in the war industries, continued to receive relatively satisfactory rations of all basic necessities. This was particularly true of foodstuffs, owing (1) to the excellent functioning of the mandatory deliveries system organized by the *Nährstand* in the Reich; and (2) to substantial contributions from the occupied territories. Goering promised the German nation, at the beginning of the war, that, if there should be starvation anywhere in Europe during the war, it would not happen in Germany. That promise was fulfilled by the Nazis nearly to the very end of the war, while they still had any occupied territories at their disposal. Thus, the comparative situation of Germany and the territories which it occupied can be illustrated by the comparison of rations in Germany and France. In the latter, before the war, owing to a greater balance between agriculture and industry, food standards had been higher than in the Reich.

Rations in calories per day	Germany	France
January 1941	1990	1365
" 1942	1750	1115
" 1943	1980	1080
" 1944	1930	1115

The effective difference in standards of nutrition was even greater than that implied by the comparison of the calory figures alone, as the German rations were much more generous with foodstuffs that were rich in protein and other quality factors.

In January 1944, for example, the weekly rations of basic foodstuffs in Germany and France compared as follows:

(*in grammes*)

	Germany	France
Bread	2425	2100
Sugar	225	115
Fats	185	70
Meat	250	120

Supplements for heavy workers were also much higher in Germany than in occupied territories, resulting in higher productivity. Thus, measured in percentage of normal rations, they were:

	Heavy Workers	Very Heavy Workers
Germany	141	181
France	120	129

During the war years, therefore, the German population had been reasonably well fed, especially if to these basic rations were added such foodstuffs as potatoes, the consumption of which was particularly important in Germany, where this item of food was unrationed. It was rationed in most countries of occupied Europe. In order accurately to measure the German consumption standard during the war, it is also necessary to take into account the enormous quantities of food and consumer goods sent by the German soldiers to their families from occupied territories, where several categories of such goods were available only to them. In occupied France, for instance, coupons for shoes with leather soles were exclusively reserved for Germans.

As a consequence of the reasonably satisfactory food-consumption standard maintained in Germany during the war, the health standard—in spite of deterioration of the housing conditions—remained relatively satisfactory. This was true even when, after the end of the war, German food rations had for a few years been considerably reduced. They still remained generally higher than those of the countries that the Germans occupied for five or six years. The death rate, from 1946 on, gradually dropped to the prewar level; and there was, and still is, a considerable birth surplus. On the contrary, during the war, in all countries of German-occupied Europe there had been an enormous increase in the death rate and, in particular, an increase of 40 percent in infant mortality.

The birth surplus which had existed in Germany during the war was due to the good food situation, which had kept mortality at a low level. It was due also to a very determinate demographic policy aimed at increase of population, such as substantial children allowances and regular leaves for soldiers. Owing to such measures during the first war years, the birth rate had been maintained at the high level it had reached by 1939. Comparison of the vital statistics, during this period, of Germany and of the Western European occupied countries may justify the opinion of some population experts that Hitler won the war from the point of view of demography, which was considered especially by the Germans as the basic element of power. Here are some comparative figures:

(in thousands)

	Germany			France			Belgium		
	Births	Deaths	Surplus + Deficit −	Births	Deaths	Surplus + Deficit −	Births	Deaths	Surplus + Deficit −
1938	1508	949	+559	612	647	−35	132	110	+22
1939	1633	1009	+624	614	643	−29	129	116	+13
1940	1645	1046	+599	535	735	−200	112	134	−22
1941	1528	990	+532	520	679	−159	99	120	−21

Because of the satisfactory food supply, the productivity of the German workers had been well maintained during the war. As the

211

working hours could not be substantially increased, expansion of war production depended entirely on increase in available manpower. This was achieved by introduction of a greater number of women and foreign workers in war industries, as well as by shifting workers from consumer-goods industries. The manpower situation developed as follows:

By the end of 1941, there were in Greater Germany 23.9 million workers (one million fewer than before the war), in spite of the increase (from 8.3 to 9.4 million) in the number of women employed in industry, and the utilization of 2.1 million foreign workers, as well as of a great number of youngsters and aged workers formerly retired. These figures, however, do not include about 2 million war prisoners, who were working mainly in war industries, in violation of international conventions.

During the first two winters of the war, the German Army could temporarily and partially demobilize, returning the factory workers to their jobs for a few months. This was no longer possible after Germany began war upon the Soviet Union. However, in October 1941, Hitler, convinced that the war on the Eastern Front had practically come to an end, ordered the stoppage of large-scale war production and a beginning of reconversion to peacetime production. Shortly afterwards, the winter campaign in Russia and the first defeats which the German Army suffered there proved that the Führer had committed a scandalous mistake. Though restarting of war production on an enlarged scale encountered considerable difficulties, an increase of the flow of military supplies became more than ever indispensable. Albert Speer, appointed Minister of Armaments, completely reorganized German war production for this purpose, in February 1942. This reorganization included concentration of production in the biggest and most efficient plants with the shutdown of smaller plants and the gradual elimination of a great part of consumer-goods industries, as well as of commercial and service undertakings. Regional control of economy through regional Chambers of Economy (*Gauwirt-*

212

schaftskammern) was strengthened, and revision of price-fixing for war-production orders was effected (see above).

New and even stricter measures of total mobilization were introduced after the defeat at Stalingrad, in January 1943. All men between 16 and 65 years of age who were not in the armed forces were mobilized for essential production (that is, practically war production), as well as all women between 17 and 45 years. Most of the retail shops were closed down. Another step-up toward total mobilization took place after the Allied landings in Normandy, in July 1944. It extended to women up to 50 years of age, who were mobilized for essential work. All nonessential activities were stopped; all amusement places, with the exception of moving-picture halls, were closed down. Production of all consumer goods, except food, was suspended. Even public services and administration were combed for able-bodied men who could be used in the armed forces or in war production.

The number of foreign workers had reached its maximum in 1943, with about 8 to 9 million; by September 30, 1944, there were 7,487,000. Owing to the increase in the number of women and foreign workers employed, the total manpower was maintained throughout the war at about its maximum level. The productivity of the labor force, however, was steadily decreasing. This was due to (1) the gradual replacement of experienced German workers (mobilized into the armed forces) by women; and even more to (2) the sabotage and "go slow" tactics of foreign slave workers.

In spite of these manpower difficulties, expansion of production in most industries working directly or indirectly for war requirements was very impressive. It was especially impressive in view of the fact that a great part of available resources had to be re-channeled for uneconomic production. Typical examples were synthetic raw materials (oil, rubber and textiles), whose preparation involved considerable waste of effort, compared to the use of natural raw materials.

Following are figures showing production increase for Greater Germany:

(in millions of tons)	1939	1943-44	
Hard coal	238	268.2	(main increases in Silesia, Saar)
Lignite	211	286.4	(main raw material for synthetic prod.)
Coke	49	53.4	

(in thousands of tons)		
Aluminum	200	395
Rayon	130	220
Synthetic wool	142	880

The production of raw materials reached its maximum in 1943. For finished armament products, production continued to increase until 1944, the development of production in this category being far greater. Thus, starting with February 1942, when Speer organized German industry for the struggle with the war potential of the Allied powers, especially the United States, the maximum figures attained were: (February 1942 = 100) for all armaments, 322 in July 1944; for aircraft, 367 in July 1944; for tanks, 598 in December 1944.

These increases in war production appear even more impressive when due account is taken of the fact that they were achieved in spite of the progressive disintegration of the German productive apparatus as a consequence of Allied air bombings. The transport system of the Reich, especially the railway net, was already overworked even in 1939; and the war transport had considerably increased the strain on the railways, in spite of many additions to rolling stock from material captured in occupied territories. The war on the Eastern front, which decidedly lengthened the war-transport hauls, even further aggravated transport difficulties. The transport system became the first main target of Allied bombings. Their influence on production began to be felt on a considerable scale only from the autumn of 1943 on. Air bombardments concentrated on transport reduced war production directly by de-

214

creasing the quantities of raw and semifinished materials that could be transported, and indirectly by necessitating the shifting of a steadily increasing proportion of available manpower and material to repair work.

When, at a later stage of the strategical air-force-bombing offensive, war industry itself became the main target, the German authorities had to reverse their previous centralization policy and, wherever possible, decentralize production. While such decentralization was obviously impossible for basic raw materials, such as coal or steel, finishing engineering plants were dispersed in small towns or even established underground, mostly in abandoned mines. Such a decentralization, however, increased even more the requirements of transport and implied an unimpaired transport capacity.

But in spite of all these difficulties, the organization of the German war production by the Ministry of Armaments, under Speer, seems to have been so efficient that output of most armaments continued to increase until the summer of 1944. Then a series of massive air bombardments paralyzed transport of coal from the Ruhr, and also drastically reduced production of synthetic oil (*Leuna*). Consequently, in five months, production of aviation gasoline declined from 175,000 tons (April 1944) to 5,000 tons (September). The reduction of ordinary gasoline production was nearly as drastic, and it produced most important military consequences. Thus, during the Battle of the Bulge, the Germans lacked gas for their tanks. Yet, in spite of increasing disorganization caused by air bombardments, German war production still continued on a substantial scale throughout 1944 and came practically to an end only by February 1945. At that time, the fighting was transferred to German territory in the neighborhood of the two main industrial regions of the Ruhr and Silesia.

However, the industrial capacity of Germany had not been reduced permanently to any considerable extent, in spite of all the destructions which resulted from air bombardments, and which, besides seriously damaging the transport system, had caused special devastation to housing in the big cities. Bombing of factories, even when it caused heavy damage to roofs and walls, caused much less damage to machinery. Enormous increase in capacity of heavy industry was achieved during the war. Capital-goods production was being pushed at a high rate, and no part of it was exported. On the contrary, a considerable amount of machinery from foreign plants dismantled in occupied territories was installed in Germany. As a result of all this, the industrial potential of the Reich by the end of the war actually was considerably above pre-war for most essential industrial products, such as coal, steel, aluminum, chemicals, machinery, synthetic oil, and textiles. Thus, the number of metal-working machine tools increased in Germany from 1,420,000 in 1939 to 2,300,000 in 1945, or to somewhere about the same figure as for the American industry in the United States in 1940, before the wartime expansion.

The enormous industrial potential that eventually existed in Germany by the end of the war was at that moment partly damaged and disorganized by the dislocation of transport; but it could be restored to production with comparatively only minor repairs or additions. The existence of this industrial potential, the greatest part of which is concentrated in the Ruhr, gives to the problem of production control in Germany, and in this region in particular, an immense political importance, as it could provide a new Reich, if resuscitated, with a potential of power, which, after the experience of the past, all the neighbors of Germany have good reason to fear.

IN OCCUPIED EUROPE

The Germans had very carefully prepared for their domination over Europe, which they achieved for a few years by means of military occupation. Already, in 1936, they had started to print the currency notes for occupied territories (*Kassenscheine*). While they dominated the occupied territories, they also brilliantly succeeded in extracting every possible advantage from them. In conformity with the Prussian tradition, they made both war and occupation a perfectly paying proposition. Their method of obtaining reparations from the conquered territories did not encounter the transfer difficulties which had prevented the Allies, after World War I, from obtaining the reparations due to them from Germany. The German method was simply a modernized and highly perfected version of the traditional looting of the conquered by the victors.

Their system of exploitation was extremely methodical and thorough. In Western Europe, they did not proceed, as a general rule, by means of outright confiscation, which they did use extensively in the occupied territories of the East. However, even in the West, there were important exceptions. Thus, the Germans took possession at once of the property of the so-called enemies of the Reich: Jews, Masons, citizens of countries at war with Germany, etc. They also claimed as war booty not only actual armaments, but also all stocks of food and raw materials accumulated by the conquered states for the pursuit of the war, as well as a considerable part of their transport equipment, mainly rolling stock.

In France alone they confiscated 2500 locomotives and, above all, 250,000 freight cars out of a total stock of 450,000 available. A special section of the German Army, the Economic Recuperation Unit under the command of General Thomas, was in charge of this systematic and scientific looting. Out of the city of Lyons, which the Germans had occupied in June 1940 and evacuated a few days later, according to the terms of the Armistice, they had sent to Germany 140 freight trains laden with loot. The total amount of loot obtained by Germany during the 1940 campaign in Western Europe was estimated at about 90 billion Reichsmarks, a sum roughly equivalent to the total amount of German military expenditure during the period 1933-39, after Hitler assumed power. Considered from a later viewpoint, the Nazi policy and methods used for making the war pay would appear to have made this expenditure a very profitable investment, a dividend of 100

217

percent having been obtained in a few months on the capital invested.

For the rest of the goods which the Germans wanted to obtain in the occupied territories of Western Europe, they generally paid: at first in occupation marks, which were later exchanged into the currency of the respective occupied countries; and later on, in their national currency itself, out of the enormous sums put at their disposal by the contributions, called indemnity, for occupation costs, which they forced the occupied countries to pay them. The amount of this indemnity was nearly equivalent to the cost of the military budget in the countries waging an active war; that is, it corresponded to about half, or even a greater share, of the total national income and production.

This method, however, presented for the Germans the considerable advantage of maintaining an apparent legality in their purchases. It did not entail individual spoliation, which would have spread discontent and stimulated resistance. On the contrary, tradesmen had frequent opportunities to make easy money by selling to the Germans those commodities in particular which had become scarce; and in such cases especially, the Germans did not argue about the prices. On an overall basis, such purchases were of course an outright spoliation of the occupied countries, as the goods purchased by the Germans were delivered without any substantial counterpart; were paid for by the countries concerned through the increase in inflation resulting from the currency issued and handed over as occupation indemnity to the German authorities.

The Germans also succeeded in making the terms of their purchases in the occupied territories especially advantageous, by fixing artificial exchange rates of the Reichsmark as compared with those of the national currencies concerned. These rates established an overevaluation of the Reichsmark by more than 50 percent in France and Belgium. Thus, the goods produced in these countries could be purchased by the Germans even cheaper in terms of Reichsmark. The terms of such purchases were even more

218

improved for Germany by the price freeze which the occupation authorities had imposed in all the countries concerned. On the other hand, subsidies which were formerly paid to facilitate German exports to these countries were now abolished and the prices of the German goods which they had to purchase were thus substantially increased.

But in spite of these especially favorable terms of trade, in relation to the occupied territories, German imports from this area were always greater than exports; and the exchange clearing accounts established for the settlement of claims arising out of their foreign trade with the Reich had always considerable credit balances in favor of occupied territories. These credit balances reflected sales which these territories had effected on credit to Germany, that is, without any counterpart in goods. On the other hand, the respective central banks which managed these exchange clearing accounts had to pay their exporters by issuing additional currency covered only by their claims on Germany in exchange clearing accounts. The credit balances in exchange clearing were thus another form of spoliation which should be added to the indemnity for occupation costs.

Both these items, considered together, for the greatest occupied Western European country, France, were distributed as follows:

(in billions of francs)	1940	1941	1942	1943	1944
Occupation costs	80	130	124.5	219	133
Clearing balance	..	12	33	63	52

The total amount of the sums thus taken out of the French economy by the Germans amounted to 847 billion francs. That means—even at the overvalued rate of exchange established by the Nazis—more than 42 billion Reichsmarks, or nearly 10 percent of the total German war expenditure during the period 1939-45, and more than half of the total French public expenditure during the period September, 1939-September, 1944, which amounted to 1650 billion francs. The total resources obtained by Germany from the occupied territories of Western Europe amounted to 82,394 million Reichsmarks, out of which 53,700 million had been provided by occupation-costs indemnity and 26,694 million through exchange-clearing balances.

All the resources of the economy of the occupied territories were forced completely into the service of the German war machine.

Agriculture was submitted to a system of compulsory deliveries, on the German model, with very strict sanctions for disobedience. In most occupied territories, the rations of the local population were considerably smaller than in Germany, and the surplus was reserved for German requirements. Thus, it was estimated that in France nearly 30 percent of total agricultural production was consumed by the Germans, either through direct exports to the Reich or by the German occupation troops.

As to industry, the heavy industries had been incorporated in the German war production. In 1941, 80 percent of heavy industries in occupied France—where the greatest part of the industrial capacity of the country was concentrated—was working on German war orders, as well as 50 percent of industry in the non-occupied zone. Some of these industries were also occupied in filling, for German concerns, export orders which they had received, especially from Russia and Spain, and were unable to implement themselves, owing to concentration on war production. The production of consumers-goods industries was maintained as long as raw materials were available, most of their production being exported to Germany. When the raw materials such as cotton and wool became exhausted, the Germans tried to reduce the productive capacity of these industries in order to limit their future competition with German industry. A considerable number of factories not working on German orders had been dismantled and their equipment sent to Germany.

The Nazis also made a steadily increasing effort to induce the workers of the occupied countries to follow their dismantled machines to the Reich and work there. All means were used to achieve this aim: material inducements, promises, and official pres-

220

sure, including such direct blackmail as confiscation of ration cards of workers refusing to leave for Germany, thus condemning them to starvation. Even these measures, however, which were still considered "voluntary recruitment," did not provide a sufficient number of workers. Therefore, in 1942, when the German manpower crisis became more acute, Saukel, *Reichskommissar* for Foreign Labor, took a radical step. In all occupied countries, by direct orders of the German military authorities or through local authorities, such as the Vichy government, he introduced a forced-labor service in Germany for all workers not employed in factories executing German orders or classified as essential by the occupation authorities.

Thus, millions of foreign slave workers were deported to Germany, where their standards of food, housing and wages were considerably inferior to those of German workers. This distinction corresponded to that between the hierarchy of "the master nation" (*Herrenvolk*) and other more or less subhuman-standard races (*Unter Menschen*), a distinction which the Nazis intended to establish as the permanent basis of the European "New Order."

As a result of exhaustion of raw materials and deportation of workers, industrial production in occupied territories steadily declined. The average yearly index of industrial production in France (1938 = 100) amounted to 60 in 1941; 58 in 1942; 55 in the first 9 months of 1943; and only 50 in September 1943, the last month of this period for which data are available. Production of vital raw materials, such as coal and steel, was better maintained; but consumers-goods production gradually came completely to a standstill.

The occupied territories were incorporated into the organization of the German-dominated Europe. Their relationship to the Reich was that of colonies exploited by the dominating country for her own exclusive benefit.

The economy of the occupied countries was organized on the German pattern. The corporative system was introduced, e.g., in French industry (*Comités d'organisation*) and agriculture (*corpo-*

221

ration paysanne). As to production, the tendency of the Germans was to limit the occupied territories to agriculture, to production of raw materials for German industry, and to a few specialties. They were inclined to restrict, or even to close down completely, industries competing with Germany, with the one exception—possibly intended to be only temporary—of concerns working on German orders. The Germans thus approved of the attempt of Pétain to return French industry to a handicraft system of organization, which would have reduced its productive capacity, efficiency and competitive power.

On the other hand, the Germans systematically gained control of the major business undertakings of the occupied territories, by using for purchase of important shareholdings part of the sums in local currency received as occupation-costs indemnity. In this way, in France, Belgium and other countries of Western Europe, they achieved control of the greatest companies in the fields of coal mining, production of steel and chemicals, banking, shipping, etc. Sometimes by means of mandatory sales, the Germans also bought up valuable foreign assets of occupied countries, such as the French-owned Bor copper mines in Yugoslavia and oil-mining companies in Rumania. Through these purchases they gained an inside control of key factors of the economy of the countries concerned.

The Germans also controlled the monetary policy of all these countries; German *kommissars* were attached to all the various central banks. The gold reserves of these central banks had been transferred to the Reichsbank and replaced with credit balances in Reichsmarks. The Nazis thus achieved possession' of important quantities of gold which hitherto they had pretended to consider useless. They seized 10 billion francs of gold in Belgium; most fortunately the gold reserves of the Banque de France had been evacuated out of reach of the German occupation armies.

Since Germany politically and economically dominated the continent occupied by her armies, Berlin became the center of European banking and insurance, as well as the center of trade between the different countries of Europe. Inter-European trade transactions were settled by means of an exchange clearing in terms of Reichsmarks, which became the basic European currency. This implied the necessity that all countries participating in these transactions maintain large Reichsmark balances and thus extend additional credits to Germany.

The attitude of the population of the occupied countries toward German occupation and domination can be summarized as follows:

(1) A part of the capitalist class collaborated with the Germans. These capitalists were the bourgeoisie of Western European countries; outstanding examples were Van Vlissingen, President of the International Chamber of Commerce in the Netherlands, and Louis Renault, the French automobile manufacturer. This collaboration was partly due to material incentives. The trade with the Germans, especially the filling of their war orders, was extremely profitable. But to an even greater extent psychological and political factors were important—especially the fear of Communism. Hitler was considered by this capitalist group as the only possible savior from the danger of Bolshevism, even when he was on apparently the best of terms with Stalin. Another sentiment which explains the pro-Nazi attitude of some French capitalists was the desire of revenge for the humiliation to which they had been subjected by the Popular Front, and the craving to prevent the danger of its repetition by crushing the power of organized labor. This direct treason by a part of the ruling capitalist class powerful in influence, even if small in numbers, rendered politically and psychologically impossible, particularly in France, a return to a completely capitalist order.

(2) Against the oppression by the Nazi occupants there arose, and steadily increased, the active resistance of (a) the majority of the working class, who had been especially victimized by the drive for slave-labor, deportation to Germany and the loss of their rights of organization; and (b) all other elements of the various nations which had ideals transcending purely material interest.

These ideals were religious, social or national. Thus, the great mass of the resistance movements, especially in France and Belgium, were composed of Catholics, Socialists, and, after June 22, 1941, Communists, as well as of patriots of all categories, including, for example, Army officers, intellectuals and peasants.

From 1940 to 1944, the Nazi dream of dominating Europe appeared realized. Entirely exclusive of the occupied parts of Russia, German domination during most of this period extended to nearly all the Continent with a total population of over 270 million, of which about 200 million were non-Germans, who had become enslaved colonial populations working for the benefit of "the Master Race." This German Europe had an enormous industrial productive capacity, only slightly inferior as a whole to that of the United States before its war expansion, and, for some key products, even superior. The productive capacity of steel was 45 million tons, about equal to that of the United States. Self-sufficiency of the Continent in food was nearly complete, even though at very low consumption levels for the non-German population, and requirements for imported raw materials were restricted, owing to expansion in the production of synthetic substitute materials. Nazi Germany, after the achievement of her continental conquests in 1940 and 1941, should have been completely invincible, owing to this gigantic economic potential; a much earlier start on all war production; a favorable strategic position, with transport on interior lines of communication; and last, but not least, the excellent fighting qualities and the vast source of German military manpower.

Her final defeat appears to have been due not alone to the effective superiority of American industrial production and technique and of Russian numbers on the Eastern Front. It seems to have been attributable to a great extent to the fact that, unlike the case in the Western democracies and also in the Soviet Union, where all human and material resources had been fully mobilized, the resources of German-dominated Europe had been mobilized only very imperfectly in quantity, and especially in quality. This was largely because production was impeded by sabotage and "go slow" tactics applied by foreign slave workers in Germany, and by labor and sometimes also management in occupied territories. The burden of guarding the occupied countries, too, considerably weakened German military forces available for battle. The approximately two million German soldiers kept on occupation duty in all parts of Europe were bitterly missed by the German command at Stalingrad and in other decisive battles. Thus, in the final test, the superiority of free effort over imposed domination and slave labor asserted itself.

19 THE BRITISH ECONOMIC WAR EFFORT: BRITAIN "TAKES IT"

SHORTLY BEFORE THE BEGINNING of World War II, in 1939, the great English writer, Aldous Huxley, a pacifist, had stated that, even though it might be necessary for the democracies to fight Fascism, there was a considerable risk that in doing so they would have to adopt the very methods and techniques of Fascism. Thus, he claimed, the democracies would become Fascist, if not from the standpoint of its ends, at least from the standpoint of its means, or its practical application.

The comparison of the experience of Germany and Great Britain during World War II seems to prove that Aldous Huxley's theory, in spite of its apparent plausibility, was completely wrong. Even though in the two countries there was a certain similarity of methods resulting from the necessity of solving similar practical problems, there was no deeper similarity as to substance: social and political structure and aims. Great Britain fought a life and death struggle against the most inhuman of all totalitarian dictatorships, and adopted in her war economy several concrete measures somewhat similar to those inspired by Dr. Schacht. Nevertheless, she still not only kept alive both the body and the soul of her democracy, but also succeeded in perfecting and enlarging that democracy. She thus achieved during the war a bloodless social revolution typical of the incomparable standard of civism of her citizens, a social transformation which continued even after the war, and which still has not come to an end.

226

Quite contrary to the case in Nazi Germany, Great Britain had entered the war in 1939 without having a war economy already functioning, and even without a blueprint for war economy ready to be implemented at a moment's notice. Such a plan existed even in France, with the *loi d'organisation de la nation en temps de guerre,* introduced in 1938. In Great Britain, all the organization of the war economy, and especially the controls of labor, imports and production, had to be introduced gradually after war had already begun. As a general rule, these controls started on a voluntary basis. Compulsion was introduced later, in order that those who had not cooperated in this patriotic behavior might not have any advantage over those who voluntarily cooperated.

The first Emergency Power Act, August 24, 1939, authorized the government to establish the rules of organization of the war economy; another similar Act, May 22, 1940, enlarged these powers. The control of labor was entrusted to the National Labor Supply Board, in which representatives of employers and labor worked together under the direction of the Ministry of Labor. At first, there was not even any freezing of wage rates; only after July 1940 was there compulsory arbitration in case of labor conflicts. A National Registration Act, September 5, 1939, made registration mandatory for all workers. The first measure really restrictive of the freedom of workers, however, was introduced only in 1940; it prohibited diversion of miners and farm workers to other occupations. In January 1941, a registration order had been issued for workers of war industries; dismissal or resignations of workers had to be authorized and the employment of all workers had to be effected through the medium of labor exchanges. In March 1941, a new registration of all workers, male and female, was instituted, in order to obtain all able-bodied young male workers for the armed services and to replace them with women.

Finally, the Essential Works Order reiterated the prohibition of resignations and dismissals from jobs, and guaranteed minimum weekly wages in all essential industries such as coal mining, steel, shipbuilding, etc. During the war, dilution of nonskilled

227

workers in skilled professions was used on a large scale. The procedure was at first strongly resisted by the trade unions and prohibited by their rules, which had the purpose of limiting the number and maintaining the wage rates of skilled workers. The unions finally abandoned their resistance, however, and strikes were prohibited.

The distribution of employed labor had changed in Great Britain compared to pre-war as follows:

(in millions of persons)	Middle, 1939			Middle, 1944		
	male	female	total	male	female	total
Armed forces	0.6	..	0.6	4.7	0.5	5.2
Professional activities:						
No. 1 (war industries proper)	2.6	0.5	3.1	3.2	1.9	5.1
No. 2 (agriculture, mining, transport, public utilities, food processing, etc.)	4.7	0.8	5.5	4.1	1.6	5.7
No. 3 (Building and consumer goods)	5.8	3.5	9.3	2.9	3.1	6.0
Total professional activities	13.7	4.8	18.5	10.2	6.6	16.8
Unemployed	1.0	0.3	1.3	0.07	0.03	0.1
Total population of working age	14.7	5.1	19.8	14.97	7.13	22.1

By the middle of 1944, of 7.6 million workers occupied in manufacturing industries, about 76 percent was working on government orders, which corresponded almost exactly with war production; 4 percent on export orders; and 20 percent in the consumers-goods industries providing the domestic market. In 1939, about 15 percent of the total number of workers in manufacturing industries had been working on production for export orders,

228

which was thus drastically cut (see above—4 percent), as was also production for domestic consumption. Thus, Great Britain was able to concentrate the maximum of its manpower on war production.

The control of industrial production had been implemented at first only in an indirect manner—through control of distribution of imported raw materials. First priority was being given to war production, and next to production for export; production for the home market was last. At a later stage, control and direction of manpower also resulted in an indirect control of industrial production. Finally, all raw materials, domestic as well as imported, were distributed on the basis of supply orders granted by the government authorities under the existing priorities. Building was also rigidly controlled and restricted, permits being issued only for projects essential for war production.

In March 1941, the government took the initiative in concentrating consumers-goods production in the most efficient plants, in order to reduce to a minimum the manpower required for production of indispensable consumer goods. This concentration was effected under the supervision of the Board of Trade in cooperation with representatives of workers and employers. It resulted in the closing down of a great number of plants, the owners of which had been indemnified and the equipment preserved for post-war resumption of production. For the time being, their orders were transferred to a relatively small number of best-equipped plants in each industry, which could thus start full-speed production with maximum savings of labor and cost. The total number of workers which this concentration policy liberated from consumer-goods production and transferred to war industry was about 500,000. In spite of all this, the government resisted the trend toward monopoly by big-scale producers and tried to protect small producers whenever they were efficient, by granting them raw-material import permits sufficient to enable them to maintain, or even to develop, their production.

In January 1942, the control and direction of all war production, imports, and distribution of raw materials and equipment had been centralized in the Ministry of War Production, established for this purpose.

In Great Britain, control of prices did not exist at the beginning of the war, in 1939, and even then it was not introduced at once. There thus occurred a considerable rise in prices, especially of imported goods, mainly because of increased freight and insurance rates. This price increase, at first very rapid, gradually slowed down and then even completely stopped, largely owing to measures taken by the British government, as well as to stabilization of import prices through Lend Lease.

During the first part of the war, prices, cost of living, and wage rates in Great Britain fluctuated as follows:

	June 1939 to June 1940	June 1940 to June 1941	June 1941 to June 1942
Wholesale prices	+36.7%	+13.4%	+4.8%
Cost of living	+18.3%	+10.5%	−0.5%
Weekly wages	+10.4%	+ 9.4%	+7.0%

After that, the upward trend of prices was practically stopped. Thus wholesale prices rose by 1 percent during 1943, but declined by 2 percent during 1944.

The government made a considerable effort to stabilize the cost of living and to keep it at about from 125 to 130 percent of the pre-war level. The aims of this stabilization policy were to maintain the purchasing power of the working class population for the basic necessities of life, as also to effect an indirect stabilization of wages, since, in the absence of an outright wage freeze, the level of wage rates had to be based on the cost-of-living index. In order to achieve this purpose, the government paid substantial subsidies. These had the effect of reducing the retail prices, and thus the cost to consumers, of main food products (bread, milk, bacon, meat, etc.), the weights of which were especially important in the cost-of-living index. The total cost of these subsidies steadily increased.

230

Thus, they amounted (in millions of pounds) to: 20 in 1939; 70 in 1940; 140 in 1941; 175 in 1942; 190 in 1943; and 220 in 1944. In 1941 their cost already amounted to 10 percent of all expenditures on food made during the year by the British consumers.

The financial effort made by Great Britain to pay for war expenditures had been extremely large. Even more than during World War I, the government strove to meet out of tax revenue a considerable share of total war expenditures; and the effort was successful.

Distribution of national income during the war was as follows:

(*in millions of pounds* of current purchasing power)

	1938	1941	1942	1943	1944
War expenditures	358	3700	4062	4674	4678
Other public expenditures	456	517	535	538	543
Consumers' expenditures	4153	4633	4909	4987	5216
Domestic capital investment	785	394	397	352	287
Decrease in foreign investment	—70	—795	—666	—684	—655
Gross national income	5682	8449	9237	9867	10069

If this distribution of gross national income is considered in constant 1938 prices, the results are as follows:

(*in millions of pounds*)

	1938	1941	1942	1943	1944
War expenditures	358	2960	3130	3440	3400
Other public expenditures	456	413	410	398	396
Consumers' expenditures	4153	3364	3222	3239	3322

231

	1938	1941	1942	1943	1944
Domestic capital investment	785	300	289	250	198
Decrease in foreign investment	—70	—608	—483	—486	—454
Gross national income	5682	6429	6568	6841	6862

Comparing war expenditures in 1938 and in 1944, we find that the increase measured in constant prices was financed as follows:

Increase in production	£1180 million	(1938 value),	or 39%
Reduction in consumers' expenditures	£ 831 "	(" "),	or 27%
Reduction in domestic investment	£ 587 "	(" "),	or 19%
Reduction in other expenditures	£ 60 "	(" "),	or 2%
Increase in liquidation of foreign assets	£ 384 "	(" "),	or 13%

War expenditures analyzed in the preceding tables did not include the substantial part paid for by American Lend Lease nor mutual aid received from Canada and other Dominions. Expenditures paid for by Great Britain alone absorbed about half of the gross national product (not including liquidation of foreign capital holdings), which was a proportion only slightly lower than that existing in Germany. Reduction in consumers' expenditures, however, was much less drastic in Great Britain than in the Nazi war economy.

The mobilization by Great Britain of all her financial resources, in order to cover by tax revenue the greatest possible share of military expenditures, implied an enormous increase in taxation, the greatest emphasis being placed on raising the level of direct taxes. Thus, the straight rate of income tax was increased from 5 shillings to 10 shillings in the pound, and a supertax on large incomes was added to it.

The situation of the British budgets during the war (tax receipts and expenditures and public debt) was as follows:

(in millions of pounds of current purchasing power)

	Total expenditures	War expenditures	Tax revenue	Increase in domestic debt
1938-39	1147	400	1006	142
1939-40	1904	1141	1132	782
1940-41	3971	3220	1495	2467
1941-42	4888	4085	2175	2566
1942-43	5740	4840	2992	2627
1943-44	5914	4950	3149	2745
1944-45	6190	5125	3355	2830

During the whole war period, 1939-45, the average part of war expenditures financed out of taxes amounted to 48 percent; and in 1945 it rose to 53 percent, a proportion even considerably higher than the part of taxation for the same period in the war budget of the United States, a country with incomparably higher resources and productive capacity.

The increase in the national debt was effected mainly in the form of debt certificates or bonds purchased by the banks, and to a much smaller extent through the sale of bonds to private investors. There was, however, though on a small scale, a system of forced savings somewhat similar to the one existing in Germany. It was effected by means of the so-called tax certificates, a special income-tax rate increase, which was to be reimbursed at the end of the war.

The income-tax receipts enormously increased, owing to the rise in the rates and the expansion of national income. Thus, total income-tax receipts, which had amounted to £398 million in 1938-39, reached in 1944-45 £1390 million, to which latter amount should be added £500 million of receipts from supertax. On incomes of £10,000 the tax rate was 73.7 percent; on incomes of £20,000, 84.4 per cent.

Hence, in Great Britain—where tax evasion is practically non-existent as compared with the situation prevailing in most countries of the European Continent, the cost of the war was paid to a great extent by the rich. At the same time, the cost of living for the low-income groups was being reduced by subsidies. This arrangement created confidence in the existence of social justice, and meant an equitable sharing of sacrifices. Owing to the combined influence of high-income taxes and price subsidies, there occurred during the war a considerable shift in the distribution of national income favoring the wage earners. The share of this category in the total national income increased from 41 percent to 45 percent.

During the war, food consumption in Great Britain stayed on a high level, in spite of a considerable decline in the volume of imports, which amounted only to 11,525,000 tons in 1943, instead of an average of 22,026,000 for the years 1934-38. However, while the general volume of food imports declined, imports of products such as meat and fats increased. The intake in calories per person of the British population is difficult to estimate, as the rationing system did not extend to all products and was, above all, very flexible. Not every consumer received fixed rations of all rationed foodstuffs. Instead each received a certain number of points, which could be used for the purchase of different kinds of products, each of them having a different rating in points. But it can be reasonably assumed that the average daily intake in Great Britain was about 3000 calories, or even slightly higher. These rations were very satisfactory not only quantitatively, being considerably higher than rations in all other belligerent or occupied countries of Europe, but even more qualitatively, as they included considerable quantities of proteins and vitamins.

Besides, protective foodstuffs—especially milk—were distributed to children and pregnant women at nominal prices, or sometimes even completely free. School lunches, and factory lunches for working adolescents, were also organized and dispensed at a very low price, owing to subsidies.

Because of this very rational nutrition policy, aimed at the best utilization of resources and at the protection of the health and productive capacity of the nation, consumption of several important foodstuffs even increased during the war. The trend of consumption for main foodstuffs was as follows (in percentage of increase or decrease): milk +28; potatoes +45; vegetables +34; cereals, mainly bread +19. On the contrary, consumption of meat had decreased by 21 percent; fats, by 16 percent; sugar, by 31 percent, etc.

From the point of view of health, the British food rations were entirely sufficient in all nutritive elements, having been prepared in consultation with dietitian experts. The only legitimate criticism which they might have deserved, and still deserve, was their monotony. But to remedy this was not in the power of the British authorities, limited as they were in the volume of their imports, at first by the shipping shortage during the war, and later on by balance-of-payments difficulties.

As the prices of the rationed foodstuffs were extremely low, mainly because of the subsidies, they could be purchased easily by all classes of the population. Many formerly unemployed workers and their dependents (over one million families) who previously had lived on below bare subsistence levels, were now working full time or even overtime in war production and earning fair wages. Such employment, combined with the low-cost rations, resulted in an appreciable improvement in food standards and, as a consequence, also in standards of health. In Great Britain, during the war, there was actually considerable decline in civilian mortality, something unheard of in time of war, and this resulted naturally in a substantial stimulating influence on the morale, the self-assurance and the confidence of the whole nation.

The total consumption of food in Great Britain as a whole, during the war, actually remained at about the pre-war level. However, on account of reduction in higher priced products—such as meat, exotic fruit, etc.—total value of food consumption in constant prices slightly declined. The greatest part of the decline by 27 percent in consumers' expenditures in 1944, as compared to pre-war, was due however not to food but to manufactured consumers' goods, such as clothing, furniture, household goods, automobiles, etc. The production of these products had been drastically curtailed—sometimes entirely stopped.

The maintenance of overall food consumption, while food imports had to be nearly halved, became possible only because of a tremendous expansion of domestic agricultural production. In caloric value and also in proteins, this increase amounted to about 70 percent as compared to pre-war. In 1943, when the effort of expansion had already produced its main effects, the increase in production, compared to the average of the years 1936-38, in percentages for the main crops was as follows: wheat 109, barley 115, potatoes 102, sugar beets 37, vegetables 34, fruit 55, and oats 58. The increase in crop production had been mainly obtained through ploughing in of former grassland, which expanded total acreage planted by about two-thirds. This development had been stimulated by the payment of a subsidy of £2 per acre for ploughing grassland.

The increase in acreage for some of the main crops was as follows:

	(in thousands of acres)	
	1939	1944
Wheat	1760	3230
Barley and oats	3440	5664
Sugar beets	345	434
Potatoes	704	1421

To this increase should also be added an enormous expansion in the acreage of family vegetable gardens.

Besides expansion in acreage, British agriculture underwent also a considerable technical development, aimed at increase in productivity and reduction of manpower requirements. Mechaniza-

236

tion, in particular, made substantial progress. Thus the number of tractors used on British farms rose to 150,000 in 1944 as compared to only 55,000 in 1939. This development of agricultural production was facilitated and stimulated by the attitude of the government. The policy of marketing agreements—already established before the war and even more extended later on—guaranteed to the farmers stable and remunerative prices; simultaneously, subsidies reduced the prices paid by consumers. The efforts of the government to direct labor to agriculture were stimulated by the revalorization of wages of farm labor.

Industrial production also underwent a marked development. Satisfactory food standards made possible the maintenance of a high productivity, which was also much stimulated by such morale factors as an appeal to patriotism. For example, after the disaster of Dunkerque, the stimulant given to patriotism by this national catastrophe resulted in an intensification of effort which largely increased productivity and output. In brief, in all basic industries production during the war was well maintained or even increased. The only exception was coal mining, where already for some time the labor force had been declining. Because of the constant depression from which the industry had suffered since the end of World War I, and the heavy unemployment resulting therefrom, young workers had been insufficient in number to replace those who retired.

In June 1940, when occupation of the Continent by the German troops had wiped out the main export markets for British coal, the government had mobilized part of the younger miners for military service. As a result, coal production considerably declined and, even though coal exports remained suspended during the war, as war production was being gradually stepped up coal requirements increased and supplies of solid fuel for industry began to be short. In order to remedy this shortage, the government exempted the miners from military service, and later on even gave to men drafted into the armed forces an option of going instead

237

into the mines (the so-called "Bevin boys"). In spite of these measures, coal production failed to increase to any significant extent, owing mainly to out of date and insufficient equipment and methods, as well as to the aging of the labor force. Very strict measures of rationing coal consumption therefore had to be applied, with the usual scale of priorities. Domestic consumption and consumers-goods industries received consideration only after satisfaction of all requirements of the war industries.

Development of production in the main basic industries during the war was as follows:

(in thousands of tons)

	1935-38 average	1939	1943
Iron ore	12,417	14,487	18,487
Pig iron	7,350	7,980	7,187 *
Raw steel	11,256	13,221	13,031
Aluminum	18	25	56
Newsprint	857	294	129 †
Cotton yarn	503	487	312 †
Coal	231,000	235,000	202,100

* Decline of pig-iron production was due mainly to the suspension of imports of rich Swedish iron ore.

† Reduction in production, as well as in exports, of consumer goods, such as cotton yarn, was the result of a deliberate policy. Thus, exports of cotton goods had been stopped since 1943. As to newsprint, the heavy fall in its production was also due to the suspension of pre-war imports of lumber and pulp from Scandinavian countries.

All consumer-goods production, even of articles which were most essential necessities, was drastically curtailed. Production of shoes had declined in 1943 to 90 million pairs as compared to 161 million in 1938. Production of all consumer goods not considered vital necessities—such as automobiles, radios, domestic appliances, etc.—was completely stopped.

In contrast, development of war production proper was extensive. For the main items it was as follows:

	1940	1941	1942	1943	1944 (first 6 months)
Aircraft (total numbers)	15,041	20,093	23,671	26,263	14,609
Out of which, heavy bombers	41	498	1,976	4,614	2,889
Aircraft in weight (million lbs.)	58.84	87.26	133.36	185.23	111.75
Aircraft engines (million h.p.)	17.40	31.42	59.45	72.80	41.92
Bombload (in thousand tons)	48.3	143.4	240.09	308.6	227.8
Tanks, total number	1,397	4,844	8,611	7,474	2,474
Warships (in thousand tons)	257	435	423	497	267
Merchant ships (in thousand tons)	816	1,158	1,302	1,204	...

Until 1943, production of all war material was being constantly expanded. In the latter part of the war, however, production was more selectively directed, with the main emphasis on aviation and on equipment required for invasion operations, whereas production of other material was gradually slowed down, as requirements had been already largely met.

Notwithstanding the tremendous rise in war production, the resources of the United Kingdom alone would have been insufficient to provide and pay for all the raw materials and foodstuffs needed to feed its population and industries, as well as to provide all the weapons required by its armed forces. Therefore a considerable contribution to British military effort had to be made by other countries. In this respect, the situation of Great Britain was somewhat similar to that of Germany during the same period. There was even a curious similarity between the proportions of these foreign contributions made to both countries: about 10 percent of their respective national incomes during the war period, and 15-20 percent of total war expenditures. However, the methods by which these foreign contributions became available to Germany and Great Britain, respectively, naturally were absolutely

239

different. The Reich obtained them through direct looting, or by ruthless spoliation by means of occupation-costs indemnity and forced credits on exchange clearing accounts. Great Britain had to pay for them, at least during the first part of the war, by liquidation of her foreign holdings or increase in her foreign indebtedness. Only after the beginning of 1941 was the greatest part of this contribution provided on a nonpaying basis through American Lend Lease, as well as through mutual aid from Canada, other Dominions and Allied countries. But even during this latter period, new debts had to be assumed, in particular in the Eastern countries.

A present comparison of the consequences of these different policies of Germany and Great Britain does not, from the point of view of purely material interest, agree with the proverb that honesty is the best policy. Thus, Germany is today completely bankrupt and any restitution of the enormous resources which it looted from the territories it occupied during the war is an outright impossibility—with the exception of isolated restitutions and small-scale reparations—unless methods similar to those used by the Nazis in their spoliations are applied. That is a procedure which the Russians alone appear to be following in their zone. As to Great Britain, she had to liquidate the greatest part of her foreign investments, which previously had been the main factor enabling her to achieve equilibrium of her balance of payments. In addition, she incurred a heavy foreign debt, sometimes for objectives which were not even for her own benefit.

Thus, Great Britain had incurred a considerable debt in sterling in Egypt, corresponding to the expenditure in that country, by the British armed forces, which had protected it from invasion and war devastation, while Egypt herself did not make any significant contribution to the defense of her own territory. The situation was similar, and even more unjust and more to Great Britain's disadvantage, in India, where the new British debt was incurred by paying the costs not only of British troops defending

240

that country, but of the Indian Army itself. The major part of its upkeep was paid for by United Kingdom Treasury. This generous policy was to create substantial hardships for the British economy in the post-war period.

The disinvestment corresponding to the amount of liquidation of foreign assets, added to the new debt incurred abroad, proceeded in the beginning of the war mainly in the so-called dollar countries (essentially the United States and Canada), which were the main sources of supply for equipment and raw materials. Hence, the total resources of the United Kingdom in gold and dollar securities declined from $4,483 million on August 31, 1939 to $2,167 million on December 31, 1940. It decreased still more in the following months. Only the passage of the Lend Lease Act by the United States Congress, in March 1941, prevented the complete stoppage of British purchases on the American market as a result of exhaustion of resources. In the latter part of the war, the disinvestment was mainly concentrated in the sterling area (Middle East, India, Australia, etc.). This was due partly to the fact that war expenditures in these areas were not paid for by Allied mutual aid to the same extent as in the West; it was due also to the increase in British military effort in these regions after the beginning of the war against Japan.

The total amount received by the United Kingdom as Lend Lease and mutual aid was $13,499 million; the value of reverse Lend Lease and mutual aid rendered by Great Britain to her Allies amounted to $3,796 million; the net amount of assistance received for the pursuit of the war was thus $9,703 million.

The total disinvestment of foreign assets was as follows:

(in million pounds sterling)

	Liquidation of assets	Increase in debt	Total
September 1939-December 1941	955	765	1720
January 1942-June 1944	110	1535	1645
	1065	2300	3365

241

Until the end of the war the total disinvestment of foreign resources of Great Britain had exceeded 4 billion pounds. With the addition to this amount of the value of the assistance received under Lend Lease and mutual aid (about 2.4 billion pounds), the total amount of the contribution of foreign resources to the British war effort was about 6.5 billion pounds.

Great Britain had come out of the war victorious, mainly as a consequence of an extremely intensive effort of the whole nation. This effort was manifested: on the battlefronts on land, on sea and in the air; through the stoic endurance by the people of the physical and nervous strain caused mainly by the Blitz; through the effort of production in industry and agriculture; through a courageous and drastic effort of taxation, rationing, controls, as well as in other ways. That national effort of Great Britain was reinforced to a great extent by the assistance received from her Allies. However, even though victorious, Great Britain ended the war completely impoverished—in fact, ruined in so far as her relations with the rest of the world were concerned. She had lost her traditional position in world economy as the classical creditor country, and had become a debtor country.

Equally important, however, as the change in Great Britain's economic position in the world, was the transformation of her social structure achieved during the war. This social transformation, which provides possibly the main reason for the intensity and the unanimity of the British nation in her war effort, was the establishment of equality of classes for the first time in the history of democracy in Great Britain. Until then, while French democracy had always put the stress on equality, in Great Britain the most valuable feature of democracy appeared to be liberty, the maximum of freedom for the individual. In contrast, inequality resulting from differences in the level of income, social origins and environment, education, etc., had been, and on the eve of war still was, an essential feature of British life.

During the war, however, actual equality had been introduced with respect to consumption of all basic necessities. This was made possible (1) through an extremely rigorous taxation system, which, mainly because of the admirable civic sense of the British people, was not disrupted by fraud; and (2) through an extremely just and effective rationing system, with scarcely any interference by the black market. The necessary level of consumption of basic food products and consumer goods corresponding to the rations was guaranteed to everybody, even to the lowest-income groups, owing to full employment and to the low cost of the rationed goods due to subsidies.

On the other hand, income of the higher-income groups was drastically reduced by increased income tax and supertax, and the remaining difference in income did not provide any significant privileges. In fact, the consumption of these groups in essential goods was limited to the same level as that of the rest of the population, by rationing. To some extent, these formerly privileged classes got even lower rations than the average, as higher rations were reserved for workers, such as miners in heavy manual jobs of special importance to the war effort. As to nonessential goods, which the higher-income groups would normally have been able to purchase, they were not available, since their production had been stopped.

In the masses of the British population, this equality in consumption stimulated a tremendous exaltation of pride and patriotic feeling. These emotions strengthened their will to win the war, and to make all necessary sacrifices for that purpose—the more so because they knew those sacrifices to be equitably shared, as war profiteering was also practically nonexistent. The new social equality thus was one of the main reasons for the admirable attitude of the British people even during the darkest periods of the war.

The social achievement of the war period (the guarantee for all of a minimum consumption level, achieved through full employment) provided the British with their main objectives for the post-war period. These objectives can be summarized in the titles of the two plans which were prepared during the war period by

Sir William Beveridge, and which achieved a tremendous popularity, proving their appeal to the people: social security and full employment in a free society. They consist in achieving, through expansion of peacetime production for creative purposes, the results obtained during the war by production for the most destructive and uneconomic of all forms of consumption—war. The conservative governments had been in power during nearly the whole period between the two world wars, and had failed in particular to solve the unemployment problem. The British people remembered this well. Therefore, as soon as the war came to an end, they put into power a Labor government in order to achieve their new social objectives.

20 THE SOVIET ECONOMY DURING WORLD WAR II

FOR RUSSIA, the result of World War II—the success of the Soviet armies in first stemming the onslaught of the Nazi troops and then driving them back—provided a complete vindication of the policy of the Five-Year Plans.

Industrialization, and particularly development of heavy industry, enabled Soviet Russia to produce, herself, the bulk of armaments she required. Therefore she was not dependent on assistance from the West to the same extent as was Tzarist Russia during World War I. Development of new industrial areas, as well as evacuation of industrial equipment to the East, made possible the maintenance of an industrial production sufficient to cover most essential war requirements. This, in spite of the occupation by the Germans of the greatest part of the former principal industrial regions. In fact, they went much farther east than at their maximum point of penetration in 1918. Finally industrialization—as well as mechanization of agriculture—which were made possible by collectivization, created a numerous class of young workers and peasants accustomed to handling mechanized equipment, especially trucks and tractors, absolutely essential for the establishment of a modern motorized army.

The readiness of the Russian soldiers to fight and to die for the Soviet system was obviously also a major factor in the victory. Any hesitancy that at first existed on that score was fast dispelled

245

as soon as the Russian people observed the Nazi policy of oppression and extermination. Realization of the truth very rapidly put an end to initial mass Russian surrenders and stiffened resistance.

It should be pointed out that, conscious of the mortal danger from a war with Germany, the Soviet authorities did everything in their power to placate the Nazis. In particular, they provided them with very substantial economic assistance. Thus during the first 4 months of 1941, Soviet deliveries of food and raw materials amounted to over 600,000 tons of grain; 230,000 tons of oil; and considerable quantities of cotton, manganese ore, etc. According to a statement of the German Ambassador in Moscow, the Soviet authorities expressed their readiness to deliver in 1941 up to 5 million tons of grain to Germany. However, at the same time that they were providing this assistance to the Nazis, in the hope of preventing or postponing their aggression, they were accumulating very large reserves of food and raw materials, as well as of armaments. These later proved extremely useful, when German invasion had drastically cut Soviet production.

At its maximum, in the summer of 1942, the German occupation extended to territories containing a vitally important part of the industrial, agricultural and population resources of the Soviet Union. Thus, the German hope that the Soviet capacity to wage war was nearly exhausted appeared justified. In the German-occupied territories, even after liberation, production could not be resumed to any significant extent before the end of the war. Those territories had a pre-war population of 88 million, nearly half of the total population of the country; their share in production of iron ore was 63 percent; of coal 60 percent; of steel 57 percent; and of agricultural production, 40 percent of total land sown to crops, but a much larger percentage of industrial crops, such as sugar beets, flax, etc.

As soon as the war started and the German offensive began, the Soviet authorities began to evacuate and transfer, from the Western territories in danger of invasion, to the east, equipment and key personnel of industrial undertakings and tractor stations, as well as rolling stock. They destroyed all equipment which could not be moved. More than 1,000,000 carloads were moved to the east during the summer and fall of 1941; and 1300 industrial undertakings that were transferred to behind the Volga and the Ural Mountains were put back to work in a few months. An enormous effort was also made to increase production for military purposes in the eastern areas. To that end, consumers-goods output was cut to the bone, and the resources of industrial manpower, equipment, fuel and raw materials were concentrated on the expansion of industrial capacity of heavy industry. The degree of such expansion was really extraordinary. Thus, during the 4 war years, industrial output increased in the Ural region 3.6 times; in Siberia, 2.8 times; and in the Volga area, 3.4 times. As a result of this development, in 1945, a year when production in the liberated Western territories was probably only about one-third of pre-war output, total value of industrial output was only 8 percent below that of 1940; it was estimated that production of heavy industry was 14 percent above pre-war, while production of consumer goods was only slightly more than half of the pre-war level.

Thus, production of several major industrial items in 1940 and 1945 was as follows (data for 1945 estimated by Harry Schwartz): *

	1940	1945	1945 in % of 1940
Pig iron, million metric tons	15	10	67
Steel " " "	18.3	14.5	79
Coal " " "	166	150	90
Petroleum " " "	31	20.5	66
Tractors, in thousands	31.1	7.6	24
Cotton cloth, million meters	4030	1616	40
Woolen cloth " "	124.4	57	46
Leather shoes, million pairs	230	60	26
Hosiery " "	480	83	17

* Harry Schwartz, *Russia's Post-War Economy*, University of Syracuse Press, 1947.

War production proper naturally expanded in enormous proportions; during the last 3 years of the war, Soviet industry produced an annual average of 30,000 tanks and nearly 40,000 planes, as well as 120,00 artillery pieces, 450,000 machine guns, etc.

The assistance of the Western Allies, however, was a significant factor, in increase of armaments available to Soviet armies, as also in providing the Soviet Union with food, raw materials and, particularly, equipment for expanding its industrial and agricultural production. The total amount of American Lend Lease and mutual aid received from Great Britain and Canada was $12.4 billion. It consisted not only of some 14,500 planes, 7,500 tanks and other armament items but also the following: 2 million tons of food; 475,000 motor vehicles; 11 million pairs of leather boots; 20,000 machine tools; 2,000 locomotives; power plant equipment with a total capacity of 374,000 kilowatt; over 15,000 electric motors; and over 100,000 tons of aluminum, copper and other nonferrous metals.

In agriculture, in spite of considerable effort, losses of production in the western areas could not be compensated for to the same extent as in the case of heavy industry by expansion in the east. The reason is to be found in the lack of manpower due to mobilization into the Army, and the lack of equipment the production of which had completely stopped because of conversion to armament purposes. In 1945, then, gross output of grain was only 56 percent of the 1940 harvest; sugar beets, only 43 percent; sunflower seeds (the main source of edible oil), 55 percent; and cotton, 44 percent. This drastic fall in production provides a picture of the tragic fall in consumption levels for food and most essential consumer goods to which the Soviet civilian population had to submit during the war period. This was particularly true because a priority on available supplies reserved them for consumption by the armed forces.

During the war years, strict enforcement of the collective farm system in nonoccupied territories was nearly abandoned, the main emphasis being placed on increasing production. Peasants were authorized, and even encouraged, to increase production on their individual plots, as well as the number of livestock which they kept. In many places in the occupied territories, the remaining peasants spontaneously proceeded to divide the collective farms and to return to individual farming. To some extent this was due to the fact that no fuel was available for any tractors that still remained on farms. However, the German authorities, especially in the Ukraine, very rapidly became aware that grain deliveries were much easier to enforce from collective farms than from individual peasants, and therefore in many instances imposed reestablishment of collective farms.

The losses due to war devastation in the occupied territories of the Soviet Union were estimated, by the State Commission appointed to ascertain the extent of the damage, at 679 billion rubles of 1941 purchasing power. This amount included: destruction, in whole or in part, of 6 million buildings, leaving homeless 25 million persons; destruction of 30,000 industrial undertakings employing 4 million workers; and of 65,000 kilometers of railroad track and 4100 railroad stations. Most of the agricultural buildings, livestock and equipment in the occupied territories were also lost.

To these very heavy material losses should be added the terrible loss in population: 7 million actual dead, according to Soviet official statements, most of whom were in the most productive age groups of the active population. And this does not take into account serious indirect losses resulting from increased death rate and reduced birth rate.

As a counterbalance to these losses, however, the Soviet Union at the end of the war had attained a number of advantages: It had considerably increased its territory; consolidated the gains it had obtained during the period of collaboration with Germany; added some new territories, such as East Prussia; and, above all, achieved supremacy in the greatest part of East Central Europe occupied or liberated by its armies. The Soviet Union thus not only could use the resources of these territories for the reconstruction of its economy, but also could coordinate their economic activity with its own. The result was a considerable increase in the economic resources and power of the Soviet government.

21 EUROPE AFTER LIBERATION, 1944–1945

AT THE MOMENT of liberation, the economy of all European continental countries directly affected by the war was in a state of complete paralysis and chaos. This situation was a consequence not only of material devastation, but nearly as much of dislocation of the pre-war financial and monetary equilibrium, foreign trade relations, and social structure.

The amount of actual physical destruction was on a scale beyond any comparison with that of World War I. It was comparable only to the complete havoc brought to Germany during the Thirty Years' War in the seventeenth century. The whole structure of modern industrial civilization collapsed; and economic activity practically stopped, owing to destruction of or serious damage to some of its key factors, thus giving manifest proof of its extraordinary fragility.

The most important factor in the breakdown of the economy was the disruption of the transport system, the functioning of which is similar in importance only to the blood circulation in the human organism. Railway transport was especially hard hit by the destruction of bridges—i.e., all the bridges in France from the Loire to the Seine, on the eve of the invasion of the Continent, as well as all the bridges on the Rhine and on all other important German rivers and canals—and also marshalling yards and the greatest part of the pre-war rolling stock.

251

Thus, in France, only 3000 locomotives remained in working order, of the 17,000 which had existed before the war; and 115,000 freight cars, of a total of 475,000. Belgium lost 60 percent of her locomotives and 50 percent of her freight cars. In the Netherlands, practically the whole railway system was wiped out and all the rolling stock lost. Inland water transport was just as badly disrupted by destruction, in air bombardments, of most barges and tugs, as well as by accumulation of debris of destroyed bridges in rivers and canals, making them unnavigable.

All the harbors of occupied Europe had been systematically mined and destroyed by the retreating Germans. The two most important of the very few exceptions that escaped, Antwerp and Bordeaux, owed that escape to the fact that the Germans did not have the time necessary to implement their plans of destruction. In France, more than 70 percent of the loading and landing capacity of the harbors, docks, warehouses, railway sidings, cranes, etc., had been completely destroyed. This does not at all take into account temporary obstacles that completely prevented utilization of those facilities until removed, such as the blocking of entrances by mines or by ships sunk with ballast, etc.

The merchant marine of all European countries also incurred severe losses as a consequence of the submarine warfare. France lost 70 percent of her total tonnage—2,100,000 tons out of 3 million; Belgium lost 60 percent; the Netherlands 40 percent; Norway 50 percent. The occupied countries and the Reich itself suffered from the destruction by the Germans and in Allied air raids.

The consequences of the total devastation of transport extended not only to the realm of economic life, but also to the social and political structure of the countries concerned. For example, the disruption of railway transport completely isolated the different provinces of France from one another in the fall of 1944. The result was extreme inequality in the food supply. In the food-growing provinces of the southwest, all rationing had been temporarily abolished, while in Paris and in the cities of the Medi-

252

terranean coast actual starvation had been prevented only by means of emergency supplies provided by Allied troops. Destruction of bridges on the Loire cut the supply of pit props from the Pyrenees forests for the coal mines of Northern France and thus prevented recovery of coal production. Because of the disruption of railway transport for several months after liberation, France ceased to be the highly centralized country that it had been for centuries, even before the Revolution of 1789. Instead, it became a loose federation of practically autonomous provinces, run by local resistance leaders, where orders of the central government were only imperfectly obeyed. The destruction of harbors impeded foreign trade, especially the arrival of vital overseas imports for relief and rehabilitation, thus delaying recovery.

Destruction in industry was relatively less extensive. Even in the especially bombed areas, such as the Ruhr, industrial capacity was for the most part only damaged, not completely destroyed, and needed only repairs. For the whole of Germany, destroyed or badly damaged industrial capacity amounted to 20 percent of the total. In France, extensive damage to industry, outside of the harbor areas, where everything had been destroyed, was caused mainly to the textile industry, in the north and in the Vosges, which the Germans did not care to preserve. It was of little use for their war production and a competitor of their own textile industry. Over 5,000 industrial buildings were destroyed in France.

Agriculture also suffered devastation on a large scale. In France, 132,000 farm buildings were destroyed and 270,000 damaged— more than 10 percent of the total. In the Netherlands, 219,000 hectares of arable land were flooded, 77,000 by salt water. Even after it had been pumped off, it caused deterioration of the soil fertility for several years.

Destruction of housing was one of the main results of the strategic-bombing offensive. In France, of 10 million houses, 547,000 were destroyed and 1,500,000 damaged; 709,000 families were made homeless. In the Netherlands, 92,000 dwellings were destroyed and 400,000 damaged—in all, 20 percent of the total number. In Great Britain, 4 million houses were destroyed or damaged by the Blitz and the V-1 and V-2 attacks—30 percent of the total. In Germany, nearly 10 million dwellings were destroyed or severely damaged—about 40 percent of the total.

As important as actual physical destruction was the complete exhaustion of all stocks of raw materials and semiprocessed and manufactured goods. The pipeline of production and distribution, which for many products normally supplies production for a year or more, was entirely empty. Durable consumer goods already in use by the consumers suffered deterioration. This was even more true of equipment of all kinds, since it had been used over-intensively without sufficient maintenance or replacement.

Last, but perhaps most important of all, was the fact that the human factor of production had also suffered substantially from the war. The population, especially in the countries of the Continent, was in a state of moral and physical exhaustion, a result of five years of undernourishment, suffering, strain and excessive effort.

For France, the total cost of the physical war devastation—exclusive of the losses of population and deterioration in health—was estimated at 26 billion dollars of 1938 purchasing power, an amount equivalent to nearly three times the total French national income, which had amounted in 1938 to about 9 billion dollars. In the Netherlands, the cost of the devastation was estimated at 6.3 billion dollars. Compared to the national income, this was an even higher percentage than in France.

As important as actual war destruction was the catastrophic decline in production, a direct consequence of war and occupation. In agriculture, the decrease was mainly due to several factors.

One was lack of fertilizer, the production of which had declined to 20 percent of pre-war. This decline, continued for several years, reduced soil fertility.

Another factor was insufficiency of draught power. A considerable number of horses had been requisitioned by the respective armies, and no fuel was available for the few tractors at hand.

A third factor was lack of manpower, mainly due to mobilization for the armed forces.

Thus in 1945, the time of the first harvest after the end of fighting in Europe, both the acreage of main crops and the yields were much below pre-war. Compared to pre-war (average 1935-39 = 100) the 1945 crop in the different European countries amounted to: Austria, 49; Belgium, 53; Denmark, 93; France, 53; Germany, 57; Italy, 57; Netherlands, 47; and United Kingdom, 135.

The decline in production in manufacturing, industry and mining, which was even more considerable, was mainly due to reduction in numbers and decrease in productivity of the workers. This, in turn, was caused by undernourishment; deterioration of general living conditions; and the lack of incentives. Other causes of decrease in production were lack of fuel and raw materials; dislocation of transport; and deterioration of obsolete equipment.

The paralysis of foreign trade had a serious effect on the economy. It was a factor that substantially increased already existing difficulties. Enemy occupation destroyed the pre-war pattern of foreign trade of the European Continent. On the initiative of Germany, and mainly in order to fulfil the requirements of her war production, another foreign trade pattern was established. Although far less profitable than the previous one, especially for the occupied territories, still it provided them with the essential import commodities needed for continuation of their economic activity. Occupied Western Europe thus received some machinery, mainly spare parts from Germany, cereals from Southeast Europe, etc. After liberation, this artificial pattern of trade broke down, while the previous natural pattern could not yet be reestablished, mainly because of transport difficulties and lack of export goods.

Of even greater and more disastrous influence was the deterioration of the financial and monetary situation. It resulted from the enormous currency and credit inflation, which had been the counterpart either of war expenditure or, in occupied countries, of German looting by the use of occupation-costs indemnity and of exchange clearing credits. By the end of the war, however, this

255

inflation had not yet appreciably influenced the price level. Owing to the policy of rigid price fixing and rationing, maintained through a system of rigorous penalties, prices had as yet remained relatively stable; or at least their rise had been much slower than the increase in monetary availabilities. The remaining inflationary potential was thus very considerable. At liberation, as soon as the whole price-control system imposed by the occupation authorities broke down, the enormous gap between expanded monetary purchasing power and the extremely reduced supply of available consumer goods was bound to provide a powerful stimulant for inflation.

The social and moral consequences of war and occupation were of completely incalculable impact. One of the most important of such factors was the development of black-market activities, which the Germans sometimes opposed, but more often fostered, as a source of goods in short supply otherwise unobtainable. The demoralizing influence of the black market was substantial, as gains of normal professional activity, limited by price and wage control, compared more and more unfavorably to the rising cost of living, and even more to the unlimited black-market profits, which discouraged return of capital and labor to productive activity.

Of tremendous importance, as factors of dislocation of social and economic structure, were the shifts of masses of population due to the Nazi policy: deportation of millions of foreign slave workers as manpower for the factories of the Reich, and expulsion from areas annexed by Germany of their former inhabitants. Other shifts of population were voluntary, but direct consequences of the food shortages caused by the war. There was, for instance, a sizeable migration from big cities and industrial areas to villages and small towns in food-producing regions.

Finally, there was another tremendous impact, felt at first in the occupied countries and, after defeat, in Germany itself. This consisted of a number of factors: dislocation of the pre-war fabric of national state and society; accentuation of class antagonism, resulting from differences in the behavior of the different groups of population toward the occupants; and the breakdown—especially in countries like France, the Low Countries, Denmark and Norway—of their traditional democratic order with its habits of freedom, respect for the rights of the individual, independent justice, etc. The domination, even though maintained only for a few years, of a criminal dictatorship, without any legal or moral restraint, was contagious and had a substantial demoralizing influence. It created and stimulated habits of violence and lawlessness, especially in the youth, and thus increased difficulties relative to the reconstruction of the economy, as well as of the political and social structure.

By the end of the war, the situation in Eastern Europe was in general even worse than in the western part of the Continent. It had been submitted, during the war years, to a particularly harsh exploitation by the Nazis. Major groups of population either had been deported to provide space for German settlers, like most of the population of Western Poland; or they had even been exterminated, which was the case with nearly all the Jewish population of the area. Later on, Eastern Europe had been the battlefield of two alien armies. Neither had the slightest interest in caring for the population or in preserving the resources of the countries concerned. On the contrary, when they retreated, they applied to the utmost the methods of the "scorched earth" policy.

Since the end of the war, for all practical purposes, Europe has been divided in two by the line corresponding to the demarcation between territories liberated or occupied, respectively, by the Western Allies and by the Soviet Union. Trends of development in Western Europe and in Soviet-controlled Eastern Europe, since the war, have been entirely different, and should therefore be considered separately.

IV

EASTERN EUROPE SINCE THE END OF
WORLD WAR II: POPULAR DEMOCRACY,
TRANSITION TO COMMUNISM

22 RECONSTRUCTION AND DEVELOPMENT IN THE SOVIET UNION

THE SOVIET ECONOMIC POLICY for the post-war period, as expressed in the fourth Five-Year Plan (for the period 1946-50) did not deviate from the major aims of the previous plans. Reconstruction of war devastation was viewed only as a part of the continued effort of general economic development. The stress on expansion in eastern areas was maintained, and even accentuated, as well as the emphasis on heavy-industry versus consumers-goods production. For the period 1946-60, the long-term goals of production of main basic materials had been proclaimed by Stalin to be 50 million tons of pig iron; 60 million tons of steel; 500 million tons of coal; and 60 million tons of oil. These objectives represent totals of an order of magnitude similar, or even slightly superior, to those of the whole of Western Europe, and not very much below those of the United States.

In the fourth Five-Year Plan itself, more than half of capital investment (55 percent) was to be made in areas that were not invaded by the Germans. It thus represented new development of these eastern areas, which were also to keep all the 1300 industrial undertakings that were evacuated there from the West during the war. These undertakings will, however, be rebuilt on their original sites, and will thus represent a net addition to the total industrial capacity of the country.

Comparison of planned targets for 1950 with actual production figures published for 1940 and estimates * of production in 1945 is of special interest. It demonstrates clearly that, compared to 1945, when consumers-goods production was cut to the bone, planned increase in production of this category was very considerable, 120 percent, whereas increase in capital-goods production during the period of the Plan was only 40 percent. On the other hand, compared to the last pre-war year, 1940, planned increase in consumer goods was much less than for heavy-industry products —25 percent, as compared to 60 percent. Thus, increase of supply to consumers, even though particularly urgent after the hardships of the war years, was still to remain subordinated to continued increase in the capital-goods industry, the basis of the economic and military power of the Soviet state.

Actual figures of the targets for 1950 for main industrial items, compared to 1940 and to estimates for 1945 (Schwartz) * are as follows:

	1940	1945	1950	1950 in % of 1940	of 1945
Pig iron, million metric tons	15	10	19.5	130	195
Steel, million metric tons	18.3	14.5	25.4	139	175
Coal, million metric tons	166	150	250	151	167
Petroleum, million metric tons	31	20.5	35.4	114	173
Electric power, billion kwh	48.3	40	82	170	205
Tractors, thousands	31.1	7.6	112	360	1574
Metallurgic equipment, 000 tons	27.8	...	102.9	370	...

* Harry Schwartz, *Russia's Post-War Economy,* University of Syracuse Press, 1947.

	1940	1945	1950	1950 in % of 1940	of 1945
Cotton cloth, million meters	4030	1616	4680	116	290
Woolen cloth, million meters	124.4	57	159.4	128	280
Leather shoes, million pairs	230	60	240	104	400
Hosiery, million pairs	480	83	580	121	700

In agriculture, the targets of the fourth Five-Year Plan consisted in complete restoration of pre-war production and a further expansion especially of industrial crops, in particular sugar beets and cotton. Planned increase for grain seemed hardly sufficient to cope with the increase in population. However, in order to reach these goals from the very low levels to which agricultural production had declined in 1945, the effort of expansion had to be very substantial.

Actual production figures for 1940, estimates for 1945, and goals for 1950 for main products were as follows:

(in millions of tons)

	1940	1945	1950	1950 in % of 1940	of 1945
Grain	119	66.5	127	108	191
Cotton	2.7	1.2	3.1	115	258
Sunflower seed	3.3	1.8	3.7	112	205
Sugar beets	20.9	8.9	26	124	292

Besides the effort made to achieve increase of production, postwar agricultural policy in the Soviet Union was characterized by a return to a strict implementation of collective farming rules. All relaxations in favor of individual farming tolerated during the war were again prohibited. Hence, provisions limiting individual plots of collective farmers and the number of livestock which they were authorized to keep were strictly enforced. Moreover, land that had been taken over for individual cultivation was returned to the collective farms. The effects of such a policy on production seem not to have been particularly satisfactory, especially as regards livestock breeding.

Nevertheless the Soviet authorities are moving a new step ahead in transforming the Russian peasantry into a proletariat of land workers similar to that of the industrial workers. Until the beginning of 1950, the collective farms had been established on the basis of the existing villages; and the members of these collectives continued, in fact, to farm the land which had been owned by the village community, the *mir,* during the time of their forefathers. Now, however, a drive has been started to combine several village collective farms into much bigger units. This arrangement may have some advantages for the utilization of mechanized equipment. It may also permit a decrease in the requirements for farm labor, and thus make available additional manpower for industrial development.

However, as important from the point of view of the Soviet government, is the progress which such a consolidation will be able to achieve toward destruction of the traditional attachment of the peasants to the land of their particular villages. This consolidation will eventually lead to regrouping of the old villages in new farm laborers' towns, from which teams of workers will be sent impartially to work on the lands of this or that former village. In theory, the new giant collective farms will remain cooperative undertakings of their many hundreds or even several thousands of members. In fact, however, these collective farmers will be nothing more than landless farm laborers in complete dependence upon the state, and directly under its control.

There was another important measure which strengthened the control of the government over the economy, and over all classes of the population. It was the liquidation, by the end of 1947, of the wartime monetary inflation. The monetary reform implemented was a drastic deflation, consisting in an exchange of cur-

264

rency in the proportion of 10 to 1; much more favorable rates, 4 to 1 and even 1 to 1, were applied to bank deposits and government bonds. This reform practically wiped out all savings which had been accumulated by individuals, mostly peasants or members of independent industrial cooperatives, the production effort of which had also been encouraged during the war. Other classes of the population were less affected. As a partial compensation for this spoliation and the disappearance of the liquid resources of individual consumers, the general level of prices was somewhat reduced and rationing was abolished.

During the post-war period, the productive effort of the Soviet Union itself received considerable contributions from other areas of the Eastern bloc. The most important of these contributions were received as reparations. They consisted, to a great extent, in industrial equipment of all kinds, as well as rolling stock dismantled and removed to Russia: from all the areas occupied by the Soviet armies; from the Soviet Zone of Germany; from the countries of East and Southeast Europe; and from Manchuria and North Korea. It is obvious that such equipment, especially of railroad, coal mines and engineering plants, brought a significant increase in Soviet capacity in the first post-war years. The amount of these direct reparations is unknown, but it was probably in the neighborhood of several billion dollars. To this should be added the amounts agreed upon in the peace treaties with the satellite countries: $900 million, of which there was $300 million each for Rumania and Finland, $200 million for Hungary, and $100 million for Italy.

As to Germany, under the Potsdam Agreement the Soviet Union was entitled to receive as reparations the surplus, over peacetime requirements, of industrial equipment in her zone, as well as 25 percent of the reparations from the Western Zones. Of that latter amount, however, 15 percent had to be compensated for by deliveries from the Soviet Zone to Western Germany; reparations from current production were completely prohibited. But disagreement between East and West rapidly put an end to equipment deliveries from Western Germany. At the same time, the Soviets, not satisfied with dismantling the greatest part of the industry of their zone, used the remainder to produce goods that they sent to the Soviet Union. They were able to do this because Soviet authorities took over all German assets in Russian-occupied territories. In Eastern Germany these assets included plants which were considered as surplus over peacetime capacity, but which the Soviets agreed to leave in the country on the condition that they become Russian property.

In accordance with the same principle, they obtained possession of a major part of oil fields in Austria, Hungary and Rumania, of shipping on the Danube, and of many other important undertakings, the products of which were sent to Russia. Besides, the general control of the policy of these countries by the Soviet authorities enabled the latter to direct the economic planning and the foreign trade of all the countries of this area in accordance with the interests of the Soviet Union. The interests of these countries were entirely subordinated to those of the Soviets, as will be shown below.

The fragmentary data (in percentage of unpublished annual targets) published about the implementation of the fourth Five-Year Plan seem to show that (as during the preceding Plans) development in particular of main industrial raw materials and heavy-industry products seems to be roughly conforming to the Plan. Indeed, some of the goals have been reached even in advance, compared to the schedule. Thus, according to a statement of Marshall Bulganin, quoted in the *New York Times,* production of coal, steel, oil and electric power during the first 10 months of 1950 was in excess of the goals, or targets, of the Plan. Compared to 1940, increase in coal production was 57 percent, instead of 51 percent as planned; in steel, 48 percent instead of 39 percent; in petroleum, 21 percent instead of 14 percent; and in electric power, 82 percent instead of 70 percent.

Progress in consumers-goods industries seems to be less spectacular. Automobile production in 1949 reached less than 60 percent

266

of its 1950 target. The situation of housing, especially, seems still very unsatisfactory, in spite of considerable effort.

For agricultural production a few absolute figures have been given in the statement of Marshall Bulganin. Increase appears to be less than expected. Thus, total production of grain in 1950 reached only 121.7 million tons, as compared to a target of 127 million tons; and production of sugar beets 23.4 million tons, as compared to a target of 26 million tons.

The situation of Soviet consumers is far from being comparable with that of the average of Western Europe. Still it is undoubtedly true that it has considerably improved in relation to the absolutely catastrophic low levels of wartime and the immediate post-war period. It will probably continue to improve.

23 SOCIALIZATION IN EASTERN EUROPE

IN ALL THE TERRITORIES of Eastern Europe under Soviet domination, including the Soviet Zone of Germany, the general policy pursued since the end of the war has followed the same pattern of gradual socialization which has been used in Russia since 1917. This process can be divided into two main phases.

The first creates in the countries concerned an economic balance of power somewhat similar to that which existed in Soviet Russia during the period of the Nep. By drastic land reform, it eliminates the main elements hostile to Communist domination, the big landowners, completely confiscating their estates and dividing them between the peasants and the farm laborers. It also eliminates the capitalists, through nationalization of all large-scale industry, banking and trade concerns. Thus, the state is able to achieve domination of the key sectors of the economy. As land reform is implemented mainly as a political measure—to win the allegiance of the peasants but without any real intention of establishing a strong class of independent farmers—nothing, or very little, is being done to assist them to develop production on their newly acquired plots by supplying them with equipment, draught power and other aids. They therefore have to face very serious difficulties and become somewhat disappointed in the immediate results of their new status as owners of their new individual farms.

This disappointment provides the psychological basis for the

268

second phase, consisting, in agriculture, in a drive for organization of collective farms on the Soviet pattern. In most of these countries, however, they are being called *cooperative farms,* the word collective farm being very obnoxious to most peasants. This drive for collectivization is supported by inducements of supply of mechanized equipment, fertilizer, and financial assistance. In a degree varying according to local conditions, certain threats are made against those opposed to collectivization, described as kulaks and enemies of the state. These threats imply sanctions, and even confiscation of the land.

During the same phase, nationalization is being extended to the rest of private industrial and commercial undertakings, thus placing all productive forces of the economy under the direct control of the state. At present, the different countries of Eastern Europe are in varying stages of this development, though none of them seems to have reached as yet the final stage of complete nationalization of economy. The second phase, however, was given a general start after the Communist *coup d'état* in Czechoslovakia, early in 1948.

Organization of agriculture on the Soviet pattern involves state-owned machine and tractor stations supplying mechanized equipment to farm labor cooperatives—that is, collective farms. The greatest progress in this direction, up to the present, seems to have been achieved in Bulgaria. Here, by the end of 1949, about 80 percent of all mechanized equipment available in the country was concentrated in 86 stations. At the same time, there were 1,605 collective farms, cultivating 560,000 hectares. Under the Bulgarian plan, the number of collective farms is to be increased, by 1953, to 4,000, with 5 million hectares producing 72 percent of all marketed grain. In Yugoslavia, the number of farm cooperatives in December 1949 was 6,500 as against only 500 in 1947; and about 30 percent of all land was under collective cultivation.

In other countries of the area the collectivization movement is in a less advanced stage; thus, in Hungary collective farms cultivate only about 7 percent of all land. However, it is necessary to add to the collective, or cooperative, farms the state farms established on some big estates which had not been divided, but were taken over directly by the state. In Hungary, the area of these state farms is 224,000 hectares, or about 4 percent of all available land. In Poland, particularly in the western areas conquered from Germany, the state farms amount to 10 percent of all lands under crops.

The Soviet pattern has also been very closely followed in industrial development, in which development the plans adopted by the different countries put a nearly exclusive stress on expansion of heavy industry. In itself, industrialization in this area was perfectly justified from the standpoint of the following objectives: to provide employment to the surplus rural population; to develop, for the benefit of their whole population, existing natural resources; and to make their economy more balanced, and less dependent on foreign markets for their produce and foreign supplies of manufactured goods, especially equipment. This dependence had enabled Nazi Germany to enslave the area in question, and to transform it into an economic colony of the Reich.

But post-war industrial development seems to be aimed much less at improving the people's standard of living than at increasing their productive capacity in heavy industry. Such an increase will enlarge their contribution to the industrial power of the Soviet Union, with the economy of which all their plans are coordinated, and to which they appear also to be completely subordinated.

This subordination of the economic interests of those countries to the political and the economic interests of the dominating power, is even much more apparent in the post-war reorientation of their foreign trade. Before World War II, nearly all foreign trade of the area was with the West, mainly with Western Europe, which absorbed all its exports of food and raw materials, and supplied most of its imports of manufactured goods. On the contrary, trade with the Soviet Union was practically nil, as the economies of Russia and of Eastern Europe were competing with and not

270

complementary to each other, their main export products being similar.

Even the one mainly industrial country of this area, Czechoslovakia, traded above all with the West. Most of her exports of manufactured consumer goods, such as glass, textiles, leather, etc., were exported to Western Europe or to overseas, wherefrom she also received her imports of manufactured goods and raw materials. Only a lesser part of her exports, consisting mainly of products of heavy industry, went to other countries of the area.

It has been the policy of the governments of these countries, subservient to the Soviet Union, to try to reorientate their foreign trade toward that country and the other countries of this territory. While they did not oppose recovery of East-West trade, especially when it could provide them with equipment for their industrialization, they refused to resume consumers-goods imports. In Czechoslovakia, a structural shift is in process of being achieved. This shift is from consumer goods, the main markets of which were in the West, to heavy industry for export to other countries of the same group. A coordinated expansion of heavy industrial capacity is taking place in Czechoslovakia, Poland and Eastern Germany, designed to establish an integrated industrial entity, similar to the Ruhr, and capable of supplying most requirements for industrialization of the area.

The result of such a policy, however, for the population of the countries concerned, is that, while formerly proceeds of exports brought consumer goods, at present, in spite of increased industrial production, imports do not contribute anything to current consumption. Thus, not only do they not improve, but they even reduce, the standard of living of the mass of the population, including even the workers. This is especially true in Czechoslovakia, where the standard had been relatively high.

In addition, the countries of the area seem to be submitted by the Soviet Union to an exploitation somewhat similar to that from which they had suffered from Nazi Germany. After the end of World War II, the Soviet Union, not yet recovered from war

271

devastation, and suffering from a shortage of raw materials, absorbed all or a great part of the surpluses of countries of the territory. She took these over, either completely free of charge, as reparations (such as oil from Rumania) or at nominal prices ($1 for a ton of Polish coal). About 15 million tons of coal were exported to the Soviet Union during 1946-47 at this price, while the regular export price applied to other countries was about $12-15.

Later on, even as shortages in Russia decreased, the Soviet authorities pursued this policy. They used their dominating position in order to obtain, at relatively low prices, considerable quantities of export goods from the different countries of this area. The surplus of such goods, in excess of their own requirements, they resold to other countries of the area or even to outside countries. Thus, a study the results of which were published in the Belgrade paper *Politika* revealed the following: Under trade agreements concluded in Moscow in February 1950 by Poland, Czechoslovakia, Hungary, Rumania and Bulgaria, these five countries agreed to deliver to the Soviet Union 75 percent of their export surpluses. Hence, Rumania sells her oil at world prices, while the Soviet Union resells this oil to Czechoslovakia, Bulgaria and Hungary at Soviet domestic prices, which are considerably higher. Similar monopolistic broker profits are obtained by the Soviet government on all items of her trade with the satellite countries, which tends to become the greatest part of the foreign trade of those satellites.

Such exploitation is not without an element of risk, as witness the example of Yugoslavia. The unfair terms of trade—raw materials exported to, and industrial equipment from, the Soviet Union —were considered by Tito a most serious impediment to the implementation of his industrialization plan. Thus, those terms were a major factor in his rebellion against the domination of the Kremlin.

However, from Russia's standpoint, other countries of the area seem to be well in hand, at least for the present. This pattern of foreign trade not only brings handsome profits, but also tends to equalize standards of living of countries such as Czechoslovakia, Eastern Germany and Poland (which formerly had been higher than in the Soviet Union) with the level of the latter or even to put them below the latter. This trend, together with the development of industry and agriculture, increases similarity in conditions in this area with those of the Soviet Union, and thus brings nearer the moment when all the countries of the area will be ripe for complete absorption into the Soviet empire.

V

WESTERN EUROPE SINCE THE END OF
WORLD WAR II: RECONSTRUCTION
AND ATTEMPTS AT UNIFICATION

24 SOCIAL AND POLITICAL CHANGES AND TRENDS

WORLD WAR II had shattered the social and political organization of the countries of the European Continent and resulted there in basic changes of social structure of a really revolutionary character. Changes nearly as important and somewhat parallel had occurred during the war period in Great Britain.

In countries such as France, the war and the German occupation had caused psychological and political conditions which made impossible the complete reestablishment of the pre-war capitalist structure of society and economy. As to Great Britain, the experience of the war had convinced the majority of the nation of the need for basic reforms of the economic structure to give community control over the key sectors of the economy. This general trend toward nationalization, planning and state control was not (as generally supposed in the United States) due only, or even mainly, to theoretical motives of socialist doctrine. To a very great extent it was due to concrete factors in the situation of the countries concerned.

The main reasons for this trend in Europe can be classified in three categories: those resulting from past experience; those prompted by desire for future reform; and those made necessary by conditions of the present moment. These reasons can be further specified and analyzed as follows:

(1) The failure of the capitalist economy to overcome, before

277

the war, depression and continuous mass unemployment, as also to prepare efficiently for war and thus to preserve national independence—in contrast to the success achieved in both respects by the planned and state-controlled economy of Nazi Germany. This failure had a tremendous influence in the occupied countries of Western Europe. The contrast between the two systems influenced not only the workers, but also the members of most nonsocialist patriotic resistance movements, who considered that the failure of capitalism to plan and organize for victory, as well as for prosperity, was to a great extent responsible for the defeat of their countries. In Great Britain, also, the contrast between full employment together with enormous increase in production reached by planning in state-controlled war economy, on the one hand, and pre-war stagnation on the other, led to similar conclusions. A natural consequence of these very widely held opinions was the conviction that post-war reconstruction and reconversion to peacetime economy should not be completely abandoned to private enterprise, but should be planned and directed at least in part by the state.

(2) The resulting aggravation in France and, to a lesser extent, in other occupied countries of Western Europe, of class tensions, due to the difference in attitude toward the German invader. The collaboration of a considerable number of leading capitalists with the Germans, the psychological background of which has been analyzed above (Chapter 18), was expressed in the drive of many employers for increased production for the benefit of the Nazi war machine. Thus, the Renault factory manufactured tanks for the German army during the occupation at a higher rate than for the French army before the occupation. A similar production drive had been attempted in the French and Belgian coal mines and in many other big concerns. Other employers, or often the same ones, pressed their workers into deportation for slave labor in Germany. This attitude resulted after the war in a natural patriotic reaction which implied considerable social changes. Thus, plants where employers had been obvious collaborators were con-

278

fiscated and the owners were put on trial. The plants themselves were generally organized as state-owned companies run by a manager appointed by the state, and with a considerable degree of participation of worker representatives in the management. This method was applied, at least partly, to Renault and even more completely to the Berliet automobile factory in Lyons. Such social reaction against economic collaboration was also one of the main reasons for nationalization of the French coal mines, where workers had refused to work any more for private owners.

(3) Nationalist reaction against German penetration of national economy effected before, but especially during, the period of occupation when, with the proceeds of the occupation indemnities, the Germans bought up controlling interests in most of the biggest concerns in the key sectors of the economy. After the liberation, these German properties became the property of the state, thus in some countries considerably enlarging the nationalized sector.

(4) Efficiency. This motive for nationalization was especially important in old decaying industries, e.g., coal mining in Great Britain, where private ownership appeared unable to make the necessary investments and was incompatible with the comprehensive reorganization required in order to achieve the desired expansion of production. A similar aim of rationalization was also one of the main reasons for the nationalization of the big French banks, which had an enormously overexpanded apparatus with considerable duplication. In nearly every small town, for example, each of the four big banks had a branch. Rationalization of the banking apparatus would be effected either through combination, which would have created a complete monopoly of banking, or through nationalization. The latter solution was adopted.

(5) Monopoly. In Europe, before World War II, there was already a widespread belief that in economic activities where a monopoly existed private ownership was not only useless but harmful and dangerous. Useless, since the advantages of free enterprise, in the traditional meaning of this term, could not be obtained in the absence of competition. Harmful and dangerous, be-

279

cause of the possibility of abuse of monopolistic power for the sake of private profits or political influence. (See above the description of successful attempts of French financial capitalism, represented by the big banks, to prevent social reforms of Leftist governments.) Such antimonopolistic tendency had been considerably strengthened since the war; and in France a special paragraph of the new Constitution states that all economic activities where a monopoly exists, or might be created, should be owned by the nation. This motive, the desire to abolish private monopolies, was to a great extent responsible for nationalization of the railways in France (effected already before the war) and in Great Britain; as well as of public utilities in both countries since the war; and of the big banks and insurance companies in France.

(6) Social and economic security. During the war, the hope of improved social and economic conditions in the post-war period was the greatest compensation and the main stimulant to the effort, action and endurance of the workers as well as of the soldiers of Great Britain, and also of the fighters of the underground resistance in occupied countries. This hope envisaged abolishing the main defects of the pre-war capitalist order, such as unemployment and the lack of a sufficiently comprehensive system of social security guaranteeing individuals against all the risks existing in modern industrial society. The implementation of the pledges, made during the war, for the fulfilment of the craving of the masses for economic and social security, corresponding roughly to the two Beveridge Plans, implied an orientation of economic activity to a great extent with a view to reaching social objectives. Such results obviously could not be obtained through automatic functioning of a free market economy, but required definite planning and direction.

(7) The desire of the majority of the people represented in parliaments and by governments (owing to one or all of the reasons above, as well as to arguments of socialistic doctrine) to give to the state the control of the general orientation of economic activity, which implied direct control, by nationalization, of a few key sec-

tors. This argument accounted, for example, for the nationalization of the Bank of England. That step gave to the Labor government the possibility of controlling credit for current production and investment; in France, the Banque de France had been brought under state control before the war. The same motive constituted practically the only major reason for nationalization of such a key industrial activity as the British steel industry.

(8) Absolute necessity. After the end of the war, all Western European countries, with the exception of a few neutrals such as Switzerland and Sweden, were suffering from shortages in nearly all categories of commodities: food, fuel, basic raw materials and manufactured goods. Even more important than any of the former was a shortage of hard currencies, that is, mainly of dollars. Such shortages had implied everywhere—even while they persisted in the United States—a policy of planning, at least for utilization of resources in short supply, by rationing, priorities, etc. In Western Europe, because of the structural changes and losses due to the war, most of these shortages were of a permanent or at least long-term character, even if they could be rapidly somewhat alleviated. A policy of long-term planning and state intervention and direction was thus indispensable.

All these reasons are to some extent responsible for government direction of economy and for the measures of nationalization undertaken in Western Europe, mainly in Great Britain and France. It should be emphasized, however, that with the exception of a few cases (such as Renault, where nationalization had the character of a penalty) compensation had been paid to owners and shareholders at a reasonable rate, in France on the basis of the average previous dividends. Nationalization had also been carried out by democratic procedure. It should be stressed, too, that there had been no attempt to establish a completely socialistic economy by nationalizing all means of production. This was true even in France after the liberation, when there was no important party favorable to a return to capitalist economy, since the three major parties (Communist, Socialist and M.R.P.) agreed on the necessity of important structural changes in the economy and a considerable degree of state control. All parties, including the Communists, recognized that complete socialization did not conform to the wishes of the great majority of the nation, while at that moment a limited degree of state control and nationalization undoubtedly did.

Such a democratically planned and directed economy encounters much greater difficulties than a totalitarian economy of the Communist or Nazi pattern. There the state is in complete control, whether directly or indirectly, and the wishes of the people, if they oppose the will of the state, can always be neglected and opposition crushed.

In spite of these special difficulties, this policy had achieved no little success in Great Britain, the country where it had been steadfastly applied since the summer of 1945, and where political and psychological conditions had been most favorable. As a matter of fact, in Great Britain, class tensions, if any, were limited; nationalization had been effected and the nationalized industries organized in the most businesslike and efficient way, without any corruptive political influence or patronage. Opposition of the conservatives, even though severe, was not obstructive and Communist disruptive influence was very limited. Still the British achievements in this field are especially impressive, considering the tremendous difficulties of the economic situation of the United Kingdom since the end of World War II.

In France, the situation in itself was much less favorable and, partly because of this, the policy pursued had been much less wise. The nationalizations, though achieved with the agreement of all major parties, had been implemented to a great extent under the influence of the Communists. They considered nationalization a first step in a gradual conquest of power, and used their influence with complete neglect of considerations of productivity in the respective industries, mainly for obtaining the maximum of key positions. However, at the beginning and until the spring of 1947, the Communists were actively participating in, and even

282

leading the drive for, reconstruction of the economy and increase of production, expecting with a very shrewd reasoning to gain popular favor through this attitude. Their slogan was "Communism, the party of French recovery." But it should be pointed out that, even while striving to expand production in industry and mining (for which the Communist Minister of Industrial Production expected to give credit to his party), the Communists had steadily opposed all such financial measures as blocking part of the currency. This step might have ended inflation and thus consolidated the existence of non-Communist democracy.

From the spring of 1947 on, however, they completely reversed their previous policy of working for economic recovery. At that time, after the break between the Communists and all other parties, they were put out of the government. After France's acceptance of the Marshall Plan and its rejection by the Soviet Union, the Communists became more and more rabidly opposed to economic rehabilitation. They feared that it would destroy their chances of winning power and would enable the other parties to develop and make prosperous there a social democracy. Such a democracy is the most dangerous and most feared competitor of the Communist order, as it is an alternative solution of the same problem, achieving the same aim of liberation from capitalist oppression without the terrific material and moral sacrifices required by Communism, and especially without forcing the individual to abdicate his rights and his freedom. This fear provides the explanation of their deep hatred of any attempt to establish a social democratic economy, and in particular their loathing of Labor Britain. Hence also their violent opposition to the effort toward French economic recovery and their use and abuse for this purpose of their influence on the labor unions. Thus twice, by the end of 1947 and of 1948, they had organized extensive strikes, especially in the coal mines, which caused a considerable set-back to French recovery.

On the other hand, because of the importance of political factors, and especially of Communist influence in the nationalized industries in France, there had been a considerable amount of mismanagement, low productivity and excessive cost, and, as a consequence, a substantial deficit to be paid by the state. This deficit, however, was due to an appreciable extent to general inflationary difficulties. For example, costs of utilities increased more rapidly than rates could be readjusted, and also it was impossible to finance by bond issues new expansion of capacity. These deficits of the nationalized industries have given the opportunity to the now revived pro-capitalist parties, most important of which are the radicals, to claim that those industries should be returned to private ownership, or at least to private management, by renting them to private industrialists. But such a solution would encounter the opposition not only of the whole working class, but also of all those who approve of the principle of the nationalizations even though recognizing the defects of their implementation. The present French government therefore intends to reform the organization of these industries. This step, if accomplished, will maintain their status of ownership by the nation and of their management in the national interest. At the same time, it will abolish the abuses resulting from the Communist influence (such as the excessive number of administrative personnel in the coal mines) and will model the industries on the pattern of business undertakings, similar to that of the British nationalized industries. The success of such a reform, however, would require a considerable measure of freedom from political and social strife and disturbances.

But neither planned economy nor nationalization of key industries provides a satisfactory solution to one of the major social and moral problems of modern industrialized society—what is called in the United States the problem of human relations in industry. This problem results from the fact that the masses of workers refuse to continue being just "manpower," anonymous cogs in the productive apparatus, without any active participation in the life and management of the plants to which they devote their energy

284

and efforts for years, sometimes throughout their active lives. The normal organization of all big business concerns is on a strictly hierarchical basis, the participation of the workers consisting purely in taking and executing orders, just like privates in an army. This pattern of organization applies, whatever the ownership of the plant may be, whether it belongs to a private company or, as in Soivet Russia, to a state-owned trust.

During and after the war, however, a strong tendency developed in Europe in favor of a more active participation of the workers. This was due both to the desire of the governments to stimulate productivity by this method, and to the will of the workers to gain self-respect as well as power in industry.

Thus, during the war, in Great Britain (and to a smaller extent in the United States) in most big war plants joint production committees were created, at first by private initiative; later on they were extended by law to all industries. As a result, representatives of labor and management cooperated in the effort to increase production. Since the war, this law, considered as a temporary measure, has expired, and most production committees have been abolished. The British unions, however, demand their reestablishment, with enlarged powers.

In France and Italy, similar committees were created after the war, with very considerable authority. The French undertaking committees (comités d'entreprise), established by the law of March 1945, exist in all business concerns, of public as well as of private ownership, employing more than fifty workers. Their members are elected by the staff, but their chairman is the manager or his representative. Their functions extend not only to cooperation for increase of production and improvement of efficiency, but to all important matters that concern the activity of the undertaking. They have to be consulted, even though their opinion can be rejected. In particular, they are empowered to receive information on the accounts of the undertaking, and are to be consulted on the distribution of profits. They also delegate two of their mem-

285

bers to the company's Board of Directors, where, however, they act without voting power.*

The French unions have established special training facilities for members of these undertaking committees, in order to enable them to acquire the competence necessary for them to exert an effective influence on management. The unions expect to increase the influence of these committees, and in particular to obtain for them an active participation on the Board of Directors. Surprising as it may appear, this plan of the unions is entirely approved by the Rightist elements of the De Gaulle movement. They propose to have business undertakings administered by a board consisting of representatives of capital (the shareholders) and labor (the workers and employees of the undertaking). In nationalized concerns of French industry, such as Renault, the importance of these committees is considerably larger than in private undertakings.

The possibility of active participation in the operation of the undertakings offered to members of the *comités d'entreprise* has considerable attraction for most of them, and makes them conscious of the interests and needs of the respective concerns. Thus, the Communist-led General Confederation of Labor, which at first was extremely eager to elect its most active members to those committees, recently complained that these members showed a tendency to defend the interests of the undertaking, thus adopting the point of view of management and forgetting the principle of the class struggle. This is the best proof of the fact that these committees offer the best opportunity—if only employers are aware of it and intelligent enough to grasp it—of reestablishing cooperation in each business concern between labor and management. Such cooperation would reduce the class tensions which for a long time have had a paralyzing effect on the French political, social and economic situation.

* Similar but even more far reaching proposals aiming at giving to representatives of the workers an active participation in management (*Mitbestimmungsrecht*) are being discussed by the parliament of Western Germany.

286

Many other forms of the organization of relationship between labor and management giving to the former a more active participation, as well as a greater responsibility, are at present subject to experiment in Western Europe, particularly in France. These attempts range from a pure decentralization of authority and financial responsibility by the workshop-autonomy system (invented by the Czechoslovakian industrialist Bat'a and introduced in more than one hundred undertakings in France) to the most idealistic type of production cooperative. The best example of the latter was the *Communauté Barbut* at Valence, in Southern France, where a team of workers in a medium-sized watch factory organized themselves into a community for work, life and education, at the urging of their former employer.

There is still much confusion and limitation in these very varied and numerous attempts and experiments made with a view to solving the problem of human relations in modern industry and emancipating the workers from oppression by management— experiments which do not always imply state direction, and sometimes completely reject it. Still they may offer guidance toward some resolving of this, one of the most important problems of modern civilization, especially as there should not necessarily be only one general solution, but undoubtedly many different ones, depending on different factors, such as the size and character of the respective undertakings.

25 RECOVERY OF PRODUCTION, AND ITS DIFFICULTIES

AT THE MOMENT of liberation, or at the end of military operations, in Europe the level of economic activity on the Continent was catastrophically low. Though exact statistical data on production are not available, it has been estimated that the general index of industrial production was at about 20 percent of pre-war in France and Belgium by the spring of 1945—that is, nearly a year after the liberation of those countries. Naturally, it was at an even much lower level in Germany at the moment of unconditional surrender.

Since the end of the war, the effort exerted in all countries concerned in order to restore their production and to expand it above pre-war level has been tremendous. It has proceeded under the guidance and control of the state, more or less direct and severe in the different countries, but applied everywhere, particularly during the early stages of recovery, because of the necessity of overcoming the key bottlenecks impeding expansion of production. To that end, all available resources have been used for the most important tasks; and minimum consumption levels for all classes of the population have been maintained through rationing.

The first task of recovery, as indicated above, was to overcome the main key bottlenecks on the continent of Western Europe. In the order of urgency they were transport, food, fuel and steel.

(a) *Transport*. Restoration of minimum transport facilities was the most urgent task facing all governments of Western Euro-

288

pean countries, as soon as their territory had been liberated or military operations had stopped. This was a prerequisite not only of full recovery or even simply of *resumption* of economic activity, but also of receipt and distribution, throughout the countries concerned, of overseas imports. These imports were required in order to begin industrial production again; to maintain minimum food standards—even to prevent actual starvation; and to restore normal political organization and adminstration.

Hence, in all countries involved the greatest effort was energetically directed at once to reconstruction of transport, on which all available resources in manpower and materials in short supply, such as steel and cement, were concentrated. As a result, there was unexpectedly rapid restoration especially of railway transport, upon which, owing to its paramount importance, the largest amount of attention was centered.

Thus, in France the first railway bridge over the Loire in Orléans was temporarily restored as early as December 1944, less than four months after the work had been started. Upon its replacement had depended the possibility of supplying pit props to the Northern coal mines. It was permanently rebuilt in July 1947. By the end of 1946 more than 90 percent of all railway bridges destroyed in France had been reestablished on either a temporary or a permanent basis; and during 1947 and 1948 permanent reconstruction of all important bridges, marshalling yards and railway track destroyed had been completed. In spite of repairs, considerable construction of new equipment, and substantial orders for locomotives and freight executed in the United States, rolling stock still is considerably below pre-war (about two-thirds of pre-war), as well as below requirements.

But owing to a better utilization of existing loading space—by a speedier rotation of freight cars and also by greater loads being put on each car—the total amount of freight carried, compared to pre-war (1937-39) average had increased already in 1946 by 10 percent and in 1947 by 25 percent. This excessive use, however, causes a rate of deterioration of equipment above normal. (Monthly average in 1937-39, 2.434 million ton kilometers; in 1946, 2.695 million ton kilometers; in 1947, 3.088 million ton kilometers. The number of passengers carried increased even more, though, because of decline in rolling stock, the average standard of comfort was still for several years much below pre-war, and started improving only after 1948.

The increase in railway goods and passenger traffic, however, was to a great extent due to the sizeable reduction in motor transport.

In most countries of Western Europe devastated by the war, restoration of rail transport proceeded with similar rapidity. It was considerably slower only in Germany, which was due to (a) an even greater volume of destruction suffered; (b) a lesser recovery of heavy industry and, as a consequence, a greater shortage of materials necessary for reconstruction; and (c) a lack of co-ordination between the different military governments.

As to the harbors, the most urgent task of making them accessible to shipping by de-mining and suppressing obstacles, such as sunken ships, loaded with sand, accumulated by the Germans, had been achieved comparatively promptly. However, reconstruction of all the facilities destroyed (docks, piers, cranes and harbor installations of all kinds) could be only started, as the complete job involved the expenditure of enormous sums, as well as the use of considerable quantities of materials in short supply. Still, in all major ports of Western Europe the main task of reconstruction of harbors was completed, in so far as the capacity to receive ships and handle cargo had been restored. Of course, the facilities do not possess all their pre-war convenience and efficiency. The volume of freight effectively handled is still below pre-war, but this is due more to difficulties of foreign trade and especially of balance of payments than to serious limitation of port capacity.

As to merchant marine, badly depleted by the losses of the war, it had been increased (1) by salvage (over 300,000 tons of shipping had thus been recovered in France alone, including the ocean

290

liner *De Grasse*); (2) by new construction; and (3) by purchase in the United States, whose merchant tonnage of Liberty ships had enormously expanded during the war. France had bought 75 and Italy 50 of these ships, which, though uneconomical for peacetime traffic, as well as short-lived, still provided the countries concerned with the cargo space necessary for carrying their imports without having to pay freight charges in dollars. Still the total tonnage of continental Europe, as well as of Great Britain, remained during the immediate post-war period considerably below pre-war. The French merchant marine, however, exceeded its pre-war tonnage by mid-1950.

Road transport is the field where the slowest and least progress was achieved, as revival of motor traffic had been hampered, first, mainly by lack of tires, and then by shortage of gasoline. Most of the actual destruction due to the war, such as of bridges, has been already restored but, because of the stoppage during the war of practically all maintenance and repair work, owing to lack of materials, the roads are generally still much below their pre-war standard. The truck fleet had been heavily depleted, and all trucks in good condition had been requisitioned for the armies. Trucks being especially indispensable while railway transport was still in bad shape, their number has been restored to, and even above, the pre-war level by imports from overseas, particularly through the purchase of a great number of United States Army surplus vehicles, as well as by concentration on good vehicles of local automobile production. This was true in France, in Italy, and to a lesser extent in Great Britain.

On the contrary, passenger motor transport remained for a longer period considerably below pre-war. Thus, in France, the number of registered passenger automobiles, even though rapidly increasing, is still below the 1938 level, owing mainly to the shortage of gasoline, which can be purchased only in hard currencies, and these are in very short supply. Also, automobile production in most Western European countries is directed mainly

291

toward export, and as far as possible toward hard currency countries. Hence, over two-thirds of total British, and about 80 percent of all French, automobile production since the end of the war has been exported.

(b) *Food.* The food shortage was the most dangerous of all shortages, and also had the greatest economic, social and political implications. Insufficient food supply was a present as well as a future menace to the health of the population in the countries concerned, in particular for the children. It also stimulated discontent, and increased social and political tensions. Finally, as a purely economic factor, it decreased the productivity of labor. The direct and most obvious consequence of food shortage was the decline in productivity due to undernourishment. An even more important, though indirect, consequence was the considerable increase in the rate of absenteeism, which in the two years immediately after the war was about double pre-war in France, and even greater in Germany. This increase in absenteeism was due mainly to the fact that the workers made trips to the countryside in search of food, which they bartered against industrial products, like coal, that they had legally or illegally obtained at their place of work. In all coal-mining industries the miners usually received as part of their pay a very liberal allocation of coal, well above their own requirements having thus at their disposal a comfortable margin for barter trade. After the war, several consumers-goods industries, such as textiles, in order to attract workers, tried to pay part of the wages in manufactured goods which could be used for barter. Other results of the food shortage were (1) the diversion of labor from the industries most essential for reconstruction—such as production of steel or mechanical equipment, which could not provide the workers with objects appropriate for barter—to consumers-goods industries, where manufactured goods for barter against food could be easily obtained; and (2) the considerable, and even more obnoxious, shifting of labor from productive work to black-market activities.

The most urgent task therefore was to increase food production in order to meet fully at least the requirements in essential foodstuffs. Immense efforts were put forth to this end, but impediments to success were considerable. In France, there was at first a shortage of labor due to war losses, as well as to a reduction in foreign labor caused by repatriation and deportation to Germany during the war. A temporary solution of this manpower shortage was the utilization of about 400,000 German war prisoners on French farms. All of them had been repatriated by the end of 1948, but about 80,000 stayed as free foreign workers. Immigration of farm labor also had been resumed, the main categories of foreign workers being Italians and displaced persons from Germany. A permanent solution of the manpower shortage could be achieved only through increase in mechanization, which was difficult because of the dispersal of production in small lots, as well as the highly individualistic tradition of the French peasants. Still a considerable development of cooperation for use of farm machinery has occurred since the end of the war. Another obstacle in the way of mechanization was insufficient production of mechanized equipment. This production had been too small to cover needs of the domestic market, even before the war, and had been handicapped, during the first two years after the liberation, by shortage of steel. Production increased only slowly, but, benefiting from high priorities for fuel and raw materials, it rose considerably above pre-war level. Also large quantities of equipment, particularly tractors, had been imported from the United States and the United Kingdom.

In Great Britain, an appreciable degree of mechanization had been achieved during the war, a fact which had been the main cause of the increase in production. After the end of wartime measures of mandatory direction of labor, which had resulted, in particular, in the drafting of a great number of women for agricultural work, agriculture had begun to suffer from shortage of manpower. Employment of foreign labor—especially Poles

293

from the former military forces who refused repatriation, and displaced persons from Germany—was the main measure taken to alleviate this shortage, while the drive for mechanization was being actively pursued.

In Germany, after the end of the war, agricultural production was effected by the departure of the foreign slave workers, and by the decline in production of fertilizer. The high yields of German crops were due mainly to an especially substantial consumption of fertilizer.

The fertilizer situation in Western Europe, which had been absolutely tragic in 1945, as all production had practically stopped, gradually improved. In the main fertilizer categories (potash, phosphate and nitrate), the situation improved first for potassium, as production of the mines of Germany and France was restored to pre-war level, in spite of difficulties which had been due principally to lack of coal. As to phosphates, production of phosphate rock in French North Africa also rapidly recovered, and even exceeded pre-war level. On the other hand, production of phosphate, as a by-product of the production of pig iron out of phosphatic iron ores of Lorraine and Luxembourg, recovered more slowly and reached pre-war level only during the second half of 1948, owing mainly to shortage of coke. Before the war, production of nitrate had been developed mainly in Germany. This expansion was due, to a great extent, to military motives, since nitrate was used for explosives as well as for fertilizer. Germany was the greatest supply source of fertilizer for the other countries of the European Continent. For some time after the end of the war, the marked decline in German production caused a shortage of nitrate, even though production in all other countries was being actively stimulated and expanded. One particular reason was that requirements had considerably increased, owing to the necessity of restoring soil fertility depleted during the war years. Substantial quantities of nitrate therefore had to be imported from the United States.

294

During the first two years after the end of the war, shortages of smaller items, such as pulp for bagging and jute for reaping-cord, had also been considerable obstacles to the recovery of agricultural production.

A real vicious circle existed, during this period, between agricultural and industrial production, as shortages of industrial products like equipment and fertilizer impeded agricultural recovery, and were due, themselves, to a great extent to decline in labor productivity resulting from insufficient food supply, that is insufficient agricultural production. Thus the vicious circle was complete.

Nevertheless, in spite of all these obstacles, agricultural production had already considerably recovered by the 1946 harvest. In 1947, however, while the supply of agricultural requisites had continued to improve, terrible weather conditions completely ruined the crops of the year. Frost in France destroyed more than half of the total French wheat plantings, and floods in England inflicted serious damage. This crop failure had most disastrous consequences (a) on the food supply; (b) on the balance of payments—food imports had to be considerably larger than expected; and (c) on the monetary situation, increasing inflationary pressure as food prices rose.

In 1948, on the contrary, climatic conditions were very favorable, and, as supplies of fertilizer, equipment and other agricultural requisites had improved even more, the harvest in most Western European countries nearly reached the pre-war level. This can be reasonably assumed, especially as the official figures, based mostly (as in France) on declarations of peasants, are more likely to understate than to overstate the actual results.

In 1949, the general improvement in agricultural production continued, even though climatic conditions, in particular in France, had not been as favorable as in 1948. In 1950, climatic conditions were satisfactory and production made new progress with a few exceptions, such as wheat in France.

WESTERN EUROPEAN CEREAL CROPS *

(in thousands of metric tons)

	Pre-war 1934-38		1945		1946	
	Wheat	All cereals †	Wheat	All cereals †	Wheat	All cereals †
France	8,213	15,270	4,209	7,926	6,756	12,247
Germany (pre-war)	4,077	16,508	....	....	2,367‡	10,039‡
Western Zones	....	....	....	....	....	....
Great Britain	1,743	5,474	2,211	7,710	1,999	6,983
Belgium	450	1,619	310	943	366	1,282
Italy	7,255	11,153	4,176	6,070	6,125	8,827

	1947		1948		1949	
	Wheat	All cereals †	Wheat	All cereals †	Wheat	All cereals †
France	3,266	7,790	7,419	12,919	7,850	13,204
Germany (pre-war)	....	....	....	....	....	....
Western Zones	1,234	5,917	2,049	8,120	2,430	9,458
Great Britain	1,694	5,909	2,318	7,304	2,170	7,170
Belgium	122	981	341	1,097	425	645
Italy	4,674	7,321	6,189	9,303	6,666	9,791

* Source: Food and Agricultural Organization of the United Nations Statistical Yearbook and Bulletin.
† Wheat, rye, barley, oats and maize.
‡ Post-war frontiers.

(c) *Fuel.* In Western Europe, because of the absence of other sources of energy, such as gasoline or natural gas, coal is to a much greater extent the basis of all industrial activity than in the United States. Thus, in the Marshall Plan countries, 82 percent of all energy consumed before the war originated in coal, as against only 58 percent in the United States. The fuel problem in Western Europe is therefore essentially a coal problem.

Before the war, Western Europe was a net exporter of coal to other continents. These exports originated in Great Britain and, to a smaller extent, in Germany. The average annual quantity of the net exports was about four million tons.

During the war, production of coal in Great Britain materially declined and did not recover, in spite of all efforts, such as drafting into the mines of young recruits ("Bevin boys"). In Germany, on the contrary, coal production slightly increased, while in the occupied countries it was at least maintained near pre-war level, owing to overexploitation of mines. The richest veins were used without any consideration of future production, and there was massive use of slave labor.

By the end of the war, the situation in the main coal-mining districts of Western Europe was as follows:

GREAT BRITAIN

The British mines were mostly old, dispersed, and with obsolete equipment, owing to the lack of new investment, during the inter-war period, because of the depression in the industry. The manpower aspect of the coal-mining situation was as unsatisfactory as the technical one; the available labor force was insufficient to achieve production equal to pre-war, as well as inappropriate in its age composition. The proportion of aged men was very high, because during the depression the young generation had refused to go into the mines. This labor force, insufficient and aged, was also overworked, having sustained heavy effort during the war. From the end of the war, and from the arrival of Labor into power, events which occurred nearly at the same time, British miners naturally expected an opportunity to obtain a relaxation of their efforts, and in particular a reduction in the number of working hours. Such a state of mind was especially inappropriate at a moment when a particularly great effort for increase of production was an absolute necessity.

297

FRANCE

The French mines and their equipment were also old and to a considerable extent obsolete, though not so obsolete as those of Great Britain, as most of the mining installations in the northern coal district, destroyed during World War I, had been replaced during the early 1920's. On the other hand, French mines were generally much poorer, with narrow seams especially difficult to exploit and, in some cases, near exhaustion. As to the manpower situation, already before the war most of the underground workers had been foreigners, mainly Poles. During the war, this foreign labor had been depleted by deportation to Germany, while after the end of the war the Polish government made a claim for the repatriation of Polish miners and a considerable number of them returned. Labor productivity had considerably declined, compared to pre-war, owing to undernourishment of the workers, as well as to the very high rate of absenteeism and the deterioration of equipment because of lack of maintenance.

GERMANY

In the Ruhr and Saar districts of Western Germany, seams of coal were mostly large, especially in the Ruhr, which considerably facilitated exploitation of mines. As to the mining equipment, it was generally modern and efficient. But war devastation caused by Allied bombings was greatest in Germany. Even though the mines themselves had suffered little damage, devastation of the railway net of the Ruhr had paralyzed production and the tremendous destruction of housing had made living conditions for miners most difficult. After the Allied occupation, the German mines lost the mass of foreign slave workers who, during the war, had been the greatest part of the manpower available.

298

As to German miners, by the end of the war a substantial proportion of them was in Allied war-prisoner camps. The productivity of the remaining German labor had considerably deteriorated because of insufficient food, the general deterioration of living conditions, and growth of absenteeism. Increase in German coal production was of vital importance to the rest of Western Europe, but especially to Germany itself. During the first two years of Allied occupation, the low productivity in this most vital of all German productions was due to a certain extent to a nationalist feeling of resentment of labor and management. Both management and labor were somewhat reluctant to make the maximum effort of production required, management mainly because they resented foreign control (in the Ruhr), and labor because of the widespread belief of the miners that their effort would mainly benefit, through increased exports, foreign interests —that is, other Western European countries. As a matter of fact, however, exports of coal from Western Germany, with the exception of the first period of liquidation of accumulated stocks, were at their maximum of about 20 percent of total production.

During the immediate post-war period, insufficiency of coal resources was the main bottleneck impeding recovery of industrial production. Therefore, in all coal-producing countries of Western Europe, the greatest possible efforts were made to increase coal production.

In Great Britain, the plan for restoration of the coal-mining industry was based on its nationalization, which had been implemented by the end of 1945. Nationalization made possible the adoption of a unified program of rationalization and modernization of organization, methods of production, and equipment of mines. The implementation of this program is being financed by state investments. While the technical progress of the program has so far been satisfactory and the greatest part of the equipment required is being manufactured in Great Britain, only a small part being imported from the United States, the attitude

299

of labor toward this plan at first caused considerable difficulties. As stated above, at the end of the war British miners wanted to relax their efforts. They expected that, as forecast by the social-ization labor propaganda of the inter-war period, the main targets and results of the nationalization of the mines would be improve-ment in the lot of the workers (higher wages and, above all, shorter hours), and not a drive for increased production.

Thus, the psychological attitude of mining workers—and this is also true of the attitude of British labor in general—was still adjusted to the situation of the inter-war period, when the chief difficulty to be overcome was unemployment. The latter was often considered as due to lack of purchasing power, and not to in-adequate production; and the natural remedies appeared to be reduction of working hours and increase in wages, that is, in purchasing power. This lack of adjustment between the psycho-logical attitude of the workers and the changed situation, and consequently the methods of action required, was a natural con-sequence of the deep and lasting impact on the British working class of the sufferings and frustrations of the preceding period. In the beginning, this attitude materially increased the difficulty of mobilizing the full support of labor in the drive for maximum production. The final success in obtaining this support was due mainly to the fact that the government in power, which de-manded this new effort from the workers, was a labor govern-ment and enjoyed their confidence. Therefore cooperation of the workers with the government, which at first was rather un-satisfactory, steadily improved.

In coal mining, the attitude of the workers had at first obliged the government, after the nationalization, to introduce in 1946 the five-day week. It had been promised to the miners as a correlative of nationalization, and came to be considered by them as a symbol of emancipation from capitalist oppression. At first, too, opposition of the miners impeded rationalization meas-ures implying speeding up of production (a five-weeks strike had been called in Yorkshire against such measures). The opposition was an obstacle, also, to concentration of production on the most productive pits, and even more to admission into the mines of foreigners, in particular of Poles from the armed forces who had rejected repatriation. Introduction of such foreign workers was advisable in order to reinforce the insufficient numbers of the labor force. Gradually, however, all these difficulties were ironed out as the miners' unions increasingly cooperated with the government in convincing the members to accept all measures necessary to expand production. Thus, the miners agreed to lengthen the hours of labor by working on every other Saturday, and accepted the admission into the mines of demobilized Polish soldiers and displaced persons from Germany. Traditional resistance to the introduction of labor-saving devices, formerly resulting from fear of unemployment, was also abandoned. Hence, production as well as productivity steadily increased, especially after the middle of 1947, though still remaining below pre-war.*

An appreciable difficulty in this respect resulted, however, from the lack of incentives for increased production, due to the democratic rationing and price system, as well as to the austerity policy. The miners who earned without any considerable effort the amount necessary for the purchase of their extremely inexpensive rations, could do very little with the extra pay received for increased production, as very few nonrationed consumer goods were at first available. Since, on the other hand, the rate of income tax on these surplus earnings was increasingly higher, most miners were somewhat weary of making special efforts that resulted mainly in increasing their income-tax payments. But gradually a method was worked out which, while maintaining the general principle of equitable rationing, still provided miners with sufficient incentives for increased effort. Accordingly, they received priority for allocation of new housing, as well as extra coupons for rationed consumer goods.

* During 1950, however, production leveled off, owing to a decline in number of miners.

In France, the technical problems were somewhat similar to those in Great Britain, but the labor conditions were extremely different. The French mines also required modernization and rationalization of productive equipment and methods, implying a heavy outlay of investment and overall planning, which would be difficult to achieve if private ownership were maintained. The nationalization of the coal mines, implemented by the end of 1944, a few months after liberation, had been motivated, however, not only by technical efficiency, but even more by political expediency, with a view to stimulating the effort of the miners. As a matter of fact, the miners refused to continue working for private owners who during the occupation had forced them to a strenuous effort of production for the benefit of the Germans. Nationalization thus resulted in the dismissal, enforced by the miners, of a great number of engineers and foremen who were accused of collaboration, but who were mainly disliked for strict enforcement of working discipline and productivity standards.

The decline in working discipline which would have been the natural consequence of such a development did not materialize to the extent that might have been feared, as the miners' unions under Communist leadership at first not only supported, but took the lead in the drive for increased production. Besides, the mass of the French miners, in a country devastated by the war and four years of enemy occupation, could be much more easily convinced of the necessity of a maximum effort to restore coal production to or above pre-war, than workers in Great Britain. The latter still liked to imagine that the victory achieved would bring relief from the necessity of continuing the effort which had brought that victory. Because of this attitude of the French miners, weekly working hours—which during the war had been restored to forty-eight—could be maintained at this level. However, the French authorities also made a much greater effort than the British in order to provide the miners with an extremely privileged status, as to food, consumer goods, new housing, etc., in spite of a considerably lower level of general rations, than in Great Britain.

The labor shortage in the French mines had been temporarily overcome by the employment of some 60,000 German war prisoners (out of a total of 220,000 underground miners), who received the same rations as other workers, but part of whose wages were retained by the Treasury. When repatriation of the war prisoners started, agreements were negotiated to replace them with new immigrants: Italians (20,000) and displaced persons, even though the employment of the latter, in particular, had been violently opposed by the unions, owing to the anti-Communist tendencies of these workers. All of the war prisoners were gone by the middle of 1948, with the exception of a few thousand who had volunteered to remain as free workers.

Through these measures, and also through the gradual implementation of a vast plan of reequipment and modernization, for which a considerable quantity of equipment had to be imported from the United States, the results obtained in the French coal mines were very satisfactory and as early as 1946 the production of 1938 had been exceeded. The decline in productivity was compensated for by the increase, by 40 percent, in the number of underground miners.

Since then, however, the attitude of the main miners' union following the Communist line completely changed and strikes, slow-down of production, and even sabotage of mining installations, as manifested during the October 1948 strike, were used as methods of political struggle. As a consequence, production naturally declined. This obstruction of the Communist-led unions delayed, but did not prevent the recovery of production owing to gradual improvement in production equipment. Thus, in 1949, coal production reached 51.2 million tons, that is, nearly a million tons above pre-war record production achieved in 1930. While, during 1950, production did not increase again, this was due to the fact that the shortage of coal having come to an end,

303

the principal efforts were put on rationalization of production by concentrating it in the most efficient pits and closing down those where production was justified only in case of absolute need. Thus, while volume of total production remained stable, productivity considerably increased during 1950.

In Western Germany, reconstruction of the railway system, especially in the Ruhr—the first condition of a revival of coal production—was rapidly achieved, even though on a temporary basis. However, during the first two years, coal production was hampered by shortage of equipment, even of spare parts, a result of the very low level of steel production. The Allied authorities gave the miners a privileged status for food and vital consumer goods, an advantage which slowly but steadily contributed to the increase of recruitment of new miners, as well as to an improvement in productivity. At the same time, former war prisoners were gradually being repatriated, and some returned to the mines. However, as long as the general level of German food rations remained low, coal output fluctuated in a manner strictly parallel to that of the general rations and not to that of the miners' extra rations, as they naturally shared those with their families.

Recovery of production, which had been very strongly stimulated by the currency reform of June 1948, had previously been much greater in the Saar than in the Ruhr. In the Saar, since the beginning of French occupation, the mines had been under the direct administration of French mining authorities and production had reached pre-war level by the fall of 1948. The Ruhr, on the other hand, had remained all the time under German administration, with only a superficial supervision by British authorities. This discrepancy appears to have been due not only to considerably greater destruction in the Ruhr than in the Saar, but also to some extent to the lack of interest of German managers and technicians in increasing production.

Production, foreign trade and apparent consumption (production + imports — exports) of the leading coal-producing countries of Western Europe, compared to pre-war, were as follows in the first five post-war years:

COAL IN WESTERN EUROPE *
(monthly average in 000 metric tons)

	1937	1945	1946	1947	1948	1949	First 9 months 1950
Great Britain							
Production	20,354	15,475	16,092	16,719	17,732	18,217	18,085†
Exports	3,680	299	420	96	972	1,334	.....
Apparent consumption	16,674	15,176	15,672	16,623	16,760	16,883	.....
France							
Production	3,696	2,776	3,934	3,770	3,608	4,267	4,179
Net Imports	2,403	321	871	1,335	1,606	1,608	.....
Apparent consumption	6,098	3,097	4,805	5,105	5,214	5,875	.....
Belgium							
Production	2,488	1,319	1,899	2,032	2,223	2,321	2,242
Net Imports	144	99	184	290	96	−100	.....
Apparent consumption	2,632	1,418	2,083	2,322	2,319	2,221	.....
Netherlands							
Production	1,193	425	693	842	919	975	1,023
Net Imports	192	...	238	282	242	293	.....
Apparent consumption	1,385	425	931	1,124	1,161	1,168	.....
Germany							
Ruhr production	11,465	...	4,497	5,927	7,368	8,734	9,072
Saar "	1,114	...	657	874	1,040	1,181	1,244
Exports (Western Germany)	2,160	...	1,060	930	1,710	2,039	.....

* Source: Economic Commission for Europe, Coal Committee Bulletin.
† First 10 months.

While production in coal-importing countries, such as France and Belgium, had rapidly recovered to pre-war levels, the two greatest coal-producing and -exporting countries of Western Europe—Great Britain and Western Germany—had in 1946, compared to 1937, a production deficit of some 120 million tons; in 1947, a deficit of nearly 100 million tons; and in 1948 a deficit of 80 million tons. This decline in production resulted in a deficit of coal exports from these two countries (mostly to other Western European countries), compared to pre-war, of nearly 60 million tons in 1946 and 1947, and only a slightly lower figure in 1948.

The decline of coal production in Great Britain impaired even domestic consumption, which had appreciably increased during the war owing to expansion of heavy industry. Consumption during 1946 having been above current production, the level of stocks became dangerously low; and during February 1947 when, owing to heavy frost, coal production temporarily stopped, Great Britain suffered a severe coal crisis which caused a temporary setback in her industrial production and exports. In Germany, also, domestic consumption, which had enormously expanded before and during the war, because of development of war industries, fell off sharply at the end of the war. It picked up only very slowly, keeping tune with the rather slow rhythm of recovery of industrial production in the first two years after the end of military operations. However, already, during this period, the question of distribution of German coal production between domestic consumption and exports became one of the most vital for the economic future of Western Europe. This was the period when German coal production, consumption and exports originating mainly from the Ruhr (the main source of fuel for production of heavy industry in all Western Europe) were still at a very low level.

The brunt of the coal crisis during the two or three years immediately after the end of the war was born, however, by the coal-importing countries of Western Europe, countries where—as in France, Belgium, Netherlands and Luxembourg—domestic production was insufficient to meet requirements; or where, as in

306

Italy and the Scandinavian countries, no domestic coal supplies at all were available. In order to implement a distribution of available coal supplies as equitably as possible, the Western Allied powers established in London, by the end of 1944, the European Coal Organization. It was empowered to allocate coal available for export to Western Europe, either in the exporting countries of Western Europe or in other areas, and especially in the United States. As a result of these allocations, the shortage of coal on the continent of Western Europe was somewhat alleviated. For about three years after the end of the war, however, it still remained the principal factor limiting all industrial activity, particularly production of heavy industry. Steel, cement and chemicals, of special importance in reconstruction, were among the chief products to suffer most.

The deficit in coal exports originating in Western Europe was partly compensated for by imports from the United States which made a very important contribution to the recovery of industrial activity—in spite of their sometimes inadequate quality (being different from coal types traditionally used), excessive cost (due to high freight charges), and, above all, to their having to be paid for in dollars. Total imports of coal from the United States amounted to 5.7 million tons in 1945, 17 million tons in 1946, and a maximum of about 35 million tons in 1947. They declined to 20 million tons in 1948; slightly below 10 million tons in 1949; and nearly stopped altogether in 1950.

From the end of 1947, slowly but steadily the coal shortage began to decrease in intensity, largely owing to the revival of exports from Poland. In 1948, that country exported to Western Europe about 10 million tons, which were paid for, under bilateral agreements, by means of exports of industrial goods requiring no dollar outlay. Coal requirements had also been somewhat reduced by the increase in fuel-oil consumption for industrial purposes, as well as by efforts coordinated by the Coal Committee of the Economic Commission for Europe. That body had taken over, by the end of 1947, the functions of the Eu-

307

ropean Coal Organization, in order to use coal in the most economical and rational way, reserving, for example, all metallurgical coke for steel production, etc. As a consequence of these developments, and in spite of the fact that total coal availabilities of continental Western Europe were still below pre-war, by the end of 1948 the coal shortage had ceased to be an obstacle to the development of industrial production, and coal imports from the United States could be substantially curtailed.

The question of the distribution of German coal resources between domestic and export markets had been settled by the agreement concluded, during the Moscow Conference, between the United States, Great Britain and France. By its terms, the Saar with its coal resources was incorporated into the French economic territory, of which it had been a part from 1919 until 1935, and there was established a sliding scale of coal exports from the Ruhr, which were to increase from 25 to 33 percent of total output as production increased.

(d) *Steel.* Requirements for steel, the basic material for reconstruction of all war devastations—such as for railway and motor transport, shipping, agricultural machinery, industrial equipment, housing, etc.—at the end of the war were considerably above pre-war, while actual production of steel in the countries of the Continent, where devastations had been greatest and requirements were the most urgent, was practically at a standstill and recovered only very slowly. Steel production was hampered at first by shortage of coking coal and, later, of scrap and high-content iron ore required in order to reduce consumption of coking coal. As to Great Britain, where sufficient domestic coke supplies were available, expansion of output of finished steel was to some extent hampered by the shortage of semi-finished products of which, before the war, considerable quantities had been imported mainly from Belgium and France.

Production of raw steel, since the war, in the main producing countries has fluctuated as follows:

308

(in million metric tons)

	1937	1946	1947	1948	1949	1950*
Great Britain	13.2	12.9	12.7	14.9	15.8	16.4
France	7.9	4.4	5.7	7.2	9.1	8.4
Belgium-Luxembourg	6.4	3.7	4.6	6.4	6.1	5.9
Western Germany	19.4	2.9	3.6	5.7	9.1	. . .

* Yearly rate based on figures for 10 first months.

By the end of 1948, the steel shortage was not yet overcome, though already considerably alleviated; while during 1949 production, which had again considerably increased in most producing countries, reached equilibrium with effective domestic and export demand.

Another important bottleneck shortage was lumber, which previously had been imported to a great extent from the Soviet Union and the Balkans, where, owing to war damage, domestic requirements had increased and exports practically stopped. Of the other main sources of supply of lumber to Western Europe, in Scandinavia, owing to shortage of coal, consumption of wood for fuel was considerably expanded, thus reducing exportable lumber resources, while imports from Canada were limited by the dollar shortage. Lack of lumber considerably slowed down reconstruction, especially of housing, and was also the main cause of the newsprint shortage which reduced the dimensions of European newspapers.

On the other hand, for most raw materials which were mainly imported from overseas, shortages did not result in bottlenecks limiting production, as available supplies only were limited by import possibilities depending on dollar resources.

Shortage of manpower was to a certain extent a limiting factor in production in France, particularly for agriculture and mining, as well as to a lesser extent in Great Britain and Belgium. At the same time, there was a considerable surplus of labor and unemployment in Italy and Western Germany, and a smaller surplus of labor in the Netherlands.

In spite of all these limiting factors, production steadily recovered and as early as 1948, in all the principal countries of Western Europe, with the exception of Western Germany, it exceeded the pre-war level. The fluctuations of the general index of industrial production were as follows, 1946-50:

	Year of reference = 100	1946 average	1947 average	1948 average	1949 average	1950 for 9 months
Belgium	1937	72	86	98	94	93
France	1937	73	87	102	112	110
Germany (bi-zone)	1936	34	40	60	89	106
Netherlands	1937	75	95	114	127	138
Great Britain	1937	90	98	109	116	124

26 NATIONAL PLANS OF RECONSTRUCTION

THE TARGET of recovery of production to the pre-war level, or even slightly above, appeared by the end of 1948 either to be already achieved or within easy reach of achievement, in most countries of Western Europe. Such production, however, was not at all sufficient to reestablish the pre-war standard of living, and even less to make possible the implementation of promises made during the war for the achievement of progress in economic standards and in social services claimed by the public.

This insufficiency was due, to a great extent, to the increase in requirements, particularly for capital goods to be used for reconstruction of actual war devastation as well as to compensation for the lack of maintenance, replacement and new construction during the war. It was to an even greater extent a consequence of: (a) the loss of the pre-war creditor position in relation to other continents, especially for Great Britain, but to a lesser extent for all other industrialized countries of Western Europe; and (b) the loss of receipts from shipping, tourist traffic and all other services, which, before the war, compensated for the major part of the deficit of the balance of trade of Western Europe.

In order even to regain their economic independence from overseas assistance by reestablishing the equilibrium of their balance of payments—to say nothing of recovering their pre-war prosperity—all the countries of Western Europe had to face the

311

necessity of an enormous increase in exports. At the same time, imports had to be reduced to a level below pre-war or at least the expanded level of immediate post-war years. For all these countries, especially for Great Britain, it was an absolute necessity, not only for recovery of pre-war standards but for sheer survival, to make a tremendous effort to develop production in order to provide these increased exports, or the replacement of reduced imports.

In order to achieve the development of their economic activity toward these ends, several countries of Western Europe, even at the beginning of the post-war period of reconstruction, had adopted more or less detailed plans of action. These plans contained the goals to be reached, and a description of the methods to be used for attaining them. In most cases, the methods to be employed combined guidance by the state to a certain extent (i.e., state-directed investments or development of nationalized industries), as well as control of the price level, with an appeal to private initiative in most other sectors of the economy.

Great Britain, although administered by a socialist government since July 1945, did not adopt such an overall plan for her economy and only proclaimed the main target to be achieved by 1950. This target was the increase of exports by 75 percent above the level of 1938, which would insure payment of the imports necessary for production and consumption at pre-war standards, but taking into account maintenance of full employment. Achievement of this objective implied increase of the labor force working for export to 25 percent of the number of all British workers, as well as modernization, rationalization and expansion of industrial and agricultural production, and reconstruction of shipping.

Nationalization of some of the most important key industries (coal mining, public utilities, transport and steel) had been effected to a great extent, in order to facilitate rationalization of their organization. For several other industries, which also were in great need of rationalization, it had been effected without na-
312

tionalization, but with the assistance of the state, which provided the funds for the investments required. The absence in Great Britain of a published overall plan, extended over several years, does not imply the lack of a carefully coordinated and planned policy. This policy, and the effort to be accomplished every year, have been made public in an economic survey published at the beginning of the respective years since 1947. The publication contains very detailed and painstaking descriptions of the targets in all main categories of production, foreign trade, balance of payment, national income, consumption and investments. Toward the end of 1948 a British plan for the period 1948-52, disclosing the long-term objectives toward which all planning in Great Britain had been directed from the beginning, had been prepared for the Organization for European Economic Cooperation, to be incorporated in the general master plan of the participating countries. The trends and targets of the plan will be described below, in the discussion of the Organization for European Economic Cooperation.

The Netherlands had adopted, shortly after the end of the war, a four-year plan of economic reconstruction with the objective of achieving by 1950 a return to pre-war standard of living. This not only would restore all war devastations, but also would compensate for the losses of income from investments in, and trade with, Indonesia, and the greatest part of the transit trade with Germany. It would also provide for the considerable rate of population increase. The Dutch plan is concentrated mainly on investments; it is intended to expand industrial production in order to replace many former German imports, as well as to develop exports, and also to mechanize agriculture.

The most important of the national economic plans of the countries of Western Europe is the French plan of reconstruction and modernization (*plan de modernisation et d'équipment*), called, by the name of its main author, the Monnet Plan. By its background, as well as by its positive contents and also its de-

313

fects, this plan is fairly representative of post-war economic trends in Western Europe.

The Monnet Plan goes back to the fact, acknowledged during the war and the German occupation, that the pre-war economic structure of France, based mainly on a balance between agriculture and industry, had been proved by events to be a source of weakness and not of strength. Until the war, dominant French opinion had believed that this structure was both a factor of social and economic stability in time of peace, making the country less vulnerable in case of depression, and a factor of strength in time of war, owing to relative independence from overseas food imports. The Nazi invasion proved that these advantages of the pre-war economic structure were relatively negligible, compared to the enormous handicap resulting as a necessary consequence of this economic structure: namely, a quantitatively as well as qualitatively insufficient development of industrial capacity, pre-war conditions in France being favorable neither to industrial expansion nor to technical progress. The inferiority of French industrial capacity was to a great extent responsible for (a) the inadequacy of economic war preparation, and (b) the difficulties and delays of reconversion to war production, which were undoubtedly one of the main reasons for the military disasters of May-June 1940.

French public opinion during that period—among the Free French, as well as in the resistance movement in the interior—became convinced of the necessity of a complete transformation, after the war, of the economic structure of the country by the establishment of a highly developed large-scale industry, especially heavy industry. Such a structural change was deemed essential in order to restore the political and economic independence of the country and to reestablish her position as a great power, as well as to make possible the implementation of the program of economic and social reform planned for the post-war period.

These reasons were of capital importance for the acceptance of such a program by all political parties, and for its appeal to the
314

general public. But besides all that, such a development also provided the only possible solution for the post-war difficulties of the French economy. In order to rebuild the ruins of her enormous war devastations, France, during the period of economic reconstruction, needed imports on a scale considerably above pre-war. Her previous international means of payment, other than exports, had been reduced or completely wiped out (income from foreign investments, tourist traffic, and other services) and she had become a debtor, instead of a creditor, country. The only possibility of reestablishment of the equilibrium of the balance of payments consisted in an expansion of exports to about double the level of 1938, and this could be achieved only as a consequence of a similar development of industrial production.

The Monnet Plan had been prepared on the basis of studies made by eighteen modernization committees, consisting of government officials and representatives of farmers, industrial employers, and labor unions of the respective most important economic activities. The plans prepared by these committees had later on, in turn, been coordinated in a general plan. This, however, still did not apply to the whole economy, but contained detailed programs only for the most important key sectors, where development of production was especially necessary. The final Monnet Plan was put into effect on January 1, 1947.

It was based on two most important international assumptions:

(1) That production of German heavy industry, in particular iron and steel production, would remain limited at or about the very low level established by the Potsdam Conference and by the level of the industry agreement of March 1946. It was also assumed that, in order to fill the considerable gap resulting from the drastic curtailment of German production and exports, France, and to a lesser extent Belgium and Luxembourg, would expand their production. This, in turn, would thus result in the transfer to the West, from the Reich, of the greatest concentration of steel production on the continent of Europe and, as a

315

consequence, concentration of the economic power and military potential based on such production. Aside from the considerable political advantage of reducing the military potential of Germany, and thus providing her neighbors with more security against a new aggression, such a transfer had also objective economic justifications, in so far as it is more economical to transport coke from the Ruhr to the iron furnaces of Lorraine and Luxembourg, located on the ore deposits, than to transport much greater quantities of iron ore in the opposite direction. As a matter of fact, however, the most economical solution consists in dividing production between both centers, which implies a two-way traffic of iron ore and coke.

(2) The second assumption was that sufficient quantities of coke and coking coal would be made available by exports, mainly from the Ruhr, to provide the fuel necessary for this increased steel production.

The program for the development of steel production was thus the most ambitious, as well as the most basic, part of the Monnet Plan. French steel production had reached its pre-war maximum in 1929, with 9.7 million tons; it had amounted to only 6.9 million tons in 1938, and even considerably less, 4.6 million tons, in 1946. The plan was to expand its maximum capacity by 25 percent and to reach in 1951 a total production (in terms of raw steel and cast iron) of 12.7 million tons. Such an accomplishment would enable France to resume steel exports on a considerable scale, 1.9 million tons, and provide the necessary raw-material basis for a similar and sometimes even more considerable development of steel-consuming equipment industries.

The machine-tools industry was planned to be the object of an especially sizeable expansion. Before the war its capacity, as well as the range of its production, had been very limited (maximum output was only 15,000 machines) and a great part of the equipment requirements of French industries had been satisfied by imports, mainly from Germany and the United States. In spite of these imports, and owing to the slow rate of progress of French

316

industry, the total number of machine tools was insufficient in quantity 475,000 (against over 2 million in Germany at the end of the war, and in the United States in 1940). The tools were also out of date; the average age of French machine tools in 1945 was 25 years, while it was less than 10 years in the United States. All this resulted in a relatively low rate of efficiency of industrial production. The plan for machine-tools production consisted in increasing the annual capacity, by 1950, to 45,000 metal-working machine tools; and in reducing, by domestic production and imports, the average age of the machine-tool part to 16 years.

The output of agricultural machinery was planned also to undergo a considerable expansion. While the plan for agricultural production was intended simply to restore by 1950 pre-war level of production, that is, approximate self-sufficiency for most important foodstuffs (wheat, sugar, meat, etc.), the plan for manpower employed in agriculture was to reduce it considerably and divert to industry a great number of farm workers. Such a procedure implied a considerable development of mechanization in agriculture. Thus, the intention was to put 200,000 tractors at the disposal of French farmers by 1950. It was planned to import some of these tractors at first, but most of them were to be manufactured by domestic industry, production of which was to be expanded by 500 percent. A similar expansion was to be effected for production of farm machinery.

Increased steel and equipment production was expected to facilitate expansion of the insufficient fuel and energy resources of French industry. In coal mining very considerable investments were planned, the new equipment required being at first mainly imported from the United States and at a later stage manufactured in France. Mining was supposed to expand its production up to 65 million tons by 1950. Production was back to 47 million tons in 1946 as compared to a pre-war maximum of 50 million tons in 1930. However, it was figured that by 1950, taking into account the planned expansion of all industries, consumption of coal should reach 87 million tons, thus leaving import requirements at over 20 million tons.

Production of electric power, which had increased from 20.7 billion kwh in 1938 to 23.1 billion kwh in 1946, was planned to expand to 37 billion kwh in 1950, mainly by building new hydro-electric plants, as well as modern thermic plants consuming low-grade fuel.

As to other key industries included in the Monnet Plan, production of building materials was planned to expand to a level more than double that of pre-war, in order to provide for the requirements for reconstruction of public works, railways and harbors, as well as of housing, and for new projects in industry and public utilities. Of the other main industries, production of automobiles and of textiles was planned to increase by 20-30 percent, mainly for exports.

The implementation of the Monnet Plan implied a considerable expansion of the industrial labor force (by about 1,200,000 workers) between the end of 1946 and 1950. This expansion was expected to be achieved by the transfer of manpower from agriculture and unproductive occupations, as well as by immigration. Arrangements for immigration of Italians and D.P. ("displaced persons") workers from Germany had been made and agreements concluded for this purpose.

During the period of implementation of the Monnet Plan, a substantial deficit of the balance of payments was considered to be inevitable. This was because very sizeable imports of raw materials and equipment for modernization had to be made, mainly from the American Continent, while exports could be increased only gradually, as production recovered and expanded. The gap between the imports required for the implementation of the Plan and the available means of payment (proceeds of estimated exports and of liquidation of remaining foreign assets) had been evaluated at $540 million for 1947, $420 million for 1948, and $190 million for 1949. It was expected that a state of equilibrium would be reached by 1950, and that in the following years a sur-

318

plus sufficient for gradual repayment of the debt incurred would be attained.

The general estimates of the Monnet Plan, and particularly of its balance of payments had been examined and approved by the United States government. The latter considered them feasible as well as desirable (in view of the estimated influence of the Plan on the economic recovery of France) and appropriate for the shift in the economic balance of power in Europe due to result from implementation of the Plan. This approval was the basis of the Blum-Byrnes agreement of May 1946, concluded in Washington, according to which the Export-Import Bank granted to France a credit of $650 million for the purchase of equipment required for the implementation of the Monnet Plan. France, for her part, agreed that, once the Plan was implemented and her economy back on a normal competitive basis, she would accept the American program of return to international multilateral trade formulated in the United States draft of the Charter of the International Trade Organization.

During the period elapsed since the beginning of the implementation of the Monnet Plan, appreciable strides had been made toward achieving increase of production approaching its goals in several important industries. However, several important defects of the plan also became apparent, such as the much too early start of a drive for maximum exports of consumer goods. This premature effort frustrated the domestic consumer of the long awaited satisfaction of requirements—some of them postponed for the whole duration of the war—and thus considerably reduced incentives for efficiency and increase of production, as well as indirectly increasing inflationary pressure.

An even much more important unfavorable factor was the failure of the French economy, during the first two years of the implementation of the Plan, to overcome inflation and to reach financial and monetary stability, which the experts of the Monnet Plan team had considered to be a condition essential to the success of their Plan. Financial instability hampered implementation

319

of the Plan, mainly by discouraging private savings and rendering most difficult, and sometimes even impossible, the financing of investments in the private sector by issue of loans. The only possible alternative method therefore was autofinancing by reinvestment of profits of the respective concerns. The inflationary rise in prices also discouraged French exports, and several devaluations brought only temporary improvement in this respect, as a new rise in prices after a few months rapidly wiped out the benefits of price reduction resulting from depreciation of the currency. Increase of exports on a considerable scale started only in 1949, when monetary stability had been established; it gained momentum during 1950.

Another factor, which in 1947 had handicapped implementation of the Monnet Plan, was the catastrophic failure of the wheat crop, which obliged the French government to spend $200 million more than had been expected on imports of cereals, and which curtailed by the same amount imports of equipment and raw materials. On the other hand, rise in the level of American prices by some 40 percent since the summer of 1946 had resulted in a corresponding increase in import prices, disrupting to the same extent the forecasts for the deficit of the balance of payments.

Another unfavorable factor of the utmost importance to the Monnet Plan is the change in Allied policy about the level of German steel production, a consequence of the split between the West and the USSR, and of the desire to make Western Germany self-supporting. The increase in authorized yearly output from 5.8 to 10.7 million tons, to which France had to agree, was implemented only during 1949, when rapidly increasing German steel production exceeded French output. Since then, it has made new strides. In the latter part of 1950, owing partly to export orders for rearmament purposes, German steel production practically reached the level of its effective available capacity of some 14 million tons. Thus, the German steel industry seems to have again become a most dangerous competitor to French production.

However, owing to the establishment of the International Authority for the control of the Ruhr, and even more to the expected adoption of the Schuman Plan, the danger of German competition might not prove as serious as had been feared. Even this substantial expansion of German steel output should not endanger arrival of supplies of Ruhr coke necessary for the planned development of French steel production, provided coal output in the Ruhr also increases as expected. But some difficulties as to distribution of coal and coke between the Ruhr and her western neighbors again arose by the end of 1950.

In the first two years of the Monnet Plan, however, insufficiency of imports of coal and coke from the Ruhr had considerably hampered development of French steel production. When, by the end of 1948, supplies of coke became adequate, French steel production expanded appreciably and in 1949 exceeded 9 million tons; during 1950, production leveled off because of slackening demand on the domestic market.

In spite of all these difficulties and handicaps, the positive effects of the Plan have still been considerable. A most important feature was the offer to the public of a national goal, stimulating imagination and presenting an appeal for the cooperation of all classes of the nation.

The implementation of the Monnet Plan had been somewhat delayed, owing to the international and domestic difficulties and obstacles mentioned above, and the final objectives are now expected to be reached only in 1952, instead of 1950. On the other hand, implementation has been considerably facilitated by Marshall Plan aid.

Already, in 1947, worth-while achievements had been made in several industries. For example, production of electric power exceeded its goal of 25 billion kwh and reached 101 percent of the estimate laid down by the Plan, owing mainly to the construction of the Genissiat Dam on the Rhone. This hydroelectric plant, the

321

biggest in Western Europe, and only slightly smaller than the famous Dnieprogues of the Soviet Union, had been inaugurated without any comparable amount of publicity. Coal production, also—when strikes and "go slow" trends did not prevent it—already showed in 1947, and even more in 1948 and 1949, a considerable increase, due to modernization of equipment. Thus, during 1949, production reached the record figure of over 51 million tons.

During 1949, production of steel was more than double its 1946 figure, and only 7 percent below the record production of 1929. Production of cement was 6.7 million tons in 1949, as against 3.9 million tons in 1946 and 4.1 million tons in 1938. Production of tractors reached 17,000 in 1949, that is, ten times higher than pre-war. In 1949, over 100,000 tractors were available to French agriculture, against 35,000 in 1938. On the other hand, integration of too small patches of land (*remembrement*), most essential for increased efficiency of agricultural production, progressed only slowly.

Total investments for the whole duration of the Plan had been estimated at 2518 billion frances. For the first reconstruction period, 1946-48, they amounted to 1045 billion francs, and in 1949 to 475 billion francs, out of which 220 billion francs had been financed by the counterpart fund of the Marshall Plan aid. For 1950, investments were estimated at 577 billion francs, and for 1951 at 566 billion francs. Of the investments made during 1949, by far the greatest part had been financed by the state, while only a small part consisted of private investments, made mainly through the autofinancing or bank loans, as the amount of new loans floated on the capital market was very limited because of the high rates of interest due to protracted inflation.

However, there was a major defect in the Monnet Plan, as well as in the other national plans—such as, in particular, the British Plan (submitted to the OEEC). While it was not in the intention of France, of Great Britain, or of any other country of Western Europe to develop its economy toward autarchy (such as was the intention of Nazi Germany and of Soviet Russia), their plans and efforts lacked all coordination with one another. This resulted in a danger of duplication and misplaced investment. Thus, for example, most countries of Western Europe intended to develop production and exports of steel products and textiles. This lack of cooperation was especially dangerous, as it impeded the restoration of the close pre-war trade relations inside the area of Western Europe, and created even greater obstacles to an eventual intensification of such economic relationships.

27 CONSUMER DEMAND AND
POST-WAR INFLATION

THE WAR LEFT in all belligerent countries, and even in neutral ones, a tremendous potential of inflation, corresponding to a great extent to the pent-up demand for goods and services that had been unavailable during all this period. This pent-up demand was expressed by the enormous increase in the volume of money and credit—corresponding to the most wasteful and destructive of all consumptions (military expenditure)—of which only a part, more or less substantial in the different countries concerned, could be absorbed even by a drastically increased rate of taxation.

Still, as long as the war was going on, this excess of purchasing power, invested in short-term bonds, bank deposits, or even increased currency holdings, was not too obnoxious. The volume of money required for current transactions was strictly limited by price control and rationing, which were supported in most belligerent countries by moral pressure due to patriotic feelings, and also, especially in occupied territories, by the threat of severe sanctions. Thus, this surplus of monetary means was practically sterilized, and, with the exception of relatively limited black markets, did not enter the bidding for available goods and drive up the prices.

As soon as the war was over, this potential of inflation became an element of acute inflationist pressures. On the one hand, con-
324

trols had to be abolished or at least relaxed, while on the other hand most people who, during the war, had been ready to forego enjoyment of many highly desired goods and comforts, now wanted the more eagerly to obtain again all that they had missed so much during all these years. The pressure of inflationary demand was thus enormously increased, while existing barriers to inflation were abolished, weakened, or in some countries even broke down under that pressure.

The most typical cases of the different aspects of the post-war inflationary situation, as well as of different policies applied in order to remedy the situation are: Great Britain, Belgium, France and Germany.

GREAT BRITAIN

Great Britain is the country where during, as well as after, the war rationing and price control were most successfully applied. The success of British controls was due to a great extent to the admirable civic sense of the population,* but fully as much to the perfection of the existing rationing system. This provided rations sufficient in quantity for food and other vital consumer goods, equitably distributed and sold, owing to government subsidies, at very low prices which everybody could afford to pay. These rations, which provided the entire population with all that was necessary for maintenance of productivity of all the workers as well as of a satisfactory health standard, represented, even for the part of the population which was formerly unemployed, a considerable improvement compared to pre-war.

In spite, however, of the considerable increase of agricultural

* The absence or the insignificance of the black market in Great Britain was, however, also due to some extent to the fact that most of the rationed food was imported and the rest produced on large-scale farms where control could be more effective and fraud much more difficult than on the small peasant farms on the Continent.

325

production in Great Britain achieved during the war, the greatest part of the food rations distributed to the British population was provided by imports. These imports were financed at first by liquidation of foreign assets, and since the beginning of 1941 chiefly: by Lend Lease from the United States; by mutual aid received from Canada and other Dominions; and (though to a lesser extent) by the creation of a considerable foreign debt in sterling, which made creditors of Great Britain on this account out of countries such as India and Egypt, which had heretofore been her debtors. Owing to a great extent to such possibilities existing for the financing of her vital imports, Great Britain had been able to devote all her energies to the pursuit of war. Thus, by the end of the war in Europe, 42 percent of all available manpower (men and women of working age) was either in the armed forces or occupied in war production, while only 4 percent was occupied in production for export.

This financial assistance from her Allies, which liberated Great Britain for the time being from all anxiety about the situation of her balance of payment, enabled her to become the front bastion in the battle of Europe, as well as one of the main supply sources of finished armaments. That assistance was therefore considered by the British government and by public opinion to be not a sort of international or interallied relief, but a participation of the overseas Allies in the common war effort, well justified by its economic and military effects for achieving victory.

This opinion, perfectly justified from the British point of view, about the financial aid received particularly under the American Lend Lease, provides the explanation for the intense resentment created in Great Britain by the suspension of Lend Lease deliveries in September 1945, immediately after the capitulation of Japan. This sudden stoppage, was effected when the British economy was still essentially geared to war production and could not even have started reconversion to peace time activity and attempted to restore equilibrium of her balance of payments. It

326

was obviously a shattering blow to Great Britain's economic strength, and was considered by British public opinion as extremely unfair, especially in view of the heavy sacrifices supported by that country while standing alone during the first years of the war. The opinion was even expressed that discontinuance of Lend Lease had been effected as a sort of punishment of Great Britain for putting a Labor government into power. On the other hand, American public opinion had considered Lend Lease as purely a wartime measure of military aid which naturally should be terminated as soon as the war itself came to an end.

The termination of Lend Lease, together with the abandonment of the plans drawn up during the war by some officials of the State Department of the United States for a post-war Lend Lease for the purpose of reconstruction of the economy of war-devastated areas, was proved by the experience of the next few years to be extremely costly in terms of economic dislocation and social and international tension. Even though, less than three years later, the course of events convinced the United States of the necessity of providing a large contribution for the reconstruction of the rest of the free world, and such assistance was granted under the Marshall Plan on an apparently adequate scale, the interruption of Lend Lease was still most unfortunate, as well as probably very uneconomical.

The loan of $3,750 million granted by the United States to Great Britain by the end of 1945, in order to cover the deficit of her balance of payments during the period of reconversion, was only a partial compensation for the stoppage of Lend Lease. This was due in particular to the conditions which had to be accepted as a counterpart, and which pledged future British policy to adopt at a fixed date certain measures, such as convertibility of sterling, which were later proved to be unworkable and had to be abandoned. Another step considered just as dangerous was the acceptance of the principle of multilateral and nondiscriminatory trade agreements, according to the U. S. draft

327

of the International Trade Organization charter, which, though certainly not objectionable in itself, might also prove unfavorable for Great Britain in depriving her, at a moment of considerable economic difficulties, of the bargaining advantages resulting from reciprocity.

The precipitate and premature end of Lend Lease obliged the British to speed up to the utmost the reconversion of their economy, as well as to start an intensive export drive, by providing all priorities in manpower and raw materials for this purpose. This was in order to compensate, by increase of exports, for the loss of income from foreign investments, and thus to restore the equilibrium of the balance of payments. While this export drive was being pushed forward with the greatest determination, the level of imports was cut to the strictest minimum of food and raw materials indispensable for the maintenance of the required industrial activity. This reduced the level of availabilities and consumption of the British population, with respect to products entirely or mainly imported, not only below pre-war, but even below wartime rations, especially in regard to meat and fats, the imports of which had been financed by Lend Lease.

This "austerity policy," in spite of the rigorous sacrifices thus imposed on the British public, has been applied with great vigor, especially since, at the beginning of 1947, Sir Stafford Cripps became Chancellor of the Exchequer, and in fact the man with the greatest influence in shaping the economic policy. It had achieved a very appreciable degree of success, since, in spite of increasing difficulties encountered by British exports (as the sellers' market began to disappear and absorptive capacity of many countries declined), their volume steadily expanded. Also, the balance of trade deficit, having been aggravated in 1947, mainly owing to the rise in world prices of food and raw materials and deterioration in Great Britain's terms of trade, declined considerably in 1948 and even more in the following years.

328

INDEX NUMBERS OF QUANTUM OF BRITISH FOREIGN TRADE (1938 = 100)

	1945		1946		1947	
	Exports	Imports	Exports	Imports	Exports	Imports
1st Quarter	...	...	84.2	63.2	100.5	67
2nd "	...	...	98	68.7	102	78
3rd "	46.2	61.7	104.3	70.1	114	88
4th "	55.8	53	111.2	72.2	117	78

	1948		1949		1950	
	Exports	Imports	Exports	Imports	Exports	Imports
1st Quarter	126	81	158	82	172	86
2nd "	135	81	146	89	167	95
3rd "	139	82	142	92	...	...
4th "	147	80	161	89	...	...

This increase in exports, which in the first quarter of 1950 nearly reached the target of 75 percent above the level of 1938, was reflected in a parallel improvement in the balance of trade of Great Britain. The overall deficit of the balance of trade, which had amounted to £336 million in 1946 and £425 million in 1947, had declined to £207 million in 1948, £147 million in 1949, and £108 for the first half of 1950. Owing to the gradual restoration of invisible receipts, mainly of shipping but also of other sources, the improvement of the balance of payments on current account was even more striking. Thus, while in 1947 its deficit had been £558 million, it had been reduced for 1948 to £80 million and for 1949 to £38 million, while during the first half of 1950 there was an actual surplus of £52 million.

As to the deficit in current transactions (merchandise, trade and services) with the dollar area, mainly the United States and Canada, which had reached its maximum in 1947 when it amounted to £574 million, it had also been considerably reduced for 1948 to £273 million, had slightly increased in 1949 to £302 million and declined in the first half of 1950 to £52 million.

The gross national product of Great Britain in 1946 already

exceeded the pre-war 1938 level by 5-10 percent; in 1947, a further moderate increase was achieved, while in 1948 considerable progress had been realized; this increase continued throughout 1949 and 1950. Thus, in spite of the appreciable reduction in net imports compared to pre-war—as well as of the tremendous increase in government expenditures, military and civilian (e.g., for economic controls)—total resources available for consumption had been about equal to 1938 (at constant prices) in 1946 and above pre-war in 1947 and even more in 1948 and the following years. Thus, from the point of view of overall supply, there appeared to be no insufficiency that could result in a strong inflationary pressure.

In fact, however, even though overall level of consumption had been maintained, or even slightly increased, the general impression of scarcity which prevailed in Great Britain since the end of the war, and which was only very slowly alleviated, resulted from shifts in consumption, compared to pre-war, between different categories of goods and classes of consumers. Thus, limitation of supplies of food, textiles and furniture below pre-war level or effective requirements expanded, because of protracted deferment of replacement could not be compensated, for the public, by increase in consumption of liquor, tobacco and of all kinds of entertainment services.

On the other hand, the standard of living of the upper and middle classes was considerably reduced, e.g., by abolishment or reduction of luxury consumptions such as foreign travel or gasoline for motoring. This was to a great extent due to (a) rationing and production controls, which had drastically reduced available goods and services other than those which were absolute necessities, and (b) the shift in the distribution of national income through high taxation. For these classes the result of the postwar equalitarian redistribution of national income (even if its overall amount had not declined) was the same as if it had been drastically reduced. Their losses in consumption of luxuries were not compensated for by the appreciable increase in consumption of necessities by the lower income groups, whose standards of consumption, owing to full employment and low cost of living, considerably improved.

The shift in the distribution of British national income is illustrated by the comparison of the share of the different income categories in 1938 and 1946; in the years after 1946 the pattern of distribution of national income did not change, even though the total amount of it had increased. The total shift in income from higher and middle income groups to lower income categories was over 20 percent.

NATIONAL INCOME OF THE UNITED KINGDOM
(in million £)

	1938	% of total national income	1946	% of total national income	% of increase from 1938 to 1946
A Lower income groups					
Wages	1,682	...	2,720	...	62
Armed forces pay	77	...	502	...	552
Social Security benefits, etc.	270	...	737	...	173
	2,029	44.2	3,959	54.2	...
B Middle and upper incomes					
Salaries	1,054	...	1,408	...	34
Rents, interest, profits	1,508	...	1,938	...	29
	2,562	55.8	3,346	45.8	...

The reduction in supply and consumption of consumer goods and services other than necessities affected even the better paid categories of wage-earners, such as the miners, and thus reduced incentive for increase of productivity. This was because increased earnings, resulting from a more intensive effort, could not be spent on the purchase of the goods they most wanted and, from a certain level up, such earnings resulted to some extent in increasing only their savings or even their income-tax payments. This lack of incentive for the workers was one of the main

331

reasons for the considerable development of new wasteful forms of consumption, like betting, and the consequent increase in race court attendance, as well as in the rate of absenteeism. Thus, the lack of incentive indirectly increased inflationary pressures by impeding development of production and increase of supplies available for consumption. Other factors acting in a similar manner were the general weariness of the workers and all the rest of the British population, after the strenuous physical and nervous effort during the war, and the general disappointment over persisting shortages, which also created a considerable pressure on the price and wage level.

Other inflationary factors were insufficiency of savings available for investment, owing to the enormous requirements for investments in the program of modernization and expansion of the productive capacity of practically all British industries. The rate of investment in relation to gross national product had been maintained at 20 percent since the end of the war, while pent-up consumer demand had increased consumption requirements and the shift in national income from profits to wages, had also increased the ratio of consumption out of a similar income, as savings out of a given amount of wages are normally much lower than out of a similar amount of profits. Owing to all these factors, and in order to resist the inflationary pressure, the British government was obliged to restrict investment at an absolute minimum. It thus especially had to curtail considerably the initially planned very extensive housing program. After an appeal of the Prime Minister, Mr. Attlee, to the workers and employers in March 1948, the government also obtained their acceptance of a general freeze of the level of distributed profits and wages.

Owing to the still satisfactory functioning of the system of controls and to the price subsidies, the cost of which, however, steadily increased, Great Britain succeeded in keeping her price and cost-of-living level relatively stable. The main inflationary influence, in this respect, had been the steep rise in import prices of food and raw materials since the decontrol of prices in the United States, which for a period of some two years had proceeded at a monthly average rate of about 1-2 percent, while prices of manufactured goods exported by Great Britain rose considerably less. This resulted in increasing even more the deficit of British trade, especially with the dollar area.

Some improvement along these lines resulted from the fall in American prices, which started in the second half of 1948. During the year 1948 also, improvement in available supplies made it possible to abolish rationing for a certain number of basic foodstuffs as well as for industrial consumer goods. Improvement in this respect continued in 1949 and 1950. The main difficulties resulting from post-war excess of consumer demand and inflationary pressure was thus overcome in Great Britain, owing to the courageous and intelligent policy of the government, as well as to the loyal attitude of the public who acted in a manner most equitable for the whole population, as well as most favorable for the development of British economy.*

BELGIUM

Immediately after liberation from the German occupation in October 1944, the Belgian government, on the initiative of the Finance Minister, Camille Gutt (at present Director General of the International Monetary Fund), introduced a carefully planned monetary reform. This consisted in the exchange of the currency and the blocking of 60 percent of the amount presented for exchange; most of the blocked amount remained absorbed by the state as taxes or forced loan. For the time being this drastic deflation caused the population severe hardships, and even hampered recovery of business activity, as all concerns had their liquid resources depleted, and yet it resulted in liberating the Belgian economy from the inflationary pressure due to excess of

* The new difficulties which resulted in September 1949 in devaluation of sterling are discussed below.

currency supply which had affected the economies of nearly all other countries of this area during the immediate post-war period.

This anti-inflationary policy of absorbing excess liquid purchasing power was supported by a very liberal import policy. Its aim was, by creating abundance, to destroy the "psychology of scarcity" which had prevailed after the war in most other countries of Europe, and which was a most important factor in increase of prices. These substantial imports, obtained mainly from the chief source of essential supplies available during the immediate post-war period, namely the United States, were possible because of Belgium's exceptionally strong dollar position due to her creditor status in Lend Lease, which resulted from the use by the Allied forces of the port of Antwerp, as well as to the important balances accumulated owing to the substantial exports of raw materials during the war from the Congo Colony. Belgium thus became the first country in Western Europe to overcome food and consumers-goods shortages. As a consequence, the standard of living of the workers was improved, and stimulants for increased productivity were provided.

Owing to these reasons and to the fact that Belgium was able to deliver at once important commodities in short supply, such as iron and steel products, chemicals and coke, Belgian exports expanded considerably above the level of imports, especially in relation to her main customers of Western Europe. Demand for the Belgian franc being thus above supply, it became the hardest currency of all those of the war-devastated countries of Europe. After a certain time, however, the lack of harmony in the distribution of Belgian imports and exports—imports originating mainly in hard-currency countries, and exports being sent chiefly to soft-currency areas—reacted unfavorably on Belgian foreign trade and industrial activity. Several countries, customers of Belgium, such as, in particular, France, lacking the Belgian francs required to pay for their net imports from that country, were obliged, after exhaustion of all resources and credits, to curtail and even to suspend completely all their purchases. This caused considerable unemployment in Belgian export industries, a condition which persisted even when in latter years the pattern of foreign trade came back to normal.

FRANCE

At the moment of liberation there was in France, left over from German occupation, a tremendous potential of inflation resulting from the financing, by the state, of indemnities levied by the Nazis. Thus, the index of money quantity (currency and bank deposits) in September 1944 had reached 510 (1938 = 100), while the price level, which had been kept down by controls directly or indirectly imposed by the Germans, had risen much less. The index of wholesale prices amounted to 271; the cost of living in Paris, at official prices of rationed supplies, was 299 and the index of wage rates only 248. Taking into account the enormous reduction in the quantity of consumer goods available, the gap between quantity of money and value of global resources at existing prices was such that an explosive inflation appeared unavoidable unless absorption of the surplus purchasing power by a drastic deflation could be effected.

The difficulties of fighting inflationary pressure were still more increased during the period immediately after liberation, when, because of paralysis of transport, the authority of the central government was very weak—indeed, it scarcely existed at all. At that time, in most rural food-surplus areas the system of mandatory deliveries of food products at official prices—introduced on the German pattern and enforced heretofore through heavy penalties —broke down, since these penalties imposed by the Vichy government had to be abolished. Thus, it became impossible to maintain the previous level of official prices of purchase of food products from the farmers and of rationed supplies sold to consumers. Besides this rise in official prices, considerably greater quantities of

335

produce than before were transferred from the official market to the illegal, or so called "parallel," market where prices also increased in a measure similar to that of the official prices.

A program of complete deflation, similar to that which had been applied in Belgium, and based on exchange and blocking of most existing currency and bank deposits, had been prepared before the return of the French government to Paris by the Minister of Finance, M. Pierre Mendès-France. This policy, if implemented, would have absorbed the surplus of liquid purchasing power over the amount required for transactions at current prices, and thus would have completely abolished, or at least considerably reduced, inflationary pressure. Such an operation would have been much more difficult in France than in Belgium, because of the greater size of the country and of the lack at that moment of centralized government. Discontent and resistance, especially from the speculators, but also from many farmers accustomed to hoarding currency as a means of saving, might have been considerable. Still it is obvious that, in the first few months after liberation, such a program might have been successfully implemented, owing mainly to the enthusiasm of the population, which supported the De Gaulle administration and enabled it to exercise great freedom of action. Resistance to this deflation would have been easily broken, as such a policy would have been quite popular with the masses suffering from inflation, while it would have been detrimental mainly to the groups or persons who directly or indirectly profited from occupation and collaboration, and whose complaints at that moment would have had little favor with public opinion.

However, such a policy, which, as events proved would have been most useful from the monetary and financial, as well as from the political, point of view, was not adopted. It was supported only by the Socialist and the Catholic parties, while naturally all pro-capitalist elements, as well as the Communists, were opposed to it. This opposition of the Communists was already mainly due to their reluctance to consolidate, by reestablishment of monetary stability, a non-Communist democracy. It was possibly due also, to some extent, to the fear of losing, in the currency exchange, considerable funds obtained as booty from the Vichy authorities and amounting, according to some sources, to one billion francs. The main reason, however, for the rejection of a policy of deflation was the attitude of De Gaulle. He was opposed to an energetic financial policy which unavoidably would have stirred some opposition, at a moment when he wanted to concentrate the united effort of the nation on the rebuilding of the armed forces of France, and on a maximum participation in the Allied war effort, in order to regain great power status and, in particular, to obtain a share in the occupation of Germany.

For these reasons De Gaulle adopted, instead of deflation, the line of policy proposed by M. René Pleven, who became Minister of Finance after the return of the government to Paris. Pleven wanted to postpone the end of inflation—that is, the reestablishment of equilibrium between effective demand and supply—until the recovery of agricultural and industrial production would have reestablished a normal supply situation. The only measure taken immediately, and intended to absorb the surplus of purchasing power, or at least to reduce it, was the flotation of a long-term loan called a Liberation Loan. This brought to the Treasury about 80 billion francs, subscribed mainly by those having good reason to fear confiscation of illegally acquired resources (which became secure as soon as they had been invested in government bonds). There was also a rather ineffective attempt of confiscation of illegal profits. In the absence of any effective control of resources, by means of exchange of currency and checking of change of real estate property, the amount of such confiscation implemented was practically negligible.

On the other hand, after liberation, the level of wage rates was raised by about 30-40 percent. This measure, even though justified by the necessity of increasing the extremely low purchasing power of the wage-earners, nevertheless resulted in a considerable increase of inflationary pressure of effective demand on the price

337

level. While demand had thus increased, improvement in the supply situation was delayed much further than had been initially expected. This was because the hopes for a rapid recovery of production had been frustrated, owing to a considerable extent to the intensification of the war effort. That, in turn, had implied (1) the mobilization of about one million men in the armed forces and thus decreased the manpower available for productive economic activity; and (2) the absorption, for military use, of a considerable share of the meager resources of consumer goods available.

There was an enormous increase in transactions on the black market, which became the only practically available source of supply for some of the most important foodstuffs, such as, at certain times, meat. This was due to the combination of inflationary pressure and aggravated shortages, as well as to the partial breakdown of food deliveries at official prices and of rationing, which remained effective only for bread and for very small rations of sugar and fats which the authorities were able to distribute. Official prices of rationed foodstuffs had also considerably increased, as it became necessary to offer more attractive prices to the farmers, in order to obtain supplies.

Gradually, also, more and more foodstuffs were derationed and the resulting free-market prices were generally close to the level of former black-market prices, or even above. As a consequence, the level of prices and of cost of living more than doubled between 1944 and 1946; the average index of cost of living increased from 319 to 746, and of wholesale prices from 245 to 648. As a result of this rise in prices, and also (since the end of the war and mobilization) of increasing production of agricultural and industrial commodities and improvement in quantity of supplies available for consumption, the inflationary pressure on the price level, resulting from an excess of quantity of money, which had been very strong at the moment of liberation, gradually declined and finally disappeared. By the end of 1946 the ratio between money quantity and the value of global resources at current prices available to the economy, which had been over 300 during the last months of 1944 was back at 100, its pre-war level.

However, if the inflationary pressure, owing to monetary reasons, had subsided, it had been replaced by an even stronger pressure resulting from a demand for increase in the wage rates, which had been far from keeping up with the effective rise in the cost of living consisting in the increase in official prices and in the necessity to purchase an ever greater share of supplies at black-market prices. Thus, by April 1946 the level of real wages, measured in official prices, amounted to 79 percent of pre-war. As a matter of fact, the real purchasing power of wages was even lower than that, owing to the necessity of taking black-market prices into account.

In spite of the very natural discontent resulting from this situation, and reflected in the inadequate consumption levels of food and other necessities of the majority of the working-class population, especially in the big cities, the Communist leadership of the General Confederation of Labor (*Confédération Générale du Travail* or *C.G.T.*) as well as the representatives of the Communist party in Parliament and in other branches of the government, tried to restrain labor demands for wage increases. They did this because, being in charge of most economic ministries and, in particular, of the ministry of industrial production, they were most concerned with recovery of production and tried to avoid anything that might disturb it. In June 1946, however, in the elections for Parliament the Communist party failed to make the further progress that was expected, and even slightly declined, slipping back to second rank, after the Catholic party (M.R.P.); and discontent of industrial workers with the wage policy of the Communists made them fear they would lose influence to socialist or Trotskyist competitors. In view of all this, just after the elections they suddenly changed their line of action: The C.G.T. demanded from the government a general rise of 25 percent in wage rates and supported the demand with the menace of a general strike. Even though the increase finally agreed upon and granted

339

by the government (18-22 percent) was slightly less than what had been requested, it provided a considerable impetus to further price increases of industrial goods and—by a sort of psychological effect and also as a result of increase in effective monetary demand —of agricultural commodities as well.

This new progress of the price spiral was especially regrettable at a moment when the excellent harvest of 1946 and increased supplies of industrial goods, as well as reabsorption of excessive money quantity, presented technical conditions favorable to a stabilization of the price level.

Besides, under existing conditions, development of the price-wage spiral was far from favorable to the wage-earners, as the rise in prices again considerably overcame the rate of increase of wage rates. Thus, by October 1946 the purchasing power of wages had declined to 59 percent of pre-war. The comparison of this index figure with the figure of six months earlier does not, however, give a true picture of the situation, as during this period many important food items had been decontrolled; they were therefore calculated in October at free-market prices, while in April they had been estimated at official prices, even if obtainable only on the black market. In spite of the fact that decline in real wages from April to October 1946 had thus been much less than expressed in this comparison of indexes, the fact remains that the real wages by the latter date, the index of which was by far more realistic than the previous one, were extremely low.

Even though the decline in real wages was to a certain extent justified by the general impoverishment of French economy, as well as by the decline in productivity, the extent of the decrease of purchasing power of wages was far greater than could be explained by these reasons. It reflected mainly a shift, in the distribution of national income, from wages to the income of activities either producing or controlling the distribution of goods most in short supply, for which monopoly prices could be obtained on the black market. These categories were the farmers and wholesale and retail traders in food or consumer goods, such as textiles, who operated to a considerable extent on the black market. This most undesirable shift in the distribution of national income in favor of intermediary activities was a natural result of shortages and of inflation, unrestrained by any policy of effective rationing and price controls.

Comparison of the total national resources of France and of their distribution can be provided for 1938 and 1946 (in billions of francs at 1938 prices):

	Total national resources		1946 in %
	1938	1946	of 1938
Gross national product	425	359	87
Net imports	8	23	..
Total national resources	433	382	88
Gross product of government services	25	36	144
Remaining available for consumption and equipment	408	346	86
Spent for consumer goods	340	276	81
Out of which, food	160	117	73
" " " clothing, furniture, etc.	41	32	78
Total equipment	68	70	103
Out of which, mechanical	21	23	110
" " " transport	12	18	150
" " " building and public works	25	24	96
Armaments	10	5	50

According to this table, during 1946, which was the second year of reconstruction, the total resources available to the French economy amounted to only 88 percent of pre-war in spite of an appreciable increase in net imports financed to some extent by foreign loans, mainly from the United States, but even more, at that moment, by liquidation of remaining gold reserves and foreign assets. Nonproductive government expenditures considerably increased,

341

owing to expansion of the economic functions of the state; and the level of consumption, especially of food, was very low, particularly as the consumption of the rural population had increased, compared to pre-war, and thus consumption of urban consumers was not a little below the national average of 73 percent of pre-war.

Notwithstanding this drastic curtailment of consumption, the level of investment in 1946 was scarcely above the extremely insufficient level of 1938, while building activity was even below pre-war. The only increase sufficient to cover the requirements of reconstruction occurred in transport equipment, corresponding to the remarkably efficient restoration of the railway system and harbor facilities.

In 1947, the gross national product did not increase, as expansion of industrial production by about 20 percent was compensated for by the substantial decline of agricultural production. Investment increased, in accordance with the Monnet Plan, to about 120 percent of pre-war, while the level of consumption even slightly declined. In 1948, on the contrary, industrial production further increased by 14 percent, while agricultural production also considerably expanded, making it possible for consumption as well as investment to be substantially increased. In 1949, industrial production further increased by 10 percent, while agricultural production was well maintained; thus the level of investment and of consumption could both increase. During 1950, industrial production in France leveled off, owing to a slight deflationary crisis prevailing on the domestic market after the end of inflationary pressure and absorption of pent up demand.

Even to a greater extent than in Great Britain, the level of current savings in France was insufficient to cope with requirements for investment for reconstruction, modernization and expansion of her productive apparatus. Outside of the normal increase in consumers' demand for satisfying delayed requirements and for rebuilding of stocks in the pipe line of production and distribution, demand was stimulated by the flight into goods resulting from lack of confidence in the currency. This factor, on the one hand, stimulated speculative buying above real requirements and thus increased demand, while on the other hand it restricted supply, as producers and distributors tried to retain as much as possible of nonperishable goods, and for as long a time as possible, wishing to profit to the maximum extent from the rise of prices which everybody expected to go on forever. Consequently, for some time, deliveries of cattle for slaughter remained on an extremely low level, while total livestock population was nearly restored to pre-war level, because the peasants preferred to keep their livestock, considering it the safest possible investment.

The lack of confidence in the currency also deflected a considerable part of savings normally available for investment to be utilized in a manner in which they could be of no use to the economy of the country, namely, in private secret hoards of foreign currencies and even more of gold. The quantities of the latter bought and hoarded, especially in rural areas, were very substantial. Moreover, these hoards were accumulated in the most uneconomical manner, as the price of gold on the black market, where they were purchased, was considerably above its cross-rate value compared to gold currencies, such as the dollar or the Swiss franc.

In the beginning of 1947, the Léon Blum government attempted a policy of deflation which was mainly directed at breaking the psychological basis of the price spiral, the expectancy of constantly rising prices. Mandatory reduction in prices of all manufactured goods was imposed, a first reduction of 5 percent being made in January and the second, of a similar percentage, in March. These measures were intended to stop speculative buying and to slacken consumption demand, while bringing back to the market the hoarded inventories of producers, and especially of distributors, and they had at first a measurable degree of success. Thus, wholesale prices declined from February to April 1947 by 4 percent, and cost of living by 2½ percent.

The full success of this deflationary policy was prevented, however, by the unfavorable agricultural situation due to weather

343

calamities. The destruction by frost of half of the winter plantings of wheat obliged the government to increase official prices paid to farmers. This gave a new impetus to a rise in all prices, still more stimulated by the drought of the summer, which even further curtailed food production. On the other hand, the efforts of the government to balance the budget—an effort involving abolishment of subsidies for coal, steel, transport, utilities, etc.—implied an appreciable increase in their prices or rates and thus provided another stimulant to price inflation.

Wages lagging again behind prices, it became comparatively easy for the Communist leadership of the C.G.T. to start an important series of strikes, which for several weeks in November and December 1947 stopped production of coal and reduced production of most industrial goods. The increase in wages (1500 francs per month) gained by the workers did not compensate them for the loss of wages during the strike, while this rise in wages naturally provided the start of a new and substantial increase in prices of industrial goods. This price rise was required not only to cover the wage rise, but also to compensate for the losses incurred during the strike.

As a consequence of the steady rise in the French price level, French exports became uncompetitive on the main foreign markets. Therefore, the level of exports, which heretofore had recovered in a relatively satisfactory way, having reached in June 1947 91 percent of the quantum of 1938, began to fall off, increasing the gap in the balance of payments. At the same time, gold and foreign exchange reserves, as well as foreign credits, were being rapidly exhausted. Obviously, the only remedy for this situation would have been the adjustment of the exterior purchasing power of the franc (that is, its monetary parity), by means of devaluation, to its domestic purchasing power. This devaluation which had been implemented in January 1948 by the Minister of Finance, M. René Mayer, was part of a general plan intended (1) to liquidate the whole system of price control and rationing, which had been a complete failure in France, and failed to prevent the development of the inflationary spiral; and (2) to restore a free market economy, with prices established according to the natural relationship between supply and demand.

Thus, devaluation was effected with differential rates of exchange. The official rate of the dollar was established at 214 francs, as against a previous rate of 120 francs. At this rate were calculated the prices of all essential imports (food, fuel, etc.). But exporters were obliged to deliver at this rate to the exchange control office only half of the proceeds of their exports in foreign currencies, and could sell the remaining half on a so-called free market. In fact, however, this market was controlled by the government, and it was established in Paris, where foreign exchange could be freely sold, but bought only with official authorization for import of goods other than essential, or for foreign travel. The rate of the dollar on this "free" market fluctuated at slightly above 300; foreign tourists could sell on this market all their foreign exchange.

This devaluation thus established three different rates for the franc: (1) the rate for essential imports; (2) the rate for tourists and nonessential imports; and (3) the rate for exports, which was the average between (1) and (2). The main aims of this system, which had been implemented in spite of the opposition of the International Monetary Fund, the statutes of which had outlawed multiple-exchange practices, were to stimulate exports by increasing proceeds to exporters and also, through the "free" market, to provide the Treasury with foreign exchange and gold. A free market in gold, similar in character to the market in foreign exchange, was also established and an amnesty was proclaimed for gold hoarders ready to unhoard their gold on this market, thus canceling the heavy penalties which they were due to incur according to previous legislation.

At the same time, and somewhat out of harmony with these measures, a partial attempt at monetary deflation was made by the exchange of the 5000-franc banknotes, used to a considerable extent for hoarding and also for settlement of black-market transactions. The equivalent of the 5000-franc notes deposited was reimbursed only after a severe fiscal control.

The reform failed, however, to reach its main objectives. While blocking of the 5000-franc notes did not result in massive sales of hoarded goods or slackening of the black-market transactions, it did weaken even more the confidence in the currency of those classes (the peasants) most reluctant with respect to state interference and control, and increased for them the attraction of gold. Devaluation, on the other hand, through the direct repercussion of the rise in import prices, and even more because of its psychological influence, provided a new impetus to price inflation. Finally, no gold and little foreign exchange came into the Treasury, as the maximum rates of the state-controlled "free" market, where nobody could buy without due authority, were rapidly superseded by prices of the real free market, that is, the black market, where the dollar rate rose to a maximum of 550 francs, reached during the fall of 1948.

But during 1948, inflationary pressure in France gradually subsided. This was due, to a certain extent, to government policy, such as the balancing of the ordinary budget of current expenditures; the investment expenditures were expected to be covered by the counterpart fund, that is, the proceeds in francs, of the American assistance provided by the Economic Cooperation Administration, and by domestic loans. The main factor in this improvement was, however, the considerable amelioration of the supply position. The excellent harvest of 1948 enabled bread, especially, to be derationed, though remaining taxed, while other major foodstuffs became relatively abundant, especially as high prices had limited demand. Industrial consumer goods, the production of which also had considerably expanded, became, for the first time since the end of the war, abundant compared to the purchasing power of the public, while, owing to excessive prices, exports had not increased as rapidly as production. The expectancy of constantly rising prices, which until then had been the main stimulant of inflation, had finally exhausted its effect and inflationary pressure subsided. The action of these anti-inflationary factors had been only temporarily halted by the strikes of October-November 1948—which were most serious in coal mining—in spite of their heavy cost to the French economy in loss of production.

At the beginning of 1949, weather conditions especially favorable to agricultural production caused a considerable decline in wholesale food prices, which, slowly at first, began to influence the cost of living. Finally, when the government was issuing a long-term loan of 100 billion francs, a most significant symptom of the end of inflation could be observed—the black-market prices of gold and foreign exchange appreciably declined (by more than 25 percent, to less than 400 francs for the dollar). The peasants appeared to have started to revert to their favorite pre-war investments in government bonds and to be selling gold in order to subscribe to the new bonds, the amount of the loan having been oversubscribed. Though still extremely fragile, as new social disturbances could at any moment revive the anxiety of the public, the cure of the inflation that inflicted the French economy seems to be near completion.

The new adjustment of the parity of the franc, which was effected after the British devaluation in September 1949, and which is discussed below (Chapter 32), did not change the basic features of the monetary situation. Confidence in the currency was maintained, and was reflected in the continued decline of the black-market price of gold and the stability of the black-market rate of the dollar at only slightly above its official parity, during the summer of 1950, even in spite of the scare due to the war in Korea.

It is true that, in the second half of 1950, rearmament introduced new and very potent inflationary factors, through unbalancing of the budget, owing to increase in defense expenditures, as well as through the substantial rise in prices of raw materials.

On the other hand, the period of monetary stability, which had coincided with a slackening demand on the domestic market, had resulted in a very favorable development of French foreign trade, the value of exports having exceeded value of imports during several months of mid-1950, for the first time in more than twenty years. In this connection, the following table is of interest:

INDEX NUMBERS OF QUANTUM OF FRENCH FOREIGN TRADE (1938 = 100)

	Exports	Imports
1945	10	34
1946	50	115
1947	83	105
1948	96	101
1949	132	104
1950—		
1st quarter	150	114
2nd quarter	100	107
3rd quarter	158	89

The main reasons for the difference in the methods of overcoming inflation in Great Britain and in France, and for the failure in the latter country of the policy of price control, were (1) the fact that control on food distribution was easier to implement in Great Britain, but even more (2) that rationing had been accepted in Great Britain as a patriotic duty, while in France it had been imposed by a hated invader to serve his own cause. Other, and most important reasons, are however to be found in: the difference in attitude toward the state; the considerably greater civic sense and discipline of the British people in accepting payment of taxes; and the weakness of the government in France in relation to certain sectional interests, such as the peasants, who pay practically no direct taxes at all, and who even threatened revolt when in 1947 a considerable increase in their income-tax payments was under consideration. Because of the widespread habit of tax evasion, even though income tax rates in France were very high the yield of direct taxation was relatively low.

In France, the consequences of having suffered for more than three years after the end of the war from an uncontrolled inflation have been very serious and, if they did not prevent recovery of production, they certainly impeded its harmonious development. Thus, for example, the apparatus of distribution expanded out of proportion to the quantity of goods to be distributed, the number of retail trades, in particular, having increased from 800,000 in 1938 to 1,300,000 in 1948. The greatest expansion occurred in food and textiles, where black-market profits were easiest to make. This expansion occurred, obviously, at the expense of more productive but less remunerative activities. Other similar factors were the flight of skilled labor into handicrafts. There, efficiency of labor was much less, but there workers, purchasing on the black market the limited quantity of raw materials required, could make profits out of proportion to the highest regular wages which they would be able to earn. Worst of all, however, was the demoralizing influence on all classes of society of easy enrichment by illegal transactions.

WESTERN GERMANY

In Germany, after the end of the war and at the beginning of Allied occupation, financial and monetary conditions were most peculiar. On the one hand, there was an enormous supply of money in currency, issued by the Nazi government, to which were added very substantial quantities of Allied occupation marks and, above all, of bank deposits. The latter, most of their counterpart being German government war loans, practically wiped out since defeat, were in fact nearly frozen. On the other hand, most of the expenditures of the German central government having ceased, local budgets were balanced; at the same time, the price and wage freeze introduced by the Nazi government still remained effective for the prices of rationed supplies and the wages earned in legal employment. Thus, such wages could be spent, and were sufficient for the purchase of the official rations with coupons. Except for rationed supplies, however, these wages had practically no purchasing power whatsoever, as all other commodities, or quantities

349

of rationed commodities purchased without coupons, could be bought on the black market at prices of an entirely different order of magnitude. But while in France or in other countries of the European Continent, prices on the black market were 2, 3 or at a maximum 5 times above the official price level, and practically everybody could and did to a certain extent use the black market, a condition which considerably influenced official price and wage level; in Germany, *black market prices* were 100, 200 or even 500 times above the *official prices*.

There was thus no common order of magnitude, no communication between the one and the other. Normal legal incomes had no purchasing power on the black market, where purchases could be effected only by those who were selling other goods at black-market rates. The real currency of black-market transactions was no more the Reichsmark, but, owing to the lack of foreign currency circulation, simply the American cigaret, which, for the first two years after the war, had nearly all the functions of a real currency. The most serious consequence of this situation—in which there was no currency with a purchasing power in all sectors of the economy—was the complete lack of incentives for workers or for producers to sell their services or goods on the legal market, since an increased effort could not provide them with more than a very limited quantity of rationed goods.

The monetary reform of June 1948 was implemented in the Western zones only because final agreement on the procedure to be followed could not be reached with the Soviet authorities, and was intended to provide Germany with a currency fulfilling all its normal functions and stimulating, instead of paralyzing, the revival of economic activity.

The reform consisted essentially in a very drastic deflation, applying to all outstanding currency and bank deposits. Every individual received, for the Reichsmarks deposited, 40 Deutschmarks immediately, and 20 more after two months. Business firms also received 60 Deutschmarks per occupied worker, but these were deducted from the total of their converted deposits. Local authorities and Allied military governments could also convert sums corresponding to one month of fiscal revenue. The rest of cash, as well as of the bank deposits, was converted at the rate of 10 to 1. Half of the proceeds of this conversion were made free for withdrawals up to a limit, for private persons, of 5000 Deutschmarks. The other half had been blocked until October 1, 1948, when 70 percent of it had been canceled, 20 percent transferred to free account, and 10 percent made available for investment in long-term securities.

While before the reform, in June 1948, currency circulation in Western Germany amounted to 13.5 billion Reichsmarks, and bank deposits to 131 billion Reichsmarks, total money supply was reduced in July to 5.8 billion Deutschmarks, of which 2.6 billion were in currency and the rest in deposits.

The currency reform in Western Germany, especially from the economic point of view, was a great success, as it stimulated revival of economic activity, provided normal incentives for workers and businessmen alike, and put an end to the hoarding of goods. Massive unhoarding and considerably increasing production, while purchasing power was limited, put an end by the end of 1948 to the inflationary situation in Western Germany. This stimulating effect persisted, and production expanded appreciably during 1949 and 1950.

28 THE PROBLEM OF GERMANY

THE PROBLEM OF GERMANY and of her position in Europe is the key problem of European destiny. It is true that Germany emerged from the war in a state of complete chaos and prostration; that she suffered considerable losses in population, and even more in territory; even though her war devastations are most serious in housing and transport—relatively limited as regards industrial production. In spite of all this, she still possesses a potential of productive resources and power which could be either an important factor of economic recovery and prosperity to Germany herself, her neighbors, and the rest of the world, or else the source of new disasters. Which they *will* be will depend on the objectives for which they are used and the methods of such utilization.

The line of policy concerning Germany agreed upon by the Allies at Yalta and Potsdam was very different from the reparations policy pursued by the Western Allies after World War I. At that time, the European Allied countries, in particular those which had been devastated by the war, like France, and which were also under pressure for payment of their war debts to the United States, wanted above all to obtain from Germany a maximum amount of reparations. This obviously could be provided only through her current production.

Thus, when, after acceptance of the Dawes plan, the question
352

of reparations had begun to be handled in an economically realistic manner, the Allies were not opposed to the expansion of German productive capacity. This alone could make possible the expansion in production and exports required for payment of reparations, so the Allies actually facilitated expansion by enabling German concerns to issue loans, especially in the United States, but also, though to a smaller extent, on the financial markets of Western Europe. The result of this policy was that while Germany, after a short time, defaulted on reparations payments, she had in the meantime considerably increased, at the expense of candid investors of Western countries, her productive capacity, that is, the industrial basis of her war machine.

Bearing in mind this disastrous experience, the Allies decided in 1945 to put the main emphasis this time not on obtaining maximum reparations (even though they were needed even more than after 1918 by the devastated countries), but on obtaining military and political security by reducing German industrial capacity and, as a consequence, her potential of aggression. The new policy was described, by the somewhat trivial but striking metaphor, as aiming at obtaining the meat, not the milk, from the cow. This aim was expected to be achieved by the dismantling of German industrial plant and equipment, mainly heavy industry (steel, chemicals and engineering), and transferring it to her neighbors, who were also the chief victims of her aggression. Such material was considered surplus to the peacetime requirements of the German economy.

Owing to this reduction in her industrial potential, while that of her neighbors, east, west and south would be increased, Germany would lose her former industrial hegemony on the continent of Europe. With it she would lose also her key position as the only practical source of supplies for some of the most important manufactured goods for certain of her less industrialized neighbors, whom she had previously been able to maintain in a state of semicolonial dependence. It was believed that through reduction in the absolute as well as relative importance of her industrial

353

potential, as compared to that of other European countries, the danger of German aggression or economic hegemony would be made impossible, and a more balanced and harmonious distribution of industrial resources would be achieved throughout Europe.

The plan, however, had one very serious flaw: It did not give Germany any prospects of becoming self-supporting, that is, of achieving an equilibrium of her balance of payments, even on a low level of consumption. The last possibilities in this respect had been ruined by the territorial losses incurred by Germany. However, the loss of Upper Silesia, with its mainly Polish population, and of the Saar, incorporated into the French economy, was relatively unimportant, as it mainly reduced only the German surplus of coal and to a much smaller extent of steel (16.7 percent of pre-war German coal production originated in Silesia, and 7.5 percent in the Saar). Moreover, these heavily populated districts were food-deficit areas and their loss relieved, to some extent, the pressure on food resources. But any possibility of the Reich's achieving independence from food imports on a massive scale was destroyed by the loss of extensive mainly agricultural territories of Eastern Germany to Poland and the Soviet Union, without any justification other than purely strategical, and as a compensation to Poland for her own eastern territories which had been annexed by the USSR. This independence from food imports had existed to a considerable extent in pre-war frontiers, as domestic production covered more than 80 percent of consumption. The eastern territories under Polish and Soviet administration, which are separated from the Reich, *de facto* if not *de jure,* owing to the absence of a peace treaty, include 20 percent of all agricultural land of pre-war Germany. Their share in total agricultural production was 32 percent for rye, the most important German cereal; 16 percent for wheat; 30 percent for potatoes; 25 percent for sugar beets; and 21 percent for livestock products.

The situation was still more aggravated by the fact that, while territory and agricultural resources had considerably declined, the total population of Germany not only had not decreased in a similar proportion, but was even potentially slightly greater. This was due to the expulsion of Germans from the lost eastern territories and from other European countries, in particular Czechoslovakia, Hungary and Poland, as well as to Hitler's demographic policy in favor of a high birth rate, pursued until nearly the end of the war.

Thus, in spite of considerable losses during the war, the total fatal casualties having been estimated, in the absence of official figures, at 4,500,000, the population of Germany on the present territory, according to a census of December 1946, was 65.9 million (Saar included). That was as compared with a 1938 population, on the same territory, of 59.8 million, but a total population on pre-war territory of 68.4 million. However, taking into consideration the war prisoners still remaining to be repatriated at the date of the census, as well as the residue of German population in Eastern Europe still remaining to be deported to the Reich, the normal population of Germany, when all these transfers shall have come to an end, will be about 69-70 million, that is slightly above the pre-war maximum. It should also be pointed out that, while the total number of the population had increased, the proportion of able-bodied men had, owing to the war, considerably declined. The result was a weakening, in the same proportion, of the human factor of productive capacity of the economy.

The interallied agreements of Potsdam in August 1945 nevertheless ratified, in principle, the above-described policy of dismantling and removal from the Reich of its surplus of industrial capacity; and the "level of industry" agreement of March 1946 established the practical terms of implementation for that policy. The Soviet Union undertook to obtain her share of reparations from her occupation zone, as well as to satisfy from it also the claims of Poland. In addition, the USSR was also entitled to 25 percent of the reparations from the Western Zones; 15 percent, however, had to be compensated for by deliveries of food and raw materials from the Eastern Zone. As to all the other Allied powers, reparations due to them were allocated by the Reparations Agency, established in Brussels, as a result of a reparations conference held in Paris in October-November 1945.

The "level of industry" agreement implied a substantial reduction in the production of German heavy industry. Thus, total productive capacity for steel to remain in Germany was limited to 7.3 million tons. Actual production, however, was expected not to exceed 5.8 million tons, a level about equal to that of the lowest point of the depression in 1932, but only half the level of the peacetime prosperity of 1929. Production of many important products (such as aluminum, ball bearings, seagoing ships, heavy tractors, and synthetic oil and rubber) had been absolutely prohibited. For many other important items, such as chemicals, heavy machinery, etc., authorized production had been drastically reduced, as compared to pre-war output. The equilibrium of the German balance of payments, on a level of consumption not exceeding the level of her neighbor countries, not including Great Britain and the USSR, was expected to be achieved: by an expansion of production and exports of consumer-goods industries (textiles, glass, toys, etc.); by a maximum development of domestic food production; and by a reduction in luxury imports of products such as luxury food, gasoline for motoring, and so on.

The possibility of implementing such a solution was, anyhow, only slight, as consumers-goods exports are normally much more competitive and more difficult to market than exports of capital goods. As to agriculture, maximum efforts had already been made for increase of production, during the previous period, with considerable success and yields were very high. There was thus very little prospect of a further substantial increase in output, while, on the other hand, the loss of the eastern territories had resulted in a massive reduction of domestic supplies.

The realization of this program, however, had also been jeopardized, and then made completely impossible, by the non-implementation of the Potsdam Agreement with respect to German economic unity. The policy agreed upon at Potsdam implied that the whole of Germany would be treated as a single economic unit, with an unhampered flow of trade between the different zones and the pooling of all their resources to provide the exports necessary to pay for the vital imports. It also implied that reparations would be limited to dismantled capital equipment, and that nothing would be taken out of current production. None of these conditions had been carried out in the Soviet Zone, which had been practically cut off from the rest of Germany. This state of affairs was most serious for Western Germany, as the Soviet Zone is economically more balanced than the Western Zones. While containing only 28 percent of post-war Germany's population it has a much superior share of agricultural resources remaining in the Reich (38 percent of breadgrains, 41 percent of potatoes, 57 percent of sugar beets, etc.) as well as important and varied industries: textiles and machinery in Saxony; optical goods in Thuringia; electrical machinery in Berlin; and nearly 70 percent of lignite production, the basis of a most important chemical industry.

In their Zone, the Russian authorities dismantled a substantial proportion of existing industrial capacity (65 percent of the total, according to a report in the *London Times,* including all wartime addition in capacity and 45 percent of the peacetime potential). Besides, a great part of the remaining industrial plant is working for Russian requirements and its production is put at the disposal of the Russian occupation authorities as reparations. Such a procedure has been facilitated by the fact that the Russians seized, as reparations, about a third of the industry of their Zone, including the biggest and most efficient plants, which they organized as Soviet industrial trusts.

In fact, the Soviet Zone is in many respects dealt with as part of the territory of the Soviet Union. Thus in some trade agreements with other countries Russian imports are compensated for by exports from the Soviet Zone. Under these circumstances their

357

Zone could not, and did not, contribute anything to assist the rest of Germany to cover its import deficit. This area has no similar problem of its own, as its agricultural resources seem sufficient to provide the rations of the population, though on a rather low subsistence level, and even to contribute to the feeding of the occupation army. The trade of the Soviet Zone with the rest of Germany is on a strictly compensation, in fact a barter, basis and is of a relatively limited volume.

Under these circumstances, the Western Zones of Germany were left to manage for themselves the problem of their balance of payment. This was especially true because, since, even before the war, these Zones were a food-deficit area to a considerable extent, their requirements and deficit had substantially increased, owing to the afflux of refugees which had expanded their population from 39 to over 47 million.

Until the monetary reform of June 1948, recovery of production in Western Germany had been considerably slower than in the rest of Western Europe. This slow pace was due to such factors as: particularly heavy devastation and dislocation of transport; disruption of normal trade relations with the Soviet Zone; and difficulties existing for some time even in the trade between the other Zones; and sometimes conflicting policies and administrative regulations in the different Zones.

Agricultural production was especially handicapped by lack of manpower and, above all, of fertilizer, of particular importance in Germany, where very high yields depended mainly on the highest rate of fertilizer use in all Europe. Industrial activity was hampered by: low productivity of labor, resulting from insufficient rations; in a few instances, shortage of fuel; and in many cases, lack of imported raw materials. The latter was only to a small extent alleviated by the import, from the United States in particular, of cotton under a credit arrangement, the credit being repaid out of the proceeds of exports of processed goods.

Thus, for the year 1947, the average index of industrial production was only 40 percent of the pre-war (1936) level which,

358

however, had been already artificially inflated by rearmament. For the first half of 1948, this index was still at only 49. Steel production was considerably below even the Potsdam level, not only in 1946 (2.8 million tons) and 1947 (3.8 million tons), but even in the first half of 1948, when it was at a yearly rate of 5.1 million tons. As a result of inadequate resources of steel engineering production recovered also only very slowly, this slow recuperation being reflected in a shortage of equipment and even of spare parts for mining, transport and agriculture.

Because of retarded industrial production, exports of the Western Zones were considerably below expectations. But imports of food required to keep rations of the urban population at the minimum level of 1550 calories were much higher than expected. This was due somewhat to insufficient recovery of output in the Western Zones, but even more to unsatisfactory deliveries by the farmers. They were most reluctant to continue deliveries at official prices, in the absence of effective incentives, such as consumer goods or equipment; and, like farmers in all other countries suffering from inflation, they had increased their own consumption. The deficit of the balance of payment of the Western Zones to be covered by the occupying powers, thus assumed considerable proportions. It was an especially heavy burden for Great Britain, which administered the most industrialized and populated zone, and which also had the greatest food deficit. That deficit had to be covered mainly by imports from the Western Hemisphere, and thus had to be paid for in dollars. The deficit of the United States Zone was nearly as great.

For the United States and United Kingdom Zones, taken together, foreign trade developed as follows:

(in millions of dollars)

	Exports	Imports	Deficit
1946	143	643	—500
1947	222	725	—503
1948 (first half)	230	636	—406

This problem of balance of payments was much less serious for the French Zone, which had a more balanced economy and paid for food imports by exports to France. However, since the incorporation of the Saar into the French economy, the rest of the French Zone became a deficit area.

The situation, which made it necessary for the occupying powers, mainly Great Britain and the United States, to pay for the balance-of-payment deficit of their Zones, was considered by them intolerable. In fact, it looked as if, as a result of the war, the victorious powers were paying reparations to Germany instead of the reverse. This was particularly shocking for countries either devastated or/and ruined by the war, such as Great Britain and France. However, there was little or no prospect of improvement, without a substantial modification of the rules limiting the activity of the German economy. As the clauses of the Potsdam Agreement, especially concerning the economic unity of Germany, had not been respected by the Russians, the Western Allies considered that they also could violate this agreement by revising the level of industry and authorizing an increase in German industrial production. Such procedure alone could provide the exports necessary to pay for all vital imports and thus make Western Germany self-supporting. This change of attitude in Allied economic policy toward Germany was obviously also a reflection of the influence of the shift of the general political situation with respect to the German problem. While the Potsdam Agreement still reflected the wartime psychology of Allied solidarity, the maintenance of which was the necessary condition for its implementation, deterioration of relations between East and West resulted very rapidly in conflicting attitudes in Germany. Instead of being considered the common enemy, to be prevented by joint action from again becoming a danger, the Germans began to be the object of a competition, between the Western powers and the USSR, for their allegiance and support, which implied abandonment, or at least alleviation, of the rigors of the previous policy.

Therefore, for political and economic reasons alike, the United States and Great Britain, which were joined only half-heartedly and at a considerably later date by France, started as early as by the end of 1946, to remove obstacles to revival of German industrial production. They also began to favor autonomy in the economic field of their Zones, which had been combined in January 1947 in the so-called Bi-Zone.

In August 1947, the authorities of the Bi-Zone published a new list of limits of industrial production, amounting to a substantial increase in the former limits. Thus, the maximum of yearly steel production was increased from 5.8 million tons, for the whole of post-war Germany, to 10.7 million tons for the Bi-Zone (the capacity of which is about 90 percent of the total). Similar increases were authorized for many other heavy industrial products previously prohibited or severely restricted. The level of a number of engineering industries, for example, was put at or even above that of the basic year 1936, when rearmament was already in full swing. As a whole, the new level of industry of the Bi-Zone was roughly equal to the 1936 level, though it was still considerably lower in steel. The economic argument justifying such an expansion in peacetime production was the considerable increase in population resulting in an increased food deficit, and thus requiring a greater industrial production and additional exports.

In April 1949, the occupation authorities of the three Western Zones agreed to eliminate part of the remaining restrictions on German heavy-industry production. This agreement, which practically coincided with the fusion of the three Zones, approved the retaining by Germany of a great number of plants formerly earmarked for dismantling and reparations. The raw-steel capacity was unchanged, but production of many previously prohibited products, such as aluminum, ball bearings, and some categories of heavy machinery was authorized, though still limited. Thus, building of ships not exceeding 7000 tons was authorized. Finally, in the latter part of 1950, the Allied authorities tolerated, even

361

if they did not officially approve, the fact that German steel production considerably exceeded the authorized limit and was close to the capacity of about a 1.2 million-ton monthly rate.

However, even if justified by economic considerations, and indispensable in order to make Western Germany self-supporting, this restoration of German heavy industry revives for the neighbors of the Reich the threat of German economic hegemony and the danger of a new aggression. For the countries of Eastern Europe, which are firmly in the hand and under the protection of the Soviet Union, and whose strategical position was considerably improved by the changes in frontiers, anxiety, in this respect, is far less justified than for the countries of Western Europe if they remain isolated.

These countries could wholeheartedly support the plans for the rebuilding of a powerful Western German industry only if two basic conditions were fulfilled: if they were guaranteed:

(1) That Germany would not obtain any priority over their own reconstruction requirements, e.g., that the coal from the Ruhr would be divided in an equitable way between German consumption requirements and exports to other countries of the area depending on it, particularly for their steel production. Thus, France agreed to the increase in German steel production after she had obtained approval by the American and British authorities of a plan for exports of Ruhr coal according to a sliding scale, increasing the share of exports as production expanded.

(2) That the reestablished German potential of power could never be utilized against them, in either the economic, political or military field. This second condition would imply international control of the use by Germany of her resources, and in particular of the main source of economic power in Western Germany and even in the whole of continental Western Europe: the Ruhr. Such a control would be facilitated and, in fact, become natural if Western Germany were included in a united Western Europe, an arrangement which would also alleviate the anxiety

362

of all the countries of this area by abolishing the danger of any one of them having to face alone a new Reich that had recovered its power.

Since the French government in 1946 first proposed internationalization of the Ruhr, an idea opposed at that time by the USSR, as well as by Great Britain and the United States, appreciable progress has been achieved in the implementation of this objective. The French plan did not imply, as had been asserted, strangling of the German economy by withholding from her the resources of the Ruhr, but merely the control over production and distribution, a control established in order to make certain that these resources would be used for legitimate purposes and would be equitably shared by all interests concerned. However, the initial French plan, based on the assumption of Allied solidarity, proposed control over the Ruhr to be implemented jointly by the four occupying powers. Since, owing to deterioration of relations between the Western powers and the Soviet Union, the former, in particular Britain and America, would never agree to grant to the USSR a share in the control of the Ruhr without some corresponding concession, such as participation by the Western powers in the control of equivalent resources in Eastern Europe, as, for example, in the former German territory of Silesia, which is the most important coal basis of Eastern Europe, outside of the Soviet Union; in this form, the plan was unacceptable.

The situation changed materially when, after the failure of the conferences at Moscow and London, the prospect of agreement between West and East on a common policy toward Germany became remote, if indeed it still existed. On the other hand, the United States and Great Britain, for the implementation of their policy of rebuilding Western Germany, needed the full support and cooperation of France, as well as of the Low Countries, which to a great extent shared the French point of view. This was also the period when the economy of Western Germany had to be integrated into the Marshall Plan and the system of European

363

economic cooperation. Hence, on March 6, 1948, in London, a conference of the three Western occupying powers and of the Benelux countries reached agreement in principle on the international control of the Ruhr, with a view to preventing the use of its resources for rearmament, and to insure an equitable distribution of its production of coal, coke and steel between Germany and other countries of Western Europe. Another agreement, concluded on December 28, 1948, between the same countries, implemented this principle by establishing the International Control Authority for the Ruhr.

This Authority, which has since come into active being, consists of a Council composed of the representatives of the signatory governments, including Germany. In this Council, the United States, Great Britain, France and Germany have three votes each, and the Benelux countries one vote each, decisions being made on the basis of an absolute majority. The functions of the Authority include the division of the coal, coke and steel produced in the Ruhr between German consumption and German exports.

Such division (1) shall insure adequate access to supplies of these products by countries cooperating in the common economic good, taking into account the essential needs of Germany; (2) shall be in accordance with any agreements still in force between occupying powers with respect to allocation of coal, coke and steel (such as the agreement on the sliding scale of coal exports); and (3) shall be consistent with the aims and programs of the Organization for European Economic Cooperation. The Authority also has the right to examine transport, trade and price practices, quotas, tariffs, etc. and to make sure that they are not discriminatory or likely to impede access by the other countries to the coal, coke and steel resources of the Ruhr, or to distort their movement in international trade.

If the latter should be the case, the Authority shall decide a modification or termination of such practices, with due regard for requirements relative to: (a) international peace and security; (b) Germany's obligations under OEEC convention; and (c)

364

the need of German authorities to afford legitimate protection to the commercial and financial position of Germany in international trade. After the end of Allied occupation, the Authority will also inherit the powers of the Allies concerning prevention of excessive concentration of economic power and return of former Nazis to control, as well as concerning regulation of production, development and investment policies of the Ruhr industries in such a way as to prevent German aggression and to insure equitable access to the resources of the Ruhr. It was expected that the Authority would be able to enforce Germany's compliance with its decisions, by making recommendations to occupation powers and, after the end of occupation, to the signatory governments.

The establishment of the International Control Authority was widely believed to be a first very important, and perhaps even decisive, step toward the solution of the German problem of integrating Western Germany into Western Europe. It was in particular expected that it would put an end to maladjustments resulting from the tendency of American and British occupation authorities (a) to favor the economic interests of the Bi-Zone at the expense of the rest of Western Europe (even in contradiction with the OEEC plans), and (b) for the sake of efficiency, to put back into power former Nazi managers. An example of such a policy was the Anglo-American directive issued, by the end of 1948, on the return to the Germans of the control of the steel industry.

The opinion had been frequently expressed that the problem of international control might be simplified if the resources to be controlled (coal mining and the steel industry) were under public ownership, either German—as seems to be the opinion of some of the major parties in Western Germany—or international, as has been urged by some French and also German spokesmen, such as Professor Mommsen. Public ownership would abolish the danger of a return to power of pro-Nazi owners, as well as the menace of a new penetration of foreign (American) capital, which could easily invest in the Ruhr industry at bargain prices. Once such capital interests obtained ownership of considerable property in Germany, they would naturally be inclined, in order to insure their profits, to defend the interests of German industry against her neighbors. Such a danger was, at a certain moment, far from being only theoretical. A joint ownership of the Ruhr by all Western European countries would make of this industrial complex, as has been said, an economic basis of Western European unity, a sort of "dowery" for a United Western Europe.

Whether such a solution will finally prevail, or whether the only international feature will be control of the coal and steel industries of the Ruhr, it is obvious that as soon as Germany, or at least Western Germany, shall have resumed her sovereignty and shall have been admitted into the councils of governments, it will be necessary to grant her complete equality of status, i.e., reciprocity of control, in order to insure her full cooperation. The mistake of the period after World War I should not be repeated. At that time, the Allies refused to grant Germany equality in armament or disarmament, referring to the obligation to which she had subscribed in the Versailles Treaty, and which applied to her alone. This attitude stimulated resurgence of nationalist feelings offended by such discrimination, and led finally to violation by Germany of the unilateral restrictions imposed upon her.

It thus became rapidly apparent, nearly as soon as the International Control Authority for the Ruhr had been established, that this was only a first step and that such internationalization could succeed and be permanently maintained only if it were gradually extended to similar resources of other countries of Western Europe participating in the administration of the Ruhr Authority.

The demand for such reciprocity of control rapidly gained momentum. It was formulated at first by only a few individual German spokesmen, who, however, were supported nearly from the beginning by isolated but influential representatives of French public opinion, such as André Philippe, a socialist member of the National Assembly, and a courageous pioneer of Western European unity, as well as by important groups representative of American and British public opinion. The pressure toward such a solution steadily increased, as the deterioration of the international situation made it more urgent for the Western powers to win, in the economic and political fields, the complete cooperation of the people and the government of Western Germany.

The Schuman Plan for the establishment of a Franco-German coal and steel pool, under a common authority, with which all other Western European countries could combine their industries (discussed in detail below, Chapter 34), thus represents a logical means of coping with this situation. It seems certain that its implementation would be the solution of the major part of the German problem inside Western Europe, as well as an important contribution toward the solution of the problem of Western Europe itself.

29 THE DOLLAR SHORTAGE

BEFORE WORLD WAR II, the situation of the balance of payments of most Western European countries was similar to the normal pattern for highly industrialized creditor countries. Having a considerable deficit in their merchandise trade, they paid for their net imports of foodstuffs and raw materials by means of the income from their foreign investments, from shipping and from other services, including tourist traffic.

The balance of trade between Western Europe and North America was always a deficit for the former, which could not pay for a considerable part of its total imports of food and raw materials (cotton, oil, etc.) purchased in the United States and Canada, nor for some equipment (automobiles, specialized machinery, etc.) with the proceeds of its exports of manufactured goods. This gap, however, was closed: (a) by income from other sources, such as shipping (mainly for Great Britain), tourist trade (Switzerland, Italy and France); (b) by income from their investments which these countries had in North America; and (c) to a considerable extent (for Great Britain, the Netherlands and France) by income from investments in Southeast Asia, which area, owing to substantial exports of rubber and tin to the United States, was accumulating appreciable dollar balances. Dollars were also obtained through normal triangular trade with other areas, such as certain countries of South America, which had a
368

surplus of imports from Europe compensated for by a surplus of exports to the United States.

Such indirect settlement of international transactions was possible because, as a general rule, and with only a few isolated exceptions, such as Germany since 1931, the currencies of the countries participating in world trade could be converted into one another. It should also be stressed that, though depending to a considerable extent on American supplies, Western Europe had an alternative source of supplies for food and certain raw materials (such as lumber and to a smaller extent oil and copper) in East and Southeast Europe, which, in its production and economic structure was complementary to Western Europe. Imports from that area could easily be paid for through proceeds of exports of manufactured goods and income from Western European investments effected there. Until World War II, Western Europe, while it was a net importer of food and raw materials, was a net exporter of equipment, of all kinds of manufactured consumer goods, and of primary products such as coal and steel.

In the post-war period, the balance-of-payment situation of Western Europe deteriorated considerably. The import requirements had enormously increased, owing to the following factors: decline in domestic production, especially of foodstuffs and coal; and the necessity of replenishing exhausted stocks, as well as of implementing the task of reconstruction. The latter objective required many new imports, particularly of products of heavy industry—steel, steel products and equipment—in order especially to compensate for the nearly complete cessation, during the first two years after the war, of production and exports of the leading European equipment-producing country of Western Europe: Germany.

On the other hand, the resources available for payment of these increased imports had appreciably declined: The volume of exports was necessarily reduced by the insufficiency and relatively slow recovery of industrial production; the merchant marine had lost a great part of its tonnage; tourist trade recovered only very slowly because of inadequate facilities and restrictions on food and other consumptions; and, finally, the greatest part of Western European investments overseas, especially in North America, had been liquidated during, or immediately after, the war. As a consequence, in the first post-war years, Western Europe was a net debtor of the United States, even for service transactions.

Besides, the flow of supplies from Eastern Europe was at first completely stopped, and was gradually resumed only on a considerably reduced scale. This was due mostly to the enormous war devastation in this area, and to the resulting decline in production, especially of timber and food. The latter was also partly the consequence of disorganization of production caused by the land reform. Recovery of exports of this area to Western Europe was also impeded by the increase of local requirements for reconstruction, particularly for timber. It was also to some extent the result of the reorientation of trade in favor of the Soviet Union, e.g., of exports of Rumanian and Hungarian oil and other raw materials as reparations to the USSR, which also absorbed, on a barter basis, other raw materials of this area. The only exception to this reduction of Eastern European supplies to Western Europe was coal exports from Poland, which rapidly reached and exceeded pre-war level. Even this increase, however, was more apparent than real, as it mainly reflected exports from production in areas formerly belonging to Germany, which before the war were either included in German coal exports, or were consumed in other German territories now depending on coal supplied from the Ruhr.

The general expansion of imports and reduction of exports, as well as the decline in supplies available in other producing areas, caused considerable expansion of the deficit in merchandise trade between Western Europe and the dollar area, the main or even the only source of supply for most of the goods imperatively needed. While it had amounted, in relation to the United States, to only $700 million in 1938, it reached $3.5 billion in

1946, and $5 billion in 1947. The balance-of-payments situation (taking into account the invisible items), that is, the net deficit, which was $400 million in 1938, had increased to $4.2 billion in 1946 and $5.4 billion in 1947. This increase in the deficit with the United States was reflected in the increase of the share, of imports from the United States, in the total imports of Western European countries (see table below).

INCREASE IN THE SHARE OF IMPORTS FROM THE UNITED STATES AS PERCENTAGE OF TOTAL IMPORTS

	1938	1946 *
Belgium, Luxembourg	11	18
France	11	31
Greece	7	23
Italy	12	55
Netherlands	11	25
Norway	11	22
Sweden	16	24
Switzerland	8	16
Great Britain	13	17

* Excluding imports under free relief, in particular of UNRRA.

On the contrary, the share of exports sent to the United States in the total of exports of most of the countries of this area did not increase as compared to pre-war. Thus, in Great Britain it amounted in 1946 to 4 percent as against 6 percent in 1938; in France, it remained at the pre-war level of 6 percent. Besides, the general level of exports in most of the countries concerned was still below pre-war, while imports, with the exception of Great Britain, were either above pre-war or at least above the level reached by exports. As to Great Britain, the increase in her exports, even though substantial, did not compensate for the loss of income from foreign investments due to the disinvestment which had been effected during the war.

371

Some countries, mostly those not at all or only slightly devastated by the war (such as Switzerland, Sweden and Belgium) had a general export surplus, or, like Great Britain and most other countries, at least had surpluses in their relations with some other countries. But they could not use the credit balances, thus accumulated, for payment of their own debts toward other countries, such as in particular the United States, because practically all currencies, with the only important exceptions of the dollar and the Swiss franc, were unconvertible. The only attempt undertaken, during this period, to reestablish convertibility of a currency for current transactions was made by Great Britain in July 1947, in accordance with the conditions of the American loan. It proved to be a costly failure; after having lost £100 million of gold in five weeks, Britain had to suspend convertibility of the pound.

The problem of financing the enormous balance-of-payment deficit of Western Europe with the United States was a most serious one. With the exception of Italy, Western Europe did not benefit from the international relief distributed by UNRRA, which brought much asssistance to the poorer, and even more war-devastated, countries of Eastern Europe. The deficit of her balance of payment toward the United States had been covered during the period 1945-47 by the liquidation of her remaining gold reserves, and dollar resources, as well as by loans granted by the United States government.

After the end of the war, the United States government extended to most of the Western European countries considerable credits which were granted partly for the purchase of war surpluses or of Liberty ships, but the greatest part of which was provided in cash. These loans were motivated, to some extent, by humanitarian considerations, and were the expression of the desire of the American people, with their customary generosity, to assist in rehabilitating their war devastated Allies. The loans were based also, however, on a very sound comprehension of the interests of the United States economy, taking into consideration,

372

in particular, the new position of that country in world trade. The wartime expansion of American industry notably increased the possibilities and also the need of exports of manufactured goods of the United States economy, in relation to the maintenance of a high level of production and of employment.

Such expansion of American exports implied, however, the existence and development of prosperous foreign markets able to absorb them. The soundness of the argument that, since all countries depend on one another, prosperity as well as depression are contagious, and that therefore each country is interested in the prosperity of all the others, has been frankly acknowledged by the leaders of the American government since the great depression. It was thus not only generous, but also reasonable from the point of view even of hard-headed businessmen, to assist the recovery of Western European countries, which were normally among the greatest trading partners of the United States. In return for the American loans granted to them, the borrowing countries had to subscribe to the pledge that, once their recovery, for which purpose the loans had been granted, was completed and their economy was again self-supporting and on a competitive basis, they would return to the pre-war system of multilateral trade. Moreover, there were to be no import prohibitions or quantitative restrictions and, especially, no discriminations between the different trading countries.

The reestablishment of such a system of comparatively liberal foreign trade (similar to the nineteenth century pattern) embodied in the proposals submitted by the United States for the charter of the International Trade Organization, obviously would have been most favorable to the interests of the United States as that country had obtained a position of technical world leadership and economic hegemony. In like manner, during the nineteenth century, such a policy had been most advantageous to Great Britain, which then held a similar position. However, provided such a system would have been applied only after reestablishment of an economic equilibrium in international relations, it would have been nearly as favorable for the other countries that agreed to subscribe to the conditions. The only serious objections had been raised by Great Britain, which feared being obliged to abandon the policy of imperial preference and thus to weaken her economic relations with the Commonwealth. Besides, Britain had been obliged to accept the additional obligation to restore convertibility of sterling at an early date, which later developments proved to be premature and extremely harmful.

By August 15, 1947, total credits and loans granted by the United States to countries of Western Europe amounted to:

Great Britain	$4,400 million		
France	1,920	"	and $250 million from International Bank
Netherlands	413	"	and $195 million from International Bank
Belgium	205	"	
Italy	325	"	

At the time when most of these loans had been granted, i.e., by the end of 1945 or the beginning of 1946, it had been expected that their amount would be sufficient to cover the temporary deficits of the balance of payment of the countries concerned (especially with the United States) during the period of reconstruction, and until recovery in their production and exports would provide them with the foreign exchange required to pay for their imports.

These hopes, however, did not materialize, owing to the following reasons:

(1) Rise in the American price level by over 40 percent since the end of price control in June 1946. This rise reduced, in a similar proportion, the purchasing power of the dollar assets or loans received by the countries concerned, and increased the rate of spending of these dollar resources, as well as the amount of dollar requirements. (2) Catastrophic climatic conditions, from which Western Europe suffered during 1947. In particular, the

374

heavy cold and snowstorm of February of that year in Great Britain caused a stoppage of rail traffic and coal production, and the fuel crisis which resulted caused a severe, even though temporary, set-back to production and exports. In France, the winter killed half of the wheat plantings, a loss which increased import requirements for cereals by over $200 million. There were similar calamities in other countries.

As a result of all these conditions, the dollar resources and loans of the Western European countries were spent the more speedily and were exhausted considerably before anticipated. Owing to the expenditure of these dollar resources, the imports obtained enabled the countries concerned to achieve a considerable degree of recovery. But it was obvious that, at the moment when these resources would be entirely exhausted, those countries would still be far from having achieved equilibrium of their balance of payment, especially with the dollar area. Thus, if they could not obtain fresh dollar resources, they would be forced to curtail all dollar imports, even those most vital to their economy, like imports of food, fuel and raw materials. Such a contingency obviously implied not only the probability of severe economic retrogression, but also a serious danger to social and political stability.

At this period, summer and autumn of 1947, the situation and the prospects of the main countries concerned were as follows:

Great Britain had nearly exhausted the loan of $3750 million which was granted in December 1945, and which was expected to last until the end of 1949. By September 1947, only $400 million of this loan remained available, and withdrawals were suspended until the end of 1947. The total amount of the loan had been exhausted in February 1948. The increase in the rate of dollar expenditure above the level expected when the loan had been granted, was due, according to an official British statement, in a proportion of 60 percent, to the rise in the American price level. The only dollar resources available consisted of a sum of $500 million remaining out of the Canadian loan, as the gold

375

reserves of a total of $2400 million were the common pool of the sterling area and could not be drawn upon. In these circumstances, the British government, under the urging of Sir Stafford Cripps, attempted to decrease dollar expenditure by cutting all but the most vital imports for which payment in dollars was required.

France, at the moment of liberation, had gold and foreign exchange resources amounting to $2600 million, but spent most of it in order to pay for the import surplus (which was due to a considerable extent to imports of food) of France herself as well as of French North Africa, which, because of a considerable increase in population and a series of catastrophic draughts, had become a food-deficit area. By September 1947, her gold holdings had decreased to $400 million, which could be considered as an irreducible minimum, while most of her foreign-exchange reserves, in particular nearly all dollar resources, were also exhausted. Thus, the French government, even though expecting to receive a limited amount of assistance under the American Interim Aid program, was still obliged to make drastic cuts in all dollar imports, only food and fuel being excepted. These restrictions were applied even to imports, such as cotton, essential for maintenance of the level of industrial activity.

The Netherlands, as well as Denmark and Norway, had to face somewhat similar difficulties, while in Italy the situation was even worse.

Owing to these conditions, the main problem which confronted the United States by the middle of 1947, if they wanted to continue to assist the economic recovery of Western Europe, was to decide how to organize such assistance in order to make it most effective, without wasting any of it, avoiding thus the danger of a waste of effort somewhat similar to the one described in the story, from Greek mythology, of the futile attempt to fill the bottomless barrel of the Danaids.

30 THE MARSHALL PLAN

THE ESTABLISHMENT of the Marshall Plan was due to a series of considerations. One of the most important was the fact, gradually recognized by the United States government and public opinion, that it appeared more and more futile to continue granting separate assistance to individual European countries, whose production, foreign trade and investment policies, as expressed in their reconstruction plans, not only entirely lacked coordination, but were to a considerable extent competitive and contradictory. On the other hand, it was generally acknowledged that it was necessary, in order to preserve the prosperity and security of the United States, to continue to support the recovery of the non-Communist countries of Europe, which otherwise might become an easy prey to Soviet aggression. This stand was taken because of the economic reasons given in Chapter 29, and even more because of political considerations, which public opinion could grasp more easily.

The proposal formulated by Secretary of State Marshall, in his speech at Harvard on June 5, 1947 (and already forecast in a speech made several weeks earlier by Dean Acheson, then Assistant Secretary of State, in Cleveland) applied, however, to the whole of Europe without any distinction based on political criteria.

This proposal appeared to be motivated by the fact (1) that the Plan would be a logical continuation of the efforts made earlier

377

by the United States, jointly with other Allied powers, for the rehabilitation of all war-devastated countries through UNRRA; and (2) that it offered the possibility of implementing a proposal, made originally by the United States, for the establishment of an Economic Commission of the United Nations for Europe, for the main purpose of furthering economic reconstruction of the whole continent of Europe. That Commission, which had finally been established in the spring of 1947, was expected to provide the technical organization required for the implementation of the Marshall Plan. An even more important argument undoubtedly was the consideration that economic recovery, particularly if due to cooperation between East and West, would necessarily reduce political tensions and improve the prospects of maintaining peace.

The Soviet Union, however, refused to accept the Marshall proposals and forced all other countries under her control to do likewise, sometimes repudiating their previous acceptance. The reason put forward for this refusal was the fact that to request, from countries applying for American assistance under the Marshall program, a pledge to subscribe to a policy of European economic cooperation was an intolerable interference with their domestic policy and a violation of their sovereignty. In fact, it appears most probable that the Soviet authorities were afraid that the economic influence which the United States might obtain in the countries of Eastern Europe, as a result of the assistance granted to them and of the economic cooperation with the West, would counteract and weaken their own political influence in those areas.

The eagerness with which Poland and Czechoslovakia immediately accepted the Marshall Plan, before they were forced to withdraw their acceptance, under Soviet pressure, seems to prove that these Russian fears were not without foundation. As a result of the Soviet refusal, however, the Marshall Plan was restricted to European countries outside of the area controlled by the Russians. It thus became the natural economic basis of the Western Bloc, the establishment of which the Soviet statesmen appeared to want to prevent at any cost. It is interesting to note that the Plan might not have been approved by the United States Congress if, as originally intended, it had included economic assistance to the Soviet Union and the countries under its influence.

The basic idea of the Plan was the fostering of European self-help through economic cooperation between all countries accepting American assistance. This cooperation, supplementing the domestic policies and efforts of each nation concerned, would eventually make Europe more economically self-supporting, and thus reduce her requirements for outside assistance. In the meantime, during the implementation of the Plan, assistance would be provided by the United States, which, during this period, would compensate the deficit of Europe's balance-of-payment, particularly with the dollar area.

The criticism of the Marshall Plan, according to which this program of aid to Europe is purely a manifestation of American imperialism, is an obvious fallacy—at least if imperialism is considered in its traditional and generally accepted meaning, as a will for conquest and domination over other countries, effected generally by applying to those countries the old Roman rule, *divide et impera* (divide and rule). On the contrary, the Plan is directed toward uniting the countries concerned, organizing their cooperation with one another, and assisting them to regain their economic independence. On the other hand, it is obviously true that the Marshall Plan was not intended purely as an act of generosity and altruism, but was also considered, by the government as well as by Congress and the majority of American public opinion, as corresponding to the interests of the United States itself.

Seen in historical perspective, the Marshall Plan appears to be the first large-scale practical application of the doctrine of economic solidarity (characterized in the preceding chapter as indivisibility of prosperity) between the different countries and nations. Owing to this solidarity in prosperity and depression ex-

379

pressed mainly through their trade relations with one another, it appears reasonable, from the point of view of their own economic interests, for prosperous countries, able to grant assistance, to provide such assistance, for the recovery of war-devastated countries, as well as for the development of resources and the rise in standards of living in underdeveloped areas of the world. This doctrine, asserted during World War II, especially in the Atlantic Charter, is also one of the basic principles of the Charter of the United Nations. Owing to political difficulties, however, practical achievements in this field have unfortunately been limited, though by no means unimportant. In so far as Europe is concerned, the work of the Economic Commission for Europe, especially of her technical committees and subcommittees for allocating materials in short supply and alleviating key shortages, was a most valuable example of international economic cooperation achieved in spite of political tensions.

In the United States, the first schemes motivated by this doctrine had been the plans drawn up in the State Department, during World War II, under the initiative of Mr. Berle. Their objective was a post-war Lend Lease to finance reconstruction. These plans were discarded by the end of the war, but their basic idea was to revive in the Marshall Plan.

The Marshall Plan was—and herein lies its special significance—the first example of acceptance of this theory as a basis of most important national policies by a first-rate power—in fact, a power which, in the economic field, was the greatest of all powers. A second, and, in the long run, a potentially even more important, example of such a policy is provided by the program of assistance to underdeveloped areas of the world, presented by President Truman in his inauguration speech, on January 20, 1949.

The acceptance of this policy by American public opinion and the mass of the people was psychologically facilitated by their traditional comprehension of Christianity, not as a belief in a theological religious doctrine, but as a pragmatic principle of action

380

embodied mainly in assistance and charity. This tradition is probably also due to the habit of generosity, which was made possible to a considerable extent by the abundance and ample opportunities existing in an immense country and a rapidly expanding economy, a generosity extended especially to inhabitants of other, less fortunate, lands.*

As a matter of fact, the theory of economic solidarity can be easily stated in terms very similar to this American religious tradition: "The whole world is our neighbor from the standpoint of the Gospel." However, this moral principle of neighborly love, implying the duty of assistance, has been complemented by the rational argument that such assistance is, in the end, useful to those who give as well as to those who receive. Naturally, this was the main basis for implementation of the principle as a matter of practical politics, though, without this moral background, its acceptance would have been much more difficult, if not impossible.

Most critics of the Marshall Plan outside of the United States completely deny its moral and altruistic motives, and claim that its purely egotistic and imperialistic character is proved by the fact that assistance is granted only to European countries which have accepted American leadership in the field of economics as well as in foreign policy; and that it is denied to others, even if the latter are more in need of assistance, or could put to better use, in terms of increase in production, such assistance if it were granted.

Thus, it has been many times stressed by Polish spokesmen that new investment in Polish coal mines, through installation of modern American-built equipment, would yield much greater results than similar modernization financed by Marshall Plan funds and

* A striking illustration of this idea is furnished by the enormous number, and considerable importance, of American welfare organizations functioning abroad, on a religious basis, such as the Friends Service Committee and similar bodies of most Protestant denominations, as well as of Catholics and Jews, and the admirable assistance rendered by them, particularly in war-devastated countries.

381

effected in Belgian or French coal mines. However, such an argument ignores the fact that, under existing circumstances, it would be not altruism but just plain absurdity, from the American point of view, to grant economic assistance to countries, which—even though indirectly, through their connections and alliances, and for reasons that might be perfectly justified from their own point of view—appear to be hostile to the success of economic recovery, as well as to political and social stabilization of non-Communist countries, particularly in Western Europe.

The fundamental principle of the Marshall Plan was to strive to reach basic objectives by 1951—when it is to be terminated—which would insure the restoration of the economy of the countries participating in the Plan, so that they would be self-supporting and would have reasonably satisfactory standard of living for their inhabitants.

The main objectives to be reached by 1951 were the following:

I. Overall increase in production. This is the first and foremost objective of the Plan. The increase forecast in the Plan, even though large, did not seem unrealistic, as it was rather similar in scope to the expansion achieved in the United States during the war period. The main effort for increase of production was to be concentrated in key sectors of economy such as food, coal, steel, transport equipment, chemicals, etc. The effort was to be directed toward expansion of total output, as well as toward modernization of equipment, in order to achieve improvement of efficiency and lowering of the cost of production.

For food production, the planned target was, on the whole, reestablishing, or exceeding very slightly, the pre-war level of output, but with considerable variations in the different categories of foodstuffs. Thus, production of bread grains, which had declined for 1947-48 by 35 percent, as compared to the pre-war average, was expected to reach pre-war level again in 1950-51, while for coarse grains an increase of 4 percent in production, as compared to pre-war, was planned. Production of potatoes, already 7 percent above pre-war in 1947-48, was expected to expand further to 19 percent above pre-war level. Production of sugar, which by 1947-48 had approximately regained pre-war level, was to be increased by 15 percent. Total production of fats and oils, still more than 20 percent below pre-war in 1947-48, was planned to exceed it by 3 percent. As to animal products, increase in production would depend on the rebuilding of livestock, as feed became more abundant; it was expected to proceed at a much slower rate. Thus, production of milk, still 22 percent below pre-war in 1947-48, was expected to reach only a level of 1 percent above pre-war, while meat production, in 1947-48 inferior by one-third to pre-war, was expected to recover only to 88 percent of pre-war. In spite of the general increase in production, as population is expected to have increased by 10 percent as compared to pre-war, the share of total consumption of participating countries covered by domestic production and imports from other countries of that area will scarcely increase.

The realization of these production goals implies a considerable effort: development of cereals production is expected to take place mainly in Italy and in France, through a slight expansion in acreage and a more considerable increase in yields intended to be reached by a higher use of fertilizer. Production of dairy products is to be restored, and considerably expanded, particularly in Denmark, Eire and the Netherlands, but also in France, for domestic consumption as well as for export. One of the main prerequisites for increase of agricultural production consists in increased availability of fertilizer, production of which is to be considerably expanded, particularly of nitrogen, which, during the first years after the end of the war, was in especially short supply. The output of nitrogen is to be more than doubled but, in spite of that, some imports from the United States are expected during the first two years of the Plan, before production of the area will cover requirements.

A considerable development of agricultural mechanization will

383

be necessary, in order to cut down the requirements for labor and thus to make it possible to increase acreage and to improve methods of cultivation, while at the same time reducing the cost of production. Such results were largely achieved through the mechanization effected in the United Kingdom during the war; this effort is to be still further extended. Similar reforms in production methods are to be undertaken on the Continent and especially in France. In order to achieve these results, a considerable increase in production of tractors and all kinds of agricultural machinery is planned, mainly in Great Britain and in France. However, some imports of equipment, mainly heavy tractors from the United States, were considered to be necessary at the beginning of the Plan, before Western European production could reach its maximum.

Owing to the increase in population, as compared to pre-war, it was expected that by the end of the Marshall Plan, even if all production goals were fully reached, levels of consumption would be no higher, but generally slightly lower, than pre-war, especially in the more expensive foodstuffs, and that import requirements from outside the area would remain considerably above pre-war.

The increase in agricultural production visualized in the original figures of the OEEC, which were accepted in the Marshall Plan, was therefore considered to be only a short-term objective, which was expected to be considerably exceeded as a result of further efforts. Drafted at the moment when the catastrophic failure of the 1947 harvest tended to justify conservative and even pessimistic forecasts, these initial production estimates have since been revised upward, particularly in the French plan presented to the OEEC. Nevertheless, the requirements for substantial food imports to bridge the gap between total production of the Marshall Plan countries and consumption on a minimum level compatible with economic recovery, are looming as the greatest obstacle to the reestablishment of the equilibrium of the balance of payments of this area.

384

FORECASTS OF TOTAL RESOURCES, PRODUCTION, CONSUMPTION AND IMPORT REQUIREMENTS OF BASIC FOODSTUFFS

(in million metric tons)

	1934-38 average	1947-48	1950-51
Bread grains production	34.0	21.4	34.0
(wheat & rye) consumption			
requirements	47.9	43.2	49.7
Net import requirements	13.9	21.8	15.7
Consumption kg per head	192	159	179
Oils and fats production	2.8	2.2	2.7
consumption	6.0	4.6	6.3
imports	3.2	2.4	3.6
Consumption kg per head	24.1	17	22.6
Meat production	9.0	6.0	8.1
consumption	10.7	8.1	10.5
imports	1.7	2.1	2.4
Consumption kg per head	42.9	30	37.6
Sugar production	3.4	3.4	3.9
consumption	6.8	5.4	7.1
imports	3.4	2.0	3.2
Consumption kg per head	27.4	20.0	25.2
Potatoes (production = consumption, as there is no significant foreign trade)	58.8	61.6	68.2
Consumption kg per head	236	228	243

Fuel and power being the basis of all industrial activity, restoration and expansion above pre-war of all sources available in Western Europe is one of the most vital sections of the Marshall Plan. Production of coal, which is by far the most important source of power in this area, is to be increased, from 526 million metric tons (total for hard coal and lignite) for the average of the years 1935-38

385

(554 million tons in 1938), to 583 million tons in 1951. In 1947, it amounted only to 439 million tons.

The most important expansion of coal production is to be effected in Great Britain, where output in 1951 is expected to reach 249 million tons, 108 percent of 1938, as against 199 million tons in 1947, and where the most complete program of modernization of production ever attempted is to be implemented, extending to extraction, as well as to haulage, washing, etc.

In France, where a similar program is being implemented, with special stress on the Lorraine coal mines, where natural conditions are most favorable, production is scheduled to reach 67.5 million tons in 1951, as against 47 million tons in 1938 as well as in 1947. During the latter year, however, higher production was prevented by strikes. A considerable effort is also to be made to improve living and, especially, housing conditions of the miners and thus to stimulate recruitment of domestic and foreign labor. The latter are mainly displaced persons and Italians required to replace German war prisoners who have been repatriated.

Production in the Saar, which is incorporated in the French economy, is also to be expanded considerably above pre-war level, and in 1951 should reach 16.8 million tons, as against a pre-war average of 12.5 million tons. On the contrary, in the Ruhr, where the most important war devastation of mining installations and ancillary plant, as well as of housing of the miners occurred, and still remains to a large extent to be repaired, production is expected to recover by 1951 only to 87 percent of 1938—that is, 121 million tons, as against 138 million tons. In Belgium, production is scheduled to exceed the level of 1938 by 1.5 million tons, while in the Netherlands only the pre-war level is to be restored.

Besides increasing production, a considerable effort is to be made also (1) to utilize available resources in the most rational and economical way; and (2) to organize, in such matters, the closest possible cooperation between all participating countries, particularly by reserving all hard-coal coke for steel production. In spite of such most careful husbanding of coal resources, and the considerable increase in production, coal resources by the end of the Plan are expected to be insufficient, owing to an even greater expansion of consumption requirements, due mainly to the rise in industrial production. Thus, consumption is expected to reach 609 million tons in 1951, as against 530 million tons in 1938, leaving a net deficit of 26 million tons. This will have to be covered by imports from outside the area. It is planned that Poland will provide most of these imports. Before the war, on the contrary, the total coal production of all participating countries allowed for net exports, though on a limited scale (about 4 million tons).

Even though the Marshall Plan countries do not possess any significant oil resources, increase of liquid fuel consumption is planned to be much more considerable than of coal. Consumption of oil products is scheduled, for 1951, at 68 million tons, that is 20 percent of all energy consumed in the area, as against 33 million tons and 10 percent of total energy consumption during the pre-war years 1935-38. The plan for this tremendous increase in consumption appeared to be justified (1) by the fact that imported liquid fuel is considerably cheaper for the same thermic value than imported coal; (2) by the mechanization of agriculture, which is expected to increase considerably the requirements for fuel oil; and (3) by the possibility that a significant share of oil supplies would be obtained from non-dollar sources, mainly from the Middle East, which imports could be easily paid for through exports of Western European manufactured goods. A considerable increase in oil-refining capacity is also planned, in order to decrease cost of imports, and to provide raw materials for various chemical productions.

Electric-power productive capacity, which, since the beginning of the war, had not been expanded, while requirements had enormously increased, is planned to undergo a substantial development. Total productive capacity, which amounted to 39 million kw in 1938, and 42.1 million kw in 1946, is due to reach 65.5 million kw in 1951, of which 40.9 million kw (instead of 25.0 million kw in 1938) will be thermal, and 24.6 million kw (instead of 14

387

million kw) hydraulic. Total production of electric power is expected to reach 237 billion kwh in 1951, as against 130 billion kwh in 1938 and 153 billion kwh in 1946. Thermic plants are planned to be built, especially on coal and lignite deposits, in order to utilize low-grade fuel unsuited for other purposes. Besides very considerable national plans of participating countries for expansion of electric power production—in particular, by establishing important hydroelectric plants on the Rhone, the Rhine and several other big rivers—an additional international program for establishment of hydroelectric, lignite and geothermic plant has been prepared, arranging for cooperation between several of the participating countries for production and utilization of electric power.

Steel production, the basis of all equipment industries, as well as of building activity, will be considerably expanded, as compared to pre-war production, in all the Marshall Plan area, with the exception of Western Germany, and in 1951 will be 25 percent above the aggregate total of the most active pre-war year. If, however, Western Germany is included, production in 1951 will be about equal to that of the most active pre-war year for the whole area. There will thus be a considerable shift in production; compared to the most active pre-war year, raw steel-production in various countries is expected to reach the following figures in 1951: Great Britain, 15 million tons, vs. 13.2 million tons; France, 12.7 million tons, vs. 9.7 million tons; Belgium-Luxembourg, 7.9 million tons, vs. 6.6 million tons; but the Bi-Zone of Germany, 10.7 million tons, vs. 17.8 million tons. The center of gravity of European steel production was thus supposed to be transferred from Germany to the West.

Coke, which had been the key bottleneck preventing recovery of steel production in the immediate post-war period, is expected to be provided, for the increased output, mainly from the Ruhr and, to a lesser extent, from Great Britain and the Saar. Besides, modernization of industrial equipment for steel production is expected to reduce consumption of coke per ton of steel produced.

388

It is expected that, by the end of the Marshall Plan period, while for scrap and some categories of finished steel there will remain some import requirements from outside the area, the net export surplus for steel and objects in iron and steel (vehicles, equipment, etc.) will be considerably above pre-war.

Expansion of steel production will provide the possibility of effecting the development of equipment industries, required in order to supply most of the new installations and machinery for the implementation of the programs of expansion and modernization of production in all sectors of the economy. Thus, the Marshall Plan countries are due to manufacture 95 percent of the coal-mining equipment needed, 90 percent of the power-plant equipment and two-thirds of the equipment for petroleum refineries, as well as the greatest part of the equipment for modernization of the iron and steel industry; for production of farm machinery and tractors; for the building of railway equipment. etc.

Restoration and reconstruction of inland transport and, in particular, of the railways was already well advanced at the moment of the drafting of the Marshall Plan; but still a tremendous amount of permanent reconstruction remained to be achieved, as well as a considerable backlog of rolling stock to be built. The main target in this respect is to enable the inland transport system to carry, by 1951, a total freight load of 25 percent above pre-war. As to shipping, the pre-war total tonnage is to be restored by replacement of some 22 million tons sunk during the war.

Another key production of vital importance for the reconstruction of the economy of participating countries is timber, which is required for reconstruction of housing, as well as for mining (pit props) for railways (ties), and for all sorts of industrial utilization. A considerable effort is to be made to exploit, to the maximum, existing resources in Western Germany, which became an exporter in the immediate post-war period, as well as in France and in the Scandinavian countries, and particularly to increase allocations of coal to the latter countries, in order to prevent burning of timber as fuel. New resources of timber are also expected to be devel-

389

oped, mainly in Africa, by exploitation of some species of tropical timber which can provide soft wood. A considerable part of timber requirements, however, will have to be still met by imports from outside, that is, from North America; and a considerable shortage of supplies, in relation to requirements, is anticipated.

Manpower shortage, particularly of skilled workers in industry and in agriculture, as well as of underground miners, is also expected to become in several countries: France, Belgium and Great Britain an important factor limiting expansion of production. However, reserves of available manpower, mainly in Italy, and in the displaced-persons camps of Germany and Austria, are considerably superior to the requirements, which will have to be met by immigration; but in general they do not provide the professional skills required. Still, manpower treaties dealing with migration and recruitment of labor will make possible considerable progress in this matter.

All the different plans of expansion of production are obviously interdependent, and the implementation of each one will depend on the degree of implementation of the others' plans. It will also depend on the availability of the required supplies from outside, that is, from the United States.

II. Internal economic, financial and monetary stability. This is expected to be reestablished, if implementation of the Plan is to be successfully achieved. Thus, the participating countries pledged themselves to overcome inflation and to reestablish as soon as possible not only equilibrium of their budgets, but a general condition of balance between national income and national expenditure, and thus end basing their standard of living, to a great extent, on consumption of accumulated capital assets or on foreign credits. Absorption of inflation should be allowed to effect, as soon as possible, stabilization of currencies at levels corresponding to the purchasing-power parity (as compared to price level abroad) as well as to a state of equilibrium between total available purchasing power and available commodities at prevailing prices, in the domestic market of each country. At the same time, establishment of budgetary equilibrium would prevent new creation of surplus purchasing power. The governments concerned pledged themselves that, after stabilization of currencies had been completely achieved and successfully maintained, they would make their currencies convertible according to the Articles of Agreement of the International Monetary Fund.

III. Economic cooperation, viz., mutual assistance between all participating countries in the effort toward reconstruction of their economies, based on their economic interdependence. This cooperation includes (a) restoration of traditional links of trade formerly existing between them; (b) development of production of essential commodities for export to other participating countries, thus reducing the general deficit of the area; (c) coordination of investment programs for establishment of new capacity, in particular for steel production; (d) joint plans for development especially of electric-power production; and (e) measures to restore, as soon as improvement of the balance-of-payment situation permits, the free flow of multilateral trade inside the area by abolishing abnormal restriction on imports. Such cooperation could eventually extend to the creation of customs unions to include several or all of the participating countries, which has been considered as highly desirable. Finally, the most important practical form of cooperation has consisted in the establishment of a common organization for the implementation and administration of the Marshall Plan by all the countries participating in this program.

IV. Import surplus and balance of payment of the Marshall Plan countries. The implementation of this program implies a large and uninterrupted flow of supplies of food, raw materials and equipment for modernization of industry and agriculture from nonparticipating countries. As capacity for production, and exports to the outside world, of participating countries is by far insufficient to provide means of payment for the urgent import requirements, and can be only gradually restored and developed, a

391

considerable, even though steadily decreasing, balance-of-payment deficit of participating countries with the rest of the world appears to be unavoidable for the four-year period of implementation of the Plan.

The total volume of import requirements—the cost of which was estimated at about $14 billion (measured on the basis of July 1947 prices) for 1948 and slightly more for each of the three following years—was scarcely larger than the average of the pre-war period, when there were no reconstruction requirements, but many luxury imports of nonessential goods. Even though that was the case, the shift in the average geographical distribution of imports considerably increased the difficulty of bridging the gap in the balance-of-payments. It was estimated that during 1948 about two-thirds of these imports (instead of only 40 percent before the war) would originate on the American Continent, and thus have to be paid for in dollars. This reduction in the share of non-American supplies was due to: (a) war devastation in Eastern Europe and the USSR, which had stopped their exports of food and lumber; (b) the loss of supplies from Eastern Germany to the western part of the Reich; and (c) the loss of supplies and income from Southeast Asia, which became, even though temporarily, a deficit area and had to import food which was being paid for in dollars by the metropolitan countries of Western Europe.

The import estimates for the following years of the Plan assumed that the mutually advantageous complementary trade with Eastern Europe will be gradually restored, as well as that the abnormal deficit of Southeast Asia will be terminated, and that this area will at least partially resume its function as a source of supplies and income. However, in spite of these measures, even in 1951 the share of the American Continent in total Western European imports will still remain above pre-war level, while imports of equipment for reconstruction should obviously be of an order of magnitude not at all comparable to the pre-war level of such imports.

Following is the estimated balance of payment of participating countries (Western Germany included) for 1948:

(in millions of dollars)

	With American Continent	With other Non-participating Countries	
Imports	—9,170	—4,700	
Exports	+2,160	+4,300	
Net deficit (—) or surplus (+) on invisible account (services and interest payments)	— 570	+ 380	
Dependent territories surplus or deficit	— 450	— 220	
Total	—8,030	— 240	—8,270

During the pre-war period, the area of the Marshall Plan countries had an average dollar deficit, resulting from its merchandise trade with the American Continent, or $1,450 million. This, however, was compensated for, without major difficulties, by proceeds of the sale to the United States of colonial products (mainly rubber and tin) from Southeast Asia; by earnings on invisible account; and by the surplus in earnings with the rest of the world which could be easily converted into dollars. During 1947, while the Marshall Plan was being drafted, Europe's foreign investments were gone, tourist traffic was a negligible item, and shipping had become a debit to be paid for in dollars, while supplies of Eastern Europe were not available and Southeast Asia had become a deficit area, and individual export surpluses with other areas, when available, could not be converted into dollars. The situation of the Marshall Plan countries had also been aggravated by the rise in American prices since the end of price control in the summer of 1946, particularly as prices of primary commodities, which are Europe's main imports, increased considerably more than those of manufactured goods, which are her main exports.

Thus, Europe's terms of trade deteriorated. Also, even without this difference in the rate of price increase, imports being considerably greater than exports, it was estimated that, even with an equal rate of price increase for imports and exports, the European dollar deficit was increasing by one billion dollars for a 16 percent rise in prices.

According to the estimates made by the Committee for European Economic Cooperation, in its report prepared from July to September, 1947, for presentation to the United States authorities, the deficit of the balance-of-payment of the Marshall Plan countries was due to decrease gradually as production and exports were expected to expand. The total deficit with the American Continent and with the rest of the world was expected to be as follows:

(In Millions of Dollars)	1948	1949	1950	1951	Total for Whole Marshall Plan
With United States	−5,640	−4,270	−3,280	−2,620	−15,810
With rest of American Continent	−1,940	−1,820	−1,300	−910	−5,970
Net deficit or surplus of dependent territories	−450	−260	−70	+130	−650
Total dollar deficit	−8,030	−6,350	−4,650	−3,400	−22,430
Net deficit or surplus with rest of the world	−240	+250	+1,000	+1,800	....

It has been estimated by the CEEC that, during the period of the Marshall Plan, a considerable part of the imports of equipment required by the participating countries from the dollar area (amounting to $3,130 million) could be financed by loans which would be granted by the International Bank for Reconstruction and Development. As a matter of fact, these equipment imports would correspond to productive investments for which the International Bank, by its Articles of Agreement, is empowered to grant

394

loans. The remaining dollar deficit, which would thus amount to $19,300 million, could be provided only by the United States; and, through the acceptance of the ERP by Congress, that country expressed its willingness to effectively provide this sum.

The CEEC had estimated that, by the end of the Marshall Plan —provided that the assumptions on which its figures were based would be fulfilled—the dollar deficit of the participating countries would, if not completely disappear, at least be reduced to manageable proportions and thus not require any further assistance. However, the assumptions on which these estimates were based were such that complete fulfilment of them could be only hoped for, not expected with any degree of certitude.

The most important of these assumptions were: (1) expansion of production in the Marshall Plan area, as well as of exports, in particular to the United States; (2) willingness of the United States to accept these increased exports; (3) reestablishment of an important trade with Eastern Europe, recovery of shipping, of tourist trade, and of other invisible income resources; (4) general reestablishment of currency convertibility, which would enable Western Europe, as before the war, to compensate her dollar deficit by her surplus with other areas; (5) a minimum of international political stability, which would prevent a significant share of the increase in production of the participating countries from being absorbed in expansion of unproductive military expenditure.

31 THE IMPLEMENTATION OF THE MARSHALL PLAN AND THE DIFFICULTIES OF COORDINATION OF NATIONAL PLANS

THE IMPLEMENTATION of the Marshall Plan is being effected by an administration of the United States government, the Economic Cooperation Administration (ECA), established according to the provisions of the ERP (European Recovery Program) Act. In addition to its central administration in Washington, which, aside from liaison, is entrusted mainly with procurement of supplies, the ECA has a central European office in Paris and representatives in all participating countries. The European counterpart of the ECA is the Organization of European Economic Cooperation, established by a convention signed in Paris on April 16, 1948, by representatives of the 16 participating countries and of the three Western Zones of Germany. Its general objective was the achievement of a sound Western European economy, through economic cooperation of the member countries, and the immediate task of insuring the success of the European Recovery Program.

The OEEC is not an economic supergovernment of the Marshall Plan area, but only the instrument for the economic cooperation between all countries concerned and also (through the intermediary of the ECA) with the United States.

Even within those limits, however, its functions are most important. They include the following: (1) to prepare, when necessary, on the basis of national estimates or programs, such overall production, import and export programs as appear necessary; (2) to consider, in the light of national estimates or programs of development, the best use of resources to further objectives pursued within metropolitan or overseas territories; (3) to promote consultation, between countries concerned, on measures for creating the machinery for European cooperation, especially in matters of trade, international payments, and movements of labor; (4) to investigate, if necessary, methods of coordinating purchasing policies; (5) to assist members, upon request, to surmount difficulties incurred in implementing the ERP program; (6) to make such recommendations as may be appropriate to the United States government, or to other governments and international organizations, on allocation of commodities among member countries; (7) to insure the most efficient use of external aid and to contribute to insure efficient use of indigenous resources by member countries; (8) to prepare reports on execution of the ERP; and (9) to collect all necessary information.

The organizational structure of the OEEC is as follows: The supreme organ is the Council, on which all member countries are represented, generally by delegates of cabinet rank. Its first Chairman was Mr. Spaak, Foreign Minister of Belgium; its present chairman is Mr. Stikker, Foreign Minister of the Netherlands, who has also taken over important executive powers as a sort of a general coordinator of the OEEC program. At first, the sessions of the Council were very few, and its main function was formally to ratify the most important decisions that were taken by the Executive Committee, a semi-permanent body, under the chairmanship of Hall Patch, of the British Foreign Office. Finally, there is the Secretariat, which prepares the decisions and the reports, and collects information. The Secretary General is the French economist, Robert Marjolin.

The most important practical task accomplished by the OEEC, during the first two years of its existence, has been the formulation of recommendations for the allocation of the American aid among the member countries. These recommendations were ratified, after some discussion, by all the countries concerned. The OEEC has

397

also prepared the intra-European payment and compensation agreement, which was also approved by the countries concerned. This agreement was intended to facilitate and to stimulate trade between the participating countries, by granting, to countries having deficits in their trade with other participating countries, part of the American assistance in the form of drawing rights in the currencies of the countries which were their net creditors. The latter countries received, as compensation, an equivalent amount of additional dollar grants, the so-called conditional aid.

This agreement, by providing debtor countries with additional import possibilities in European creditor countries, stimulated intra-European trade and discouraged the trend to purchase from the United States, with the proceeds of Marshall Plan aid, goods which were available in Western European creditor countries. As a result of the allocation plan and the compensation agreement, distribution of ERP assistance, for the year 1948-49, between the different recipient countries is shown on page 399.

In spite of the considerable revival of inter-European trade, due to the conditional-grant system, at first there were still appreciable balance-of-payment difficulties. Thus, in 1948, in some of the countries concerned, particularly in France, continuation of the inflationary situation impeded the necessary expansion of exports, and diminished even more the receipts of their proceeds in foreign exchange, which exporters were obviously most reluctant to deliver to the authorities. Thus, her means of payment in foreign exchange being nearly or completely exhausted (even including the drawing rights provided in the intra-European payment agreement), France had to curtail drastically her purchases payable in sterling, and to suspend for several months all imports payable in Belgian francs. On the other hand, Belgium, which at first did not attempt as far as possible to concentrate her imports in other participating countries, which were her main export markets created thus for them a shortage of Belgian francs, with resulting curtailment of her exports and development of considerable unemployment.

(in millions of dollars)

Recipient Countries	Total Aid	Drawing Rights in Other Currencies Received	Granted	Net Amount of Assistance Received
Total	4,875	810.4	810.4	4,875
Austria	217	66.4	3.1	280.3
Belgium-Luxembourg	250	11	218.5	42.5
Denmark	110	11.9	5.1	116.8
France	989	333	9.7	1,312.3
Greece	146	66.8	....	212.8
Ireland	79	....	....	79
Iceland	11	....	....	11
Italy	601	27	47.3	580.7
Netherlands	496	83	11.3	567.7
Norway	84	48.3	16.5	115.8
United Kingdom	1,263	30	312	981
Sweden	47	9.8	34.8	22
Trieste	18	....	....	18
Turkey	50	8.8	28.5	30.3
Germany Bi-Zone	414	98.6	108.8	403.8
Germany French Zone	100	15.6	14.8	100.8

Another most important task which the OEEC started to handle, but with rather disappointing results, was the coordination of the short-term, as well as the long-term, economic policies and plans of all participating countries, especially as to current production and investments planned for its future expansion, foreign trade, and balance of payments. For this purpose, the OEEC requested all participating countries to submit to it their plans and forecasts for the period extending until 1952, in order to coordinate them into a single general master plan. As a matter of fact, the individual countries' plans had actually been submitted, but their integration into a single master plan had not been achieved.

The main difficulties relative to such an integration were structural changes, since the war, which affected, in particular, the economy of Great Britain and of Western Germany, and which resulted in a shift of their import requirements from other participating countries mainly to overseas primary-goods-producing countries.

Great Britain, owing to the loss of her foreign investments, had to plan to maintain global volume of imports at only 80-85 percent of pre-war, which, moreover, would have to provide the food and raw materials required to support a more numerous population at the considerably increased level of industrial activity and purchasing power of the masses implied by the policy of full employment. Requirements for imports of basic foodstuffs and raw materials thus being irreducible, the main part of the decrease in imports will have to be effected in the category of the less essential industrial or agricultural consumer goods, which, before the war, Great Britain used to purchase mainly in the participating countries of the European continent. These purchases provided the other Western European countries with a considerable surplus of sterling, which they used to pay for their net imports (such as wool from Australia) from other countries of the sterling area. The shift in the distribution of British national income, from the higher- and middle- to the lower-income brackets, also reduced the domestic purchasing power which used to be spent for such imports while increasing the effective demand for basic supplies.

A somewhat similar change occurred in Western Germany, which, with a population nearly 20 percent above pre-war level, and cut off from her former food-supply sources of her eastern territories, has thus to face considerably increased import requirements for basic foodstuffs, while her industrial exports are not expected to increase substantially above pre-war. This situation will inevitably result in a drastic curtailment of all imports, other than those most essential, which before the war originated mainly in other participating countries; the main source for food and raw-material imports will obviously be, even more than before the war, overseas countries, especially those in the Western Hemisphere.

400

These difficulties were still more increased by the strictly nationalist attitude of British planning, expressed in the Four-Year Plan of the United Kingdom submitted, by the end of 1948, to the OEEC. Great Britain had achieved the greatest recovery in production and balance of payments of all the participating countries. This was due to her austerity policy, including strict rationing of consumption, a successful fight against inflation, and a very high level of investment (20 percent of national income) made possible by such a policy, as well as to a strenuous production effort directed by Sir Stafford Cripps. She intended to continue this policy without any attempt to taking into account cooperation with other participating countries.

The British plan forecasts a general increase, by 1952-53, in industrial and agricultural production, by 40 percent, as compared to pre-war. Its main features are: increase of production of bread grains to 8.4 million tons vs. 4.6 in the average of 1934-38, and 7.6 in 1948-49; increase in production of milk and dairy products to 9 million tons vs. a pre-war level of 7.3 and 8 million tons in 1948; and restoration of meat and bacon production to the pre-war level of 1.5 million tons vs. 1 million tons in 1948. Production of coal is expected to reach 257 million tons vs. 233 for the average 1934-38 and 218 in 1948; production of raw steel should reach 17 million tons vs. 11.4 million for the pre-war average and 15 millions in 1948.

Consumption of imported raw materials, on the other hand, is not expected to increase generally, but only where it may prove indispensable for domestic investment or justified by prospects of additional exports. Thus, consumption of copper is expected to rise to 427,000 tons vs. the pre-war average of 266,000 tons, and consumption of wool should reach 232,000 tons vs. 190,000 tons. On the other hand, consumption of cotton is planned to decline to 473,000 tons vs. 619,000 tons; and the consumption of lumber will have to be curtailed drastically to 7.7 million cubic meters vs. 12.6 million cubic meters.

401

Owing to the general increase in production, exports as well as invisible receipts are expected to expand considerably; for 1952, exports are forecast to reach £1,844 million, and net receipts on invisible accounts £263 million, leaving, after payment of imports (the value of which is estimated at £2,007 million) a net credit balance of £100 million available for foreign investment. The geographical breakdown of the British balance of payment is expected to leave, in 1952, a deficit of £73 million with the Western Hemisphere, and of £43 million with the non-participating countries outside of the sterling area; while achieving, on the other hand, a surplus of £204 million with the sterling area, and of £12 million with the other participating countries, which, before the war, used to have a substantial positive balance of about £150 million in their trade relations with the United Kingdom.

The British plan was naturally violently criticized by the other participating countries, which asserted that the United Kingdom manifested the intention of pursuing a purely egoistic policy, and of aiming to achieve its recovery at their expense. They maintained that the result of the implementation of the British plan would be for the rest of Western Europe to make of the pound sterling a currency as much in short supply as the dollar, and thus still more aggravate the situation in this area. However, the British replied: that because of the deterioration of their economic situation, owing to the war, the United Kingdom was unable to maintain its pre-war imports of non-essential consumer goods from the Continent; but that, on the other hand, they were ready to accept from this group of countries exports of essential goods corresponding to requirements, if that group was able to provide them; and that they would use them as an alternative source of supplies originally planned to be imported from overseas. This last clause opened the door to a possible compromise, provided the plans of the other participating countries were adjusted in accordance with these export possibilities.

The French Four-Year Plan submitted to the OEEC was, on the contrary, intended to provide a maximum contribution to European economic cooperation by adjusting for this purpose the Monnet Plan, which had been drafted originally with a purely national outlook. It thus contained the basis for a conciliation with the British plan. Hence, while the industrial objectives of the Monnet Plan had been generally maintained, considerable stress was put on expansion of agricultural production, which was expected to increase by 1952 to 25 percent above pre-war level, while the Monnet Plan merely intended to restore it to pre-war level. For example, production of wheat was expected to reach 10 million tons by 1952 vs. a pre-war average of 8.15 million tons; production of milk and dairy products, 175 million hectoliter vs. 146 million; and production of fat and oils, 540,000 tons vs. 325,000 tons.

This planned expansion of agricultural production is expected to result mainly from increase in yields due to development of use of fertilizer and mechanization, as well as to replacement of animal draught power by tractors, liberating feedstuffs for beef and dairy livestock. It is anticipated that the results will be to increase to 21 6 percent the share of agricultural products in total French exports. In particular, it was planned to export 1.5 million tons of wheat and about 200,000 tons of meat to other participating countries, thus effecting a dollar saving for the whole ERP area of at least $200 million.

Doubts manifested, at first, as to the realistic character of the planned expansion in agricultural production and exports were somewhat dispelled by the drastic fall in French farm prices during the first months of 1949. At that time, considerable surpluses of fruit, vegetables and even meat could not be sold on the domestic market, and thus became available for export.

The policy of contracts at stable prices, pursued by the French government for the main agricultural staples, appears also to warrant further development of their production and of availability of export surpluses. Franco-British negotiations on exchange of agricultural products were started at that period and, in spite of numerous difficulties concerning prices, quality standards, etc., were undoubtedly a turning point in a most important and sig-

nificant aspect of European economic cooperation. During 1949
and 1950, a steady expansion of French agricultural exports to all
other participating countries took place. With Great Britain, in
particular, there were very satisfactory results from the first export
contracts, which were renewed and expanded.

3 2 THE BRITISH MONETARY CRISIS AND THE DEVALUATION OF THE CURRENCIES OF WESTERN EUROPE

EVEN THOUGH THE STRUGGLE against inflationary pressures had met with considerably more success in Great Britain than in most other countries of Western Europe, still the British monetary position since the end of the war had been under special pressure. This was due to the fact that Great Britain administered the "pool" of gold and dollar resources of the sterling area, that is, of the whole British Commonwealth (except Canada) and some other countries, mainly in the Middle East. The reserves of this dollar pool were used to cover not only the dollar deficit of Great Britain, but also of the rest of the sterling area.

The American and Canadian loans at the beginning of the postwar period, and the Marshall Plan aid since 1948, brought, in this respect also, a considerable alleviation of British difficulties. However, the dollar assistance received from Great Britain's share in the ERP appropriations was nearly offset by the amount which had to be released annually out of the blocked sterling balances, representing the foreign debt due to the war, for the benefit of the respective creditor countries (mainly India and the Middle East countries).

The amounts released were to a small extent converted in dollars, but were used mainly to finance purchases of British goods. These so-called unrequited exports amounted in 1947 to £140 million and in 1948 to £210 million ($840 million), that is, more than the amount which had been granted to Great Britain as unconditional aid for 1948 (£170 million). Thus, nearly all the financial assistance granted by the United States to Britain was transferred to creditor countries of the sterling area.

Another aspect of these unrequited exports was the fact that they offered ready markets for British manufactures not only of capital goods, which the respective creditor countries mainly wanted, but also of consumer goods of all kinds, which other foreign markets were growing less eager to absorb. Existence of this margin of guaranteed foreign markets discouraged British manufacturers from making the most difficult effort required in order to sell their goods, in particular in the dollar markets of the United States and Canada. On the other hand, it had been probably a support for maintenance of full employment in Great Britain, which the Labor government was most reluctant to abandon. This last reason seems to provide the main explanation of the fact that, in spite of considerable pressure of the United States authorities to settle the sterling-balances question (an action absolutely essential for establishment of the pound on a more sound basis), the British government as yet had not taken such an initiative. This action, according to the schemes considered, would have naturally implied a considerable scaling down of the amount due, the rest being partly transformed in a long-term loan and, to a relatively small extent, repaid in convertible currency. It would, of course, also have been opposed by the creditor countries concerned.

During the first year of the Marshall Plan, the dollar position of the sterling area had been maintained, with even a slight improvement, owing to: (a) the assistance granted; (b) progress of the British export drive; and, in particular, (c) the recovery in exports to the United States of raw materials of the sterling area. However, this favorable trend became reversed during the second quarter of 1949, mainly because of the considerable decline in prices of raw materials sold by the sterling area to the United States, but also on account of the slight recession which caused American purchases of such raw materials to be reduced in volume, as well as in price. To some extent, also, sales of British goods in the United States and other hard-currency markets were slowed down, owing to the end of the seller's market and greater domestic supplies (e.g., sales of British automobiles in the United States declined). Thus, while British exports to the dollar area declined in the first half of 1949 to £90 million, as compared to £95 million in the second half of 1948, the dollar deficit of the rest of the sterling area increased, during the same period, from £8 million to £44 million. Hence, during the second quarter of 1949, total dollar deficit of the sterling area was $632 million, as against $330 million in the first quarter, a situation which, in spite of ERP aid, caused the gold and dollar reserves to decline during this quarter, by $261 million, to $1651 million, as compared to an increase of $56 million during the preceding quarter.

This deterioration of British foreign trade and of the monetary situation again stimulated pressure for devaluation of the pound. Such devaluation had already been considered desirable in many quarters, in the United States as well as on the Continent of Europe, where the pound had been looked upon as overvalued. It was expected, in these quarters, that a moderate devaluation would make the pound rate more realistic and improve the British competitive position on foreign markets, thus strengthening the British monetary position and improving chances for a return to convertibility and to multilateral trade.

Under the influence of such considerations and of the unfavorable trend of British exports during the third quarter of 1949, devaluation of the pound came to be generally expected. This was reflected in the sharp decline of the black-market rate of the pound, a consequence of attempts of holders of blocked sterling balances to liquidate their holdings even at a considerable loss. Such depreciation, even though not important in itself, was nevertheless considered to be a psychologically significant development. Besides, this expectancy caused temporary curtailment or

407

postponement of purchases of goods payable in sterling as well as even payments for outstanding debts. All this contributed to aggravate even more the country's monetary position.

At first, and for a long time, the British labor government vigorously opposed any suggestion of the devaluation of the pound. It asserted that the pound was not at all overvalued, cost of living in Great Britain being, at official currency rates, rather less, than more, expensive than not only in the United States, but in most Western European industrialized countries competing with Britain. This argument, however, should be qualified by acknowledgment of the fact that low prices for basic rationed foodstuffs and consumer goods purchased by the British population were due to complete absence of taxes and payment of substantial subsidies (over £200 million annually), while non-subsidized prices in Great Britain of export goods were certainly not lower, and generally higher, than in most other countries.

The British government was also afraid that depreciation of the currency would stimulate inflationary pressure, which it had so much difficulty in resisting. It considered that devaluation would cause an unavoidable rise of import prices resulting in a new price wage spiral. It also considered probable that depreciation of the pound would cause a deterioration of Britain's terms of trade, as prices of essential imports mainly from the dollar area would increase by the full extent of the devaluation, while British export prices, in order to conquer foreign markets, would have to be maintained or increased to a much smaller extent. Such a possible development was considered to be dangerous, particularly as, compared to pre-war, Great Britain's terms of trade had already deteriorated and this deterioration was an important obstacle to a restoration of the equilibrium of foreign trade.

For all these reasons, the Chancellor of the Exchequer, Sir Stafford Cripps, several times solemnly declared that the parity of the pound would be maintained.

However the deterioration of the British monetary situation

408

continued, and very little to improve it was achieved, at an emergency conference of the sterling-area countries held at London in July 1949, even through drastic and painful measures—such as the curtailment by 25 percent of all dollar imports. During the third quarter of 1949, the dollar deficit amounted to $539 million, and total gold and dollar reserves declined, by $226 million, to the dangerously low sum of $1,425 million. In the first days of September, there was a tripartite conference between the finance ministers of the United States, United Kingdom, and Canada, held in Washington. Here any alternative solution to the problem of devaluating the pound, such as a new American loan, which Sir Stafford Cripps might have had in mind, proved to be impossible. He had to accept the inevitable. So, on September 18, 1949 the British government announced the devaluation of the pound by 30.5 percent, from $4.03 to $2.80. All other countries of the sterling area, with the one exception of Pakistan, devaluated their currencies in the same proportion.

The British devaluation had been made without any previous agreement, or even consultation, with the other Western European countries, Britain's partners in the OEEC. Such a devaluation had been widely expected, and even desired, in most of these countries. There it was believed that a devaluation of the pound to a more realistic level would offer the opportunity, and provide the basis, for a general readjustment of parities of European currencies, which would reestablish the monetary equilibrium of Western Europe and assist in restoring the equilibrium of the balance of payments.

The manner, however, in which the British devaluation was effected was most disappointing to other European countries. They had the right to resent the high-handed unilateral way of achieving it, which was most discouraging from the point of view of the ideal of European cooperation. They also protested against the rate of the currency depreciation, which had generally been considered, in other European countries, as much greater than the proportion warranted by the need for readjustment.

Instead of attempting an orderly readjustment, with the cooperation of all countries concerned, which would have reestablished balanced currency rates in the whole area of Western Europe, the British government adopted a currency rate affording to British exports an unfair competitive advantage on foreign markets. Thus, Britain had again made use of the method of competitive currency depreciation, which, during the 1930's, had been one of the main factors of monetary and economic disequilibrium, and which the establishment of the International Monetary Fund had intended to outlaw for the post-war period.

The extent of the British devaluation, and the drastic change in the competitive position of exports of British goods in relation to those of other OEEC countries, thus forced those countries to readjust, in a similar way, the parities of their respective currencies. The final effect of all these operations, therefore, was more or less similar to that which would have been achieved through an agreed action. However, owing to the very considerable extent of the depreciation of the pound, the percentage of depreciation of other currencies had to be greater than it would have been otherwise. For the same reason, devaluation had to be applied even by countries, like Belgium, whose monetary position had been sound, and where formerly currency depreciation had not been considered.

All OEEC countries, with the exception of Switzerland and Turkey, devaluated their currencies in varying degrees in a period of a few weeks after the devaluation of the pound (see table below).

Considerable progress toward achievement of monetary equilibrium in Western Europe was made as a consequence of this readjustment of parities. The result, in most cases, was to place the new rates on more realistic levels, generally near the former free or black-market rates. In France, the devaluation offered also the opportunity to abolish the multiple-exchange rate of the franc. The following table gives comparative statistics.

410

DEPRECIATION OF
WESTERN EUROPEAN CURRENCIES
(Other than £)

Currency	Old rate units per $	New rate units per $	Percentage of devaluation
Belgian franc	43.96	50.02	12.8
Danish krone	48.10	69.20	30.5
French franc	210	350	40
Deutschmarks (Western)	3.30	4.21	20.8
Greek drachma	10,000	15,000	33.33
Iceland krona	6.51	9.36	30.50
Italian lire	575	632	10
Luxembourg franc	43.96	50.02	12.8
Netherlands guilder	2.66	3.80	30.5
Norway krone	4.97	7.14	30.5
Portugal escudo	2.52	2.89	13.5
Swedish krona	3.60	5.17	30.5

As to Great Britain, the first effects of devaluation on British trade and balance of payments were favorable, owing to the fact that increase in inflationary pressure, and resulting price and wage increases had been, at the beginning, relatively limited. Thus, during the last quarter of 1949, the dollar deficit of the sterling area was reduced to $31 million, and reserves were increased by $263 million. During the first half of 1950, the improvement was even greater; thus, during the first quarter, there was a dollar surplus of $40 million, and dollar reserves increased, by $296 million, to $1,984 million; during the second quarter, the increase of resources of the sterling area amounted to $180 million.

During the latter part of 1950, the rise in prices and the increase in American demand for raw materials of the sterling area (such as, in particular, wool, rubber and tin) improved still more the position of sterling. On the other hand, it resulted in reviving again strong inflationary pressures in Great Britain and preventing maintenance of price and wage stability.

411

33 PRESENT STATE AND PROSPECTS
OF EUROPEAN RECOVERY

By THE END of the first two years of the Marshall Plan (that is, half of its originally specified four years) the results achieved were extremely impressive, especially with respect to its first objective: increase of production. American assistance of less than $4 billion, on the average, for the two years 1947-49, permitted an expansion of annual output by about $30 billion. The total output of goods and services increased, by 25 percent, from 1947 to 1949, and exceeded the pre-war level of 1938 by about 15 percent. During the same period, industrial production increased by 30 percent: coal, by 18 percent; electricity, by 16 percent; steel, by 56 percent; output of engineering industries, by 30 percent; chemicals, by 25 percent; and textiles, by 35 percent. Production of agriculture was restored to about 95-100 percent of pre-war, which was still insufficient, considering an increase, by about 10 percent, of the total population of the area. Recovery of production was much faster and smoother than after World War I, when pre-war level of production was not reached until seven years after the end of the war.

By the end of 1949, productivity of labor (excluding Germany), measured in output per man year, was 10 percent above pre-war. Owing to change from creditor to debtor position, however, and to a much higher percentage of investment expenditure required for modernization of production, consumption per head of popu-

412

lation was still slightly below pre-war, in particular in view of increase in population (see table below).

APPROXIMATE ESTIMATE OF TOTAL SUPPLIES OF GOODS AND SERVICES OF OEEC AREA
($ billion at 1948 prices *)

	1938	1947	1949
Output of goods and services	152	130	160
Import surplus paid by net income from overseas	3	...	...
Import surplus paid by grants, borrowing, or spending of reserves	...	8	4
Total	155	138	164
Investment, public and private	23	25	30
Government expenditure	18	20	21
Private consumption	114	93	113
	155	138	164

* *European Recovery Program, Second Report of the OEEC,* Paris, 1950.

Considerable progress was also achieved toward internal financial stability. By the end of 1949, in only 3 out of 15 countries prices were by 10 percent higher than in 1948, while in 4 countries they were lower. The budgetary position also was generally improved; however, inflationary pressures still persisted, and were even strengthened by the recent currency adjustments.

Improvement in foreign trade, too, was substantial. Trade between participating countries increased by 50 percent from 1947 to 1949. and reached again its pre-war level of about $9 billion. This progress was due to the assistance of temporary European payment schemes, financed by the conditional aid grants of the ERP, and was attributable also to some extent to a partial removal of quantitative restrictions on 50 percent of the trade of the

413

participating countries with one another on private account by December 15, 1949.

Progress of exports and of balance of payments of Western Europe with other areas was also decidedly marked. While exports to North America (which in 1947 covered only 14 percent of imports) increased to 22 percent in 1948 and 24 percent in 1949, exports to Latin America increased from 75 percent of pre-war in 1947 to 130 percent in 1949, and exports to non-participating sterling countries from 90 percent to 150 percent in 1949. The only area with which recovery of Western European trade was unsatisfactory was Eastern Europe; exports to that area reached only 40 percent of pre-war and imports 35 percent. The failure to obtain from Eastern Europe the food and raw materials which were received from there before the war, increased dependence of Western Europe on exports to the rest of the world.

On the other hand, between 1947 and 1949 there was a considerable development in the exports of dependent overseas territories of Western European countries. There, largely because of new investments made by the metropolitan powers, production of mainly primary materials and foodstuffs recovered to pre-war levels or exceeded them. In the case of some products, exports of overseas territories supplied an important part of the requirements of Western Europe, while, in the case of others, exports to North America were an important source of dollar exchange. The greatest increase in exports achieved in 1949 as compared to pre-war, occurred in bauxite from Guinea, sent mainly to North America, 550 percent; phosphate rock from North Africa, which covered most import requirements of Western Europe, 163 percent; rubber, mainly from Malaya, which provided the greatest dollar exports, as well as covered the area's own requirements, 152 percent; and copper from Africa which covered half of Western Europe's consumption, 115 percent.

As a result of improvement in exports of the Western European countries and dependent territories, progress was made toward

414

reduction of the dollar deficit, which decreased from over $8 billion in 1947 to $5.5 billion in 1948, and to less than $4 billion in 1949-50.

During the first half of the Marshall Plan program, the countries of Western Europe through their own efforts, and with the assistance of the ERP grants, thus achieved considerable progress toward attaining some of the main objectives of the Plan. But the remaining task is still most important and, if not in terms of material effort, at least psychologically and politically, more difficult to achieve, in so far as its success will depend mainly on the degree of economic integration and cooperation which will be accomplished.

On the contrary, results achieved during the first two years were mainly due to the individual action of the countries concerned; in the field of effective European cooperation, progress had been very limited. Thus, establishment of a common Western European master plan had not been implemented, and very little advance was made toward coordination of investment plans, and even less toward reduction of tariff barriers. Progress in economic cooperation and integration can be reached only through overcoming the resistance of powerful economic groups, whose interests might be hurt by increased competition and lower price and wage levels resulting if products or workers of other participating countries could enter freely, or at least with fewer restrictions than heretofore, into formerly protected domestic markets.

Such economic integration as will be achieved can be effected only with the loyal and willing cooperation of the principal economic groups concerned. That kind of cooperation, if it were controlled and directed by the governments of the participating countries, or, even better, by a central authority such as the OEEC, would prevent the monopolistic abuses of the former private cartels. At the same time, it would achieve the main positive results desired: (1) coordination of economic policy and investment, particularly through specialization of the future develop-

415

ment of the industries of the countries concerned, in order to avoid duplication and wasteful competition; and (2) compensation for—or at least reducing to a minimum—the effects of economic dislocation such as, especially, in unemployment in industries that would be unfavorably affected by such an integration.

In view of its object of achieving European economic integration, the insistence of the ECA on adoption by the participating countries of absolutely anticartel policies, which conform more to the theoretical American position, such as those expressed in the antitrust laws, than to actual United States practice, seems most unrealistic politically as well as economically. It is obvious that, particularly owing to lack of capital for investment in Europe, there exists an absolute necessity to make the most effective use of all available resources, which frequently can be obtained much better through coordination than through unrestricted competition.

The economic integration which it is planned to achieve during the period of 1950-52 is, however, extremely modest, as aside from continued efforts to coordinate investment plans, it consists mainly of liberalization of trade and establishment of a multilateral-payment scheme to achieve convertibility between currencies of participating countries. It was thus intended to establish a large area where trade could expand, the only limitation being low tariff barriers—that is, simply to restore the degree of relatively unhampered exchange of goods which had existed before creation, during the depression of the 1930's, of quantitative and exchange restrictions.

In liberalization of European trade, after having achieved, by December 15, 1949, removal of half of the existing quotas, the OEEC adopted on January 31, 1950, a resolution stating: (a) that, as soon as a satisfactory multilateral-payment scheme was established, participating countries would remove quantitative restrictions on 60 percent of imports on private account, in each main category of products; and (b) that as soon as possible after

June 30, 1950, removal of 75 percent of such quantitative restrictions would take place, and that quotas still existing after December 31, 1950, would have to be justified. In case an excessive import duty prevents removal of quotas from having a liberalizing effect on trade, such import duties will also have to be justified. Participating governments were also urged to attempt to harmonize their financial, economic, social, tariff, and investment policies.

So far, in the second-half period of the Marshall Plan, the establishment of a European Payment Union has been the main achievement. Such a payment union, based on the experience provided by operation, during the first two years, of temporary schemes financed through conditional grants, was intended to assist liberalization of trade, in order to facilitate transition to the post-ERP period. The Union had to be organized in such a way as to provide machinery of a permanent character for a trading area free from quotas and exchange restrictions. It is insuring complete transferability, among participating countries, of all Western European currencies earned on current account, and while providing reasonable temporary credits, discourages excessive deficits by requiring gold or dollar payments. Its facilities are not to be used to finance permanent structural deficits; the use of large resources in currency of a member country available to non-member countries could endanger the whole payment system. Existence of large sterling balances is thus one of the main difficulties which Great Britain had to face in its approach to this problem.

The functioning of the European Payment Union proceeded as follows: Each participating country had to open and to receive from the EPU a short and a medium line of credit, kept in a common unit; in addition to these resources in currencies of participating countries, the EPU started its activity with a dollar fund, in order to be able to cover temporary dollar payments to creditor countries. The ECA devoted for this purpose $600 million out of the 1950-51 ERP appropriation. Net debts on short-

417

term lines will be carried on as medium-term credits of the EPU, while net credits will be considered as credits granted to the EPU. However, as the amount of the net debt increases, the debtor will have to cover an increasing part of it with dollar payments, while similar dollar payments will have to be made to net creditor countries. In case of a permanent deficit, the net debtor country might be authorized to apply temporary trade restrictions, or to readjust the parity of its currency.

The greatest obstacle to the implementation of the EPU, the principle of which was accepted at once by the ECA as well as by all continental participating countries, was the attitude of Great Britain. She made the objection that a full participation in this system would destroy the present payment system of the sterling area, where transferability on current account already exists, as well as hamper Great Britain's bilateral agreements and create new difficulties due to the sterling balances of non-participating countries. Great Britain, therefore, wanted to join the EPU only as a sort of associate member, maintaining her bilateral agreements, and she refused the chance of gaining as well as losing dollars from her net creditor or debtor position. She would agree to settle through EPU only the sterling deficits and surpluses of different participating countries which would be compensated one against another.

In view of the importance of Great Britain's participation in the scheme, and of the fact that the objections which the British have raised were to a great extent justified, such a compromise formula had been adopted by the end of May 1950 and the European Payment Union was put into operation in July of that year.

The general implementation of the program of the OEEC for the second two-year period of the Marshall Plan was based to a great extent on assumptions regarding the future course of American policy.

The first assumption was that the United States would continue her assistance, though on a gradually decreasing scale, and

418

that this assistance would be about $3 billion for 1950-51, and about $2 billion for 1951-52. The amount authorized by Congress for the first of these two years was more or less equivalent to this assumption.

The second assumption was that business activity in the United States would remain at its present level or thereabouts, as even a small fluctuation of American economic activity could have a considerable influence on American demand for products of participating countries and for raw materials of their overseas territories, and thus reduce, in a substantial degree, total dollar earnings. Thus, between the 4th quarter of 1948 and the 3rd quarter of 1949, a decline of only 5 percent in the gross national product and of 10 percent in the index of industrial production caused a fall of 30 percent in the value of imports from the participating countries, their dependent territories, and the nonparticipating sterling area to the United States.

Realization of the dollar-equilibrium objective of the Marshall Plan also implies a more favorable attitude of the United States authorities toward imports from Western Europe, which obviously must be mainly in manufactured goods. Such change in attitude should be expressed in further reduction of tariff duties, which, though considerably reduced as compared to the completely prohibitive Hawley-Smoot tariff, are still rather high on many important items, simplification of customs formalities, etc.

The dislocation which a substantial increase in such imports could cause to competing American industries, and its impact on the American economy as a whole, should not be exaggerated. This can be the better realized in the light of the past that total imports from Western Europe, which before World War I had been equivalent to 2 percent of the gross national product of the United States, declined after World War II to only 1/3 of 1 percent of the gross national product. Thus, even if the amount of such imports were doubled, which would increase Western Europe's dollar receipts by about $1 billion, their damaging effect on the American production, if any, would be completely

419

negligible. But even small quantities of imports could have considerable importance in endangering monopolistic price levels which exist in some sectors of the American economy; for example, imports of steel products from Belgium and other countries of Western Europe could endanger the price structure of steel. Such a result, however, could certainly not be considered as unfavorable from the point of view of the United States economy as a whole, and even less from the extremely anticartel point of view of American economic policy as applied by the ECA in Europe.

Not only the United States government, but also general public opinion, and even Congress, is gradually recognizing the necessity for the United States to do her share toward increasing imports from Western Europe, in order to be able to curtail and later to terminate aid grants to this area. This attitude was best expressed by Secretary of State Acheson, in November 1949, when he said that the apparently favorable trade balance of the United States was in fact unfavorable to her consumers and taxpayers. The joint communiqué issued by the United States, the United Kingdom, and Canadian governments, after the monetary negotiations of September 1949, proclaimed that the United States and Canada should reduce obstacles to the entry of goods and services from debtor countries, in order to provide the latter with the opportunity to earn a maximum amount of dollars.

The main features of the OEEC plans for 1950-52 was continued increase of production, even though the rate of progress was not expected to be quite as high as during the preceding period; increased production was due to provide goods necessary to replace dollar imports, and to expand exports and levels of consumption. Dollar savings, particularly, were expected from development of production and imports from overseas territories, especially, of course grains, oilcakes and seeds, sugar, coffee, cotton, nonferrous metals, paper pulp, and tropical timber. As to production in Western Europe itself, the greatest dollar savings were expected from expansion of agricultural production, which

420

was due to increase from an approximate level of $19 billion, at 1948-49 United States prices, to $21 billion in 1952-53, as compared to $19 billion before the war.

It was expected that such an increase, as well as an even greater expansion over a longer period, could be achieved without increase in cost and consequent need of protection, partly through land reclamation, but mainly through: improved methods (use of such seeds as hybrid maize); increase in the use of fertilizer to 180 percent of pre-war level, as compared to 150 percent in 1949; increased modernization; improvement in the size of farms, etc. The practice of using marketing agreements between exporting and importing countries to insure stable and reasonably remunerative prices to farmers, incentives, thus, for increased production should also be generalized.

Total industrial production was expected to increase by 5-6 percent. Major developments that will be expected are: return to a net export position in coal; considerable increase in electric power; national programs supplemented by several inter-European projects and the development of a general grid to facilitate exchange of temporary surpluses of hydroelectric or thermic power; as well as an especially great expansion of the equipment industry, mainly mechanical and electrical engineering, wherefrom major increase in exports is expected, while domestic consumption will also increase to cover requirements for modernization of production.

Considerable efforts will be made to match the increase in production with an even greater expansion of exports, particularly to the dollar area. It was expected that total exports of participating countries to the rest of the world would increase from $14,279 million (in 1949-50) to $15,934 million in 1951-52, while imports would decrease from $18,722 million to $18,300 million. Exports to North America were expected to increase from $1,016 million (in 1949-50) to $1,262 million in 1950-51. The main increase was anticipated not from the former main export specialities—whisky for Great Britain, watches for Switzer-

421

land, etc.—but from a great variety of specialized industrial items, a large number of which are to be introduced for the first time in the American market. Moreover, great efforts will be made to adapt export goods to requirements of the American market.

Invisible dollar earnings were also expected to increase, net shipping receipts by $33 million; tourist receipts, from $87 million (in 1949) to $275 million in 1952.

Thus, the expectation was that in 1951-52 the dollar deficit of the balance of trade of participating countries would be reduced to $2,366 million, which, with the surplus, on invisible items, of $926 million would leave a net deficit of the balance of payments of $1,440 million. It was believed that a residue of such dimensions would be relatively easy to finance without requiring public action on a scale similar to that of the Marshall Plan.

It could probably be compensated to a large extent, or even completely, by a development of American capital investments, in some degree in the participating countries themselves, but especially in their overseas territories. As a matter of fact, in most of these territories, there are great possibilities for the development of agriculture and mining, which could open to Western Europe important sources of supply and also offer an important market for its manufactured products. However, a major difficulty in the development of these natural resources of dependent territories is the shortage of capital in the metropolitan Western European countries, while considerable capital is required for investment to be made for this purpose. Capital to supplement European resources could be provided by the United States under the Point Four program for the development of underdeveloped areas.

Such assistance, which could be most easily provided by private capital, would not have to be guided by reasons of public interest, as development of these natural resources would provide the means of making investments of this kind quite profitable. As to the natural products resulting from such ventures, they could be shared between the United States and Western Europe

422

and thus open, for the American economy a possibly considerable source of supply of vital raw materials in short supply, such as manganese, radium, uranium, copper, etc. In this way, these investments could even be of direct usefulness to the United States economy, without even taking into account their favorable effect on economy of Western Europe.

A first example of such investments is provided by the concessions recently granted to American oil companies in French North Africa, where previously, owing to the shortage of dollars required for the purchase of American-built drilling equipment, little boring could have been made as yet, while intensive exploitation of probably existing resources might provide an important contribution to oil consumption of North Africa, France, or even the whole of Western Europe and thus might effect a considerable saving of dollar imports.

Developments up to mid-1950—that is about nine months after the forecasts for the second part of the ERP period, quoted above, had been drawn up—appeared to confirm the optimism of those forecasts.

Intra-European trade continued to increase, stimulated by the establishment of the European Payments Union, the first results of which had been extremely satisfactory. In particular, the Union was able to overcome, without outside assistance, temporary difficulties due to a too-rapid expansion of trade, such as of imports of Western Germany. The balance of payment of most countries of the area, in relation to the dollar area, also showed further improvement.

The war in Korea, however, suddenly changed completely this favorable outlook and shattered the apparently heretofore well-justified hope that Western Europe by 1952 would become self-supporting, and independent of American assistance.*

* The success of the Marshall Plan had been convincingly demonstrated by the fact that in December 1950 the ECA was able to declare that Great Britain, the country where development of production had been particularly great, did not require any more ERP aid and would cease

The cognizance, as a result of this first aggression, of an acute military danger to the Western world, established massive rearmament as the first and foremost "must" objective, to be achieved at any cost. It also aroused, in the majority of public opinion in the United States, a far greater sense of imperativeness and urgency for this military preparedness than for continuation of aid for economic recovery and development in Europe or in other continents.

The results of rearmament, of which Western Europe will have to bear a major share, in order to prevent the danger of invasion, will be most detrimental to continuation of efforts toward recovery and self-support. Thus, already, the considerable rise in the prices of all raw materials which Europe has to import has caused a new deterioration of its terms of trade. As European defense production is stepped up, it will require more such raw materials, while a smaller part of its industrial products will remain available either for exports or for domestic consumption. This situation will aggravate its balance-of-payments situation, and will also cause a set-back to its standards of living, which are still as a general rule below pre-war. Consequently, its social stability will be menaced.

The rise in imported raw materials has already endangered the continuation of progress in liberalization of intra-European trade. All countries of the Continent, and particularly France, can only suffer from this rise, and not benefit at all, while Great Britain, on the contrary, benefits to some extent from the improvement in the position of the raw-materials exporting countries of the sterling area. Therefore France declared that she will be able to abide by the OEEC regulations concerning abolition

to be eligible for such aid for 1951, that is more than a year before the end of the plan. The improvement of the position of sterling, which enabled Great Britain to forego further dollar aid, was however to a great extent the result of the rise in prices and volume of raw material exports of the sterling area to the United States due to the rearmament boom.

of quantitative restrictions only if an international agreement is reached on stabilization of prices and equitable distribution of raw materials.

In the report to the President on foreign economic policies Gordon Gray, in the so-called Gray Report, has analyzed and stated with admirable clarity and logic the impact of rearmament on the recovery of Western Europe. He also points out the implications which will result from it for the United States policy, if that country is to achieve the aims of world peace, progress and stability which have been its major objectives since the end of World War II.

The Gray Report stresses, among other things, two important facts: (1) By mid-1950, it appeared that the productive ability of most Western European countries was either already sufficient, or would soon become sufficient, to make unnecessary a net addition to their own productive resources from outside aid, and that further grants from the United States would probably become unnecessary by 1952 or even earlier; and (2) the urgent need for rapidly creating defensive strength in Western Europe, as part of a joint effort to provide mutual security, forces a postponement of the time when the United States, consistent with its own interests, can end economic assistance. Adequate rearmament within the time required by the current situation, will require not only supplies of military equipment from the United States, but also a substantial diversion of Western European output from other uses and some increase in imports.

It seems clear that a sufficiently large and rapid development of military strength is beyond the capacity of Western European countries through their own efforts, or with aid only in the form of military equipment. In view of the fact that, as the Report stresses, Western Europe is the most critical area from the standpoint of American security and the security of all the rest of the free world, the United States should be prepared to extend dollar aid to meet the short-run burden of the military production

425

of those countries, in so far as it exceeds the sacrifices which it is within their ability to make.

The Gray Report therefore recommends, in particular, that: (a) to facilitate the required expansion of Western European defenses, the United States should be prepared to continue supplying aid, apart from military equipment, for another three or four years beyond the present time; (b) such aid should be planned on the basis of an overall assessment of requirements, and should be administered on a basis that will contribute to the fullest possible use of European resources, encourage intra-European trade, and help to integrate the European economic effort. Development of an effective intra-European payment mechanism, and allotting, for the time being, to the European Payments Union of a portion of the dollar aid, are also recommended. According to the Report, adequate consideration should also be given to the importance of a high volume of European exports, which are the only means whereby the countries concerned can achieve self-support.

It is as yet impossible to foresee to what extent the recommendations of the Gray Report will become directives of future American policy. However, it is to be hoped that this lucid analysis of the problem of American foreign economic policy will not be altogether ignored.

In addition, it is to be hoped that excessive stress will not be placed upon objectives of a military character, which, in spite of their spectacularly urgent nature, could only achieve security temporarily, and at the expense of objectives of economic and social recovery and progress. Only success in these latter fields can improve not only material conditions, but also, as stressed in the Gray Report, what may be even more important, the morale and the outlook of the peoples of Western Europe and of other parts of the world, thus making possible a consolidation of their solidarity inside the community of the free nations.

426

34 PROSPECTS FOR A UNION OF WESTERN EUROPE: THE SCHUMAN PLAN

CAN IT BE EXPECTED THAT, in spite of its present plight and its economic and political difficulties, Western Europe will become a healthy and self-supporting economic organism as a result of self-help, economic cooperation, and American assistance under the Marshall Plan?

Western Europe, understood in the meaning of the Marshall Plan, that is, including the sixteen participating countries and Western Germany, has considerable elements of strength. It is an area of economic power, comparable in the whole world only to the North American Continent. Its population is even considerably larger, some 270 million; its coal production amounted in 1938 to about 550 million tons—more than the production of the United States during the same year; and production of steel in 1938 was 45.5 million tons, that is, about equal to American production at that time.* Western Europe's pre-war production considerably exceeded the output of the United States in many important industries, such as shipbuilding, chemicals, textiles, etc.; and its agricultural production in most products was greater

* Compared to the Soviet Union, including even the whole of the Soviet-controlled Eastern Europe, Western Europe has about the same total population, but a considerably greater industrial production; thus, production of coal in the whole Soviet area in 1950 was somewhat less than 350 million tons and production of steel only slightly above 30 million tons.

427

than that of North America, and generally much more intensive than in the latter area. However, owing to a much larger population, production was still insufficient to cover consumption requirements.

But the maintenance of Western Europe's standard of life, second only to that of North America and of some rich and sparsely populated countries, such as New Zealand, was effected not only by the direct proceeds of its agricultural and industrial production, but by their exchange with other areas. Thus the share of Western Europe amounted to 40 percent in world exports, and 50 percent in world imports, while the share in world trade of the United States was only 13 percent. Western Europe also had under its flags the greatest part of the world's shipping, 65 percent as against 14 percent for the United States. The proceeds from shipping and other services—such as tourist trade, insurance and banking commissions, etc.—as well as income from foreign investments which, alone, paid for 25 percent of the total imports of the area, compensated the deficit in its visible trade.

To the Western European economic sphere belong also, as markets for her industrial products, and sources of supply for food and raw materials, the colonial empires of some of the countries of the area which, without counting the British dominions, and discounting possible losses in the Far East, comprise still practically the whole of Africa. The Middle East is also part of the Western European economic sphere.

If the objectives of the OEEC are reached, Western Europe, which already has more than recovered its pre-war level of production, will have undergone an expansion similar to that achieved during World War II in the United States. It will also have wiped out the shortages of key products, which, during the first years after the end of the war, impeded industrial recovery. If plans work out, this area will again become a net exporter of steel on a large scale, and will be independent of overseas supplies of coal, the only imports from outside the area being from Poland, where coal can be paid for by industrial exports. Ex-

428

pansion of industrial production is expected to result in a substantial development of exports of all kinds of manufactured goods, capital equipment, as well as consumer goods.

New sources of supply are to be developed for vital imports in areas wherefrom imports can be paid for by exports, thus reducing dollar requirements for payment of imports. Hence, oil is to be provided by the Middle East; cotton, in increasing quantities, from British and French Africa; fats from Africa (important ground-nuts schemes are being undertaken for this purpose, in particular in British East Africa and French West Africa); lumber from the forests of Central Africa; and nonferrous metals from different parts of Africa and other overseas territories.

The main difficulty in the way of the recovery by Western Europe of its economic independence will be the continued necessity of substantial imports of foodstuffs from outside the area or its overseas dependencies. A considerable increase in food production, as compared to pre-war, will be a long-term proposition. Population of the area is expected to be by 1951 about 10 percent above that of 1938. Also, owing to the policy of full employment, to which all the countries of the area are committed, the import requirements of industrial raw materials will be generally above pre-war. Most of the food imports, as well as a substantial part of imports of raw materials (such as cotton and lumber, and also some specialized equipment) will have to be purchased in North America, thus creating considerable dollar requirements.

The experience of the last two years, and the very considerable expansion of trade between Western Europe and other areas, seem to give reasonable assurance that Western Europe will be able to earn foreign exchange sufficient to pay for most, if not all, of her imports, provided world conditions do not deteriorate materially.

Development of trade with Eastern Europe may not prove to be as great as initially expected, in spite of the mutually complementary nature of the two economies of Western and Eastern Europe. These conditions have not yet been substantially modi-

429

fied by the industrialization effort and Eastern Europe, even including the Soviet Union, Czechoslovakia and Eastern Germany, remains unable to satisfy the requirements of capital goods for this industrialization. Political motives and motives of economic interest at present point in opposite directions; and foreign trade between the two areas will probably remain limited to exchange of some surplus primary products, such as lumber, coarse grain, and Polish coal from the East, in return for equipment considered of no strategic value from the West. The contribution of this trade to Western Europe's economic equilibrium will therefore probably remain relatively limited.

The main market in which all Western European countries plan to expand their exports is the American market, which, having the greatest global purchasing power, as well as the highest level of individual consumption, is able to absorb most easily the high-quality, high-price specialties of all kinds. These already, at present, represent the bulk of European exports to the United States, especially in value. Exports of such articles, which are generally not in direct competition with the main American industries, could be easily increased.

Even greater, in the long run, seem the prospects of European equipment industries to conquer important markets, by participation in development and industrialization of important overseas areas, such as Latin America, India, the Near East, etc. These areas pay for their imports of equipment with exports of raw materials (like oil, copper, cotton, etc.), as well as of foodstuffs, which Western Europe willingly absorbs. On the other hand, with a few exceptions, such as coffee, tropical fruit and jute, the markets of these products in the United States are much more limited. This characteristic of the economy of Western Europe, which is more complementary than the economy of the United States to that of most underdeveloped areas, has been the main reason for the tremendous expansion of European equipment exports to these areas, which has already been achieved, and which gives hope of further improvement.

But the success of the effort toward the economic recovery of Western Europe implies not only development of production and foreign trade, but also the fullest possible degree of economic cooperation between all the countries of the area. This includes in particular, as far as possible, economic union, which alone could insure full utilization, through intra-European trade, of all available resources, as well as the establishment of a domestic market of sufficient size to make large-scale production possible and profitable, and thus reduce costs and improve export possibilities.

Such economic union obviously is very difficult to achieve, even if only economic factors are considered. The difficulties are due to the fact that many obstacles have to be overcome, especially the stubborn resistance of all private or group interests, which fear that they would suffer from the opening of their domestic market to competition from other countries of the area. Even aside from such resistance, the technical problem in itself is difficult to solve, as customs union which was the nineteenth century technique, is today not sufficient. This is because the main obstacles to the expansion of foreign trade are no longer tariffs, but either quantitative restrictions, such as quotas or, even more frequently, monetary restrictions resulting from the shortage of foreign exchange. Thus, economic union implies a complete free trade, that is, movement of goods, capital and persons inside the area, which requires the establishment of roughly similar levels of prices, wages, indirect taxation, etc., in order to avoid excessive disequilibrium and hardships.

These difficulties provide, to some extent, the explanation why, in spite of the nearly universal acceptance, in principle, of the desirability of establishing one large economic area, progress in this field has been rather slow. Even though the idea of a general Western European economic union has been studied by a special subcommittee of the CEEC, no practical steps have as yet been taken to achieve it. Considerable progress, however, has been

431

achieved with respect to the establishment of smaller regional unions.

The oldest of such regional unions, the Benelux, had already been started in 1944, before the liberation of the territories of Belgium, the Netherlands and Luxembourg, and when their governments in exile accepted in principle their economic union. The establishment of Benelux is being achieved step by step, and is planned to be completed by the end of 1950.

Another economic union is in progress of being established between France and Italy (Francital), but its progress is even slower than that of Benelux. The first agreement was concluded in March 1948, and the economic union of both countries is expected to be completed by 1955. As a result of Franco-Italian preliminary agreements, trade between the two countries has considerably expanded. Other regional economic unions are being planned between the Scandinavian countries, between Greece and Turkey, etc.

Owing to the sizeable difficulties which confront the establishment of economic unions, and which are no less for small-scale unions such as Benelux (the benefits of which would be relatively limited) than for more general unions, the Benelux countries have manifested the desire to enter into a much greater economic group, in which they would like to include at least France and Western Germany.

However, the establishment of such a union, including the greatest part of the continental Marshall Plan area, does imply considerable political as well as economic difficulties, and both kinds are still far from being solved.

The main trouble is the attitude of Great Britain. She is still reluctant to consider herself a part of Europe, and remains faithful to her traditional policy of opposing any union of which she herself would not be a member, even though refusing to join it.

This attitude of Great Britain is due, to a great extent, to economic reasons: (a) the fear of weakening her ties with the Commonwealth, a fear particularly strong since the establishment of the sterling area; and (b) the fear of endangering maintenance of full employment and the British standards of living, by too close a cooperation with countries which pursue different lines of policy, and which have competing industries and lower standards. As important, however, if not more important, are political and psychological factors. There is, for example, the instinctive feeling of the British that, in case of emergency, they will always better manage to overcome the crisis by themselves. This traditional feeling was strengthened by the painful memories of the events of 1940, which had increased still more the average Britisher's lack of confidence in the nations of the Continent. Another traditional characteristic, and for a long time one of the basic explanations of British greatness, is their indomitable and most exasperating superiority complex.

All this, however, does not imply that the movement toward European unification did not make great headway in Great Britain. On the contrary, it found there its greatest leader and mouthpiece: Winston Churchill. Although, like any other loyal Englishman, he was 100 percent British, he still had enough vision and historical perspective to recognize that union of the free countries of Europe was necessary for their survival. His crusade for this idea in Great Britain, however, is an uphill fight.

There has been a considerable and steadily increasing influence by the ideal of European unity, which was proclaimed by the different movements, especially the Movement for United Europe, as an essentially positive one, and which stresses the common heritage of European traditions, civilization and way of life. Nevertheless, the trend toward Western European union, which even Great Britain had to follow, received impetus from United States assistance, since European cooperation was one of the major aims of the Marshall Plan. Even greater impetus, however, resulted from the fear of Soviet Russia—a fear felt by the different countries of Western Europe, isolated and helpless in relation to the Russian giant, already dominating the eastern part of the Continent, which had been united under his control. Union

433

(pooling of economic, political and military strength) was the natural, the only, way for the countries of this area to insure their security; and, as long as their own strength was not yet completely restored, the guarantee of the United States provided them with security against aggression. In contrast, their previous state of complete weakness had been a temptation for, and encouragement of, aggression.

Thus, establishment of the Bruxelles Western Union, between Great Britain, France and the Benelux countries, had been stimulated by the events of February 1948 in Czechoslovakia. It also provided the motive for President Truman's speech to Congress, which became the starting point for the North Atlantic Pact. Hence, fear of, and opposition to, Soviet Russia became an important motive and stimulant for Western European unity. It is typical of human nature to unite more readily *against,* than *in favor of,* something or somebody. While this factor creates the opposition of all exterior or interior forces under Soviet or Communist influence, by means of strikes, manifestations, etc., it is also mainly responsible for the support which the United States policy provides for the trend toward unity of the area, a most potent influence toward the achievement of such unity in one form or another.

Great Britain followed this trend in the political, economic and military fields; in fact she even sometimes took the initiative, as, for example, in the Bruxelles pact. This was true, however, only as long as there was no question of surrendering part of her national sovereignty.

The establishment of the European Council in Strasbourg was agreed to by Great Britain with considerable reluctance, and only under strong French pressure. Britain accepted the Council only because it was to be purely consultative, without any real power whatsoever.

During 1950, Great Britain succeeded in blocking the proposed extension of the powers of the Council, and violently opposed efforts exerted in the Council toward making it a nucleus of a

434

European federation. As a result of the stubborn resistance of the Labor representatives, the federalist group was confronted with the danger of seeing Great Britain withdraw from the Council. It therefore had to abandon its moves toward direct unification and seek other methods, such as functional unification. British opposition to such a method was less vehement and, while spokesmen of the Labor government appeared generally reluctant to join, themselves, such a functional group, still they did not try to obstruct its establishment by other countries of the area.

Thus, Great Britain has relinquished leadership in the efforts toward the unification of Western Europe, a leadership for which she was best qualified, since after the end of the war, she remained the only country in Western Europe with a significant military power, as well as the most productive economy, a stable financial and political structure, and a high prestige, which had been still further strengthened by the result of the war.

The initiative in this field of unification was therefore taken by France, a country whose approach to the problem was entirely different. On the one hand, to all practical purposes, France, unlike Great Britain, is purely a European power, not a world power, in spite of the importance of her overseas territories. Even at the summit of her power, during the period of Louis XIV and Napoleon, when France tried to dominate Europe, and for a short time succeeded, she always considered herself as part of Europe. Indeed, French civilization can perhaps be considered as the most purely European of all the countries of Europe. Even French imperialism was, and still is, in so far as it persists, an imperialism of culture, much more than of a specific nation or (even less) a particular race. Even though French nationalism is still a strong tradition, French culture as such is much more universalist than nationalist in its outlook.

Then, too, the idea of European unity based on a common tradition of civilization, as well as on a common interest of maintaining peace and balance of power always had a great appeal in France, not only for the philosophers and poets, such as Bernardin de St. Pierre and Victor Hugo, but also for statesmen, from Sully, in the beginning of the seventeenth century to Briand in the 1920's.

Besides, French nationalism, like the national feeling of most continental countries, including Germany, suffered from World War II a terrible blow from which it did not recover. This is understandable, since France was overrun and occupied, during the war, by a victorious enemy, with the whole traditional structure of the state, representing the nation, completely shattered. All this does not mean, however, a decline in attachment of the French to their country or to their countrymen. It merely means that traditional nationalist feeling alone no longer provides, for the great mass of the people, especially the youth, a sufficiently strong moral basis for a concept of life (called, in German, *Weltanschauung*) capable of opposing the rival appeals of different creeds, such as Communism.

A new and broader basis for nationalist feeling was necessary to revive its appeal. Thus the ideal of European union became, for a great part of the youth in many countries of Western Europe, but particularly in France, an objective which stimulated their enthusiasm and appealed to their sense of a common destiny of all the nations of the area.

Aside from these most important factors of ideology and national psychology, in most continental Western European countries, as a result of the war, the conviction became generalized that, if they remained separate they would be completely helpless in case of a new world crisis; and that, moreover, in a world dominated by giant superstates extending to whole continents (such as the United States and the Soviet Union), they would be unable to survive, in the long run, as independent states, preserving their own way of life and pattern of civilization. At best, they would be only pawns of the giant world powers in the game of world politics, instead of, as formerly, equal participants. This conviction was extremely painful for all those who in Western

Europe were still proud of the importance of the contribution made by their particular countries, and by Europe as a whole, to the achievements of the last century, when Europe not only had been supreme in political power, but also had given her civilization to the rest of the world.

The only solution capable of insuring survival of these countries of Western Europe, and of allowing them to maintain the essential part of their heritage, was obviously their union. While the differences between their respective cultures remained real, they faded into insignificance compared to the considerably greater contrast between their combined cultures and those of their successors in power. Even though the civilization of the New World had the same moral basis as the culture of Europe, of which it was an offspring, it had developed—because of different environment and trend of events—a very different pattern. And there was more than a difference—there was a moral abyss—between the culture of Europe and the totalitarian civilization of Eurasia, that is, the Soviet Union, which was radically opposed to the most basic element of European tradition: the belief in the value and freedom of the individual, and which became a mortal danger to the survival of European civilization.

Owing to all these reasons, public opinion in continental Western Europe, particularly in France, was much more interested in, and attracted by, European unification than was the case in Great Britain. Support of a definite policy for achieving this objective extended to all shades of public opinion, with the exception, of course, of the Communists. Thus, the two most active pioneers of this policy in France were a Socialist, André Philippe, and the conservative elder statesman, Paul Reynaud, while on the whole, the party which gave the most steadfast support to the European idea was the M.R.P. of Georges Bidault, which reflected their Catholic ideal of universalism.

To the M.R.P. belongs also Robert Schuman, who, with bold initiative, had taken the most practical and concrete step undertaken as yet towards achieving European unity. At the same time,

437

he tried to overcome the greatest obstacle to European unity—the problem of Franco-German relations.

The distrust of France toward Germany, which was largely born of three aggressions in a period of seventy years, each more brutal and callous than the one preceding, and which was strengthened by deep memories of personal sufferings and hardships of a great part, if not the majority, of the population, was also due to a feeling of insecurity resulting from the realization of the greater strength of Germany and of the fact that the disequilibrium between the two nations was steadily increasing. As a matter of fact, the growth of population, as well as of the economic and the military potential, was much greater in the Reich than in France. Out of this feeling of insecurity arose (1) the desire (which had such a fatal influence on French policy during most of the inter-war period) to prevent Germany by all means from achieving a status of equality, especially in armaments, but also in other fields; and (2) the refusal to make any agreement with Germany alone. The main successful attempt at Franco-German reconciliation and co-operation, the Locarno Treaty of 1925, had been made possible by the participation of Great Britain as a witness and third partner. When, a few years later, Great Britain rejected Briand's plan for a European customs federation, there was not even any attempt to build a purely continental customs federation, as France was most reluctant to stay practically alone, facing a much more powerful Germany.

After the end of World War II, while hatred and resentment in France against Germany were obviously greater than ever, and for very good reasons, the fear of Germany seemed to lose its justification. This time, Germany was not only conquered and devastated, but completely crushed and prostrated. The structure of her state was destroyed, and, above all, she was divided into separate occupation zones. Moreover, the difference between the social, economic and political conditions in Western Germany and the Soviet Zone, respectively, was so great as to make this split appear very real and, if not permanent, at least of a durable character.

438

Even more important appears the change in the psychological attitude of the mass of the people of Western Germany. Having, for once, been one of the worst-hit victims of their own aggression, they appear to have lost to a great extent, at least temporarily, their aggressive nationalist spirit. To them, also, the danger of Soviet domination, which had already engulfed a great part of their country, appeared most frightening of all. Fear thus stimulated their willingness to combine their forces with those of their Western neighbors for defense of what had been the common heritage of Europe, to which the contribution of pre-Hitler Germany had been very considerable indeed.

The French statesmen very soon realized that, as Allied determination to hold Western Germany down weakened, and finally disappeared, because of the growing tension between East and West, the favorable opportunity for France to reach a complete agreement and alliance with a Western Germany militarily helpless, politically weakened, and only slightly more populated than France herself, would not last. As time went on, they knew, the Germans would recover strength and self-assurance, and might be no longer contented with mere equality, which, for the moment, they were glad and grateful to accept as a present.

They understood, especially, that unilateral Allied control over the Ruhr would not be maintained for any considerable period. The French, after great and protracted efforts, had succeeded in establishing that control, through the International Control Authority for the Ruhr, which enabled France to reach the two essential objectives, (a) control of German steel production, and (b) a guarantee of an adequate supply of coke for French steel production. These two objectives could not be preserved permanently as a result of a treaty imposed on Germany —as the history of the aftermath of World War I had proved again and again. The only change to preserve them was through an agreement with Germany.

Thus, the idea of a pool of German and French resources of

coal and steel production was born. The plan was conceived and developed by Robert Schuman (the French statesman who best knew and understood the Germans and their psychology) and Jean Monnet, the author and directing mind of the modernization plan for the French economy.

This plan offered the Germans equality, which meant abandonment of all still existing restrictions on production of steel and steel products. At the same time, it provided for France the guarantee of adequate coal supply for her steel industry and thus insured its normal development. Further, it rendered groundless all fears concerning the possible utilization of German steel resources which would be controlled by a common authority.

On the other hand, the willingness of France to abandon, under the same conditions as Germany, part of her sovereignty in a most vital economic matter, and to transfer it to a common authority, was a most significant decision. The resulting impression on the public opinion of France, Germany and other European countries was most stimulating.

It was on May 9, 1950 that Mr. Schuman announced, in a press conference, the proposal to coordinate, under a single authority, the coal and steel production of France, Germany and all other European countries that would agree to join the scheme. The main provision of this proposal was the establishment of a High Authority, which would be entrusted with insuring, during the shortest possible time, the following: modernization of production and improvement of its quality; supplying of coal and steel, on the same terms, to the markets of all member countries; increase in joint exports; and improvement and equalization of living conditions of industrial workers in participating countries.

The basic aim of the plan was to create, for the commodities concerned (coal, coke, iron ore, pig iron and raw steel), a single market, including all the participating countries. This program implied (a) abandonment of tariff barriers for these products between the different member countries, as well as of all discrimina-

440

tory practices, such as differences in prices or freight rates for export, import or domestic consumption; and (b) establishment of a common price level, subject only to legitimate differences due to cost of transportation from the centers of production.

This aim, however, could be reached only gradually; the period of transition was supposed to be five years. In order to enable the industries to overcome difficulties arising from such change in conditions due to involve reduction in prices, an equalization fund was to be established. Its purpose was to grant temporary assistance, on a decreasing scale, to concerns whose production would have to be either modernized or reduced and, in the latter case, to facilitate use of their resources for other more economic activities. Such assistance was also to be granted to the labor of such industries, to facilitate its reorientation.

As soon as the main principle of the Schuman Plan, the establishment of a super-national authority, had been published, the Plan was at once accepted by the government of Western Germany. Chancellor Adenauer, like Mr. Schuman, stressed not only its economic importance, but also, and above all, the deep political significance of close Franco-German cooperation in such a vital economic field. The Schuman Plan had also the merit of providing a practical solution of the Saar problem, which had caused great tension between France and Germany. As the coal and steel resources of the Saar were to be included in a common pool, the question of whether the territory was part of the French or of the German economy lost a large part of its importance.

The acceptance of this Plan by Germany had, as a necessary consequence, its acceptance by the Benelux countries, whose industries are closely connected with those of France and Germany, and whose harbors are the outlet of the Ruhr, for exports as well as for imports. Italy, being mainly, if not entirely, an importing country for the coal and pig-iron required for her finished steel production, could only benefit by joining in the Plan.

The only question was the attitude of Great Britain. She could not but approve the political aim of the pool, especially in so far

441

as it resulted in cooperation between France and Germany. However, the problem of Great Britain's participation in the coal and steel pool involved a delicate decision. The Labor government was extremely reluctant to abandon to the Authority a portion of British sovereignty, especially since its decisions might interfere with British economic planning and endanger maintenance of full employment, as the establishment of a common market might make uneconomic a certain part of British coal and steel production. Great Britain considered the provisions concerning the equalization fund as an insufficient safeguard, and therefore finally refused to accept the principle of international authority, which the French had established as a preliminary condition essential to the negotiations for the practical implementation of the Plan. The British, instead, proposed to negotiate about cooperation in the field of coal and steel, for the establishment of an intergovernmental organization whose decisions would be only recommendations, and thus not binding for the governments of the countries concerned.

The French government, however, refused to accept such a basic modification of the Schuman Plan and stated that an intergovernmental organization without any transfer of sovereignty would, as experience of several such organizations had proved, be unable to achieve the aim proposed. After some hesitation, the Paris cabinet decided to start negotiations on the basis of its proposals, without Great Britain, believing that, if the Plan were finally implemented, Great Britain would be realist enough, at least to find a way to cooperate with the countries of the Pool, if not to become a full-fledged member. Otherwise nothing whatsoever could be accomplished.

On June 24, 1950, negotiations started in Paris between the six countries (France, Western Germany, Belgium, Netherlands, Luxembourg and Italy) that had agreed on the basic principle of the Schuman Plan. After several months of negotiations, an agreement was nearly reached on the following main principles:

The Plan has, as its main objective, to make available to the participating countries the maximum of coal and steel products at the lowest possible cost, and to pursue a policy of economic expansion, full employment, and higher living standards for the workers. Its aims and methods are thus very different from those of a cartel. The activities pursued under the Plan would not include interference in the management or organization of industries or individual concerns, it would aim at a gradual, overall equilibrium of cost of production, including wages, indirect taxation, and social security; but would extend to (1) establishment of investment plans for the whole area, which might serve as a guide for the investment programs of individual industries or undertakings, and (2) to assisting them in connection with financing such investments.

The executive and administrative body of the Plan would be the High Authority, the members of which would be appointed by the participating governments acting in common; thus, no member would represent a particular country.

The Authority would be responsible to a Joint Assembly, consisting of representatives elected by the parliaments of the countries concerned, to which it would present the annual report on its activity. In case of a vote of censure, the Authority would have to resign as a body. There would thus be, in matters relating to coal and steel, a sort of supernational cabinet and parliament.

It was also proposed to establish a Court of Arbitration which would render decisions, in case of complaints of states or individual concerns against findings of the Authority directly affecting them. Whenever a decision of the High Authority appeared to jeopardize the economic expansion or the foreign-trade balance of a member State, the Court could request the Authority to modify its decision.

The Authority would be assisted by consultative committees, representing employers, workers and consumers, as well as by

443

regional associations of producers created on a geographical basis, without regard to frontiers.

Agreement was reached without too much difficulty on most organizational problems. Great difficulties, however, were encountered in regard to equalization of prices and indemnification of producers due to suffer from the introduction of the Plan.

It was obvious that the producers having the highest cost would have to make a considerable effort of adjustment, and possibly have to reduce their output. Such would be the case with iron-ore mines in Germany, and with some coal mines in France, but particularly in Belgium. The latter country not having implemented a modernization program after the war, had a particularly high level of cost. The subsidy required by Belgian coal production in order that the coal might be marketed at the same price as coal from other producing areas, until, over the next five years, the highest-cost mines, producing about five million tons, would be abandoned, was extremely high. But Germany, which, under a levy calculated on output, would have paid the greatest part of the cost, refused to do so, and suggested, instead, that only a small part of Belgian coal production should be included in the scheme at once, reducing thus considerably the subsidy to be paid.

These difficulties which appeared particularly formidable in the summer of 1950, when production of coal and steel in several countries of Western Europe had been affected by a decline in effective demand were alleviated by the end of 1950. At that time, the substantial rise in steel production, due to the increase in defense demand, on the one hand, caused a rise in German coal prices, reducing their difference in relation to Belgian costs, and on the other hand resulted in a coal shortage, implying the necessity of maintaining and even of increasing the output even of the high-cost mines.

The main economic significance of the coal and steel pool, according to an estimate by the United Nations Economic Commission for Europe, was that it could enable the area to organize

444

an interchange of resources and rationalization of production. The area had reached a maximum production, more or less equivalent to its present productive capacity, of some 250 million tons of hard coal, i.e., slightly above Great Britain and about equal to the Soviet Union; and 40 million tons of steel, second only to the United States (see table below). While post-war developments and difficulties of balance of payments resulted in expansion of high-cost output of coal in Belgium and France, and of iron ore in Germany, the Schuman Plan should allow a more rational use of resources, and should make it possible to direct new investment according to economic motives only. This should enable the area to expand considerably its production of these basic materials of heavy industry at reduced cost, thus creating the basis for a general expansion of industrial activity, as well as improving its competitive position on foreign markets. In announcing his plan, Mr. Schuman had specifically mentioned the necessity of expanding the steel production of the area, in order to meet the demand for development of overseas territories, particularly of Africa.

COAL AND STEEL PRODUCTION
OF THE SCHUMAN PLAN COUNTRIES
(in million metric tons)

	Best pre-war year	Best post-war year	Highest production reached
COAL			
West Germany (Ruhr)	137.3	103.2	137.3
(Saar)	16.1	14.3	16.1
France	50.5	51.2	51.2
Belgium	30.0	26.7	30.0
Netherlands	14.3	11.7	14.3
Italy	1.7	1.1	1.7
Luxembourg	....	....	....
	249.9	208.2	250.6

COAL AND STEEL PRODUCTION
OF THE SCHUMAN PLAN COUNTRIES (*Cont.*)

STEEL

West Germany (Ruhr)	17.8	9.1	17.8
(Saar)	3.0	1.8	3.0
France	9.7	9.1	9.7
Belgium	4.1	3.9	4.1
Luxembourg	2.9	2.4	2.9
Italy	2.3	2.1	2.3
Netherlands	...	...	...
	39.8	28.4	39.8

The countries of the Schuman Plan area also have considerable resources of iron ore. The highest yearly production of iron ore measured in content of metal for the different countries of the area was:

(*in million metric tons*)

France	15
West Germany	3
Belgium	0.1
Luxembourg	2.4
Italy	0.7
French North Africa	2.4
	23.6

As a comparison it may be interesting to observe that maximum production of iron ore in Great Britain had reached only 4.5 million tons, while in the United States it was as high as 54 million tons.

At present (December 1, 1950), the approval of the Schuman Plan by the participating countries is expected to be achieved in the first months of 1951. The British government had made clear that, as soon as the plan is in force, it will start negotiations to achieve cooperation between British industry and the Authority, probably mainly as regards exports. The anticipations of the

NORWAY

NORTH SEA

SKAGERRAK

SWEDEN

BALTIC SEA

DENMARK

EAST

GERMAN
BERLIN   ODER   POLAND

REPUBLIC

SCHUMAN PLAN AREA
APPROX. MAX. PRODUCTION
IN MILLIONS OF TONS
COAL   251
STEEL   40

UNITED
KINGDOM
C 245
S 16

IRELAND

LONDON

C 14

NETHERLANDS

RUHR

WEST

GERMAN

REPUBLIC
C 137
S 18

CZECHOSLOVAKIA

BELGIUM
C 30 S 4

LUXEMBOURG S 3

SAAR C 16
         3

ELBE

DANUBE

ENGLISH CHANNEL

PARIS

LORRAINE

FRANCE C 51
         S 10

SWITZERLAND

AUSTRIA

YUGOSLAVIA

ATLANTIC
OCEAN

LOIRE

RHÔNE

PO

ADRIATIC
SEA

ITALY
C 2
S 3

ROME

SPAIN

Corsica
(Fr.)

Sardinia
(Ital.)

SCHUMAN PLAN AREA
WESTERN EUROPE
COAL   IRON
STEEL PRODUCING CENTERS
PRINCIPAL CANALS
APPROX. MAX. PRODUCTION { coal C 2
IN MILLIONS OF TONS   { steel S 5
COUNTRIES PARTICIPATING IN THE
SCHUMAN PLAN ARE INDICATED IN GREY

MEDITERRANEAN SEA

Sicily
(Ita.)

ALGERIA
(Fr.)

TUNISIA

French concerning the attitude of Great Britain seem thus to have been justified.

The example of the coal and steel pool stimulated similar efforts for functional unification in other fields, especially agriculture. Several proposals were made during 1950 in France (by the *Confédération Générale de l'Agriculture*) and in the Netherlands for establishing, between different countries of Western Europe, agreements on distribution of certain agricultural products (such as, in particular, wheat, sugar and dairy products). These agreements, which would include long-term marketing export and import obligations at fixed prices, would stimulate expansion of production in surplus countries and insure to deficit countries supplies at stable prices. On August 26, 1950, the Consultative Assembly of the Council of Europe recommended conclusion of such long-term agreements, in order to improve organization of the agricultural markets.

In November 1950, the Committee of Ministers of the Council of Europe approved this recommendation, as well as a recommendation to study the establishment of a Western European Transport Authority.

Considerable concrete steps toward economic unification of at least the continental portion of Western Europe were thus achieved during 1950, and it may be expected that, barring unforeseen developments, this trend will continue. It is also probable that, if this proves true, Great Britain, with its traditional empiric attitude and her ability to adjust herself to existing facts, will succeed in establishing a very close relationship with such a continental union, without becoming officially a member, and naturally without weakening her economic leadership of the Commonwealth. Thus she would become the link between the two areas, and possibly also their focal point.

In some quarters, unification of Western Europe alone, the first attempts at which are described above, had been recently opposed to the establishment of the larger unit of an Atlantic Community; and it had been stated that Western Europe was too

448

small a unit, especially as it was at present unable to insure either its economic independence or its military security without American assistance.

However, even if it has to be admitted that these arguments are undoubtedly true, and that the closest possible economic, political and military cooperation between the two main sectors of the Atlantic Community, that is, North America and Western Europe, is absolutely essential to preserve the Western civilization and way of life, such a cooperation does not seem to contradict, but on the contrary appears to complement, a unification of Western Europe.

As a matter of fact, if Western Europe needs the assistance and cooperation of North America not only in the military field, but also for the settlement of world-wide economic problems, such as equitable distribution of raw materials, it also requires a regional unification enlarging the scope of its domestic market and allowing a complete coordination of its productive resources. Such a unification implies a process of making uniform the economic and social conditions, and the freedom of movement of persons, inside the unified territory. Such an accomplishment is obviously absolutely impossible between Western Europe and North America, while between the different countries of Western Europe such an adjustment, even though difficult, would certainly be feasible.

449

CONCLUSIONS: IMPORTANCE OF THE SURVIVAL OF A FREE WESTERN EUROPE

THE GRADUAL SUCCESS of the at least partial attempts toward the unification of Western Europe, which alone can insure the maintenance in this area of its way of life, based on free political institutions, is of the utmost importance to the rest of the world. In fact, it is so important that the destiny of this area bears no comparison to that of any other similar in population or resources.

This importance is obviously due not alone to the overall reasons of solidarity in prosperity and stability. It is due also, to a considerable extent, to the fact that Western Europe—including Greece, which is today again, and not only for strategical reasons, part of this area—is the cradle of modern civilization, where even such main factors as originated outside of it, like Christianity, found their greatest development. In Western Europe was born and developed the tradition of individualism, implying freedom of thought and of speech; the right of the people to elect their own government; and, most important of all, respect for the value of the individual personality of each man.

That tradition is based on all of the following: the teachings of Christ and of the Greek philosophers; the humanism of the Renaissance; the Magna Charta; the Declaration of Human Rights; of the French Revolution; and the economic liberalism of Adam Smith and of the French physiocrats in the eighteenth century, which was the basis of the economic development of capitalist

450

economy, as well as its amendment in the direction of social justice by the socialist thinkers of the nineteenth century, Owen, Proudhon and Karl Marx. Western Europe was the home of most, if not of all, of these traditions and ideas. It is also the area where they are most alive and have the greatest influence on shaping the course of events.

The greatest significance of present developments in Western Europe, however, consists in the attempts which are being made, in most countries of this area, particularly Great Britain, to achieve a synthesis of what are called political democracy and economic democracy. In other words, the attempt is to combine political freedom and economic security, i.e., to combine the right to work and to achieve a reasonably satisfactory standard of living by the proceeds of labor, and the right to be protected against risks of illness and unemployment without abandoning the right to vote.

Western Europe seems to have better qualifications for such an experiment in elaborating new forms of social and economic organization than any other country or area, even than the United States. This is true, in spite of the fact that similar trends in favor of a social-welfare state begin to gain strength also in this country, even though considerably more slowly than in Europe; it is true also in spite of the undoubted leadership of America in the field of technical and economic progress. This appears to be due to the fact that the structure of the American economy and the standard of living, and also the way of life of the American people, are based on an abundance of natural resources, in proportion to the population. That abundance is greater than anywhere else in the world, with the result that Americans have greater opportunities than any other people, and are free from the necessity of facing and overcoming difficulties which have to be overcome by the peoples of other and less opulent countries. Therefore, the experience of Americans in organizing their social and economic structure, even though it might be extremely interesting and in-

451

structive, as well as most satisfactory for the people, could never become a model for the rest of the world, as some of its basic features could not be duplicated outside of North America.

On the other hand, Western Europe's natural resources, especially in proportion to the population, are much more limited. Its main difference, however, compared to the rest of the world (outside of North America), that is, essentially with respect to the underdeveloped areas, consists not in the level of natural resources, which can not be changed, but in the level of civilization, and of technical and scientific knowledge, where progress may be expected gradually to decrease these differences. The experience of Western Europe, which will have to overcome difficulties that are likely to be encountered in most other countries of the world, seems thus to offer an example of the greatest possible significance.

In this attempt at the synthesis of political and economic democracy, success is obviously much more difficult to achieve than either in a purely capitalist or in a completely planned totalitarian economy. As a matter of fact, it would be much easier to do one of two things: (1) either to abandon the economy to the laws of competition and the play of the free market, even though such an economy might very often be unworkable, owing to political and social pressures, and might result merely in domination by monopolies, (2) or, on the contrary, to submit to a totalitarian and disciplinarian organization of state economy, without any more freedom or "say" for the individual than for a private in an army on the battlefield; but this would be an army in which the individual would be conscripted for life to wage the battle of production.

Even though much more difficult, this attempt to reach a synthesis of political and economic democracy—until now apparently contradictory and equally valuable conditions for human dignity, development and happiness—appears much more worth while.

452

Moreover, in the prospect of its success resides the greatest hope for a world worth living in.

The success or the failure of this experiment in Western Europe seems thus to be of decisive significance for the destiny of mankind in the near future.

INDEX

459

461

465